❧ PLANTS IN ❧
GARDEN HISTORY

PENELOPE HOBHOUSE

PLANTS IN GARDEN HISTORY

PAVILION

First published in Great Britain in 1992
This paperback edition published in 2004

PAVILION BOOKS LTD

An imprint of **Chrysalis** Books Group plc

The Chrysalis Building, Bramley Road
London W10 6SP
www.chrysalisbooks.co.uk

ISBN 1 86205 660 9

Art Director: Bernard Higton
Project Editor: Helen Sudell
Picture Editor: Jenny de Gex

A CIP catalogue reference for this book is available
from the British Library

Printed and bound by: Imago PTE Ltd (Singapore)

CONTENTS

INTRODUCTION

To what degree has the introduction of new garden plants influenced developments in design? To what extent have any great movements of garden history been set in motion by plant novelties, with design philosophies having to adapt to accommodate whole new ranges of plants and plant types? How often have new plants merely been fitted in to existing patterns and used to furnish or decorate familiar, well-tried layouts? How often were they treated as collectors' items rather than being integrated into a deliberate design?

The very stuff of the history of gardening, from ancient Egypt to the present day, consists largely of plants that have been displaced and transplanted to new situations, that have succeeded in acclimatizing – sometimes with the help of a considerable degree of horticultural skill and care – and that have made their way into gardens through a variety of channels – often being 'improved' in some respect along the way. Whenever and wherever they have been introduced from foreign regions, new plant discoveries have had at least a temporary rarity value while being judged by prevailing standards and assessed for their beauty, 'curiosity' or potential for use. But to be adopted on any scale and grown by gardeners – and, moreover, to become sufficiently important to influence the

An early seventeenth-century painting on a spinet cover by Frederick van Valchenborch (c.1570–1623) shows a typical contemporary garden scheme. Gardeners are being directed, presumably by the owner and his wife, in various occupations which include tree planting, planting of 'greens' in pots, and tending and tidying the flowerbeds which are enclosed into geometric patterns by low-growing box. The hedge which surrounds the garden area, separating it from farming activities, gives the appearance of careful 'laying' or pleaching, a practice known since very early times.

appearance of those gardens – plant novelties had to prove their garden worthiness, and to be recognized and promoted not by mere plantsmen but by enthusiastic gardeners in pursuit of some ideal of garden beauty. In this book it is tracing this process that is my main interest: I am concerned here with plants *growing in gardens* – as opposed to exotics nurtured in artificial conditions or mummified in herbaria.

Parallel with the history of plant introductions and availability runs the story of the evolution of garden styles – particularly the emergence in the West of the more overtly ornamental garden of pleasure, where plants were appreciated for their beauty, rather than the more utilitarian plot in which grew plants for medicine, flavouring and food. These two themes are reflected in the vast body of previous scholarship on which I have leaned heavily in writing this book. On the one hand there exist many detailed works tracing the history of gardens and garden design – to some aspects of which the presence of plants seems almost incidental. On the other hand there exists a wealth of anecdotal documentation focusing on the plants themselves – dating discoveries and introductions, describing the efforts of the plant hunters, the enthusiasts who experimented with the novelties, and the agents who in various ways disseminated them – publicizing their virtues, or more practically passing them around for other gardeners to grow. Treasured at first by great collectors in the grandest gardens, these 'rarities' would be propagated and – until nurseries made them more generally available – distributed slowly. Meanwhile, there needed to be publicity, knowledge – a demand: from the Renaissance onwards this was fanned by a proliferation of garden literature, in which plants were illustrated and described, culminating in a nineteenth-century explosion of horticultural periodicals, which brought plant and garden knowledge to the masses. The twin strands of scholarship continually converge and intersect. My aim in this book has been to meld them together in an attempt to establish clearer pictures of planting in gardens in successive eras – to infuse the design theories with life, and to put the dry data of plant introductions into some context.

Faced with the vast amount of material I have had to be selective. I have chosen to concentrate on the periods and plants which seem to have spread their influence beyond the common run of horticultural development. I have confined myself to the evolution of western gardens. The development of garden design

and use of plants in the Far East are outside the scope of the book. To discuss the garden philosophy of China and Japan and their planting would be beyond my capability. Indeed, it should be remembered that even the plants growing in Islamic gardens are seen through western eyes. By the exclusion of the desert the Muslims expressed their deep antipathy to and fear of nature's forces; without the essential ingredient of water and its manipulation the garden would wither and die. In our western world 'nature' also has to be kept at bay in countries with higher rainfalls, but any gardening neglect leads rapidly to a return to a strongly growing living wilderness, a sort of primeval forest (today complicated by the naturalization of foreign plants), rather than the nothingness and aridity of sand. Nevertheless the modern enclosed garden envisaged as a haven, whether laid out in old-fashioned formality or evoking more natural scenes, has much in common with both the Islamic paradise and the Christian *hortus conclusus* of the Middle Ages.

I have broadly followed historical sequence for the themes in the book, although some topics overlap and two chapters – that on Islam and that on America before the twentieth century – are special cases, taking the discussion beyond the chronological framework. Each chapter ends with a series of more detailed illustrated essays as digressions on particular themes, people and fashions and their interrelationships with plants.

The first recorded gardens of the western world, often for very practical reasons of safety and for making irrigation simple, had what we would today call a formal aspect, with outer perimeters, inner flower-beds and canals parallel and at right angles. Plants, both useful and decorative, were arranged inside this basic structure, and, although the appearance of the gardens would have varied somewhat according to the particular plants grown, those recently introduced from foreign countries would have been integrated into the pre-existing scheme rather than playing a determining role in how garden styles might evolve.

The Muslim gardens of Islam were all of similar pattern, with water, fruit trees and flowers arranged to fulfil certain religious as well as secular needs. Cultivated ornamental trees and flowers were essential features for beauty and scent but did not influence the accepted fundamentals of design. However, by identifying the actual plants it is possible to get a clearer picture of how Islamic gardens of a particular age and place might have looked.

All through the Middle Ages, while Arab botanists and gardeners were studying and cultivating fruit trees, flowers and bulbs, in the Middle East and in the Iberian peninsula, western European gardeners jogged along with quite a small palette of plants, and most of these were grown only for their useful qualities for medicine or food. All this was to change with the Renaissance, with a new scientific attitude to the study of plants – given impetus by the invention of printing. Since then, in the western world, there have been some three or four main periods of plant arrivals, each of which has in turn had a strong influence on the way in which design would develop: the influx of bulbous plants into Europe from the eastern end of the Mediterranean in the sixteenth and seventeenth centuries, the flood of arrivals of North American trees, shrubs and perennials in the seventeenth, eighteenth and early half of the nineteenth century, the brightly coloured annuals and tender plants, many from South America, which transformed mid-nineteenth-century garden appearances, and the discovery and introduction of the plant treasures from the Far East which, from the nineteenth century onwards, promoted plant-collecting manias in new forms.

By the second half of the sixteenth century new bulbs, corms and tubers arrived in Western Europe from the Middle East. These were often already cultivated garden plants, grown in Islamic gardens for centuries, and they were to transform gardening possibilities. In the west they were first valued like works of art for their intrinsic beauty and their rarity. Specimens were grown in rows in geometrically shaped flower-beds or in specially prepared long narrow borders for individual admiration. They fitted happily into existing schemes in which, increasingly through the seventeenth century, malleable plants such as box, yew and hornbeam came to be treated as green architecture and were regimented into perspective views and elaborate ground patterns, often to frame the rare bulbs. The manipulation of plants into patterns in the French formal style could be on a vast scale, and avenues of native European trees, now augmented by the newly arrived horse-chestnut and hybrid Dutch elms, stretched across whole countrysides.

The second great era of introductions was of plants from the New World. By the middle of the eighteenth century the concept of landscape was paramount, at least in England, and the wealth of trees and shrubs arriving from North America contributed to the new naturalistic compositions that embodied the picturesque vision. The great design theorists and practitioners allowed these trees and shrubs to develop their natural shapes – after all, growing them in Europe was experimental – in groups and groves, rather than in regimented lines, to augment the native species that were already growing in exuberant splendour.

The nineteenth century saw the third period of plant introductions on an unbounded scale, which influenced gardening fashions in quite different ways. A host of new flowers came from western America, Mexico, South America and the Cape of Good Hope, and seasonal bedding schemes were enamelled by bright-hued annuals – by now being improved by scientific breeding – to prove the power of horticultural skills and moneyed resources. Simultaneously dark-hued conifers from the American north-west, from Chile and from the Himalayas, with rhododendrons and other woodland plants, arrived to stimulate a new era in plant collecting and the establishing of arboreta. Here, too, experimentation could assume bizarre forms – with monkey puzzles being used to implement a formal parterre planting (recently reinstated by the English National Trust) at Biddulph Grange in Staffordshire. The influx of good plants from the Far East towards the end of the nineteenth century gave a new impetus to developing great garden collections both in Europe and in North America, many of which are still thriving today. Since the end of the Victorian era garden artists have woven hardy perennials – augmented by splendid Asian species – into the flowering glory of the herbaceous border.

Substantial numbers of new plants continued to arrive in western gardens during the first decades of the twentieth century, and by today the expertise of the plant breeders has reached new heights, yet in many ways the prospect for gardeners has narrowed. Even though new garden plants continue to arrive from places such as China and from the mountains of northern Mexico, many of the nineteenth-century introductions have long ceased to be available to gardeners, and some of the best old hybrids and garden cultivars are at a premium. Modern marketing methods and the economics of plant production make it less attractive to growers to offer a wide range of plants. As natural habitats all round the world are destroyed by man's activities some plants, now rare in the wild, assume ecological importance, and, by the end of the twentieth century, it is accepted that only plants grown from seed collected in the wild have true scientific interest. In

A.M.3267.ᵉ'56.   demorogues (V. A. M.

The French Calvinist, Jacques Le Moyne de Morgues (1530–88), became a refugee in England after the massacre of St Bartholomew in 1572. The water-colour depicts the wild daffodil or lent lily (*Narcissus pseudonarcissus*), found in western Europe and England, and the red admiral butterfly. Le Moyne's book of watercolour drawings, with his signature 'demorogues', remained unidenti-fied in the Victoria and Albert Museum until the 1920s.

many gardens, especially in parts of North America, Brazil and in Australia, all countries with an exciting range of flora, natives are planted to create 'wild' and 'natural' gardens in which imported exotics have little place.

Many of the plant introductions throughout the centuries, especially those too tender for growing outdoors and those craving alpine conditions, were taken up by enthusiasts but can hardly be said to have influenced trends in garden design. A good example of lack of adaptability would be the sensational plant discoveries made by Sir Joseph Banks with Captain Cook during the voyage of the *Endeavour* between 1768 and 1771 and the comparative unim-portance of the plants – of the greatest interest to botanists – as a general influence on gardening styles. Extremes of heat and cold, length of growing periods and soil types all play their part in determining how plants will adapt to new situations. The history of ornamental gardening is also the history of exciting experimen-tal planting and developing horticultural knowledge which made it possible to grow plants with different and specialized needs. And it was the nurseries, growing and multiplying in number, which made the plants available to an increasingly aware public, as well as playing their part in hybridizing and selecting plants for garden use. Sometimes plants, especially perennials, of little beauty in the wild, have been improved by selection and breeding to become brilliant partners in border schemes and thrive to their best effect in garden conditions rather than in their wild habitats. Many soft-stemmed North American natives considered weeds at home, 'improved' in Europe, have returned to American gardens to flourish in European-style perennial borders.

The plant collectors, although often regimenting bulbs and herbaceous plants, have always allowed exotic trees and shrubs to realize their true forms and extend the levels of romantic natural-ism. The conflict between a delight in logical rhythms of planting and in more natural free effects – between considering the art of gardening as 'nature perfected' and using gardening to re-interpret the roles of plants in order to imitate the wild – remains as topical today, when whole landscapes are threatened, as it has through the ages. But both old and new plants can be used equally satisfactorily to please the formalist or the lover of naturalism. There is no right or wrong way to use plants. To me, the successful garden – whatever its style, whatever its planting – is one where an enlightened overall vision prevails. In the hands of an individual who appreciates plants and sees the garden as an entity, the form of the layout and the character of the plants become inseparable: whether formal, natural or something else, the concept of the garden as a work of art retains its supremacy.

CHAPTER ONE

THE ORIGINS OF GARDENING IN THE WEST

The first western gardens were those in the Mediterranean basin. There, in the desert areas stretching from North Africa to the valleys of the Euphrates, the so-called cradle of civilization, where plants were first grown for crops by settled communities, garden enclosures were also constructed. Early gardens, surrounded by walls or palisades to give protection from marauders and desert winds, were mainly utilitarian; to garden and grow for beauty alone implies a degree of luxury well above subsistence level. But fortunately trees and flowers fulfil dual roles; the useful fruit trees, herbs and medicinal plants, laid out in rows and symmetry for ease of irrigation and culture, at once assumed a further decorative character. Gardens emphasized the contrast between two separate worlds: the outer one where nature remained awe-inspiringly in control and an inner artificially created sanctuary, a refuge for man and plants from the burning desert, where shade trees and cool canals refreshed the spirit and ensured growth. From these beginnings, through four thousand years of history, ornamental gardening, with plants often assuming symbolic and religious meanings, has developed as an art form.

No actual records exist of garden layouts before the second millennium BC, but the use of flowers and leaves for personal ornament and to decorate buildings and pottery is far older. Before 2000 BC the ancient Egyptians used the lotus (the scented blue

Nymphaea caerulea) and papyrus (*Cyperus papyrus*) for motifs in architecture and jewellery; a gold pendant found in a tomb from the Early Minoan period (*c.* 2800–2400 BC) is shaped in the form of a flowering lotus, while other jewellery was moulded as clearly recognizable daisies, lilies, roses and sprays of olive leaves. We must assume that at least some of these decorative plants were grown in gardens along with the more mundane 'produce' plants. These floral images were often symbolic of both spiritual concepts and the necessary growing of crops and fruit for survival. Flowers and fruit were grown as religious offerings. Pottery decoration by the Minoans in Crete, from the period 1900–1700 BC, was even three-dimensional, with flowers curiously moulded on the rims and stems of vases.

These early stylized versions of trees, flowers and leaves seem to hint at an appreciation of plants for their beauty. But the plants used most frequently as decorative motifs (and which have continued to be employed through the ages), such as the invaluable palm (*Phoenix dactylifera*) which provided shade for the garden, dates for food and had plenty of more mundane uses (the Greek geographer Strabo mentioned 36 useful qualities) also had religious significance. The palm was deified as a symbol of fertility and was an important tree in the sacred temple gardens both in Egypt and in the Euphrates and Tigris basins. The Egyptians especially believed in the magical qualities of imitation; they expressed this in the use of papyrus, the symbol of resurrection, in tomb paintings and funeral bouquets. A strong cross-fertilization of ideas between different civilizations spread through trade connections and conquest. The palmetto (*Chamaerops humilis*) was known in Egypt in 2800 BC as decoration and, inserted in volute capitals, was further developed in Assyria between 1000 and 600; the lotus, with both

In a tomb painting of *c.* 1475 BC showing an Egyptian funeral ceremony, a canopied funeral barge bears the body of the deceased through lotus-filled waters edged with papyrus. Date palms and sycamore figs surround the temple garden. Funerary bouquets of leaves of persea, olive and papyrus have often been found in tomb excavations, together with jars of wine, fruit and nuts, honey, herbs and spices, all designed to sustain the tomb occupant's body during its journey through the afterlife. Bodies were mummified with oils, resins and perfumes and stained with dyes all made from plant materials.

flower and leaf sacred in ancient Egypt, was also used by the Minoans and in the Assyrian empire. Decorative styles from Mycenae in mainland Greece were revitalized under later Egyptian dynasties to be used in the tomb paintings which first reveal 'real' garden outlines and plant arrangement.

The existence of these decorative plant motifs and their dating show us which plants were considered beautiful, useful and of symbolic importance in each period. Papyrus flowers and stems moulded as columns at Karnak[1] in ancient Egypt, lotus decoration in personal ornament and architecture, carved capitals of acanthus, oak, ivy and grape vines on various Greek orders (motifs which were copied and extended by the Romans), and later more elaborate and stylized fretwork flowers and leaves in early Muslim architecture, representing palmettes, irises and lotus, are all indications of contemporary taste. Even without actual visual records of gardens they offer us clues to contemporary garden planting. Most representations are of plants symbolically connected with the idea of the oasis offering shelter from the desert heat.

The plants were mainly native to the Mediterranean basin or were very early introductions, and ranged from the delicate bulbs of crocus and lily, which became totally dormant during the hot summers after flowering, to water-loving lotus and marsh-growing papyrus (from Southern Nubia on the upper Nile) which depended on irrigation, and more imposing shrubs and trees such as the pomegranate, fig, date and olive, all of which have questing roots to search out water at low levels. The cypress trees (*Cupressus sempervirens*), symbols of mortality and eternity (today in Greece they are found only in cemeteries), were planted to make sacred groves around temples in both Mesopotamia and Greece. The oriental plane (*Platanus orientalis*, Virgil's plane tree 'that roofed drinkers with its airy shade') was already grown by Sargon II in his botanic garden near Nineveh by the eighth century BC; it probably originated in the more northern hills – and spread east and westwards to establish its major role as the shade tree *par excellence*, whose canopy provided patterned shade for philosophers and shepherds alike.

EGYPTIAN GARDENING

Perhaps the wealthy Egyptian's stock petition inscribed in tombs of the New Kingdom best expresses his appreciation of his garden.

He asked that 'I may each day walk continuously on the banks of my water, that my soul may repose on the branches of the trees that I have planted, that I may refresh myself under the shade of my sycamore.'[2]

The first actual record of a garden layout comes from a model found buried in the tomb of Meketre, chancellor to King Mentuhotep II in *c.* 2000 BC; in doll's-house size, sculpted in wood and painted green, it shows a walled garden including a fish pond shaded by sycamore figs (*Ficus sycomorus*, the 'sycamore tree' of the Bible, also called mulberry fig). The pillars of the house portico are moulded to resemble bunched papyrus canes. During the period of imperialist expansion and conquest of the New Kingdom after 1085 BC, artists began to portray trees and flowers quite skilfully. The tomb paintings do not depict real gardens but serve as symbols of the necessary refreshment of the soul on its long journey through the afterlife, imitation 'earthly' gardens in which fruiting trees and flowers combine beauty with usefulness as offerings to the gods. The layout is simple; a high wall protects the garden from intruders and a formal rectangular pool, with flowering lotus, is edged with flower-beds and flanked symmetrically with tall shade-giving trees. The basic formula portrayed by the tomb artist is one which in modified forms will be used as a garden pattern again and again throughout history.

Paintings of whole gardens are found on the walls of tombs and date to around 1400 BC (see pp. 32–33). Both the garden painting found in the tomb of an official at the time of the Pharaoh Amenhotep and that known as the Garden of Nebamun, 'a scribe who keeps account of the corn of Amun' at Thebes, show the symmetry of a contemporary rich man's garden with trees in rows and flowers in square beds or straight borders.

While bouquets and wreaths of dried flowers, fruit and seeds actually found in the tombs provide evidence of what plants were available, visual representations of gardens and flowers give us some idea of what the actual gardens looked like. All settlements had to be on raised ground to avoid flooding, and garden walls gave protection from persistent searing winds. Shade was so important that houses and their garden courtyards were sometimes built around existing trees so that large date palms or sycamore figs dominated the garden from its inception. The lotus-growing pool (either the blue-flowered *Nymphaea caerulea* or the white-flowered *N. lotus*) was also inhabited by fish and waterfowl;

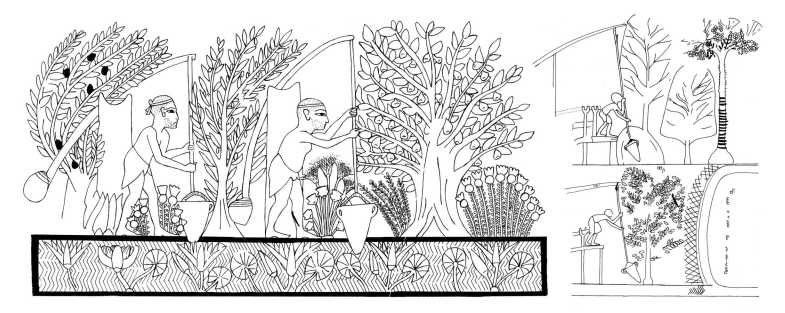

The Egyptians employed nursery gardeners to supply the flowers and herbs necessary for medicine, cooking, cosmetics, perfumes and other purposes. The layout of these gardens is unknown but the plants were probably grown in quite utilitarian market-garden style and watered by a *shaduf* (*above*). This contraption, still used in Egypt, was depicted in wall paintings in Theban tombs. A long pole, with a jar for water at one end and a container of mud at the other, is balanced over a stand to enable water to be distributed without the necessity of lifting.

at its edge tall papyrus flourished in moist mud. A canal often gave access to the garden through a grand water gateway, providing water for the pool or for irrigation. Water was moved upwards to irrigate the garden by the device known as the *shaduf*. The soil was extremely fertile and trees grew rapidly if sufficient water was available.

In the almost rainless Egyptian climate, then as now, annual flooding of the Nile allowed winter crops to be grown as the waters receded. Native annuals flowered in the relative humidity following in spring, and some plants introduced from regions with a more typical Mediterranean climate where rain fell in winter adapted well to those conditions. From about 1500 BC, after the establishment of the New Kingdom, native trees and flowers were being steadily augmented by foreign introductions from the east and south-east of the Mediterranean. Pomegranates and mandrakes were among those that proved suited to the climate and produced their exotic flowers and fruits for bouquets, garlands and decorative collars worn by both men and women. Pomegranate

(*Punica granatum*) was introduced in about 1550 from the Caspian Sea area and its many-seeded fruit became a symbol of fertility; mandrake (*Mandragora officinarum*) was depicted grown as a cultivated plant in a tomb painting of about 1000 BC that also showed spring-performing cornflowers (*Centaurea depressa*) and poppies (the scarlet-flowered *Papaver rhoeas* from the eastern Mediterranean). In summer trees which obtained water with long questing tap-roots or were fed from irrigation canals produced their fruit and also provided essential shade. Indigenous trees included different sorts of date palm, both sycamore and common fig (*Ficus carica*), carob (*Ceratonia siliqua*, the supposed source of the locusts eaten by John the Baptist in the wilderness), the horse-radish tree (*Moringa aptera*, syn. *M. peregrina*, from which 'ben oil' was extracted) and grape vines.

Incidental attempts at experimenting with new plants from abroad are recorded. During the Eighteenth Dynasty (*c.* 1470 BC) Queen Hatsepshut, 'for whom all Egypt was made to labour with bowed head', brought 31 frankincense trees (*Boswellia sacra*), their roots balled up in baskets, from Somalia – known to the Egyptians as Punt – to decorate her temple at Deir-el-Bahari in western Thebes and provide the valued incense, but they did not survive. Tuthmosis III, her co-monarch and successor, collected other plants during his campaigns in Asia Minor. Few are likely even to have survived the journey home, but his artists drew them at the time and later carved their reliefs on the walls of a room in the temple of Amun at Karnak – perhaps the oldest herbal in the world, and known as 'the Botanical Garden'. This shows contemporary enthusiasm for exotic plant collecting, but is of little help in teaching us what was being grown in the gardens. The pomegranate is among the plants depicted as new, but was already being grown in Ineni's Theban garden a hundred years earlier (see below).

The oldest written description of a garden dates to more than a thousand years before the garden tomb paintings: Methen or Amten, governor of the northern delta district in Egypt during the reign of Sneferu (c. 2600–2576 BC, first king of the Fourth Dynasty of the Old Kingdom), left a record of his life's work inscribed on the walls of his tomb. His garden, of which he seemed especially proud, extended to approximately 1 hectare/$2\frac{1}{2}$ acres (with a vineyard of more than a further 405 hectares/1,000 acres); it had a 'very large lake' and 'fine trees' were 'set out'; his house, pool and trees formed the core of his estate and would almost certainly have been laid out in formal style to match the geometry of walls and pool. The sands of Egypt have helped preserve traces of the foundations of temples, houses and garden plans. Excavations of the early temple garden at Deir-el-Bahari reveal trees planted in a formal pattern framing the ramp leading to the entrance. The tree pits show that three rows of seven sycamore figs and tamarisk trees were planted to give an avenue effect. Statues of the king were placed in the shade of the figs and there were separate geometric flower-beds. Excavations have also uncovered the roots of perseas (not the avocado, Persea gratissima, but an Egyptian tree, Mimusops laurifolia, given the name 'persea' by Dioscorides) later planted in groves lining the approach to the queen's terraced temple. Part of the plan for the temple garden was sketched out on one of the floor slabs and confirms in detail the pattern made by the surviving root system. Stories written on papyrus in the period of the Middle Kingdom (before 1600 BC) tell us of an earlier king boating on his 'pool' which is large enough to allow twenty beautiful ladies clad only in nets to row him. Another part of the series shows a crocodile lurking in the pool to catch the king's wife's visiting lover.

There are no paintings of gardens in the royal tombs, but some scenes carved on ivory panels set in frames decorated with individual flowers were found in Tutankhamun's tomb, from the Eighteenth Dynasty, and show him and his wife in a garden setting (see pp. 34–5). Further evidence of plants comes from wreaths and other items discovered in Tutankhamun's tomb.

Nigel Hepper and Lise Manniche have separately provided identifications for the plants grown in ancient Egypt. Hepper's flowers include those used in some form or other in Tutankhamun's tomb, while Manniche has reconstructed a herbal including 94 species of herbs and trees used from before the pharaohs to the Coptic Period; the list, of course, includes all the useful plants grown for food, cosmetics and cures as well as those which appear to have a decorative role. It is almost certain that among all the latter even the most beautiful will have had some other function. These two sources list and identify many of the plants in the tomb wall paintings or described in hieroglyphics. Ineni, builder to King Tuthmosis I (1528–1510 BC) listed his orchard trees two hundred years before Tutankhamun. He grew Phoenix dactylifera, Ficus sycomorus and other shade-giving fruit trees such as Mimusops laurifolia, a favourite garden tree, the fruit and branches of which were used as decoration, moringas, carob trees, and the Christ thorn (Zizyphus spina-christi, one of the plants from which the 'Crown of Thorns' was said to be made) as well as shrubs such as pomegranate, grown for fruit and for its flowers and leaves to be used for bouquets, and myrtle (Myrtus communis) with scented flowers. Besides those mentioned above, he grew one specimen of the now almost extinct argun fan palm (Medemia argun), eight willows (Salix subserrata), ten tamarisks (the indigenous Tamarix nilotica or T. aphylla) and five 'twn' trees (perhaps Acacia nilotica), grown for their gum and valuable hard reddish wood, and five other unidentified kinds of tree. His garden was walled and contained a house, granaries, a pavilion and a pool; the trees were arranged neatly in rows but in no particular order. The garden of the temple of Aten, the Egyptian sun god, in the city of Tell-el-Amarna, built by Akhenaten and Nefertiti (c. 1367–1350 BC), was laid out to delight the god rather than for usefulness, although providing shade was, as always in Egypt, an essential feature. The garden, with plentiful trees growing in tubs, is portrayed on the wall of the tomb of Merye the high priest. Among the shrubs and trees are pomegranates, dates, doum palms (Hyphaene thebaica) and grape vines. Excavations in Akhenaten's city have uncovered rooms of houses painted with naturalistic plants, birds and water beasts looking out on to courtyards with pools.

Although there are few native Egyptian flowers they grew

poppies, both the ordinary red annual field poppy (*Papaver rhoeas*) and the opium poppy (*P. somniferum*), a white daisy, possibly a mayweed or camomile (a form of *Anthemis pseudocotula*), blue annual cornflowers (*Centaurea depressa*) and mandrakes. By the seventh to the fourth centuries BC an unidentified species of lily had arrived and the flowers were being pressed to yield perfume.

Egypt was invaded by the Assyrians in 671 BC and from 525 was under Persian rule until the conquest by Alexander in 332 BC, after which its cultural development ran on Hellenistic lines.

A mid-nineteenth-century painting by Marianne North shows the date palm (*Phoenix dactylifera*) and the branching doum or *dom* palm (*Hyphaene thebaica*) growing together on the Nile above Philae in Egypt. Both are native date-bearing trees and are shown in the wall paintings of gardens in Egyptian tombs, in which their fruit was also preserved. Many parts of both palms were utilized for food and medicine. Theophrastus mentioned that the Egyptians made bread out of doum to cure stomach ailments. Today the decorative date palm is grown in many Mediterranean gardens.

MESOPOTAMIA: THE FERTILE CRESCENT

Western man's evolution from nomad hunter to settled agriculturist began ten thousand years ago in the foothills to the north of the Mesopotamian plain. Later the Sumerian tribes moved south into the delta, where they made the first settlements. In the cool north there were forests of scrub oak, oriental plane and species of box, cedar, cypress and poplar, while willows only grew in the northern river plains and date palms only in the delta. In the swamps between the rivers Tigris and Euphrates nothing grew except a giant reed, *Phragmites australis*. Even before 3000 BC the Sumerians became skilled in constructing canals to serve as drainage between the great reeds and to irrigate the more desert-like regions in the fertile plains.

Ur, the royal city of Sumeria, lay to the west of the lower Euphrates which, like the Nile, flooded annually. Cities were

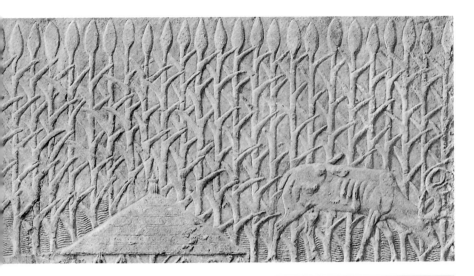

A relief from Sennacherib's palace at Nineveh, dating to c. 700 BC, has a dense backdrop of stylized giant reeds, *Phragmites australis*, in which animals take cover – this detail shows a browsing deer. The reeds, growing to a height of 7·5 metres/25 feet, were originally found in the marshy country between the Euphrates and the Tigris and were introduced by the Assyrians to areas around the more northern cities where they made their hunting parks and landscaped their gardens. Like the papyrus of the Nile delta, these reeds were an essential source of building material for boats and mats, and provided fodder and fuel as well as cover for wild life.

walled for defence and fruit trees and vegetables were grown in the space between the inner and outer fortifications. No records of actual gardens, useful or ornamental, survive from the earliest periods but the foundations of a typical ziggurat, a raised temple built in stepped terraces, have been uncovered. Shade trees will have been planted at each level.

Ornaments discovered at Ur include a woman's latticed gold headdress with a circlet of leaves and prongs of daisies which dates to the third millennium BC. A Sumerian poem *The Epic of Gilgamesh* of about 2000 BC describes the city of Uruk: 'One third of the whole is city, one third is garden, and one third is field with the precincts of the goddess Ashtar.' The poem also tells of the groves 'of the plain' with willow and boxwood and the hills with 'forests stretching ten thousand leagues in every direction'. Of course 'gardens' would have been primarily useful, with orchards of fruit and vegetables and herbs. A fable of the time relates how a king planted a date palm and a tamarisk in the courtyard of his palace and held a banquet in the shade of the tamarisk. In temple gardens fruit was grown for offerings. An early Babylonian text proclaims,

'I planted a pure orchard for the goddess and established fruit deliveries as regular offerings.'

The Akkadians succeeded the Sumerians and ruled until 2000 BC; a 'Temptation Seal' from their period shows a subject akin to Adam to Eve and confirms the sacred nature of trees. Two horned figures, one female and one male, sit on either side of a central tree, perhaps the sacred Tree of Knowledge, while a serpent lurks in predatory fashion behind each figure. By the time of the return of the Assyrians at the beginning of the tenth century, the warlike invaders from the northern plains gradually extended their empire to dominate most of western Asia including Persia in the east, and, by the fourth century BC, Palestine and Egypt. It seems clear that sacred tree gardens, planted around temples, had a special significance. Palm trees, pines and pomegranates assumed symbolic personalities and special rites took place 'under every garden tree'. Apart from trees, the Madonna lily is the most identifiable plant in Assyrian art motifs.

The narrative bas-reliefs of the Assyrians in the ninth to seventh centuries are records of war and pillage, but the landscapes depic-

In a relief dated about 645 BC Sennacherib's grandson King Ashurbanipal (668-27 BC) and his Queen are depicted feasting under an arbour of grape vines in the royal park at Nineveh flanked by pine trees. They are served with wine and food by their servants. In a neighbouring part of the garden the decapitated head of the conquered king of the Elamites hangs from a tree. Ashurbanipal introduced many new trees from foreign countries.

A seventh-century relief from Nineveh shows a lioness resting under a pine tree garlanded with vines. Daisies grow under the tree and a Madonna lily is recognizable on the far left, and another on the right beyond the lion. As an imported bulb, probably from the countries around the eastern end of the Mediterranean – it has been so long in cultivation that its exact origin is unknown – the lily would have been highly prized as a rarity. It was also 'useful'; the Egyptians extracted scent from its flowers and the Romans used the crushed bulbs as an ointment for corns as well as for food.

ted give a vivid picture of natural mountains and rivers, marshes, parks and gardens all alive with luxuriant trees, flowers and fruit. Many of the representations must have been of neighbouring countries to the north and east where the climate encouraged a wider range of native flora. It is easy to see why later chroniclers placed the Garden of Eden somewhere in these regions.

Although there is no record of small intimate gardens such as we find portrayed in the Egyptian tombs, the Assyrian kings, inspired by foreign landscapes, began to lay out great hunting parks on the banks of the Tigris in the northern region. By the end of the second millennium plant collecting was obviously in fashion. King Tiglath-Pileser I (1114–1026 BC) wrote of 'Cedars and Box I have carried off from the countries I conquered, trees that none of the kings my fore-fathers possessed: these trees I have taken and planted in my own country, in . . . Assyria.' His trees included oaks, cedars, box and rare fruit trees. The flowers in these gardens were both wild and cultivated; some were from the west and others came from the lower Euphrates valley and beyond. They may have included the jasmine and rose, lilies, irises, tulips, hollyhocks, mallows, anemones, buttercups, daisies, camomiles, helichrysums, crocuses and poppies. A red flower – known as an *illuru* – with a red berry is often held in the hands of kings, courtiers and deities but cannot be identified.

Although archaeologists have found few traces of inner palace gardens it is thought that the Assyrian kings probably had private courtyards to which they could retreat, where palms, pines and fruit trees provided shade; these were almost certainly laid out in a

A detail from a seventh-century relief showing orchards and a variety of trees in the hilly country near Sennacherib's Nineveh, founded in 700 BC. Rather than being used for hunting, the park was both a pleasure ground and a nature reserve with figs, pomegranates and vines. Around 710 BC Sennacherib's predecessor, Sargon II, had laid out parks to the north, around Khorsabad, where he had grown a good mixture of trees for timber, fruit and shade. These included cedars, cypresses and junipers as well as dates, olives, almonds, apples, pears, quinces, figs and grapes, together with ebony and oak trees, terebinth, ash and tamarisk, oriental planes, willows and poplars.

geometric pattern. Most of the houses were low horizontal buildings raised on a podium to avoid possible flooding. Trees and flowers are often depicted growing on the roof gardens to which water was raised from the river, the whole ensemble resembling the pyramidal ziggurat at Ur or the arrangements later implemented by Nebuchadnezzar II for the famous Hanging Gardens of Babylon. The ramped or stepped access was framed with palms and other trees in much the same way as the temples in Egypt, early examples of a 'designed' approach focusing on a main entrance. Excavations of the temple garden at Assur, the first capital of the Assyrians, reveal the formal layout of flower-beds which filled the centre of an inner court and extended around the outside; the royal gardens would have had a similar pattern. The flowers were for cutting to provide fresh offerings to the gods.

At the end of the seventh century the later Assyrian centre of Nineveh was destroyed by Scythians, Medes and Babylonians, banded together to humble the proud Assyrians. All its garden beauty was abandoned and the city became a series of 'ruined mounds'. The grandson of the leading Babylonian warrior was the famous Nebuchadnezzar II (605–562) who established his new capital at Babylon, and created his Hanging Gardens overlooking the Euphrates.

From the ninth to the fourth centuries the Medes and Achaemenians established their own civilizations in Persia and it was in their lands east of the Mesopotamian settlements that gardens first developed as the enclosures to which the Persians gave the name *pairidaeza*, from which the English word 'paradise' is ultimately derived. Originally it simply meant an enclosure or park. The Persian was translated into Hebrew as *pardes* and the first translations of the Bible into Greek gave the word as *paradeisos*.

The early Persian paradise gardens were surrounded by walls and would have been planted with many trees, as well as being parks for isolating animals from the world outside. The trees and orchards were watered by irrigation systems, with the garden architecturally integral with its palace or pavilion. What seems almost certain is that Persia, situated on the trade route from China, the spice route from India and the salt route from Arabia, will have been influenced by garden developments both in the west and in the orient. Excavations of the sixth-century BC palace of the Achaemenian Cyrus the Great at Pasargadae near Isfahan show it as having a rectangular columned hall and multi-columned porticos designed to provide shade in the extreme heat, as the nucleus of the walled rectangular garden. The sixth-century Private Palace and the fifth-century Audience Hall, with a garden pavilion, are connected by a network of narrow gravity-fed stone watercourses, opening up into pools at regular intervals. The porticos of each building were designed to give the maximum protection from the sun's rays during the midday heat. There is no record of plants or planting patterns, but it seems likely that avenues of shade-giving trees will have been planted in the outer areas and flower-beds will have framed the narrow water rills. After capturing Nebuchadnezzar's Babylon in 538, the Persian empire expanded to stretch across the known world, its borders reaching to Greece and Egypt in the west and to China in the east. Reconstructions of the layouts of both Achaemenian palaces at Pasargadae and at Persepolis, only 48 kilometres/30 miles to the south-west, show how the complex irrigation system made it possible to grow plants in the most inhospitable sites. The garden-makers must have been familiar with the many glorious flowers to be found in spring in the fertile snow-watered valleys between the rolling upland hills – flowers which were gradually collected and

The famed Hanging Gardens of Babylon, constructed by Nebuchadnezzar II for his Median wife Amytis, who missed the hills and meadows of her native country, were considered one of the Seven Wonders of the ancient world. Described by the Roman historians five hundred years later, when already in decay, the terraces of baked brick were said to extend in total to 1·4 hectares/3½ acres. They were waterproofed with layers of reed and stone slabs and a complicated hydraulic system made possible a thick planting of trees, which, as Diodorus said, 'could give pleasure to the beholder'. Camels give a sense of scale in this nineteenth-century French artist's impression.

cultivated and later became some of the greatest treasures of western horticulture. Situated high on the Iranian plateau, 1,200–1,500 metres/4,000–5,000 feet above sea level, and ringed by mountain ranges which kept annual rainfall down to some 50–250 millimetres/2–10 inches, the gardens suffered harsh winds throughout the year and summer and winter extremes of burning heat and searing cold. Vita Sackville-West summed up the needs of the desert dweller in every century as: 'coolness at the end of the day's journey: coolness and greenness; the sound of trickling water after the silent plain. That is his idea of paradise.'

The Achaemenians were also responsible for expanding the existing underground watering system, the *qanats*, which although superseded today by mechanized wells and large-scale dams (if not damaged by conquerors from the east during the Middle Ages or running dry through changes in the water level), can still provide essential water for crops and gardens.

Alexander destroyed Darius's Persepolis in 330 BC, in doing so bringing Greek culture to western Asia and as far as India – but also establishing a cross-fertilization of gardening ideas and plants which travelled back westwards. The earliest written description of one of these gardens was even provided by the Greeks a century before Alexander's conquest. The enclosed park at Sardis, in western Turkey, planted by Cyrus the Younger, King of Persia (d. 401 BC), was described by Lysander the Greek envoy from Sparta to the Greek general Xenophon; he was shown it by Cyrus himself. He marvelled how the paradise was laid out with fruit trees in formal rows: 'the beauty of the trees all planted at regular intervals . . . in perfect regularity – the rectangular symmetry of the whole and the many thousand scents of sweet flowers which hung about them'. Besides the planning of the garden, much of the actual labouring was done by Cyrus, who grew trees from seed, transplanted them to the garden and watched over their progress.[3] As Alexander and his Greek army travelled eastwards through Persia

in the fourth century, they had an opportunity to see the wild flowers in the high plateaus in spring (among them the saffron crocus, native to eastern Iran) as well as the sophisticated gardens of regional palaces.

Within a few hundred years irrigation channels, fruit-bearing orchards and flowers had become so much a feature of Persian gardens that their presence was being reflected in carpet-making even before the expansion of the Islamic garden themes. At Ctesiphon, on the river Tigris just outside modern Baghdad, Khusraw Nushirvan (known to the west as Chosroes) built his

Sassanian palace in the sixth century AD. The famous Spring Carpet of Chosroes, cut up as booty at the fall of the city in AD 637, was reputed to be 55 metres/180 feet square, and was one of the glories of Ctesiphon. The carpet, woven flat rather than with the elaborate knots which were used by the sixteenth century, represented the archetypal Persian garden, a theme used ever since in garden carpets. It depicted a garden with the main canals, the four rivers of life, represented by wavy lines, crossing at the centre with flowers and trees worked in silk, gold and precious stones. Pavilions, shaded by spreading *chenars* – oriental planes – are set across water intersections where cooling breezes and scents would please the senses. Cypresses, symbolizing mortality, and fruit trees, representing life and the fertility of spring, grew in the flower-beds. Excavations have revealed that a contemporary garden layout at Imarat-i Khusrau had many of these features.

ANCIENT GREECE

Although the Greeks have never been gardeners in the horticultural sense, the mountainous terrain and lack of rain hardly providing an encouraging aspect, the whole of Greece is a natural garden. Native wild flowers cover the hills in spring; anemone, asphodel and crocus are followed by scarlet lilies; more substantial shrubs and climbers such as cistus, periwinkle (*Vinca*), honeysuckle (*Lonicera*) and ivy (*Hedera*), with aromatic myrtle (*Myrtus*) and brooms (*Cytisus* and *Genista*), provide further vegetation and sweet-scented flowers through the seasons.

The ancient Greeks showed a grand perception of landscape in their choice of sites for temples and theatres. They gave their buildings awe-inspiring panoramas, nurturing groves of native trees around each one to retain a naturalistic aspect. Stories of Greek gods and other mythological characters were often associated with grand forest trees, bosky shrubs and the more fleeting seasonal flowers. The sacred grove (*alsos*)[4] contained shade and fruit trees, repeating the pattern of temple gardens both in Egypt and in the Fertile Crescent, with trees and bushes deified.

The laurel of antiquity was, of course, the aromatic native bay (*Laurus nobilis*) which early on was dedicated to Apollo at Daphni near Athens; Daphne had turned herself into a bay tree in order to escape the god's pursuit. Many other figures from mythology were transformed into flowers at their deaths.

The spirit of Homer's landscapes pervades his eighth-century poetry. Sacred groves, trees, caves, springs of water and herbs with magical powers give background rhythm to the *Iliad* and to the travels in the *Odyssey*: the 'silver trickle' of water over a cliff, the 'black wind' on the sea and 'the meadow of asphodel, which is the dwelling place of souls, the disembodied wraiths of men' are all evocative images from nature which still convey something of the drama of the wooded mountain ranges and herb-scented valleys of mainland Greece.

Although only two gardens are described in the epics – those of Alcinous, King of Phaeacia, and of Laertes, father of Odysseus – there are plenty of allusions to a garden concept, either as a place of divine happiness and pleasure for the gods, or as enclosed orchard-gardens – in direct contrast to surrounding uncultivated land and woods – of extravagant fertility. The plants grown in them are all useful and yet Homer's descriptions make their beauty implicit. Having first waited with Nausicaa – who he describes as 'a fresh young palm tree shooting up by the altar of Apollo' – in a grove of stately poplars surrounded by a meadow, Odysseus visits Alcinous, whose enclosed garden, outside the courtyard, extends to about 1.5 hectares/4 acres. 'Here, with a hedge running down on either side, lies a large orchard ... where trees hang their greenery on high, the pear and the pomegranate, the apple with its glossy burden, the sweet fig and the luxuriant olive. The fruit never fails nor runs short, winter and summer alike. It comes at all seasons of the year, and there is never a time when the West Wind's breath is not assisted, here the bud, and here the ripening fruit; so that pear after pear, apple after apple, cluster on cluster of grapes, and fig upon fig are always coming to perfection. In the same enclosure there is a fruitful vineyard, in one part of which is a warm patch of level ground, where some of the grapes are drying in the sun, while others are gathered or being trodden ... Vegetable beds of various kinds are neatly laid out beyond the farthest row and make a smiling patch of never-failing green. The garden is served by two springs, one led in rills to all parts of the enclosure, while its fellow opposite, after providing a watering place for the townsfolk, runs under the courtyard gate towards the great house itself. Such were the beauties with which the gods had adorned Alcinous's home. Stalwart Odysseus stood before the house and eyed the scene. When he had enjoyed all its beauty, he stepped briskly over the threshold and entered the palace.'[5] In this descrip-

Wall paintings discovered on the island of Santorini (the modern Thira), just north of Crete, are a unique portrayal of recognizable plants. Almost destroyed by an earthquake and then by volcanic eruption in *c.* 1500 BC, the frescos, representing religious rituals, have been assembled from fragments and are now in the National Museum in Athens. Red lilies, probably *Lilium chalcedonicum*, grow on spectacular rocks; with bending stalks the lilies are depicted both in bud and in flower, and swooping swallows add to the natural-istic effects. Another fresco is of women collecting crocus (*Crocus sativus*) for the saffron crop; in a third room the walls are decorated with papyrus.

tion are contained all the elements of garden topography – abundant fruit trees which give sustenance and shade, a vineyard, trim flower-beds and a 'channelled' water supply.

But even earlier the Minoans in Crete between 2100 and 1600 BC, in a civilization parallel to those of contemporary Egypt and Mesopotamia, had used floral decorations on pottery (examples have been found on both Crete and other Aegean islands). Two of the plants used, rather than the wild flowers growing on the Cretan hills, were those patronized by the neighbouring Egyptians with whom they traded: the date palm, later to become a symbol of victory, though it did not fruit as far north as Attica, and the marsh-loving papyrus. A fresco in the Minoan Palace of Knossos shows lilies, irises and the autumn-flowering sea daffodils (*Pancratium maritimum*) which grow by the island shores.

The nearest approach to an historical record of practical ornamental gardening comes when archaeologists discovered that plants for decoration were grown in terracotta pots, their watering facilitated by irrigation channels, outside the Minoan palace. They were probably arranged much like those, over one thousand years later, along the south side of the third-century Temple of Hephaistos in Athens (see p. 23). The plants in the pots could have been exotic palm trees, native *Myrtus communis* with scented flowers and leaves, pomegranates or roses; they may even have been planted with the Madonna lilies (*Lilium candidum*) and irises portrayed in the fresco, both probably introduced from the neighbouring Asian continent.

The rose, although first portrayed much earlier at Knossos, became a popular motif by the fourth century. Both the single dog rose (*Rosa canina*) and the cabbage rose (*R. centifolia*), probably from Macedonia, were grown with crocus, dianthus, hyacinth, iris, lilies, narcissus, scented violets and all the usual aromatic herbs such as basil, marjoram, mint, rosemary and sage. The island of Rhodes, where by the end of the classical period roses were cultivated intensively, was legendary for the scent of the petals, which were crushed for their fragrance.

It is obvious that the ancient Greeks were by no means insensitive to the beauty of flowers. From the Bronze Age onwards their literature and art express an appreciation of both landscape and plants. But it was not until Alexander's soldiers in the fourth century brought back stories of Persian paradise gardens that the aristocrats of Athens even considered gardens and plants as adjuncts to their houses, to be enjoyed and savoured, rather than as 'necessary' cultivated orchards and vineyards which existed as an extension of agriculture.

Sophisticated Greeks of Plato's time (*c.* 388 BC) introduced shade trees from the forests to make comfortable walks for their philosophical discussions, just as in later years the Christian cloister performed a similar function of giving shade and shelter to ambulatory monks. Pupils in Plato's Academy and Aristotle's Lyceum, walking among the *peripatoi*, the avenues and groves of plane and poplar, olives and bay laurel, became known as the 'peripatetic' philosophers. There were groves of native cypress (*Cupressus sempervirens* 'Fastigiata' and the more spreading *C.s.* 'Horizontalis'), olives, both the evergreen holm oak (*Quercus ilex*) and deciduous *Q. robur* and Kermes oak (*Q. coccifera*), the Aleppo pine (*Pinus halepensis*) and the umbrella or stone pine (*P. pinea*), the Grecian fir (*Abies cephalonica*) and the white and black poplars, combined with lower-growing evergreen shrubs such as native bay, arbutus and myrtle. Spreading *Platanus orientalis* from Asia Minor provided shade in the summer; tradition has it that Hippocrates taught his students under the branches of a plane tree in the island of Cos.

Plato established his Academy in the valley of the Kephissos, outside the walls of Athens to the west. It was turned into a 'well-watered grove with trim avenues and shady walks' by the states-man Cimon. Later Aristophanes described the valley as 'All fragrant with woodbine and peaceful content and the leaf which the lime blossoms fling, When the plane whispers love to the elm in the grove in the beautiful season of spring.' Nearby, the small Garden of Epicurus was one of the few private gardens we know of – a vegetable garden cultivated by Epicurus himself to give practical expression to his philosophy. It was laid out at a cost of 7,000 *drachmai* (1 *drachma* was a labourer's average day wage), but regret-

At Knossos in Minoan Crete surviving frescos, painted in the early part of the second millennium before the civilization was destroyed *c.* 1450 BC, include a rose (top left of picture), the earliest known representation of the flower. It may be the Abyssinian rose from regions of the Upper Nile, which could have been brought to the Minoans through trade with the Egyptians. Other flowers portrayed at Knossos include white lilies, irises, crocuses, violets and lotus. Irrigation channels discovered in excavations round the palace of Phaistos seem to confirm that there were gardens for flowers and vegetables, and large pots with holes may have been for decorative shrubs and bulbs.

tably there is no record of the plants he used or of their arrangement in the garden.

Cimon also gave plane trees to provide shade in the Agora, the market place of Athens within the city walls, where sacred groves

Another Minoan fresco, restored by Sir Arthur Evans, shows a warrior with more stylized representations of lilies. These may be of the white Madonna lily (*Lilium candidum*) from the lands of the eastern Mediterranean, or the Scarlet Turk's cap lily of Thira (a form of *L. chalcedonicum*), a native in the Greek Islands as well as in Chalcedonia.

of bay and olives surrounded the Altar of Pity, a sanctuary for runaway slaves. Both the Agora area and that of the Temple of Hephaistos lying to the west have been excavated and partially restored. The Temple Garden is the first formal layout to have been revealed in Greece. Planting in its gardens probably took place in the early years of the third century. The shattered remains of terracotta pots were found in square pits, cut 88 centimetres/35 inches into bedrock, in two rows along three sides of the temple, each row separated by narrow unpaved walks. The woody trees or shrubs for these sites were layered straight into the pots, which were broken up at planting time to allow the roots to spread. Cato described the method: 'To make shoots take root while on the tree, make a hole at the bottom of a pot and push the branch you wish to root through it. Fill the pot with earth, press it thoroughly and leave it on the tree. When it is two years old, cut off the branch beneath the pot . . . shatter the pot and plant the branch in the pit together with the pot'.[6] The garden also had small beds for flowering plants, and ivy and grape vines may have been grown against the outer walls of the precinct. The Temple Garden, with quite an elaborate aqueduct watering system, survived until the Augustan period at the end of the first century AD; it has now been restored, with myrtles and pomegranates growing in the original plant pits.

In his *Oeconomicus*, written a generation after the death of Socrates, Xenophon drew attention to the King of Persia's attitude to husbandry, ranked with the art of war as 'two of the noblest and most necessary pursuits', reminding the reader that the 'Great King . . . in all the districts he resides in and visits . . . takes care that there are "paradises" as they call them, full of all the good and beautiful things that the soil will produce, and in this he himself spends most of his time, except when the season precludes it.'[7]

The naturalist Theophrastus (*c.* 370–*c.* 286 BC) succeeded Aristotle at the Lyceum. Author of *An Enquiry into Plants*, Theophrastus made a systematic classification of all known plants, the first in western literature, with their uses in medicine. Until this moment herbal lore had been transmitted verbally and memorized. His herbal included plants from the east such as Levant cotton or the cotton bush (*Gossypium herbaceum*, introduced by Sennacherib to Khorsabad on the upper Tigris in 700 BC) and the banyan tree (*Ficus benghalensis*), already described by Alexander's admiral Nearchus, who saw it growing in the plains of India, as well as mangroves in the Persian Gulf and great spiny euphorbias in Baluchistan. Plants from Egypt particularly interested Theophrastus, while plants from northern Greece and Asia Minor were described to him by his students who accompanied Alexander the Great on his expeditions. No illustrated copy of Theophrastus survives, but Pliny the Elder reported in the first century AD that some of the herbals of his period were illustrated, although seldom with completely original pictures. The most important herbal is, of course, that of Dioscorides the Greek – *De Materia Medica*, written in the first century AD in the reigns of Nero and Vespasian (see pp. 36–37). Laboriously hand-copied and translated into almost every language including Arabic, this herbal remained a standard work for consultation well beyond the sixteenth century and was studied by botanists trying to identify his plants for a further two hundred years.[8]

Theophrastus left his own garden to slaves who were to be freed on condition they looked after it. It may have been an early version of a botanic garden with plants arranged in some sort of systematic order to facilitate the study of medicine and their use as cures. Recently its site on the north side of Constitution Square was revealed in excavations but it has now been covered in.

Besides mentioning plants in poetry, Hellenistic Greeks used them as motifs for architectural decoration. The most familiar is the wild Greek acanthus, moulded into the Corinthian column. This is *Acanthus spinosus*, which has distinctly fretted leaves, unlike the more smooth and glossy Italian *A. mollis*. It is said that a fifth-century sculptor, Kallimachos, adapted the leaf design after seeing how an acanthus on a Corinthian girl's grave had grown through a fisherman's basket to make an elegant pattern. By the middle of the fourth century wreaths and swags of myrtle and ivy, friezes of grape vines and flowers and leaves were all painted on pottery, and writers such as Aristophanes and Demosthenes alluded to small domestic gardens (*kepoi*) annexed to town houses of the wealthy. Simple gardens had shade trees and flower-beds lining pathways.

The spread of Hellenism east to Asia and west to Italy was not a one-way traffic. The Greeks, in search of empire, discovered a new garden culture in the great paradise parks of Persia. In 408 BC Lysander had been shocked to discover that Cyrus the Younger worked in his own garden at Sardis in Turkey; all physical work, except in war or athletics, was considered degrading by the Greek upper crust, which depended on slave labour. In another hundred

Sea daffodils (*Pancratium maritimum*) were depicted in wall frescos at the Palace of Knossos in Crete, which date to before 1500 BC. These large bulbs – edible, according to Theophrastus, and used in various cures – grow on the shores of many of the Greek islands and produce sweetly scented flowers in summer. Those illustrated (on the right in the picture) were drawn by the Dutchman Emmanuel Sweert and published in his *Florilegium* in 1612 in Frankfurt. With no text, the drawings – named in Latin, German, English and French – are probably a form of nursery catalogue. On the left is the related *Pancratium illyricum*.

years Alexander himself was sending seeds of exotic trees and flowers to be germinated by Aristotle's students at the Lyceum. Both the peach and the lemon (*Citrus limonia*) were introduced to Greece at this time. Shortly after Alexander's death in 323 BC Megasthenes visited the Gupta empire in India and wrote of the parks surrounding the 'royal residences' where exotic evergreens – 'their leaves [which] never grow old and fall' – have their 'boughs interwoven by the woodman's art'. In Alexandria, Thebes and Antioch, expatriate Greeks copied the 'idea' of oriental pleasure gardens; exotic timbered parks were laid out combining Greek ornament and decoration in buildings with more romantic naturalistic effects culled from Asia. The tyrant Dionysius (430–367 BC) is said to have created a Persian-style pleasure park in the Greek colony in Sicily.

One of the most sumptuous of gardens was made by a Greek potentate, Heiron II (269–221 BC), in the Sicilian colony of Syracuse; it was laid out on his boat. In it there were garden beds of every sort, luxuriant with plants, and watered by ingenious lead pipes hidden from sight. There were shade bowers of white ivy and grape vine, the roots of which got their nourishment in casks filled with earth, receiving the same irrigation as the garden beds.

More important to the future of ornamental gardening style was a Greek 'peristyle' villa and garden constructed on the island of Delos in the second century BC; this may have been the prototype for the villa gardens made by the Romans in Pompeii and the surrounding countryside in the next hundred years or so.

ROMAN GARDENING

The gardens of classical Rome, crumbled to ruins for a thousand years or so, were a major source of inspiration to the great garden-makers of the Italian Renaissance. Not only were their patterns copied and their remaining statues rifled to ornament new layouts, but the whole spirit of classical literature and learning animated poets and thinkers of the new humanist age. It is not so well known that it was the agricultural writers of imperial Rome who provided most of the details of husbandry and garden lore known to western man during the Middle Ages: the works of Cato (234–149 BC), Varro (116–27 BC), Columella from the first century AD, and fourth-century Palladius (writing *c*. 380–95) were constantly referred to. Columella, although the most systematic of

all the writers, went far beyond the utilitarian; Book X of *De Re Rustica*,[9] written in hexameters, dealt with gardening as a sort of supplement to Virgil's fourth *Georgic*; it was a poetic evocation of spring rather than a purely useful text and demonstrates a sensitivity to the beauty of plants:

> Now when the earth, its clear divisions marked
> As with a comb, shining, from squalor free,
> Shall claim her seeds, 'tis time to paint the earth
> With varied flowers, like stars brought down from heaven,
> White snow-drops and the yellow-shining eyes
> Of marigolds and fair narcissus blooms,
> With Fierce lions' gaping mouths and the white cups
> Of Blooming lilies and the corn flag bloom,
> Snow-white or blue. Then let the violet
> Be planted, which lies pale upon the ground
> Or blooms with gold and purple blossoms crowned,
> Likewise the rose too full of maiden blush . . .

Unlike the gardens of Greece, of which we can discover comparatively little actual detail, the development of gardens during the time of classical and imperial Rome after the second century BC is well documented. Archaeological finds continually reveal garden layouts and planting patterns; modern archaeological methods, including pollen analysis, carbon dating of plant remains and making casts of root cavities aid plant identification. Contemporary practical authors, although writing primarily about crops, including flowers being grown for commerce, and more poetically about the countryside, are an educated source for studying known plants as well as evoking something of the Roman's attitude to his garden. Wall paintings of gardens found at villas near Rome and in the peristyle gardens at Pompeii, Herculaneum and Stabies are probably fairly accurate reconstructions of contemporary layouts as well as being stimulating pictures of more visionary distant landscapes. Then there are the herbalists and encyclopaedists, such as Pliny the Elder, a contemporary of Dioscorides, and the poets, the latter providing an inspirational stimulus to the 'good' life devoted to rural pursuits and appreciation of landscape.

Plants were obviously considered as decorative. The statues of gods, carved in marble or cast in bronze, which looked out from niches, lined colonnades and presided over fern-filled grottoes and mossy nymphaeums in the gardens, were often garlanded with ivy and grape vines. Periwinkle, myrtle and bay were made into wreaths and crowns. Many of the Roman gods (often 'adaptations' of those from other civilizations) had an interest in the fertility of the soil and in particular flowers or even parts of flowers.

In the town-house gardens, the architecture of the house surrounded a 'garden room' or series of rooms, in which fruit trees, vegetables and flowers were grown. Gardens of this type are best exemplified by the villas and gardens 'mummified' at Pompeii where the town, destroyed by a major eruption of Vesuvius in AD 79, was preserved under volcanic ash. In these small gardens an extra dimension is added by the wall paintings showing garden views. These give us a clue towards understanding the contemporary Roman's vision of ideal gardens of the 'imagination'; extending sometimes beyond a *trompe l'oeil* presentation of garden space, possibly mirror images of the garden setting, they depict exotic scenes of trees and animals evocative of the Persian *paradeisos*, which Romans of the second century BC might have glimpsed during expeditions into Hellenistic Asia.

Quite different from the inner courtyard gardens were the great public layouts where trees framed temples, civic buildings and amphitheatres, which echoed the universal form of Greek architecture. Just as in Egypt, Mesopotamia and Greece, such gardens provided essential shade and a place for repose and now became an integral part of town planning. The great villa gardens laid out from the first century BC by the patrician Romans and later by the emperors were a private extension of the idea of the sacred garden but also provided opportunities for experimenting with new plants introduced from foreign expeditions. From the first century AD many of these gardens were set in the countryside round Rome but others were also made in distant colonies.

Pompey, returning to Rome in 62 BC, built a theatre in front of which he planted trees to make a shady wood, as well as making his own garden below the Pincian Hill. Lucullus had a Roman garden to which he retired in 63 BC, on the Pincian Hill above the Spanish Steps, on the site of the Villa Medici and its seventeenth-century gardens. Although it was renowned at the time for its luxuriance and evocation of Epicurean pleasure, nothing is known of its layout; Lucullus, however, is credited with introducing cherries, peaches and apricots from the east after his campaigns.

Mithridates, ruler of most of Asia until conquered by Lucullus, had Crateuas as his medical attendant; both physician and master had an extensive knowledge of poisons derived from plants. It is even possible that Lucullus could have acquired some special plant knowledge from examining Crateuas's learned writings and famous drawings of plants, all lost to succeeding generations. We do know that the garden of Lucullus was only one of many on the hilltop, which was known by contemporaries as the 'hill of gardens'. The historian Sallust, also rich from foreign spoils, created a garden slightly to the east of that of Lucullus, where he had paintings of scenes taken from the Nile valley as well as a collection of Egyptian statues of pharaohs and queens. The umbrella or stone pines (*Pinus pinea*) which guard the hills of Rome today and are a particular feature of the Pincio may be descendants of trees from Roman times. Less than a hundred years later pines, tall distant cypresses and fruit trees as well as flowers and birds were painted on the walls of the Empress Livia's villa at Prima Porta just outside Rome. The plane tree brought from Greece to Italy in spite of warnings from Dioscorides, later repeated by Galen, on its possible danger to health (it was thought to affect breathing and the lungs) was used for shade in every garden.

The development of country estates was influenced by poetic themes from writers such as the earlier Cato (*De Re Rustica* of 160 BC), Cicero, Catullus, Horace and Virgil, all of whom expressed a deep love of the countryside and a joy in natural beauty – themes inherent in the Epicurean creed of withdrawal from public life. With new wealth and often a deep cultural sense acquired from service and travel abroad, these aristocratic owners could live in luxuriant ease. In a *villa rustica* where the pure life and country air allowed the experience of true *otium* – 'surrounded by nature man became the master of his own destiny' – owners could lay out increasingly sophisticated gardens where they could grow both useful and ornamental plants. Instead of being enclosed as inner peristyle courtyards, their gardens were open to the surrounding

Trees and flowers are realistically depicted in the frescos painted round the walls of a subterranean garden room in the Empress Livia's villa at Prima Porta from the first century AD. In this section a pomegranate in fruit is readily identifiable, and roses and ox-eye daisies flower above the low inner wall. Birds flutter between the flowers or alight in the trees. Elsewhere in the room oaks, pines and soaring cypresses frame the garden to give the impression of a landscape setting.

landscape; views of distant mountains, rolling hills, vineyards and agricultural land or the sea were an integral part of the whole scheme. What began in poetry as an exaltation of pastoral and agricultural life and a yearning for the countryside, was further developed by Virgil in the *Georgics* (written between 38 and 29 BC) with detailed descriptions of the seasons and the crops.

Virgil celebrates country life and agriculture, the actual working of the earth, as 'a happy compulsion that makes labour sweet'. This idealization of the countryside influenced the development of a patrician villa life-style made possible by vast wealth. In these villas ornamental gardening played a greater role than true farming activities (although many villa owners also retained a real farm

where the peasants could be watched tilling the soil). In place of the original small-holdings around Rome, large estates were developed throughout Latium as sumptuous country retreats – their owners such as Lucullus also retaining smaller town gardens in Rome – while corn for actual consumption had to be imported from Sicily or Africa. These magnificent layouts were also built in the far reaches of the Empire and excavations at Coimbra (the Roman Conímbriga) in Portugal, Vienne in France and Fishbourne in England have revealed their grandeur. Tree-shaded colonnades became settings for statues brought from Greece or Hellenist cities. Cicero had his own country garden but, in 54 BC, supervised the making of one for his brother Quintus at the family home at Arpinum where it was 'marvellously pleasant with a fishpond, spouting fountains, an open space' and a plantation of trees, 'Your gardener has so enveloped everything with ivy, not only the foundation walls of the villa, but also the spaces between the columns of the promenade, that I declare the Greek statues seem to be in business as landscape gardeners, and to be advertising ivy.'[10]

While poets such as Virgil wrote about the natural countryside and native plants, as well as of fruit orchards, olive trees and vineyards, other writing remains a reliable source for the history of garden planting. Pliny the Younger's letters[11] with their descriptions of plants and planting, bring these gardens alive and convey their special atmosphere. In both of Pliny's country estates villa and garden were integrated in one unit for function and comfort as well as for beauty; dwellings and terraced garden seem to have been designed together. The more formal and symmetrical layout (including topiary box) outside the actual living areas was very much integrated with the purpose for which the rooms were built; plane trees provided shade and cool sparkling fountains cascaded into marble basins. Beyond the edges of the 'hippodrome' at the Tusci villa, its fringes planted with ivy-garlanded plane trees with

At the Paul Getty Museum at Malibu in California, where the climate resembles that of Naples, the main peristyle garden of the Villa dei Papiri, probably belonging to Lucius Calpurnius Piso at Herculaneum at the end of the first century AD, has been reconstructed in as much detail as possible. Judging from recent excavations and assessment of contemporary gardens at Pompeii, it seems likely that the manicured garden of clipped box, myrtles and bay trees as well as the geometric flower-bed patterns of mounded ivy, roses, oleanders and irises have a more formal character than the original.

Excavations at provincial Pompeii, preserved under volcanic ash since AD 79, have revealed the patterns of contemporary gardens, and science has made it possible to identify plants grown in the town's public and private gardens, orchards, market gardens and nurseries. Fruit trees, including lemons, were planted out around the edge of the peristyle courtyards. Surviving wall frescos portray ideal gardens, their perimeters marked by a fence or wall, and romantic Persian-style hunting parks. In this imaginary garden scene painted on the walls of the Casa del Bracciale d'Oro, tall oleanders and arbutus shelter twining convolvulus, pinks and white lilies.

an outer ring of evergreen bay, planting patterns were loosened. Pliny's 'winding alleys', flanked with boxwood hedges, criss-crossed the fringes of the garden, which were never far from the meadows of wild flowers (see pp. 38–39).

The other country garden we know most about in Italy is the villa-city of the Emperor Hadrian at Tivoli, laid out between AD 118 and 138. Here in the plain just below ancient Tivoli, for long a setting for villas of wealthy Romans, Hadrian chose a site sheltered in winter but cool in summer. Near by stood Horace's first-century villa with views over grove and lofty town and a stream from the 'clearer than crystal' spring which fed the Aniene river. Pine trees grew on the highest hills and olives clothed the slopes. Although much plundered for almost two thousand years, Hadrian's villa has had its main outlines revealed by excavations. Far from being a private garden for retreat, it was almost an extension of a public building and reflects Hadrian's thinking on town planning; all the major buildings alternated with wide garden spaces punctuated with fountains and canals. On a vast scale, this garden became a manifestation of Hadrian's (and Rome's) imperial power and experience, incorporating features such as Greek temple architecture and the Academy in Athens, as well as the Egyptian Canopus, which may have been intended to express Rome's domination of other civilizations.

In fact, although inspired by ideas from Greek and Hellenistic traditions, Hadrian's vision of a central plan was original and innovatory, later influencing the development of both Renaissance and Baroque architecture. Little if anything is known of its planting, only that each major building was linked with a garden area. (Unfortunately on the island theatre, surrounded by the circular canal, there was no space left for flower-beds to imitate the profusion of planting in the earth- and flower-filled watertight compartments found at Coimbra.) Today tall cypresses, umbrella or stone pines and olives grow free to decorate terraces and frame the ruins to make a romantic landscape in very different style from its original appearance, when gardens and orchards would have been diligently tended.

None of the excavations or pictorial representations, nor Pliny's two garden descriptions, can reveal more than a hint of how the gardens looked when overflowing with flowers and vegetables in summer. From other Latin authors we can fill in some of the gaps. Both Varro's *De Re Rustica* (*c.* 40 BC) and Columella's *De Re Rustica* (*c.* AD 60) were practical farming manuals in which plants, including flowers grown as crops, were mentioned. Varro particularly stressed that farming should be for both profit *and* pleasure; he said little about actual gardens, although he did advise laying out commercial nursery beds for growing roses (the rose gardens of Paestum were the most famous), violets (in a later passage he explained how difficult it was to keep a raised violet bed, the *violarium*, safe from erosion by rain storms) and herbs in order to

supply the demand for flowers and garlands in Rome. Certain identification of Varro's flowers is not possible as the Romans gave the name *viola* to more than one plant; scented stock-gilliflowers or stocks (*Matthiola incana*) are one alternative. He gave the time of the year for planting lilies (presumably the Madonna lily, *Lilium candidum*), crocus and rose bushes. He also recommended gardens for pleasure and mentioned elaborate gardens such as those of Lucullus near Frascati and in Campania. In his own aviary at Casinum (reconstructed in 1614 by J. Laurus to illustrate Varro's description in *Roma Vetus et Nova*), there was a domed casino in which a table 'revolved so that everything to eat or drink is placed on it at once and moved round to all the guests'. He also spoke of 'dwarf trees' which alternated between the outer stone columns of the surrounding colonnade.

Columella's Book X *De Re Rustica*, besides being poetic, is the more practical treatise on both vegetable and flower cultivation. A somewhat older contemporary of Pliny the Elder (who frequently quoted him), Columella gave considerable details of the culture of plants. In Book XI he dealt with winter-pruning not only of vines but also of briar hedges. In February poplars, willows, elms and ash trees should be planted before they put forth leaves, new rose beds should be planted; in early March 'broadcast of the berries of laurel and myrtle and the other evergreens in beds' as well as 'upright and other kinds of ivy'. By the end of October 'if anyone is minded to make a wilderness, that is a wood where various trees are planted together, he will do well to plant it with acorns and seeds of the other trees'.[12] He even gave tasks to be accomplished by artifical light in the dark November and December days. One was to sharpen tools and make handles for them of the best wood, with holm oak, hornbeam (described by Pliny as 'yoke elm') and ash being preferred in that order. His famous description of how best to establish a hedge composed of brambles, roses and Christ's thorn (*Paliurus australis*) is in Book XI III –8: 'The seeds of these briers must be picked as ripe as possible and mixed with meal of well-ground bitter vetch . . . sprinkled with water [and] smeared either on old ships' hawsers or any other kind of rope, and these are dried and put away in an attic . . . when midwinter is passed . . . the ropes . . . are produced from the loft and uncoiled and stretched lengthways along each furrow and covered up in such a manner that the seeds of the thorns . . . may not have too much earth heaped upon them but may be able to sprout' – a method of

At Coimbra the excavated foundations of magnificent houses and gardens from the time of Septimius Severus (AD 146–211) have revealed design elements with flower-beds made into self-contained islands in the central pool within the peristyle surround. Packed with earth for planting, these provided opportunities for a profusion of shrubs and flowers, kept cool and fresh with constantly playing water jets. Formal in outline, in a series of semicircular and right-angled indentations, the islands are entirely geometrical. Fountain jets curve to complete an architectural sequence.

hedge-making still being recommended in the England of the Tudors.

Pliny the Elder (c. AD 23–79), the naturalist, was the younger Pliny's uncle; he died from fumes while observing the eruption of Vesuvius which engulfed Pompeii in AD 79. His *Naturalis Historia*,[13] in 37 volumes, is extraordinarily comprehensive. Quoting extensively from any previous literature available to him, it is a mixture of uncritical acceptance of earlier superstitions as well as being immensely practical. Pliny described the art of ornamental gardening as *topiara opera* or *opus topiarum*; *topia* comes from the Greek meaning elements of a place and was used to describe the scenes depicted inside the peristyles of Pompeii, on outside garden walls and on the inner walls of the larger villas. In Pliny's time tree-clipping and hedge-cutting were but one part of the whole and the

ordinary labouring gardener was called the *topiarius*. Pliny referred to cypress trees being cut 'into tableaux of *opus topiarum*; hunt scenes, fleets of ships, and all sorts of images'. He ascribed the practice of tree-clipping – *nemerosa tonsilia* – to a Roman, G. Matius, who lived at the end of the first century BC. Pliny borrowed freely from the works of Theophrastus to describe trees and plants he may never have seen. He wrote of the plane tree, an 'exotic' first brought to Sicily from the Ionian Islands, which with the banyan (*Ficus benghalensis*) was supposedly used in Greece to make shady bowers for shepherds. Although Pliny's manuscript did not survive, a copy was available in England in the eighth century and a fine illustrated manuscript copy was produced in Italy in the fifteenth century (see Chapter Three).

In the fifteenth and sixteenth centuries, when Italian Renaissance architects looked for inspiration in garden making, it was to the Latin authors that they turned. Vitruvius's work on architectural principles (*De architectura*, 30 BC), in which he also described the art of landscape painting as already well developed, Hero of Alexandria's *Pneumatica* (first century AD) on hydraulic devices, with Varro's and Columella's more farm-orientated works and Pliny the Younger's description of his two country villas all became standard references for expansion into a new humanist idiom.

The paintings found on the walls of tombs from the expansionist period of the New Kingdom (beginning in the sixteenth century BC), although probably realistic portrayals of contemporary gardens, do not represent any exact garden or location. Instead, by imitating growing plants in earthly gardens, they serve as symbols of the magical refreshment of the soul of the departed on its journey through the afterlife while waiting for the day of judgement. The fruiting trees and flowers were also considered as offerings to the gods, all of whom had mystical associations with the fertility of the earth. Delight in

TOMB PAINTINGS

flowers was particularly associated with the sun-god Amun-Re, and the divine king had also 'created the fruit tree' and 'made the green herb and sustaineth the cattle'.

The tombs belonged to substantial merchants or officials and these 'luxury' gardens were usually sited outside the walls of the town, with their own walls a firm barricade against animals and wind. Their formal symmetry was in part dictated by the need for irrigation channels. The rectangular or square pools placed usually in the centre of the

enclosures were dominant features, with the dwelling house of almost minor importance placed to one side. The pools were filled with water plants – both lotus and papyrus – and there were fish and ducks, presumably for food and sport. Plants, including grape vines, fruit trees, figs, pomegranates and date palms, grew in profusion around the edge of the pools as well as against the walls. Other gardens were necessary enterprises, run by nurserymen, providing vegetables as well as cut flowers for religious festivals, leaves and flowers for funeral wreaths in addition to oils and perfumes for embalming.

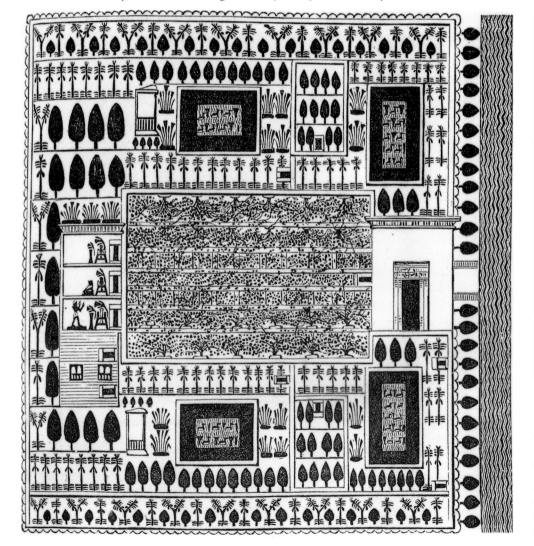

Left; The walled garden painted in the tomb of an Egyptian official of the Pharaoh Amenhotep in *c.* 1400 BC shows a symmetrical plan with papyrus-fringed pools shaded by trees and other plants. An imposing gateway is reached by boat from an outer canal, which is used to irrigate and to fill the four inner pools. The house itself, surrounded by vegetation, is set deep in the garden and two viewing pavilions look out over the small pools. Both the date palm and the doum palm are shown and vines are trained on a central trellis.

Above left: The papyrus (*Cyperus papyrus*), originally a marsh plant from southern Nubia on the Upper Nile, with yellow-green umbels clasped by green bracts held on tall stems, can grow to 5 metres/15 feet in height. As well as being shown growing in the tomb paintings of gardens it frequently appeared as a decorative motif on capitals and columns – those of the great hall at Karnak are the most familiar. Among its useful products were writing materials and sailcloth. The illustration of papyrus growing in the marshes in the south of Sicily is by Marianne North and was painted in 1865.

Above: The painting of the garden and ornamental fishpool in Nebamun's tomb at Thebes dates to *c.* 1400 BC. It is one of a series on the walls in which the importance of the sacred lotus flower is clear to see. Around the pool rows of palms (both the single-stemmed *Phoenix dactylifera* and the branched doum, *Hyphaene thebaica*) bear clusters of dates. Conically shaped sycomore figs (in the upper right hand corner the sycomore goddess, Hather or Nut, is arranging the fruit as offerings in the Hereafter) and ordinary figs (*Ficus carica*) provide both fruit and essential shade. The papyrus planted around the margins of the pool is a symbol of ultimate rebirth.

PLANTS OF TUTANKHAMUN

The treasures revealed in Tutankhamun's tomb at Thebes after its discovery in 1922 had lain buried for 3,000 years. Tutankhamun reigned for only eight years between 1339 and 1327 BC in the Eighteenth Dynasty; when he died at the age of eighteen he was buried with his worldly possessions for his enjoyment during the afterlife. Also buried with him were the ingredients necessary for survival – bread, fruit, wine, ointments and other materials of plant origin which have been identified.

Even the plants used for the wreaths placed in the tomb are known, preserved in the dry climate: soft branches of olives were intertwined with willow (*Salix subserrata*, which grew in the moist soil of the Nile delta), wild celery, lotus, cornflowers and mandrake fruits. There were bouquets of persea and olive leaves tied to a stick of the common reed (*Phragmites australis*), which was also used for making arrows. Bows were made of both the flowering or manna ash (*Fraxinus ornus*) and the Syrian ash (*F. syriaca*). Oils (including olive, linseed, almond, sesame and ben oil, the latter from *Moringa aptera*) were used for anointing the head and body. Resin was probably obtained from one of the native acacias and from Mediterranean mastic (*Pistacia lentiscus*) and coniferous resin, important for mummification, from Aleppo pine (*Pinus halepensis*), although the Egyptians also had access to Cilician fir (*Abies cilicica*) and oriental spruce (*Picea orientalis*). Incense came from the frankincense tree (*Boswellia sacra*) from southern Arabia or Somalia and myrrh from *Commiphora myrrha*. Native trees were used for making tomb furniture but ebony from farther south and cedar from the Lebanon were also employed for the chests. Other soft woods such as cypress, juniper, fir and pine were used, while for hardwoods the Egyptian woodworkers preferred imported box, oak and ash, decorating their work with birch bark.

Carved ivory panels found on a casket in the king's tomb show him and the queen in a garden setting. The frame of the panel is bordered with scarlet-flowered poppies (*Papaver rhoeas*), cornflowers and mandrake, while in the lower panel children pick poppies and mandrakes. The queen hands Tutankhamun two bouquets containing papyrus, white-flowered lotus (*Nymphaea lotus*) and gilded poppies. Behind the figures vines bearing clusters of grapes grow over a pergola.

On the back of the seat of the golden throne Tutankhamun and his Queen Ankhesenamun are shown wearing floral collars similar to those found in the tomb. Huge floral bouquets of papyrus, lotus and poppy are shown at the side of the throne, the wooden frame of which is overlaid with sheet gold. More botanical motifs showing a papyrus swamp are carved on the back panel of the chair. The floral collars include thin strips of date and pomegranate leaves, berries of golden nightshade (*Withania somnifera*), blue water-lily petals (*Nymphaea caerulea*), cornflowers and some fruits of persea (*Mimusops laurifolia*).

The lotus is a recurring theme both in garden portrayals and in all decorative art. The scented blue lotus (*Nymphaea caerulea*) is the sacred lotus of the life-giving Nile; its pointed petals open in the morning and close at evening, allowing the sun god Amun Re to enter the flower at night and be reborn at dawn. The white water-lily (*N. lotus*), symbol of the god Osiris, has rounded petals and sharply toothed leaves; its petals open in the afternoon and close in the morning. Both are natives of Egypt, the blue lotus being portrayed as early as 2000 BC in stone carvings. This Roman mosaic now in Naples shows the pink-flowered Indian lotus (*Nelumbo nucifera*), introduced to Egypt in Hellenistic times and already naturalized near Alexandria by Strabo's day.

THE *DE MATERIA MEDICA* OF DIOSCORIDES

Dioscorides, a physician and contemporary of Pliny the Elder, was born in Asia Minor in the first century AD. Although written in Greek, his famous manuscript herbal is more familiar under its Latin title, *De Materia Medica*. It contains names, descriptions and healing virtues of herbs – he mentions 500 plants, actually seen by him, together with recommendations for observing their growth at all seasons of the year, instructions on how to gather them – only when the weather was fine – and on how to store 'flowers and sweet-scented things' in 'dry boxes of Lime-wood', and 'moist medicines' in other suitable ways. The earliest copy in existence has magnificent full-page coloured paintings of plants, probably taken from earlier copies of the work (the original manuscript may not even have been illustrated) or from that of Crateuas. It was made in the sixth century AD and discovered in Constantinople in the 1560s. The ambassador from the Emperor Ferdinand to the Sultan, Ogier Ghiselin de Busbecq (1522–92), first saw the manuscript in 1562 and it was finally purchased for the Emperor Maximilian II in 1569 and taken to Vienna. Known as the *Codex Vindobonensis*, this version of *De Materia Medica* was accepted as an infallible authority at least until the Renaissance. By the sixteenth century, the compilers of herbals, although still dependent on Dioscorides, gradually had begun to include a wider range of plants (from more northern parts of Europe); but both text and illustrations from *De Materia Medica* were still used in the earliest printed woodcut herbals. The Italian botanist Pierandrea Mattioli is the most renowned of the commentators; his *Commentarii in sex libros Pedacii Dioscoridis de medica materia* identifies many of the original plants, while incorporating new plant descriptions (and descriptions of their medical properties).

Left: Asphodelus ramosus from the oldest surviving copy of *De Materia Medica*, the *Codex Vindobonensis* in the Österreichische Nationalbibliotek in Vienna. Made and illustrated in Constantinople about AD 512 for Juliana Anicia, daughter of the Emperor Flavius Anicius Olybrius, the codex has 400 full-page coloured illustrations of plants, besides other more general representations. In one, Dioscorides himself receives a mandrake; others show Crateuas and one depicts an artist and easel. Some of the more naturalistic of the plant illustrations may have been taken from Crateuas's *Rhizotomikon*, written in the first century BC, which was certainly known to Dioscorides.

Right: Physalis alkekengi franchetii and two different mulleins (*Verbascum* species) in the *Codex Neapolitanus*, written in Greek in the seventh century and now in the Biblioteca Nazionale in Naples. The drawings in this version of *De Materia Medica* are smaller than those in the *Codex Vindobonensis* and several are grouped on a page.

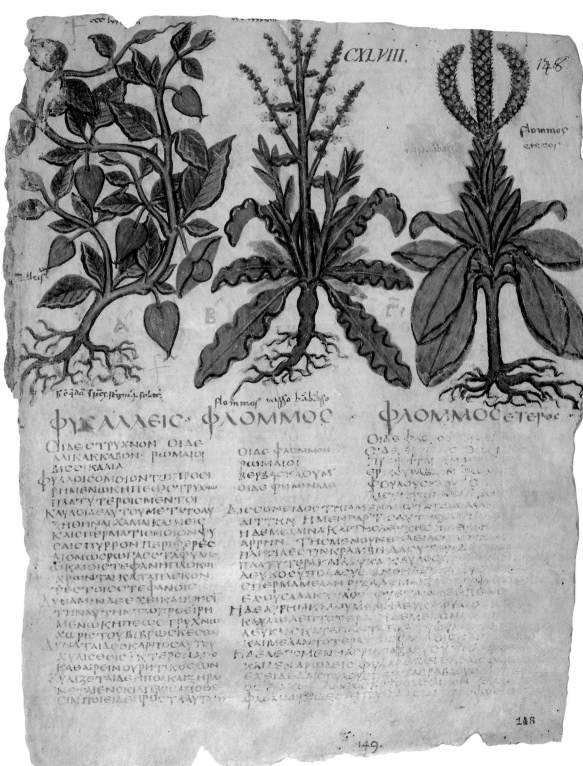

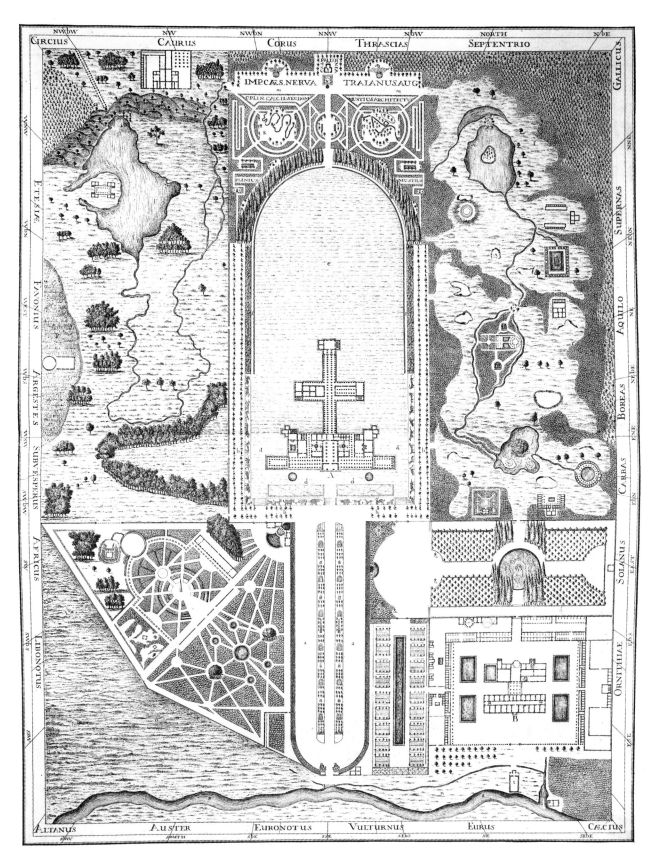

THE YOUNGER PLINY'S COUNTRY VILLAS

Pliny's letters written between AD 97 and 107 describe the gardens of his two country villas, at Laurentum near Rome and Tusci at Tifernum Tiberinum in the upper valley of the Tiber. Surrounded by 'woods of ancient trees' – European or sweet chestnuts, ash, poplar, linden, elm, and suckering cherry (and what Virgil called 'the common oak, the oracle tree of the Greeks') – and meadows of wild flowers, the garden at Tifernum had orchards and vineyards as well as pleasure grounds. 'In front of the colonnade is a terrace laid out with box hedges clipped into different shapes from which a bank slopes down, also with figures of animals cut out of box . . . On the level here waves – or I might have said ripples – a bed of acanthus. All round is a path hedged by bushes . . . trained and cut into different shapes, and then a drive oval like a racecourse, inside which are various box figures and clipped dwarf shrubs.' The 'hippodrome' at the villa was open in the centre but 'is planted round with ivy-clad plane trees, and outside there is a ring of [bay] laurel which add their shade to that of the planes'. Planting at the back becomes 'darker and densely shaded by the cypress trees [the fastigiate *Cupressus sempervirens*]'. Roses grew in the more open sunlit area. Winding alleys were lined with more box 'clipped into innumerable shapes, some being letters which spell the gardener's names or his master's'. Obelisks of box alternate with fruit trees, perhaps Virgil's 'thorny plum' and 'hardening pear' and the many kinds of apple grown in Virgil's 'Alcinous' orchard' (*Georgics* Book IV). The open space is set off by low plane trees. Vines are trained to shade a curving dining seat, and to shade a whole building in which 'you can lie and imagine you are in a wood'.

Opposite: In *The Villas of the Ancients*, published in 1728, Robert Castell showed a reconstruction of Pliny the Younger's villa, today the site of the modern Città di Castello. Although more or less faithful to Pliny's own detailed descriptions, Castell, influenced by contemporary changes of fashion from the strict formality of French-inspired gardens to a more relaxed landscape image, portrayed Pliny's garden to resemble Stephen Switzer's recommendation in *Ichnographia Rustica* (1718). The plan, showing the surrounding countryside visible from the villa, is dominated by the central 'hippodrome', with axial alleys leading through lateral garden areas.

The painting of a garden by the sea from a fresco discovered in the excavations at Pompeii shows a Roman seaside villa which will have had many of the characteristics of Pliny the Younger's Laurentine villa on the shore near Ostia, only 27 kilometres/17 miles from Rome. Planting was less ambitious than in his more northern garden, probably due to the exposed site. Pliny wrote that 'all round the drive runs a hedge of box, or rosemary to fill any gaps, for box . . . dries up if exposed in the open to the wind and salt spray'.

CHAPTER TWO

THE GARDENS OF ISLAM

A hundred years after Marco Polo's almost legendary reports, the sophisticated splendours and beauties of gardens in the eastern outposts of the Islamic world were confirmed by another western observer. Ruy Gonzalez de Clavijo was one of the first European travellers to record his impressions of the city and orchard enclosures laid out on a vast scale for receptions and festivities by the great Tamerlane (or Timur). Raised in the courtly circles of Castile, Clavijo was sent by Henry III of Castile and Leon as ambassador to the Timur emperor at Samarkand in central Asia (now Uzbekistan). After long months of travel, the Spanish ambassador reached Kash, beyond which the fertile plains stretching towards Samarkand sustained five yearly crops of corn, besides cotton, grape vines and melon yards between orchards adjacent to the road. He and his companions arrived in the outskirts of Samarkand at the end of August 1404 and were received in a great park-like orchard: 'We found it to be enclosed by a high wall which in its circuit may measure a full league, and within it full of fruit trees of all kinds, save only limes and citron trees which we noticed to be lacking . . . Further there are here six large tanks for a great stream of water flows from one end of the orchard to the other. Five rows of very tall and shady trees have been planted beside the paved avenues which connect the pools and smaller paths lead out of these avenues to add variety to the design.' In the

In this eighteenth-century miniature painting the Mughal emperor Shah Jahan (1628–58), great-great grandson of the emperor Babur, the founder of the Indian dynasty of garden-makers, is shown holding a seal. The flowers which decorate the border include lilies, irises and tulips. Shah Jahan, builder of the Taj Mahal as a mausoleum for his wife, was the father of Dara Shikoh who gave the album of Mughal miniatures, including the paintings of flowers, to his bride Princess Nadira.

centre palaces were built as almost impregnable fortresses on an artifical mound surrounded with deep ditches. Beyond the orchard another equally large area, ringed with 'tall and beautiful trees', was planted as vineyards. After his weary journey across the high and desert-like Persian plateau, Clavijo must have been captivated by the beauty and luxuriousness of Tamerlane's court and by the extent of the garden oases: 'so numerous are these gardens and vineyards surrounding Samarkand that a traveller who approaches the city sees only a great mountainous height of trees and the houses embowered among them remain invisible.' On arrival at another great garden known as Dilkusha (or Heartsease), Clavijo and his troupe found Tamerlane in residence in his palace. The emperor, by now seventy and nearly blind (he died the following February), was seated on cushions on a raised dais in front of a fountain from which the jets of water fell into a basin on the surface of which floated red apples. Within a few days Tamerlane moved to the Plane Tree Garden – both these gardens are described by the Emperor Babur a hundred years later – and then to another garden entered by a majestic gateway ornamented with tile-work in blue and gold. Clavijo described scenes of celebration in gardens made in the plain.

Soon after Tamerlane's death in 1405 his son Shah Rukh moved the capital to Herat (now in Afghanistan) and constructed another fine garden, covering 40 hectares/98 acres, which was also described later by Babur, with its pools, red tulips and roses. Both the garden at Samarkand and that at Herat deeply influenced the youthful Babur and became the prototypes of Babur's own gardens around Kabul and in the Indian plains (see pp. 64–65).

Tamerlane's gardens, although grand as befitted a great emperor, were not unusual in the world of Islam; their extent may have surprised the Spanish ambassador but Clavijo may well have known, at least by report, the Moorish gardens in Toledo, Cordova and Seville, cities which were all by then in Castilian hands. Even Granada, although nominally Muslim until 1492, was often an ally of Castile, and its gardens, laid out only between 1319 and 1390, must have been at their peak by the turn of the century. Henry III's predecessor, Alfonso X of Castile, had been a distinguished scholar (producing scientific treatises and the Alfonsine astronomical tables for which he is best remembered). He it was who arranged for translations to be made into Castilian Spanish of the works of the great Arab botanists, Ibn Wafid and Ibn Bassal, who worked in the Toledo gardens in the eleventh century.

Although Christian gardeners were, like the Muslims, inspired by symbolic elements in the Bible, most actual gardening in Clavijo's Europe was utilitarian and the renaissance of scholarship and learning which was to flower in gardening as in all the arts was still only a stirring. When in the early sixteenth century new attitudes did emerge, Europeans were able to build on the foundations laid by the Muslims who had taken advantage of the strength of earlier cultures to create new civilizations in which a synthesis of religious precepts with the practicalities of everyday life led to a distinctive attitude to the beauty of flowers and gardens.

tect all of nature, which had a divine source.

Islam inherited and extended many aspects of the cultures existing in the conquered territories. In taking Sassanian Persia in the eighth century, the Arabs found themselves heirs to many sophisticated traditions in garden making (see Chapter One); they also discovered in the fertile valleys and uplands a wealth of wild flowers new to them, as well as many garden flowers already cultivated by the Persians.

Backed by serious botanical scholarship – by the ninth century the Greek text of Dioscorides was translated into Arabic – the Muslims built on the basic fourfold format of the Sassanian paradise garden to develop the Islamic garden according to Koranic teaching as a sensual experience, a terrestrial paradise, a foretaste of heaven for those who followed the word of the Prophet. To the nomad's dream of cool shade, running water, fruit and scent inside protective walls was added a new symbolism that enhanced the garden as a private place for contemplation where man could try to find an equilibrium between himself and God, temporarily removed from the human worries and turmoils of the outer world.

The development of garden fashions under Islam is best viewed against a background of the scientific pursuit of knowledge combined with the influence of the teachings of the Koran. Trees and

THE SPREAD OF ISLAM

The spread of Islam was rapid indeed. Within a hundred years of the prophet Muhammad's death in 632, the areas covered by the ancient civilizations of Sumeria, Babylon and Assyria, Persia and Egypt were all under one rule. The Arab conquerors dedicated to the expansion of the new religion were remarkable for their restraint in some aspects of warfare: their first caliph, Abu Bakr, issued orders to his soldiers that no palm trees were to be cut down, cornfields burnt or orchards ravaged during their victorious progress, since the Koran taught that it was man's duty to pro-

Above: Illustrating the fifteenth-century poem *Halnamah*, the miniature painted for the future Emperor Jahangir (1605–27) in 1603–4 shows a typical Islamic garden, enclosed behind high walls and with access through an imposing gateway. At its centre the four rivers of life, which divide the garden into quarters, meet at a square basin. Cypresses and almond trees with sunken flower-beds are also typical features of the *chaharbagh* or fourfold garden.

Right: The rose of Muhammad from the Turkish manuscript *Akhlaq-i Rasul Allah* produced in 1708. The rose was of special significance to the Muslim. By tradition it was created from the drop of perspiration that formed on the prophet Muhammad's brow during his heavenly journey. In Islam the whole of nature becomes a symbol with each flower admired not so much for its individual beauty but because it is a reminder of the spirit of God. The idea of paradise as a reward for the Muslim faithful was expanded in the Koran so that an earthly garden became an anticipation of heaven to come.

flowers, unless they had some religious or symbolic appeal, were still grown and described mainly for their usefulness: the oriental plane – the mighty *chenar* – offered shade; fruit trees provided sustenance, and herbs and roots furnished medicines; however, fruit blossom and flowers assumed a more luxuriant purpose in the concept of the 'heaven on earth' prescribed by the Prophet. Under Islam the very layout of the Persian gardens became instilled with rich symbolism. The basic quadripartite plan of the *paradeisos* parks had its origins in the geometry of irrigation canals: gardens were divided into four quarters (sometimes each further subdivided into four) by water channels which met at a central circular basin or fountain (*haud*). For the Arabs the number four assumed a cosmic importance based on traditions inherited from Babylonian, Pythagorian and Hindu sources. The interaction of the cube, representing the multiplicity of nature's manifestations, with the heaven-inspired dynamic circle, dictated how sacred Muslim architecture developed. The fourfold garden can be considered as an open-air version of this theme – not only a place of refuge and beauty, but also an expression of spiritual understanding of the universe.

This basic format remained stable through the centuries, enriched and inspired by Muslim teaching and interpretation. Over the next thousand years or so many gardens of this pattern were developed in three continents – Asia, Europe and Africa; they even influenced Spanish mission gardens established at the end of the eighteenth century in the hot and dry western States of America. Especially in the territories included in Safavid Persia, in Andalusia and in the empire of the Mughals in India, the Islamic gardens developed as a high form of art in which religious meaning and teachings as well as poetic imagery combined with a genuine love of flowers and beauty to produce exquisite compositions. The basic elements of geometry and symmetry reflected a remarkable unity of concept throughout Islam. Variations in garden appearances in the different countries depend more on local climate and planting possibilities than on variations in the fundamental features of style. The early Abbasid gardens in Baghdad, those of the Umayyad dynasties in Spain from the ninth to the end of the fifteenth centuries (the last Arab foothold in Andalusia was held against the Christians until 1492, when Ferdinand and Isabella captured Granada and with it the exotic paradise gardens of the Alhambra and Generalife, the gardens of the Timurids, sultans in central Asia in the fourteenth and fifteenth centuries, those of the Safavids in

western Persia from 1501 to 1732 and of the Ottoman Turks from the early 1500s to the twentieth century have all been 'worked' inside this tradition. Perhaps the great Mughal emperors, descendants of Babur and dominant in northern India for three centuries from the early 1500s, built the most breathtaking gardens of all on the plains at Delhi and Agra and on the shores of the shimmering Lake Dal in Kashmir (see pp. 66–67).

THE PATTERN OF ISLAMIC GARDENS

Water, the fundamental element without which no plants could flourish, was for the Muslim the purifier and symbol of life itself, just as the geometric layout dictated by the practicalities of irrigation also became symbolic. But the enclosed oasis garden exploited other properties of water. Excavations at Pasargadae show that as early as the sixth century BC Cyrus I had had gravity-fed channels and basins of stone incorporated in the design for their beauty; a separate system of watering devices ensured that plants had adequate moisture. In sophisticated Islamic gardens the sound and movement of water rippling over specially carved stone or mosaic patterned channels or cascading over constructed screens (*chadars*), sparkling in fountain jets (the jets had a practical use in keeping away insects) or bubbling in low spouts, added a further dimension to the visual pleasures. The *chabutra*, a stone or marble platform, was often placed above the meeting point of the four main channels, and was a resting place for contemplation, an integral part of garden appreciation. An owner might sit for hours or days with his own thoughts, lulled by the musical sounds of water, the presence of dark-eyed houris and the scents and colours of ephemeral seasonal flowers. The provision of deep shade by spreading *chenars* and the more dappled foliage effects of fruit trees, contrasting with dark columns of cypress, added a further element of sophistication and beauty.

For the first Islamic 'desert' gardens we have no exact images. The earliest tradition in Persian and Mughal miniature painting, representing a highly idealized and poetic view of gardens, dates only from the fifteenth century. Archaeological reconstructions together with manuscript sources can, however, give us at least a clear idea of the general layout and the relationship between buildings and water features. Occasionally, as we have seen in Chapter One, written descriptions of trees and flowers are sup-

The Mughal miniature of c. 1610–15, painted during the reign of the Emperor Jahangir, shows a private enclosed garden where friends meet at the intersection of the water canals. Cypresses, fruit trees, bananas and other exotic trees and bushes grow in the sunken beds below the level of the main pathway. Jahangir was the greatest gardener and flower-lover of all the Mughal emperors, commissioning a collection of paintings of Kashmiri wildflowers from his favourite artist, Mansur. Between them, Jahangir, his son Shah Jahan and his courtiers, constructed 177 gardens on the lakesides and foothills of Kashmir during the first half of the seventeenth century.

plemented by surviving decorative carvings which identify the most popular plants.

John Harvey's analysis of al-Biruni's lists of plants of AD 1050 provides us with a limited idea of which plants may have been cultivated in the eastern Islamic gardens.[1] To these might reasonably be added the plants of eastern origin mentioned by two Spanish Arab botanists. These plants had travelled westwards as had the more familiar plants of Dioscorides and Pliny, which were certainly known to the Baghdad scholars in the ninth century.

In the middle of the eleventh century fruit known to have been in cultivation included almonds, apples, apricots, bananas, brambles, cherries (*Prunus avium*) and morello cherries (*P. cerasus*), figs, grape vines, jujubes (*Zizyphus jujuba*), mulberries, olives, oranges and plums, while terebinth (the mastic, *Pistacia terebinthus*) was grown for its nuts. Dates and pomegranates had been grown for centuries. Not all these trees would have been grown in enclosed gardens; some would be planted in rows in orchard-style meadows and irrigated by open-channelled *jubes*. Al-Biruni wrote of roses of numerous types: single and double in white, yellow (*Rosa hemisphaerica*), deep red and 'black' as well as pink, and there were musk roses (*R. moschata*) and briars. Among other purely ornamental woody plants he mentioned white and yellow jasmine (*Jasminum officinale* and *J. fruticans*), lavender, myrtle, rue, moisture-loving willows and, of course, the oriental plane tree. Among al-Biruni's flowers and herbs are forms of *Anemone coronaria*, camomile, colchicums, coriander (*Coriandrum sativum*), cumin (*Cuminum cyminum*), elecampane (*Inula helenium*), fumitory, mallow, sweet marjoram, marshmallow, mints, mugwort, narcissus species, opium poppies, southernwood, thyme, alexanders (*Smyrnium olusatrum*) and asparagus, as well as the more utilitarian chickpeas, cabbage, carrots, celery, cucumber, leeks, lentils and turnips. The economic plants included hemp, indigo and safflower (*Carthamus tinctorius*) used for dyeing, and saffron (*Crocus sativus*) used medicinally, as a condiment, as a disinfectant and as a dye. To this list violets, the Madonna lily and oleanders would seem to be obvious additions. Gertrude Bell's 'tiny rills of water fringed with violet leaves' spotted in an old garden near Tehran in 1892 in the shade of ancient plane trees, with briar roses 'a froth of white and yellow', must have been a thousand-year-old reality.

We can conjure up a visual image of the gardens as they will have looked in this early period with flowers growing in the sunken beds under the fruit trees. The flowers would have been planted singly – not massed in drifts as in modern gardening – to spread on their own, sometimes in the 'lawns' mentioned by Clavijo, between drifts of clover. In early spring, almonds with pink blossom on leafless branches would open the season, a symbol of annual regeneration and, in Persian poetry and painting of a later period, often intertwined round the dark cypress spires which represented mortality. Under the spreading branches of the almond trees, white and yellow narcissus would be in flower to be followed by scarlet crown anemones; in summer opium poppies might be a crop in garden or orchard, with roses or jasmine to add sweet scent and colour.

The fourfold Islamic garden, its high surrounding walls pierced by a monumental doorway, had a principal canal of constantly flowing water dissected at right angles by smaller channels. The plantations of fruit trees, roses and other flowers lay in geometrically arranged beds below the level of the flanking pathways – usually at the depth of about 1 metre/3 feet, but sometimes, for fruit and citrus trees, as in the eleventh-century Alcázar in Seville, as much as 4.5 metres/15 feet – so making irrigation simple and to provide the sensation of walking on a carpet of flowers. Some trees planted in 'basins' would be deliberately stunted in growth, but most, including the inevitable *chenar* and cypress and fruit trees such as almond and plum, were essential for shade. Four *chenars* often surrounded the centre pavilion or mausoleum. Most of these elements are visible in many of the small illustrations, known as miniatures, in the manuscript memoirs by the Emperor Babur describing the gardens near Kabul, and other manuscripts in both Persian and Indian literature (see pp. 62–63).

As information travelled, many of the characteristics of the Muslim garden were adopted in medieval Europe. In the *hortus conclusus* there were often central pavilions and vine- and rose-covered pergolas and arbours, although, due to the colder and wetter climate, there were obvious planting differences. In northern Europe flower-beds were often raised for practical reasons of drainage, a practice also recommended by Roman writers on husbandry and commercial flower-growing.

The Islamic garden, in its emphasis on high enclosing walls which created an inner, isolated, private paradise, differed essentially from the European garden styles which developed after the Renaissance. In the west man either openly demonstrated his control over nature with vast geometric layouts such as those of Le Nôtre, which stretched out into the forests of France, or strove to express his oneness with it as exemplified in the romantic English landscape tradition. The Muslim, seeking to create a personal paradise in anticipation of the heaven to come, effected a compromise between these extremes. He used a pre-established geometry, providing in its structure flowing water, green shady trees and abundant fruit, not only for the enrichment of his *inner* garden, the garden of the soul, but also to make possible the growing of fruits, trees and flowers in the material garden, the garden *without*, which gave immediate solace. The same sense of enclosure appeals to modern westerners who are constantly in search of privacy and withdrawal from an increasingly alien and public world, and whose often urban gardens also offer a pre-established geometry.

ISLAMIC SCHOLARSHIP IN THE MIDDLE EAST

Under the Abbasid caliphate who claimed descent from the prophet, and was the ruling dynasty from 750 to 1258, scientific studies were encouraged during a time when Europe had retreated into Dark Age chaos. By 762 the Abbasids had transferred their centre of operations to Baghdad and the city became respected for its pursuit and dissemination of knowledge. Ancient Greek texts, the heritage of centuries, were translated into Arabic and became available to eastern readers. Although philosophical works by unbelievers were banned, scientific studies of medicine and plants were not felt to be in contradiction of religious principles. In spite of prohibitions on image-making it was permissible to make representations of plants in the form of floral and vegetal motifs. Indeed, plants were considered to be a valuable part of the divine creation which should be shared by all human beings; Christian and Jewish scholars were invited to participate in Muslim botanical studies of plants and their practical uses.

By the ninth century AD the Islamic world was already divided

A page taken from the thirteenth-century Arabic *Kitab al-Diryaq* (*diryaq* being the Arabic translation of the Greek *theriak* – an antidote to the poison of a venomous serpent) has exceptionally beautiful miniatures of plants and superb calligraphy. The plants portrayed are all those for pharmaceutical use; the manuscript, derived from Galen's work and earlier Greek studies, is a collection of preparations and cures for snake venom. There are thirteen illustrated pages of plant portraits, each containing six panels of different herbs.

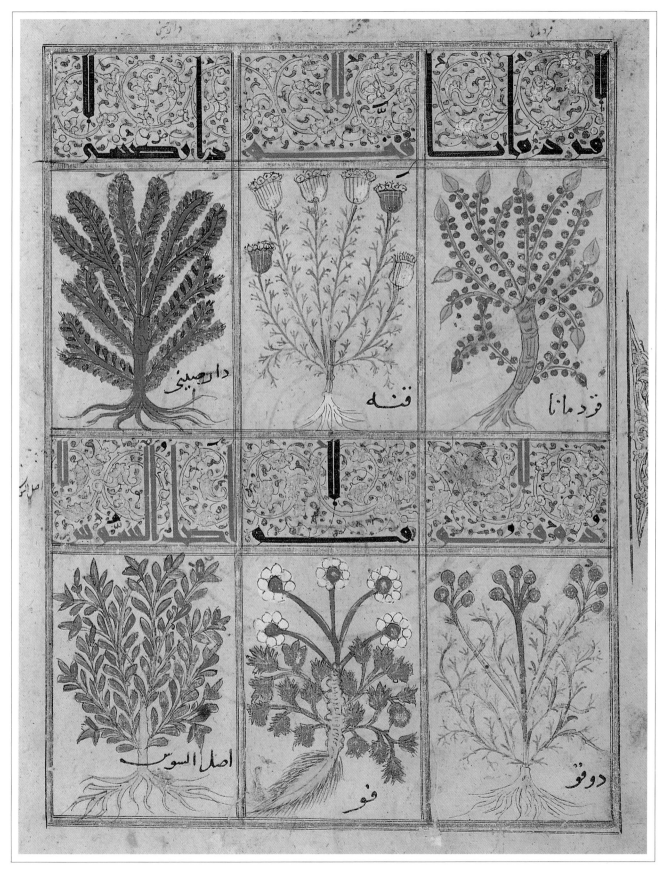

up into power blocks. Its main cultural centre under the Abbasid caliphs remained in Persia, Iraq and northern Syria, but the Umayyad caliphs in Cordova made Andalusia the centre of European learning. Travelling scholars such as al-Harran not only brought the latest knowledge to the outlying regions but also took with them living plants and medicinal drugs. It is not surprising that the plants found growing in the Umayyad gardens in Toledo, Seville or Cordova, recorded in the eleventh century by Ibn Bassal and a hundred years later by Ibn al-Awwam (see pp. 58–59), included many which grew wild in the mountains of Persia as well as those long 'cultivated' there in gardens.

THE MOORS IN SPAIN

Although finally expelled from Spain in 1492, the Moors' cultural legacy in architecture, agriculture and gardening remained of lasting importance throughout the Iberian peninsula; plant lists drawn up by Arab botanists enable us to conjure up real visions of how gardens appealed to all the senses. Many of the Muslim gardens in Spain, completed from the tenth century onwards, made use of or copied irrigation features which remained from the Roman occupation; besides Spanish wild flowers, these gardens grew many eastern Mediterranean plants, and some from farther afield, including the exciting mainly bulbous plants brought by Arab travellers from distant Persia. Long before the Islamic penetration into Spain, many oriental plants had been introduced to southern Europe by the Romans and the Visigoths. These plants will have come from as far east as India and China as well as from Persia, Ethiopia and other parts of Arabia; they will have been introduced over many centuries through Egypt, Greece, Rome and the Byzantine empire. Plants mentioned by authors such as Pliny the Elder and Columella in the first century, and Isidore, Bishop of Seville in the sixth century, would be familiar in gardens well before being chronicled by these Arab botanists. Bay, tamarisk, pine (both *Pinus pinea* and the Aleppo pine, *P. halepensis*) and palm trees (including the date palm) were all plants well known before the eleventh–century writings of Ibn Bassal. Pliny and Columella both mentioned the plane tree, olives, artichokes, figs, cypresses, dates, violets, roses, white lilies and, of course, the pomegranate. Isidore (*c*.560–636), who introduced a form of monasticism in Seville, and made a special point of having a garden within the cloister, spoke

Thirteen Arabic translations of Dioscorides's medical encyclopaedia, *De Materia Medica*, were made between the ninth and fifteenth centuries, the first at Baghdad under the Abbasid caliphate. An incomplete Arabic translation from Spain held in Paris dates to the twelfth or thirteenth century and is almost certainly copied from the manuscript which was translated in Cordova in AD 950 (see below).

of the saffron crocus, sugar cane, ginger, the camphor tree (*Cinnamomum camphora*) and mulberries.

A further translation of a fine illustrated copy of Dioscorides's *De Materia Medica* was undertaken at Cordova in 950 by the monk Nicholas for the Caliph Abd-al-Rahman III (912–61). The manuscript had been sent as a gift by the Byzantine Emperor Constantine VII Porphyrogenitus (913–59). We can get some idea of its splendour from two surviving copies of Dioscorides, the *Codex Vindobonensis* of AD 512 and the *Codex Neapolitanus*, which dates from the seventh century. Naturally Dioscorides had been able to include only plants from Greece and southern Asia Minor, but within a few years Juljul, the personal physician to the Caliph Hisham II (976–1009), compiled a supplement to include local Spanish plants identified from his personal 'botanizing' expeditions. This was issued in 983.

In 939 the Caliph Abd-al-Rahman III, known as Defender of the Law of God, had begun to build the great garden city of Madinat az-Zahra a few miles north of Cordova on the lower southern slopes of the Sierra Morena (see pp. 56–57). Its history has been chronicled by both Arab and Spanish historians, but excavations in this century have revealed the more detailed layout of buildings and the patterns of garden beds, pools and water channels. These grand gardens at Medinat az-Zahra were not the only important Moorish gardens in Spain, but the date of their construction coincides with a peak in plant introductions from the east and an upswing in the development of a scientific attitude towards gardens and agriculture. We have no exact knowledge of their planting but we do have two main sources for establishing what plants could have been grown in tenth- and eleventh-century gardens,[2] or in those of a slightly later date such as the Alhambra and Generalife in Granada, the last outposts of the Muslim world in Spain (see pp. 60–61). From the tenth and eleventh centuries Arab botanical scholarship was most closely connected with Spain and two important sources for known plants after AD 1000 survive there. The first work was written in 1080 by Ibn Bassal, a botanist in Toledo; the other a hundred years later by Ibn al-Awwam. Both convey a practical attitude to agriculture and gardening, giving details of how to grow plants and move them, and some of the plants listed seem purely decorative rather than merely useful.

Other literature of the period, of which little survives, also gave lists of cultivated Spanish flora. A great encyclopaedia by Ibn al-Baitar (d. 1248 in Damascus) concerned the medical virtues of plants, but much more charming and evocative is *Novelties in Description of the Spring* by an eleventh-century Spanish Muslim, al-Himyari, which gives the flowers most commonly grown in gardens rather than newer rarities. This has a special appeal as it may indicate the plants which might have been found in quite humble rather than palace gardens: the pheasant's eye narcissus, which rivalled the rose in the affections of the Arabs, as well as trumpet narcissus, yellow and white jasmine, mauve stock-gilliflowers or stocks, yellow wallflowers, violets, red roses, water-

lilies, camomile, scarlet poppies, bean-flowers and, of course, the delicate blossom of almond trees and sweet-scented myrtle, with ubiquitous pomegranates grown for flower and fruit (as well as the less domesticated 'wild' form). Al-Himyari reminds us how for contemporary garden lovers the fragrance of fruit blossom in spring was almost as important as the later fruits.

The Cordova caliphate came to an end in 1031 (the palace and gardens of Madinat az-Zahra were virtually destroyed) and the Spanish Muslim world was split into separate states, among the most important of which were Toledo and Seville. The royal garden at Toledo, the Huerta del Rey, was created by Ibn Bassal's predecessor during the eleventh century. Ibn Bassal remained in charge there until the Castilian conquest of 1085, after which he moved to Seville where he worked for the Sultan, sowing newly imported seeds and carrying on his work in horticulture.

A poem composed in 1348 by Ibn Luyun (1282–1349) from Almeria in Spain, and later known as 'the Andalusian *Georgics*', drawing heavily for plant and gardening information on al-Awwam as well as on Greek and Roman classical authorities, provides contemporary plant lists and advice on propagation. Most importantly the rules for pleasure gardening are laid down in simple verse, effectively a fourteenth-century summary of the garden as it had developed under Islam (all of its precepts could apply to Tamerlane's garden), as a refuge from the heat and winds found in open desert sites; but the poem also brings the garden alive with suggestions for planting, evoking a strong visual image of shade trees, twining vines and roses and flower-beds. A house should be set in a garden with a southern aspect and 'a watercourse where the water runs underneath the shade', with evergreen shrubs next to the reservoir and 'somewhat farther off, arrange flowers of different kinds and farther off still evergreen trees, and around the perimeter climbing vines . . . and under [them] let there be paths which surround the garden to serve as a margin . . . plant any fruit tree which grows big in a confining basin so that its mature growth may serve as a protection against the north wind without preventing the sun reaching [the plants] . . . In the centre of the garden let there be a pavilion in which to sit . . . clinging to it let there be roses and myrtle, likewise all manner of plants with which a garden is adorned and this last should be longer than it is wide in order that the beholder's gaze may expand in its contemplation'.[3]

It seems likely from the details of design and planting later incorporated in his writing that the poet was familiar with the gardens of the Alhambra and the Generalife.

ISLAMIC GARDENING IN THE EAST

After AD 1000 the history of central Asia is turbulent. Wandering Turkish-speaking nomads, culminating in 1218 with Genghis Khan, the forerunner of Tamerlane, pushed their way westwards, destroying traditional irrigation systems and with them the prosperity of the desert lands. Surprisingly these violent tribesmen often became patrons of the arts and encouraged local artisans to add brilliance to the new courts they established. Genghis Khan's descendant Tamerlane at Samarkand and Tamerlane's son at Herat developed their own distinctive cultures around 1500. Gardens, first called *bagh* or *chaharbagh* at the time of Genghis Khan's invasion, were now developed for receptions and festivities, giving a more public feeling to the basic format of the enclosed oasis garden. The Samarkand gardens and orchards had become extensive by 1400 and by the middle of the next century Herat had become a centre for producing beautiful illustrated manuscripts

and glowing faience tiles portraying flowers. Peonies introduced from China appeared as motifs in many artefacts. Farther west, at Tabriz, in what is modern Iran, the Ilkhans laid out the garden of the Golden Horde in 1302 with a square walled enclosure providing a meadow for the sojourn of the emperor. Avenues of willows and poplars were specially planted round the garden perimeter to control the populace while central pavilions joined together by water channels were for the use of the court.

Nearly a century after Clavijo's visit to Tamerlane the young Babur (1483–1530), a descendant of Genghis Khan through his mother's family and of Tamerlane through his father, and founder of the mughal dynasty in the early 1500s, also visited Samarkand and went on to stay for forty days at Herat, by then a centre of arts and culture. The gardens which he later laid out and loved near Kabul and in the flatter Indian plain near Delhi were based on the format of those he admired in these cities: 'arranged symmetrically, terrace above terrace and . . . planted with beautiful *narwan* [fine trees], cypresses and white poplars. A most agreeable sojourning place, its one defect is the want of a large stream'. In the following two centuries his descendants brought the *chaharbagh* garden to its finest flowering in both India and Kashmir. But Babur was not only a garden maker; his memoirs show his keen interest in nature and in the plants, including ornamental trees and shrubs, fruit trees and flowers, which he could grow successfully. Babur knew at least 25 sorts of fruit, including some he found in India. He knew cypresses, elms, holm oaks, planes, poplars and

In Iran the art of silk weaving reached its peak under the Safavid Shah Abbas I (1588-1629). The detail of a woven coat (*left*) with its design of realistic-looking golden flowers and fresh green leaves against patterned silver threads, shows the African marigold (*Tagetes erecta*), newly introduced from Mexico via Europe. During his reign Shah Abbas constructed walled gardens in the city of Isfahan as well as the great Chaharbagh Avenue which, edged with plane trees and poplars and with a central watercourse, ran for a mile to the river. He also laid out gardens along the route to his summer palaces on the Caspian Sea (where much of the silk was produced), which were explored in 1626 by Charles I of England's envoy and his companion Sir Thomas Herbert.

Right: The detail of an eighteenth-century Rajput miniature of an Indian princess in a garden reveals typical features inherited from the ideal of the Islamic and Mughal garden. Within high enclosing walls with imposing entrance gates there are pavilions and lotus-filled pools, and cypresses and flowering fruit trees as well as colourful flowers flourish in the geometrically arranged beds. Beyond the outer walls irrigation from the river has made it possible to grow a shrubbery which includes cypresses and bananas and perhaps other exotic trees and flowers as well as those native to India.

willows; he mentions oleanders, jasmine and roses as well as pandanus palm or screwpine (*Pandanus tectorius*), tulips and violets, and clover spread to carpet the ground beneath the branches of the fruit trees.

We do not have only Babur's memoirs as a source for garden activity in the period. His contemporary Kasim[4] writes of gardening techniques and on the design of a typical *chaharbagh*, its pavilion and the relationship of the plants to the geometric layout. A main canal, opening out to make a wide pool, flows down the centre of the garden past a pavilion, with two streams each a cubit in width (a cubit was about 50 centimetres/19 inches) and three cubits apart lining the perimeter. Poplars line the edge of the outer water channels and roses, apricots and peaches flank the inner garden edge. Clover is to be planted as a substitute for grass (as recommended by Babur for his Garden of Fidelity) between flower-beds. In four main plots Kasim recommends planting single species of fruit such as pomegranate, quince, pear and peach. Of the greatest interest are his recommendations for specific flowers to be

planted in each of nine beds; it is the first positive mention in literature of flowers specially cultivated in beds rather than allowed to spread and 'naturalize'.

By the seventeenth century travellers with European attitudes produced more realistic eye-witness accounts of gardens and plants to augment the idealized versions seen in miniature paintings, capturing what it felt like to be actually *in* the garden. Persia remained almost inaccessible to foreign visitors until the time of

The famous garden carpets produced throughout the Islamic world reveal a typical pattern of the terrestrial garden and of the garden expected to be found in heaven to come. With beautiful colouring, these carpets brought the delights of the summer garden indoors during winter. The design of the Wagner Carpet in the Burrell Collection, dating to the early seventeenth century portrays a characteristic layout with a central pool as well as strong parallel water channels, flanked by pairs of pyramidal cypresses and *chenars* or oriental planes, in which waterfowl and fishes swim. The flowering trees and flowers demonstrate an appealing theme of luxuriant profusion designed to contrast with the harsh, dry conditions of the surrounding desert.

the great Safavid Shah Abbas I (1588–1629) who re-established the country as a formidable power. After that time travellers from the west also brought plants; summer-flowering four-o'clocks or marvels of Peru (*Mirabilis jalapa*) and tuberose (*Polianthes tuberosa*) recently introduced from the New World and the tropical amaranthus (*Amaranthus caudatus*), already mentioned by Kasim, reached Persia and central Asia. Revelling in the summer heat, they added a wider range to seasonal flower displays, supplementing the mainly winter- and spring-flowering natives.

The shade and cooling waters attracted the traveller as they had the nomad through the centuries. Sir Thomas Herbert accompanied Charles I's ambassador, Sir Dodmore Cotton, to Isfahan in 1626. Before a hasty departure for the Caspian sea Sir Thomas was able to appreciate the great Shah Abbas's new garden city: 'Gardens here for grandeur and fragour are such as no City in Asia outvies; which at a little distance from the City you would judge a Forest, it is so large; but withall so sweet and verdant that you may call it another Paradise; and Agreeable to the old report, *Horti Persarum erant amoenissimi*.'

Sir John Chardin, an Anglo-French jeweller travelling in Persia in the 1660s, visited Isfahan and described the Persian garden more critically. Knowing the profusion of native Iranian bulbs and flowers available for gardeners, Chardin complained, 'I have found it to be a general rule that where nature is most easy and fruitful, they are very raw and unskilful in the art of gardening . . . The most particular reason one can assign to this is that the Persians don't walk so much in gardens as we do but content themselves with a bare prospect and breathing the fresh air: For this end they set themselves down in some part of the garden, at their first coming into it, and never move their seats till they are coming out of it.' There were essential differences between European pleasure grounds which were meant to be walked in and appreciated in a theatrical sense, and the gardens of Islam which represented paradise and the devout Muslim's deeper inner vision. Elsewhere Chardin continued: 'The gardens of the Persians commonly consist of one great walk . . . bordered on each side by a Row of Plantanes [bananas], with a bason of Water in the middle of it . . . and likewise of two other little Side-Walks, the Space between them is confusedly set with Flowers, and planted with Fruit-Trees, and Rose-Bushes; and these are all the decorations they have.'

Some of the gardens Chardin saw were those laid out by Shah Abbas, who had made ancient Isfahan into one of the most beautiful cities of its time, its glittering domes, tiled with floral arabesque patterns, towering over wide shaded avenues and spacious terraced gardens watered by a complicated irrigation system. Most impressive of all was the mile-long Chaharbagh Avenue cutting through four vineyards to the river. The central water channel, faced with onyx and intersected with secondary rills, was flanked with eight rows of stately plane trees and soaring poplars which shaded flower-beds of roses and poppies. A description of the Chaharbagh written two hundred years later by Sir Robert Ker Porter captures some of its grandeur and serenity.[5] 'We passed through the most charming parts of the Chahar-Bagh; taking our course along its alleys of unequalled plane trees, stretching their broad canopies over our heads . . . Thickets of roses and jessamine, with clustering parterres of poppies and other flowers embanked the ground; while the deep-green shadows from the trees, the perfume, the freshness, the soft gurgling of the waters, and the gentle rustle of the breeze, combining with the pale golden rays of the declining sun, altogether formed an evening scene, as tranquilizing as it was beautiful.'

The seventeenth-century poet Ramzi was asked by Shah Abbas II to write a poem in praise of the garden of Sa'adatabad of which the Chaharbagh Avenue was a part. Besides the billowing fruit blossom and mauve-flowered Judas trees, Ramzi praised scented narcissus, violets, hyacinth, sweet sultan (*Centaurea moschata*), poppy, anemone, larkspur, iris, tulips, white and gold lilies, damask and musk roses with red and yellow petals, white jasmine, sweet basil, marigolds, hollyhocks and *Jalapa mirabilis* in addition to tuberoses from the New World recently introduced through Europe.

All travellers in the lands of Persia and Central Asia mention the searing heat and cold of the high plateaus. Only a few penetrated beyond the Elburz range of mountains and descended the northern slopes to the Caspian shore 30 metres/100 feet below sea level, encountering there a very different subtropical climate. Charles I's ambassadors made the arduous journey to the north. Along the route the shah had built a series of oasis gardens as stopping places for his own annual migration. One of these, known today as Taj Abad, was described by Sir Thomas Herbert: 'The garden is north from the house yet joining to it, it has severall discents, each part giving eightie paces, and seventie broad, this watered by a cleare rivolet (tho little) by whosse vertue it abounds in Damask Roses and other flowers, plentie of broad spreading Chenars (which is like our beech) with Pomegranates, Peaches, Apricockes, Plummes, Apples, Pears and Cherries . . . it enjoys a Hot-house well built and paved with white Marble, and these are the rarer, because they are seated and walled about, in a large even Plaine rich in nothing but Salt and Sand.'

Today only poplars outline the remaining three terraces but gnarled rose bushes and grape vines tumble over the crumbling water channels. The old *qanats* still bring water from the mountains; it runs clear and cool through the open *jubes* in the village built against the wall of the garden. Once over the rocky Elburz range the travellers found themselves descending into a subtropical wilderness above reptile-infested malarial swamps. Here Shah Abbas had laid out steeply terraced paradise gardens with rushing water cascades. He entertained his guests in the garden pavilions but we have no records of the planting other than Chardin's later travel notes.

Chardin, although unimpressed in general by the gardens, enthusiastically described some of the flowers he saw growing in them and growing wild in the fields: 'The flowers of Persia by the vivacity of their colours are generally handsomer than those in Europe, and those of India . . . Along the Caspian coast there are whole forests of orange trees, single and double jasmine, all European flowers, and other species besides. Towards Media and the southern parts of Arabia [on the western side of the plateau], the fields produce of themselves tulips, anemones, single ranunculus, of the finest red, and imperial crowns. In other places as round about Isfahan, the jonquils grow of themselves . . . they have in the proper season seven or eight sorts of daffodils, and there are flowers blooming all winter long . . . white and blue hyacinths . . . dainty tulips and myrrh . . . in spring yellow and red stock and amber seed [?] of all colours and a most unusual flower called the clove pink, each plant bearing some thirty blooms.' Besides these Chardin noticed 'the lily of the valley, the lily and violets of all colours, pinks, and Spanish jasmine of a beauty and perfume surpassing anything found in Europe . . . There are beautiful marshmallows [probably hollyhocks], and, at Isfahan, charming short-stemmed tulips . . . The rose which is so common among them is of five sorts of colours besides its natural one, white, yellow, red and others of two colours *viz* red on one side

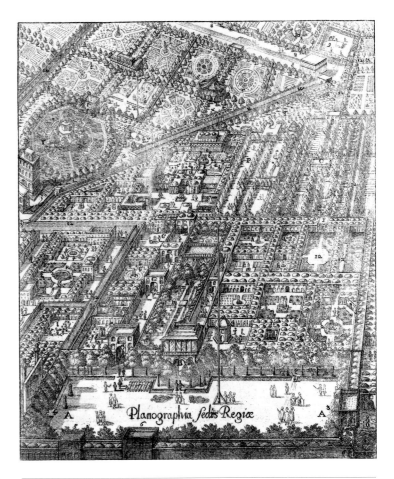

An engraving by Engelbert Kaempfer (1651–1715), the German botanist, for his *Amoenitatum exoticarum politico* of 1712, shows the city of Isfahan with the grand avenue of the Chaharbagh and individual gardens laid out around palaces and pavilions by Shah Abbas during the early part of the seventeenth century. Visiting in 1637, Alfred J. Mendelslo describes the king's garden as 'what they call a Tsarbagh . . . one of the noblest in all the World. It is above half a League in a perfect square, and the River Senderut, which hath spacious walks on both sides of it, divides it in a cross, so that it seems to make four Gardens of it.'

and white or yellow on the other . . . I have seen a rose tree which bore upon one and the same branch roses of three colours, some yellow, some yellow and white, and others yellow and red.' Chardin noted the largest specimens of cypresses, plane trees and pines in the gardens at Shiraz which he visited in 1674. Most of the flowers he mentions can be identified in the Persian miniatures of the period; among these the rose, as a special favourite of the Prophet, is the most frequently painted.

PLANTSMANSHIP IN TURKEY

Many of the plants seen by Chardin in the seventeenth century, as well as their cultivated garden forms, were already in Europe, introduced over centuries by soldiers, pilgrims and travellers through the Levant and Anatolia. After the fall of Constantinople in 1453 newly opened relations with the Ottoman Turks led to an acceleration in introductions from east to west as well as in the opposite direction. In 1558 the Frenchman Pierre Belon, the first to describe the cherry laurel and the lilac, expressed admiration of the gardens which he had seen during his travels in the Levant between 1546 and 1548 and of the Turk's appreciation of flowers: 'There are no people who delight more to ornament themselves with beautiful flowers, nor who praise them more, than the Turks. They think little of their smell but delight most in their appearance. They wear several sorts singly in the folds of their turban; and the artisans have often several flowers before them, in vessels of water. Hence gardening is in as great repute with them as with us; and they grudge no expense in procuring foreign trees and plants, especially such as have fine flowers.'

The Turks, Hittites who came from far-distant Asia to found their Seljuk empire were nomads and during their sweep eastwards absorbed the tradition of the Persian garden paradise; their gardening activities ran parallel to the Turkish-speaking dynasties who stayed in central Asia. Gardens were enclosed and symmetrical with flowing water, cypresses and plane trees for shade. Since 2000 BC the Hittites had grown bulbous plants – the useful onion, leek, garlic and the saffron crocus – holding annual spring festivals as the snows melted and the first flowers appeared on the mountain slopes. Although we have few records of Ottoman gardens before the seventeenth century, we know that the Turk developed a special interest in flowers and in cultivating them for their beauty; bulbs sent to western Europe in the sixteenth century were already 'garden' plants, not wild species. Early public records reveal large-scale cultivation of bulbs and of roses in the palace gardens in Constantinople and Edirne in Adrianople in the last quarter of the sixteenth century (see pp. 68–69). In May 1593 50,000 white and 50,000 blue hyacinths were ordered from Maras. In September 1593 rose trees for the garden at Edirne were ordered by weight: 400 *kantar* of red roses and 300 *kantar* of white, making a total of nearly 40 tons of rose bushes. The meadows of tulips at Manisa are of legendary fame. These vast consignments would seem to confirm reports that the sultan grew flowers for profit in the gardens of the Topkapisaray, selling roses, violets and vegetables from the royal enclosures. The Turks were to carry the tradition of a love of flowers with them through the Balkans to the gates of Vienna. By 1526 the Ottoman empire extended over Asia Minor, Egypt, Greece, the Balkans and Hungary. It was certainly commonplace for potted plants to be part of the baggage train of any Ottoman army; it was at the second siege of Vienna in 1686 that Kara Mustafa Pasha planted a garden in front of his tent for the duration.

Mehmed II had laid out a garden round his palace at Edirne in 1451–52, before he conquered Constantinople. His contemporary biographer Kritovoulos describes how 'around it he planted gardens decked with all sorts of shrubs and domestic trees bearing beautiful fruit.'[6] In the city after the conquest Mehmed created pleasure grounds to surround the Topkapi Palace in much the same style: 'large and lovely gardens abounding in various sorts of plants and trees bearing beautiful fruit' were set among 'conspicuous and beautiful groves and meadows'. Mehmed's vizier, in improving the Byzantine city, insisted that gardens and fruit should be provided for 'the delectation and happiness and use of many'.

Ogier Ghiselin de Busbecq, ambassador from the imperial court at Vienna to Sultan Süleyman the Magnificent from 1554 to 1562, not only discovered the sixth-century illustrated manuscript of Dioscorides (see p. 57), but also introduced the cultivated garden tulip to Europe. The following years were exciting ones for European gardeners as trees, shrubs and bulbs long familiar to Islam began to flood into Europe. The story fits best into the history of gardening after the Renaissance (see Chapter Four), but it was centuries of Muslim gardening development and scholarship that made these plants and knowledge of their cultivation readily available to a newly civilized western world. The Turks, people who had originally come from Central Asia, with cultural contacts with China, India, Afghanistan and Iran, first had encountered Islam at the turn of the tenth century as their migrations to the West began. The tulips were said originally to come from Central Asia and were brought west during the Turkish migrations (tiles decorated with tulip designs date from the twelfth-century Seljuk period), but twenty wild species also exist in Anatolia.

The vast palace and gardens, the remains of which lie five miles outside Cordova, the Umayyad capital of Muslim Spain, existed in their full glory for only forty years between 936 and 976. It was given the name of Zahra after the most beautiful of the caliph's wives. Situated under the southern slopes of the Sierra Morena and with plentiful water provided by aqueducts, the gardens could grow all the rare plants and seeds brought from the east.

MADINAT AZ-ZAHRA

The pleasure city of Madinat az-Zahra was created by the Caliph Abd-al-Rahman III between AD 936 and 976, when Cordova was the centre of learning in western Europe. After his death it was destroyed in the civil wars between rival dynasties. It covered 120 hectares/300 acres but most of the dwellings, including the caliph's palace and dependencies, were on three main terraces with market gardens, a mosque and gardens with pools and fountains as well as cages for wild beasts and birds lying on the flatter ground at the base of the hill. The royal dwellings and reception rooms, made from limestone blocks with pink marble columns, faced a square pool on the lowest of the three terraces. Colonnades supported arches of stone work carved in graceful floral patterns which were reflected in the shimmering water. The gardens, covering one third of the whole area, with walkways raised above the sunken flower-beds (but due to surface rock not as deep as in many Islamic gardens), were surrounded by water channels painted in red ochre. On the western side these, controlled for irrigation purposes, descended in noisy cascades. Narrow irrigation channels fed from the central reflecting pools watered the flower-beds (an outlet has even been discovered at the corner of a bed). Water for the gardens, as well as for the vast throng of 20,000 courtiers, administrators and slaves who lived at Madinat az-Zahra, was brought 15 kilometres/10 miles by aqueduct from springs in the neighbouring hills.

There were avenues of cypress, groves of bay trees, pomegranates (coming from Damascus through North Africa), rose gardens and flower-beds of tuberoses and lilies and almost certainly orange trees. The Red Fort at Delhi, constructed under the direction of Mughal Emperor Shah Jahan seven centuries later, closely resembles the layout at Madinat az-Zahra.

The painting by Dionisio Baixeras, showing the arrival in AD 951 from Constantinople of the monk Nicholas who has come to translate the Greek text of Dioscorides's *De Materia Medica* into Arabic, hangs in the great hall of Barcelona University. In AD 949 an envoy from the Byzantine Emperor Constantine VII Porphyrogenitus (913–59) brought a copy of Dioscorides's work to Cordova as a gift to the Umayyad sultan. In 983 under Hisham II (976–1009) the sultan's physician Ibn Juljul added an important supplement to include the plants at that time known in Spain.

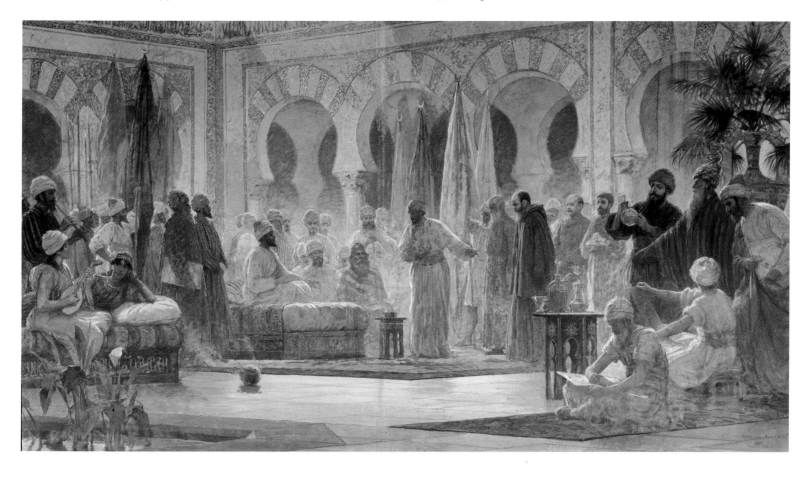

ARAB BOTANISTS: IBN BASSAL AND IBN AL-AWWAM

Two manuscripts, written in Spain in the eleventh and twelfth centuries, are hand-books on agriculture and gardening. In spite of difficulties in interpreting names, they provide a remarkable list of known plants, particularly fruit. Among the more exotic of the latter were bananas, azarole (*Crataegus azarolus*), the apricot (*Prunus armeniaca*) and citrus. Other trees included azedarach (*Melia azedarach*), today naturalized throughout southern Spain. *The Book of Agriculture* was compiled by Ibn Bassal in about 1080; during his career Ibn Bassal travelled widely on botanizing expeditions, visiting Sicily, Alexandria, Cairo, Mecca, Khurasan (in northern Persia) and Valencia in eastern Spain. He experimented with growing oranges (the bitter orange *Citrus aurantium*, known today as Seville orange), figs and vines. The second book, on Andalusian agriculture, was written by Ibn al-Awwam a hundred years later and shows a considerable increase in the species cultivated, with new introductions including lemons, the Judas tree, oleanders, hibiscus, mallows, medlars and the water-lily.

Al-Awwam is one of the first writers to encourage gardeners to think of design; his ideas were taken up in the fourteenth century by Ibn Luyun in his poem (see p. 49). Al-Awwam recommended growing cypresses to mark corners, and as avenues along the main walks, and also using cedars and pines planted in rows to make shady alleys, with citrus fruit and sweet bay presumably in more open areas. Jasmine was to be trained on trellis or over pergolas while water pools could be shaded by pomegranates with taller elms, willows and poplars (known as black and white elms). Hedges were of box and bay laurel as well as composed of intertwining climbers such as ivy, jasmine and vines. He also encouraged taking plants from the wild to use in gardens, suggesting moving ivy (*kissus*) in February and planting it near water channels.

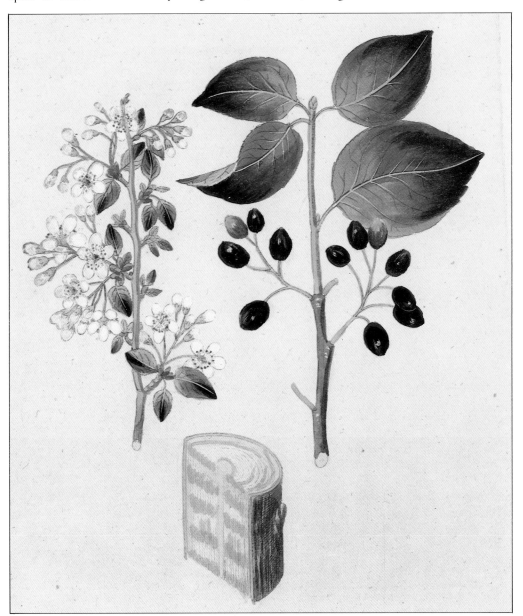

The St Lucy cherry (*Prunus mahaleb*) is first mentioned in Ibn al-Awwam's *Kitab ab-filaha*. It is described as 'a savage tree, cultivated in the gardens, where it grows quite well, strongly, and if its roots are implanted, it is difficult to destroy it or take it off. Even oldness can nothing against it; only complete lack of water dries it and kills.' Its origin seems to have been in Abyssinia and it was acclimatized in gardens of Seville in the eleventh to thirteenth centuries. In Spanish-Arabic documents it is mentioned as having been used for grafting stock for fruiting plums and cherries.

The readily identifiable and naturalistic picture of camomile is from the Bury St Edmunds codex of the Apuleius Platonicus *Herbarium* of the sixth and seventh century and dates to *c.* 1120. The portrayal is thus contemporary with the Arab botanists in Spain and the camomile is one of the plants mentioned by Ibn Bassal. Ibn Bassal and Ibn al-Awwam provide a lengthy list of bulbs, flowers and useful herbs. Bulbs included white and yellow narcissus, iris, white lilies, saffron and sea daffodils. There were many 'useful' plants besides camomile: anise, balm, basil, coriander, cumin, mandrake, marjoram and twelve different kidney beans. *Nigella sativa* or black cumin was grown for its aromatic spicy seeds, violets (both wild and cultivated) for scent, and wormwood for its pungent leaves. Wallflowers (*Cheiranthus cheiri*) and stock (*Matthiola incana*), camomile and marguerites were admired for their scent and beauty.

A plan of an orchard, included in a manuscript of a poem copied in 1685, is typical of the delicate paintings executed in the Deccani region of India. Many of the plants portrayed were mentioned by the Arab botanists writing in Spain seven hundred years earlier. Included are fruiting figs, pomegranate and citrus trees underplanted with poppies, lilies and narcissus; willows and cypresses flank the garden pavilion through which the central canal flows. The fundamental features of an Islamic garden have remained constant throughout the centuries.

B est preserved of all the Moorish gardens in Spain, even if not retaining authentic planting, both the Alhambra, constructed in the fourteenth century by the Nasrid sultans, and the Generalife on the hillside above, built in the middle of the thirteenth century and used as a summer residence, still retain their magic. Breezes from the snow-covered Sierra Nevada keep the gardens cool in summer. High walls protect and hide a series of unroofed enclosures in which water rushes through marble channels or curves in

THE ALHAMBRA AND GENERALIFE

graceful arching jets to cool the air and fill it with sparkling beauty. The water, without which the whole ambience and the luxuriant planting could have no existence, was channelled from the River Daro some distance above Granada. Although much altered over the centuries, the gardens of the Generalife may best convey the true spirit of the Muslim

garden; a true terrestrial paradise, 'a place of delight' almost unequalled in any other garden in the west.

The Court of the Myrtles and that of the Lions are part of the original garden complex – the former with canal, today edged with *Myrtus communis*, the latter planted only with orange trees in the four corners. Much of the rich honeycomb decoration surrounding each courtyard has been destroyed in intervening centuries. Recent planting in the outer patios and the Generalife are colourful pastiches of what might once have grown. Ibn Luyun's fourteenth-century poem gives clues to the planting and organization of the gardens when first constructed. He advised that 'next to the reservoir plant shrubs whose leaves do not fall and which rejoice the sight; and somewhat farther off, arrange flowers of different kinds and farther off still evergreen trees and round the perimeter climbing vines . . . and under climbing vines let there be paths which surround the garden to serve as a margin'.

Left: The painting of the Patio de la Acequia – sometimes called the Patio de la Riada – in the Generalife gardens above the Alhambra is by Ludwig Hans Fischer and was painted in 1885, forty years after the American writer Washington Irving had encouraged restoration of the Moorish monuments and gardens. The Generalife was laid out at the end of the thirteenth century as a summer residence for the caliphs. Today the tall cypresses no longer exist and much of the planting is of summer-flowering annuals rather than the aromatic Mediterranean plants shown by the artist. The multiple water jets usually shown are a recent innovation.

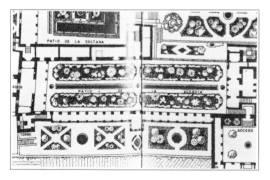

This plan of the Patio de la Acequia in the Generalife shows its medieval layout, with beds flanking the central water rill divided to make a quadripartite shape. The excavations carried out by the archaeologist Jesus Bermudez in 1959 revealed the pavement of the Arab paths and the level of the flower-beds 50 centimetres/20 inches below them, discovered under five centuries of accumulated debris and earth; they are unfortunately now buried once more. The water supply to the Generalife, channelled in the top of the walls, runs diagonally across the steep hillside to fall to feed canals and jets in the patio gardens.

A modern photograph of The Court of the Myrtles – the Patio de los Arrayanes – in the Alhambra shows the central canal appropriately lined with bushes of the aromatic Greek or Mediterranean myrtle (*Myrtus communis*), planted in the nineteenth-century restoration but possibly authentic. The pool serves as a mirror to the porticos of the Comares, the caliph's official residence, and to Charles V's Renaissance palace at the farther end, built in the early sixteenth century, after Granada was captured from the Spanish Moors.

PERSIAN LITERATURE AND MINIATURES

At Tabriz distinctive painting styles developed in which miniatures portrayed gardens with spring blossom and carpets of flowering bulbs as a favourite theme – idealized to illustrate inspirational love poetry and legends, many of which had been written or 'told' centuries earlier. The delicate paintings of stories of romance or war, such as the *Shahnama* (Book of Kings) written by Firdawsi in about AD 1000, Nizami's stories and poems written a hundred years later (in the *Khamsa* he recounts the story of Khusraw and the Armenian princess Shirin), and stories of the love of Humay for the princess Humayun, show plants set both in 'natural' landscapes and in formal walled gardens. The earliest miniatures date to about 1396. Sometimes individual trees and flowers play roles in the stories. Legends are interpreted in different styles in succeeding eras; after the end of the sixteenth century Persian miniaturists portrayed scenes from the Indian Mughals, with more elaborate formal-style gardens with pavilions, water channels and flower-beds usually planted with only one type of flowering plant. Often the garden scene is mirrored in the pool with garden dimensions dissolving in the reflections. Courtly owners are seen lounging on cushions and gardeners are shown working against a charming back-

This miniature was painted in the 1590s to illustrate a copy of Firdawsi's *Shahnama*, and shows Zal climbing up to Rudaba's balcony. The artist portrays the lovers against a background of flowering trees, flowers, willows and two tall cypresses. A plane tree is clasped by a twining vine heavy with grapes. The pavilion is decorated with narcissus, violets, roses, lilies and jasmine. In the poem Rudaba is first described to Zal at the court of Mihrab, her father, as having cheeks like Pomegranate blossoms . . . cherry lips, her silver breasts bear two pomegranate seeds, her eyes are twin narcissi in a garden'.

ground of fruit blossom backed by more statuesque planes, cypress and poplar trees. Fruits portrayed include almonds, apricots, cherries, figs, peaches, plums, pomegranates and quinces, with citrus fruit such as lemons, limes and oranges. Nuts were filberts, hazels and pistachios. Flowers such as the rose – the 'queen of flowers' and always given pride of place – iris, poppy, peony and hollyhock are favourite subjects, both for depiction and for mentioning in poetry.

Miniatures portraying the romance of Khusraw and Shirin, a beautiful Armenian princess, are taken from the manuscript of Nizami's *Khamsa*, written in the twelfth century. This particular miniature, showing Khusraw and the Princess Shirin in a garden, a scene of peace and tranquillity, was illustrated by an artist in Shiraz in 1410–11.

A miniature painted in the Punjab by Abd al-Hakim Multani in 1686 illustrates the Persian manuscript poem *Khavarannama* by Muhammad Ibn Husam. Lavishly decorated with gold, it shows King Khavar, disguised as a gardener, being attacked by his enemy, Mir Shyyaf, on behalf of Ali, son-in-law of the prophet Muhammad. A silver stream flows in the foreground, backed by elegant cypresses, willows, pomegranates and other trees often depicted in paintings of the period.

THE GARDENS OF BABUR

A copy of Babur's memoirs produced during the reign of his grandson Akbar was illustrated by Persian miniatures of the gardens and with some paintings of individual trees and plants which were new to him when he went to India. Babur wrote of the beauties of wooded slopes and of the fruit grown in the meadows which lay near the crest of the Hindu Kush. Of Kabul itself, where today vineyards provide important crops of grapes for wine and raisins, he said, 'If the world has another [place] so pleasant, it is not known.' For garden-making Kabul's climate was excellent, hot days being succeeded by cooler nights and a blanketing cover of snow giving winter protection. Today in one of Babur's gardens called Nimla 40 kilometres/ 25 miles from Jelalabad tall green cypresses and ancient plane trees line the now dry water channels and soar above mud walls to give a welcome to the weary traveller. Orange trees thrive in the garden plots; in spring the ground beneath them is carpeted with fragrant narcissus. To another garden near Kabul, already planted with willows in 1505, Babur brought cuttings of the sour cherry (*Prunus cerasus* – the *alubalu*), and of plane and *tal* (possibly ivy – *Hedera colchica*), setting them above a large round seat. He planted oranges, citrons and pomegranates in his Garden of Fidelity, and added plantain bananas, other fruit trees and sugar cane. In yet another garden he instructed his governor: 'the best of young trees must be planted there, lawns arranged, and borders set with sweet herbs and with flowers of beautiful colours and scent.' Babur's love of flowers and trees was renowned and he recorded two occasions when he made a collection of tulips found growing wild.

Babur was equally influential as a great garden designer in India, introducing fruit trees and other plants from Kabul and lining the roads with trees to shade the traveller.

Left: A miniature shows Babur enjoying the pleasures of his garden as he sits reading. Arriving at Agra in India in 1526 Babur looked for a site for a garden in the unpromising terrain. The whole of the Jumna river area was 'so ugly and detestable' that he nearly gave up the attempt. He described how the garden and others near it were made, and how he sowed roses and narcissus in each. He died at Agra in 1530 but was buried in one of his earlier gardens near Kabul, where *chenars* (one of which is 14 metres/45 feet in circumference) may have been planted by him.

Above: Babur's favourite garden was the *Bagh i-Wafa*, the Garden of Fidelity, probably near Jelalabad. In October 1519 Babur wrote of 'the days of the garden's beauty; its lawns were one sheet of trefoil [clover]; its pomegranate trees yellowed to autumn splendour their fruit full red'. He noticed 'a few purslane [poplar] trees in the utmost autumn beauty' and by November found one young apple tree so beautiful that 'it was such that no painter trying to depict it could have equalled [it]'. The pair of miniatures shows envoys waiting outside the garden while Babur gives directions to his gardeners.

Above right: The oleander (*Nerium oleander*) and the screwpine (*Pandanus odoratissimum*), painted by Ibrahim Naqqash in *c.* 1590, are two of the plants illustrated in a copy of Babur's memoirs (the Vaqi'at i-Baburi) now in the British Library. Babur described the oleander as 'both red and white like the peach flower' and 'five-petalled, blooms well and profusely in the rains and also is had throughout most of the year'. He said that the screwpine had a very agreeable perfume. Other miniatures in the manuscript show the gathering of the almond crop near Khodjand, some 240 kilometres/150 miles from Samarkand.

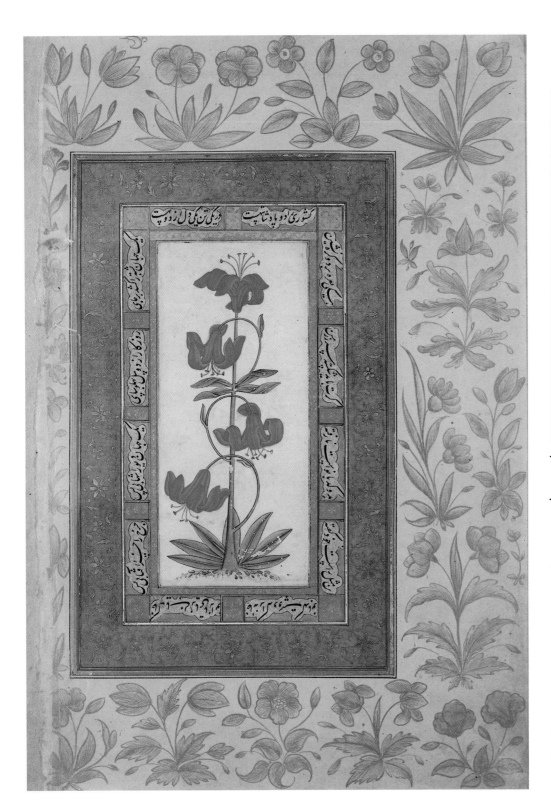

THE MUGHAL GARDENS IN INDIA

Islamic garden art reached its peak with the development of the Mughal gardens in India. From the time of Babur, who founded the dynasty in the early 1500s and was the first 'gardener', through the reigns of his six descendants, Humayun, Akbar, Jahangir, Shah Jahan and Aurangzeb, to the end of the seventeenth century, some of the most beautiful gardens ever seen were laid out both in the hot plains of northern India and in the lake landscape of Kashmir. There are few portrayals of the actual gardens but trees, shrubs and flowers as well as garden layouts, showing quadripartite canal systems and sunken flower-beds, are well represented in Mughal miniatures of both Persian and Indian subjects. In the gardens of the plains high walls make secluded and shady enclosures and gardening is difficult, totally dependent on irrigation. Trees included the usual cypress, plane and willow familiar in Persian miniatures from Tabriz but other trees which dominate the Indian landscape such as mango, pipla, banyan, plantain (banana) and palms are also frequently shown. The pink-flowered Indian lotus (*Nelumbo nucifera*), with irises, day-lilies and poppies as well as oleanders, are all much in evidence. Kashmir gardens jut out into the landscape, embracing panoramic views of low-lying orchards in spring flower, wild red roses, violet irises and saffron fields in autumn – which Akbar recorded as a 'sight that would entrance the most fastidious' – and mountain slopes clothed with pines (*Pinus wallichiana*), all of which delighted the Mughal emperors. On the site of Nasimbagh, Akbar's giant *chenars* still survive from the 1,000 trees he had planted to make a green oasis on the lake shore at Srinagar; an avenue of poplars remains at the Shalimar gardens. His son Jahangir kept the court painter Ustad Mansur busy drawing the wild flowers of which 'there were picked fifty kinds . . . in my presence'.

A page from the album of Dara Shukoh, a collection of superb miniatures and calligraphy which the prince, eldest son of Shah Jahan, had prepared for his bride *c.* 1635, shows exotic flowers and insects (*right*). Another miniature (*far left*) portrays a red lily. None of the pictures are signed with the name of an artist.

Top left: Of all the buildings and gardens constructed by the Mughal emperors in India, the pavilion and gardens of the Taj Mahal, built by Shah Jahan as a tomb for his wife (1632–54), are the most splendid. The garden, a traditional four-fold pattern, divided by canals lined in white marble representing the four rivers of life, lies to the south of the main pavilion. On a higher terrace the tomb seems to float between the paradise garden and the river landscape below. Originally cypress avenues and fruit trees – the first symbols of death and eternity, the second of life and fertility – lined the main pool, and bulbs and other flowers decorated the sunken flower-beds.

THE GARDENS OF CONSTANTINOPLE

Although there are no real records of gardens in Constantinople in the early years after the Turkish conquest, the passion for flowers seems to have led to a degree of specialization in a few sorts rather than in many different ones. Gardeners were concerned to grow roses, carnations, tulips, hyacinths, narcissus, jonquil and cyclamen, considering others as simple flowers of the field. Ebusuud Effendi (d. 1574), grand mufti under Süleyman the Magnificent, became a narcissus specialist and produced both yellow and white varieties from his garden at Karaagac near Edirne (Adrianople). By 1630 the famous Turkish traveller Evliya Chelebi described the city as having 80 flower shops and 300 florists besides being rich with vineyards and orchards. On the Bosporus waterside villas had flower-beds planted with tulips and hyacinths, both of which, with roses, feature in contemporary poetry.

On 1 April 1717 Lady Mary Wortley Montagu wrote to Alexander Pope from Adrianople: 'For some miles round Adrianople the whole ground is laid out with Gardens, and the Banks of the River set with Rows of Fruit Trees, under which all the most considerable Turks divert themselves every Evening: not with walking, that is not one of their Pleasures, but a set party of 'em chuse out a green spot where the Shade is very thick, and there they spread a carpet on which they sit drinking their Coffee.' Her letters also des-

The interior of the Kubbealti Tower and the gardens of the Topkapisaray are shown in this sixteenth-century miniature. The palace and gardens were begun in the fifteenth century after the fall of Constantinople in 1453. Although the scene is conventional, with cypress, almond and other fruit trees and flowers scattered in the grass, it is recorded that in 1593 fifty thousand white roses were ordered for planting in the series of open courtyards. Busbecq reported that the Grand Vizier Rustem Pasha conducted a commercial operation, selling roses, violets and vegetables for profit. In the eighteenth century tulip festivals were held in the gardens.

cribe the magnificence of the gardens of the sultan, with walls of the Topkapisaray encrusted with emeralds and diamonds and parterres enamelled with flowers. Alas, visitors later in the century throw some doubts on her veracity, ascribing the scenes to her brilliant imagination. It seems likely that the gardens declined after the revolution of 1730, before which Ahmed III had his version of 'tulipomania', importing cultivated European tulips back to the city for his displays.

Sixteen-century Iznik tiles in the harem of the Topkapisaray portray elegant lyre-shaped spotted tulips, closer to the appearance of wild species than the more globular shapes which developed in

Europe after the tulip's introduction there in the second half of the century. (Frescos from a hundred years earlier show specimen tulip flowers with sepals which are even more pointed.) The panels of these Iznik tiles portraying flowers brought the garden as a concept indoors in the same way that garden carpets provided garden interest even in winter.

Above: A detail from an eighteenth-century mural in the apartment of the queen mother in the harem of the Topkapisaray in Istanbul, shows an idealized garden with rectangular rose-beds and vertical cypresses intertwined with flowering almonds, a typical Muslim garden motif. The central kiosk, pool and garden are integrated to seem one. The formal garden, surrounded by a wilderness, demonstrates the contrast between control and nature. In many Muslim gardens the layout reflects the attitude of a society which preferred living in tents, represented by garden pavilions, to houses.

CHAPTER THREE

THE MEDIEVAL GARDENS OF CHRISTENDOM

Except for those made by the Moors in Spain, no actual garden made in the period which covers the withdrawal and conquest of the Roman empire in the fifth century until after 1500 exists today in Europe. Nor, in the area of the Continent linked together by the Roman Catholic Church and by a common Latin language, have even the remains of medieval garden beds been uncovered for the archaeologist to interpret – unlike the many gardens of classical Rome, preserved as if in aspic by volcanic ash at Pompeii, or built over as far afield as Vienne in France, Coimbra in Portugal and Fishbourne in the south of England. In Spain it is possible to trace clear lines of descent between Roman layouts and later Islamic-type gardens, but gardens in the north of the empire such as Fishbourne seem to have had no perceivable continuity in style. Three hundred years of chaos not only obliterated any sophisticated Roman conception of a pleasure garden but also left contemporaries with little practical experience of earlier horticultural achievement. What knowledge existed depended on hearsay or derived mainly from thinly distributed copies of the classical agricultural and horticultural manuscripts.

Catering at the time they were written for a far-flung empire, these texts are surprisingly comprehensive and relevant to more northerly climates. For instance beds could be raised and edged with boards or woven panels of willow to improve drainage, just as Columella recommended for wetter regions, and for the cultivation of specific plants (such as garlic). All evidence of any such techniques has, however, disappeared, and what we know of European plant use and gardening practice in the thousand years up to 1400 is refracted through scanty written authorities and after this, pictorial records only reflect hypothetical gardens until at least the mid sixteenth-century.

We do, however, know some of the plants which, with indigenous ones in each region, were available to the gardeners in the era before the first millennium. Fortunately the Romans had brought fruit trees as well as grape vines with them north of the Alps and many of these, already well established as the empire collapsed, are likely to have remained in continuous cultivation, especially in regions with sufficiently hot summers. The Romans probably introduced sweet and sour cherries, plums (*Prunus domestica*), mulberries, peaches, almonds, cultivated pears, figs and European or sweet chestnut and even tried to grow the Mediterranean umbrella or stone pine (*Pinus pinea*) and olives, neither of which survived. They also introduced roses (probably *Rosa gallica* and possibly *R. alba* types; dog roses and *R. pimpinellifolia* are natives of northern Europe), the Madonna lily (its bulbs used by Roman legions for food and as ointment to cure corns) and forms of cultivated violets, periwinkle (*Vinca*) for wreaths and garlands (in medieval times a victim on the way to the gibbet wore a crown of periwinkle) and the Christmas rose (*Helleborus niger*). Among their edible vegetable introductions were dill and fennel, and beet, kale and other 'coleworts' from the cabbage family; they grew hemp for making rope and canvas but not, as far as we know, as a drug. They are given the dubious credit for first growing goutweed or ground-elder (*Aegopodium podagraria*) in England for use as a salad.

The painting known as *The Garden of Paradise* is by an unknown Rhenish artist and dates to between 1410 and 1420. In the grass or 'flowery mead' grow borage, cowslip, rose campion, daisy, purple flag iris, hollyhocks of two different colours, Madonna lily, lily-of-the-valley, peony, sweet rocket, violet, periwinkle and spring snowflake (*Leucojum vernum*), as well as strawberries in flower and fruit. The scene represents a walled *hortus conclusus*, in which the Virgin Mary and various saints perform ritual tasks. St Dorothy picks cherries from the Tree of Life.

The red rose (*Rosa gallica*), with the white lily, were probably the most popular flowers during the Middle Ages, celebrated in both secular and sacred literature and in paintings. Primarily associated with the Virgin Mary, the rose signified divine love. It was grown on arbours and over trellis, while wild roses such as *R. canina* and *R. rubiginosa*, the sweet briar or eglantine, were used for hedging. The illustration portrayed here in black and white is a print of a hand-coloured wood block from the *Hortus Sanitatis* (Vicenza, 1491).

After AD 280 the Emperor Probus encouraged the cultivation of vineyards throughout the empire to prevent his soldiers from being idle; before that commercial growing of grapes for wine was forbidden outside Italy. Other plants such as oranges and lemons, pomegranates and Mediterranean myrtle (*Myrtus communis*), were also brought north by the Romans as the empire expanded, but

they succumbed to neglect during the Dark Ages to be re-introduced as hot-house plants centuries later; they were possibly grown by Albertus Magnus in the winter garden he showed to William of Holland in Cologne in 1259.

EARLY DOCUMENTATION OF PLANTING

Until the thirteenth century we have no written description of pleasure gardens, but we have long known that flowers and fruit were appreciated for delight even as Europe emerged from the Dark Ages. Our small knowledge of any gardening activity in this early period derives from laws and legal records relating to useful plants, several authoritative lists of plants known and grown in the period, and literary references.

St Isidore of Seville (*c.* 560–636) specified the need for a garden within his monastery, attached to the wall at the back of the cloister. St Fiacre from Donegal, later to become the patron saint of gardening, founded a monastery and made a fine garden near Meaux in France in the seventh century. We have no record of the extent of planting in either garden but that in Seville may have grown the citrus fruit described by Pliny the Elder, while St Fiacre might have had access to most of the plants which the Romans had earlier brought across the Alps.

In the laboriously hand-copied herbals of the Middle Ages the plant emphasis was primarily on medicinal herbs, although edible plants and herbs for seasoning also find a mention (many plants had dual 'useful' and symbolic roles) but from these and other sources it is possible to extract references to more ornamental gardening.

Fruit was grown everywhere; in the south round Naples and in Andalusia pomegranates, citrus oranges and then lemons were additions to the more ordinary apples, pears, peaches, apricots and almonds. The aromatic myrtle is frequently mentioned. Although rarely giving any idea of how plants were arranged, some of the reports of extensive orchard planting reveal a significant degree of aesthetic pleasure found in the beauty of organized rows of trees (probably staggered in a quincunx pattern to allow maximum light and air) and in the colour and scent of fruit blossom in spring.

The coming of spring would have had much more significance in the north than in the relatively warm south. Even in northern Europe trees were chosen specifically for shade; in 1180 William

FitzStephen described how elms, oaks, ash and willow were planted along watercourses and to make shady walks in London, and in Germany and central Europe linden (lime) trees were most often mentioned. Pollarding and pleaching – the latter from the French *plessier*, meaning to plait or intertwine – was practised all through the Middle Ages; recorded in England in 1324, workmen were paid a penny for every two perches completed. Pleaching became common practice by the end of the period with intertwined trees – sometimes reinforced with a framework of laths – used to make openwork pavilions and bowers. Grafting is discussed by the classical authors and seem to have been generally practised, although some outlandish ideas of grafting fruit on plane trees seem to have had little reality.

In northern Europe flowers were mainly valued for altar decoration, just as the pagan Romans grew them for victory chaplets, garlands and wreaths. They are mentioned principally in cultivated gardens and orchards tied to monasteries or establishments large enough to include some sort of 'luxury' planting.

Throughout Christendom roses were scattered in churches to signify the gift of the Holy Spirit; in Germany St Dorothy was always portrayed with a coronet of roses on her head or a bunch of roses in her hand. Roses were not only symbolic of the Virgin Mary, they also had medicinal properties, and were valued for their fragrance. The poet Venantius Fortunatus (530–609), an Italian who became Bishop of Poitiers, was befriended by Radegunda, widow of Clotaire I (d. 561), at her nunnery in Poitiers. There, tables were strewn with roses and the poet wandered among the 'apple, and the tall pear, which now pour forth their fragrant scent' and sent flower posies to the queen: 'none of the sweet-smelling herbs I send can equal the nobility of the dark violet. Flowing in royal purple, their petals bring together perfume and loveliness.' Fortunatus also wrote of the gardens in Paris of another widowed queen, Ultrogotha, noted for their fragrant roses. The Venerable Bede (673–735) described the Madonna lily as the emblem of the Virgin, the white petals representing the purity of her body and the golden anthers the glowing light of her soul.

Alcuin of York (*c.* 735–804), scholar and founder of the palace school for the Emperor Charlemagne (the earliest university in north-western Europe) was also a flower lover; his last eight years were spent as Abbot of St Martin at Tours, where his cell was

The white lily (*Lilium candidum*) traditionally associated with the Virgin, and later often portrayed as symbolic of the Annunciation in early Renaissance paintings, is illustrated in a manuscript copy of the Apuleius Platonicus *Herbarium* in the Eton College Library in Windsor, dated to the beginning of the thirteenth century and executed in Germany. Most of the plant portrayals are difficult to identify. Originally compiled much earlier, possibly in the sixth century and originally written in Greek, the herbal is an illustrated medical recipe book, mainly derived from Dioscorides and Pliny's older works.

adorned with white lilies and red roses. This Alcuin corresponded with Benedict of Aniane (near Montpellier) who was almost certainly the author of the list of plants in the famous *Capitulare de Villis* (see pp. 86–87), formulated by Charlemagne after he was proclaimed Holy Roman Emperor *c.* 800. The decree insisted that each city in 'all the crown lands' should have a garden planted with 'all herbs', a total of 73, as well as 16 different fruit and nut trees.

It seems certain that from Charlemagne's time onwards attitudes to pleasure gardening were stimulated and enriched by Arab influences. Charlemagne's list of plants, issued more than 280 years before the lists of the Spanish-Arab botanists, Ibn Bassal and Ibn al-Awwam, is neither a gardening book nor even a careful compilation of all plants known at the time. Nevertheless it is the earliest record of plants in northern Europe to emerge after the Dark Ages. Taken together with the plan found at St Gall in Switzerland and Walafrid's garden poem, it is possible to get some idea of ninth-century gardening practices, which probably differed little from those implicit in the instructions in the four classical Roman manuals and in Pliny's *Naturalis Historia*.

Such works were available only to Latin scholars in the libraries of religious establishments and to the rare private individuals fortunate enough to own copies. In the eighth century the Venerable Bede possessed a Pliny, and Alcuin had access to one. Of the four agricultural treatises termed *De Re Rustica* and the fourth-century works of Palladius, all containing specific gardening instructions, that of the latter, with much of the best material based on Columella's work, was most frequently found. The St Gall plan shows separate gardens for medicinal herbs and for vegetable beds arranged just as Columella specified: the 'ground is divided into beds, which, however, should be so contrived that the hands of those who weed them can easily reach the middle of their breadth, so that those who are going after weeds may not be forced to tread on the seedlings, but rather may make their way along paths and weed first one and then the other half of the bed.'[1] Fruit and nut trees were grown both as standards and against walls.

THE EXCHANGE OF PLANTS AND PLANT KNOWLEDGE

There are plentiful records of a flourishing exchange network of seeds and cuttings between monastic houses throughout Europe during the twelfth and thirteenth centuries, much of it emanating from Burgundy and with the Normans spreading to England, where, by Henry I's reign, there were nurseries for grafts and for growing on seedlings. The wallflower (*Cheiranthus cheiri*) was reputedly brought to England during Norman building works, but its first mention (with other garden plants such as columbine and

heartsease) in cultivation north of the Alps comes in the twelfth-century Low German *Glossarium Helmstadtiense*.

Although Charlemagne had contact with the Abbasid rulers in Baghdad, the centre of Muslim scholarship in the Middle East, and received a gift of an elephant from Harun al-Rashid in 802, we have no record of exchanges of plants or even of items of scientific knowledge travelling to medieval Europe from this source. Yet at this time Dioscorides and other ancient classical texts, unavailable in Europe, were being translated into Arabic, and botanical books with additional contemporary information were being written. These works travelled to southern Spain in the tenth century. After this any access to Arab learning for Christian Europeans is likely either to have originated in Spain or been obtained from Arab settlements in southern Italy (and the University of Salerno), and particularly from Sicily after the Norman take-over in 1072. By the eleventh century scholars, pilgrims and merchants were travelling across the Pyrenees to study Arab medical science in Spain and it is possible that plants as well as philosophical ideas were brought north on their return. Certainly this trade continued during the succeeding centuries with seeds and dormant bulbs and rhizomes of flowers such as lilies, irises and narcissus, and even cuttings of plants such as rosemary.

Gardens such as those at Granada were so admired by Christian rulers who succeeded the Moors that, at Seville, Pedro I (1344–69) had Arab craftsmen make the Alcázar; at the end of the fourteenth century the royal gardens of the kings of Navarre, whose kingdom stretched across the Pyrenees and as far north as Cherbourg, were made at Olite and Tafalla. In the gardens at Olite, built by Carlos III (1387–1425) whose sister Joan married Henry IV of England in 1401, there were pine trees and a plantation of oranges, and surrounding cloisters were planted with cypresses and pomegranates. Some of the horticultural exchanges recorded from this period stem from such links; there must have been more. The double clove carnation (*Dianthus caryophyllus*) came north from Valencia in about 1460 and first appears in France, known as *oeillet*, in the 1470s, while the single pink had been in cultivation earlier. In contemporary paintings it is shown growing in pots with semi-circular hoops of willow and tall stakes for support. Some plants were sent as gifts between sovereigns. The famous orange (*Citrus aurantium*) at Versailles, known as the 'Grand Connétable', sown in about 1411 in Olite by Leonora, wife of Carlos III, was one of the

tion of the west with tales of open courtyards and fountains in crystal basins. By the middle of the thirteenth century the Emperor Frederick II had hanging gardens built on the buttresses of his castle at Nuremberg and established what must have been an oriental-style park (destroyed in 1494), as he employed an expert gardener to supervise the plants he had acquired from the warmer south through contacts with Saracens and Spaniards, his domains stretching from the south of Italy to Germany.

Arab influence also percolated northwards from southern Italy, especially through trade with the Saracens at the port of Amalfi. At nearby Salerno the medical school predated that of Montpellier and it seems likely that Islamic-type parks established in the area influenced travellers from the north, even before the Normans' conquest of Sicily in 1072.

The Arab botanists writing in eleventh- and twelfth-century Spain (see pp. 58–59) listed many plants which could not easily transplant into northern Europe. Others would readily adapt to the colder conditions. Most of the 'botanical' treatises were compiled in more southerly latitudes, but the climate in northern Europe was several degrees warmer during most of this period – a comparison of probable temperatures between the sixth century and 1300 with records for 1900 suggests that there may have been an additional month's growing time. The extra degrees of warmth may for this period have made it possible to grow olives successfully as far north as Great Britain and perhaps the date palm although it could not have produced fruit.

Plant improvement and horticultural technology were also important and particularly concerned improving strains of fruit. Although oranges were used for hedges in Valencia, in northern Europe citrus fruit had to be overwintered in special sheds warmed with coal fires; by 1537 a garden near Llandaff in South Wales had a furnace built into its wall.

THE GARDEN AS A SOURCE OF PLEASURE

From Norman times references to the beauty of plants become more frequent. The English story of William Rufus's visit to the gardens of the nuns at Romsey in about 1092, is well known; even though his real reason was to glimpse Edith of Scotland, the heiress of the Saxon line, his plea to admire the roses and other flowering plants was obviously an acceptable one and indicates

Taken from a Flemish Book of Hours of c. 1500, the illustration shows a wheelbarrow (first mentioned as a garden aid in the thirteenth century), with a vast pot containing a single red carnation, being pushed by the gardener's wife. When Geoffrey Chaucer mentioned the 'clowe-gilofre' c. 1400, he had in mind the oriental spice clove and not the clove gilliflower or carnation, which was introduced to northern Europe only in the last quarter of the fifteenth century. Although carnations were undoubtedly grown in Turkey and the Middle East at an earlier date, the Spanish grew carnations at Valencia only by 1460 and in France the *oeillet* is first mentioned in the 1470s.

five trees sent in 1499 as a wedding present to Louis XII and Anne of Brittany. In the twelfth century contacts were re-established between the German emperor Frederick I Barbarossa (reigned 1152–90) and Baghdad; embassy reports stimulated the imagina-

The symbolic theme of the garden and its flowers found expression in some of the great fifteenth-century Flemish Madonna paintings of artists such as Memling, van der Weyden and van Eyck. In the painting of the Virgin and Child by Dieric Bouts, a follower of Memling, executed in about 1490 for Isabella of Spain, a contemporary Flemish formal garden and house are shown in the background. The garden is neatly divided up into raised rectangular beds, each four bricks high, and sanded walks, with estrades – trimmed plants trained over tiered hoops – carnations supported by frames, and a railed bed, perhaps of massed lavender. Irises grow beside the river.

contemporary attitudes to garden pleasures. Perhaps the flowerbeds he saw would have been 'adorned with roses and lilies . . . violets and mandrake,' as suggested in the Englishman Alexander Neckam's list a hundred years later. Fortunately the princess, disguised as a nun, escaped his observation.

Although the description by Albertus Magnus of a pleasure

garden in the thirteenth century is something new, there are several earlier plant lists or catalogues which imply that certain plants were being considered at least in part for their beauty. Neckam, born in 1157, wrote his prose work *De Naturis Rerum* while a young man; in it he spoke of 'adorning' the garden with specific flowers. The work was in circulation well before 1200 and became the most used plant encyclopaedia in the religious houses of Britain for three centuries. One chapter was devoted to flowers, herbs and trees for growing in the garden. Some of his plants may not have actually been cultivated in England; nevertheless the breadth of varieties Neckam mentions implies familiarity at least by hearsay. Bearing in mind the warmer climate until approximately 1300, this list contains few introduced plants that would not thrive in his native country. Out of a total of 77 plants, fewer than ten of ornamental value are either slightly tender, such as acanthus and pomegranate, or, like the date palm and orange, unable to survive without some sort of heat in winter; even the latter could be grown from seed in pots. Today pomegranates often flower in England and their fruit may have ripened regularly in the warmer twelfth century; for the rich they were a popular imported delicacy. Neckam avoided the usual emphasis on utility crops and instead struck a more aesthetic note, recommending flowers which seem only to have been grown for their beauty. To roses, lilies, violets and mandrake he added borage and daffodils (the latter may have been the wild *Narcissus pseudonarcissus* or the martagon lily, which was called a narcissus in some Continental sources), the first listing of either in England. To his original prose list Neckam appended a section distinguishing plants often confused in contemporary works: common or blue chicory (*Cichorium intybus*) from pot marigold (*Calendula officinalis*), mugwort (*Artemisia vulgaris*) from feverfew (*Chrysanthemum parthenium*, now correctly *Tanacetum parthenium*) and house-leek (*Sempervivum tectorum*) from stickadove (*Lavandula stoechas*), all of which at the time had very similar Latin names. Myrtle or *Myrtus*, when quoted in a northern context, normally meant the aromatic bog myrtle (*Myrica gale*) of peaty swamps and not the classical Greek or Mediterranean myrtle (*Myrtus communis*), which is distinctly tender in northern Europe. (In the United States what Europeans call periwinkle – *Vinca minor* – is colloquially known as myrtle.) 'Dragons' in Neckam's list probably means the hardy snakeweed or knotweed (*Polygonum bistorta*, now classed in the genus *Persicaria*). In his poem *De*

Laudibus Divinae Sapientiae, Neckam gave a further number of trees with which he seemed familiar. Some, however, were definitely not hardy in England even in the warmer climate of the 1200s; others are thought to be much later introductions. Officially the Italian cypress (*Cupressus sempervirens*) and oriental plane (*Platanus orientalis* – the sacred *chenar* of the Muslims) did not reach England until the end of the fourteenth century; the cedar of Lebanon (*Cedrus libani*) not until the seventeenth. It is always possible that attempts were being made to grow all these trees in Neckam's time from seed brought back from the Levant and Italy.

A fair number of written accounts of gardens exist from the twelfth century onwards, their tone more explicitly suggesting an enthusiasm for the various pleasures they afforded. A contemporary of St Bernard described the grounds of the Cistercian Abbey of Clairvaux in Burgundy at the beginning of the twelfth century: 'behind the abbey but within the wall of the cloister, there is a wide level ground; here there is an orchard, with a great many different fruit trees, quite like a small wood. It is close to the infirmary and is very comforting to the brothers, providing a wide promenade for those who want to walk, and a pleasant resting place for those who prefer to rest. Where the orchard leaves off, the garden begins, divided into several beds or (still better) cut up by little canals, which, though of standing water, do flow more or less . . . The water fulfils the double purpose of nourishing the fish and watering the vegetables.' Early in the twelfth century the Saxon theologian Hugh of St Victor described a garden or *hortus* (probably in France) ditched about and 'beautified with the adornment of trees, delightful with flowers, pleasant with green grass . . . offering the benefit of shade, agreeable with the murmur of a spring, filled with divers fruits, praised by the song of birds'.[2] At about the same time William of Malmesbury went a little further in gardening appreciation: 'the flowers of the plants, breathing sweetly, give life'; he described 'the smooth stems of the fruit trees, that stretch up toward the stars'. His remark that 'there is competition between nature and art, and what one fails in the other produces',[3] is one of the first allusions to horticultural work as an 'art' form. All these descriptions, although seldom mentioning trees or flowers by name, seem not only to discover beauty in utility, but to go a step further towards recognizing the powers of enchantment of flowers.

The earliest description of a medieval 'herber' or pleasure

The illustration from the *Grimani Breviary* of *c.* 1510 shows a garden enclosed by a trellis-work fence and an outer landscape in which there is an olive tree and a well-head; a castle sits on a rock in the background. This *hortus conclusus*, with beds and paths in disciplined shapes, was a place of luxury but was also a symbol of the Virgin Mary with her special flowers, the white lily and the rose, growing in it.

garden *per se*, with layout and plants designed only for delight, is found in a chapter of the *De Vegetabilibus et Plantis* of Albertus Magnus, Count of Bollstädt, written in about 1260 (see pp. 88–89). This may itself be a copy; it is probably based on a now missing section contained in the encyclopaedic work by the Englishman Bartholomew de Glanville completed in 1240. Within fifty years Albertus's own definition was copied almost verbatim by the Italian Pietro de' Crescenzi in the first chapter of Book VIII (On

A garden recently laid out at Winchester behind the Great Hall of the castle honours two English queens, Eleanor of Provence, married to Henry III, and Eleanor of Castile, wife of Edward I. The flowers in the garden are all plants known to have been in cultivation in their time. Among them are two 'new' plants – the hollyhock, introduced from Spain by Eleanor of Castile in 1255, and sweet rocket, first mentioned in Europe by Pietro de' Crescenzi at the beginning of the fourteenth century. The garden with its plants and features encapsulates the 'idea' of an enclosed medieval garden.

gardens survive until about 1400, we know from contemporary reports and literature that they existed. In the fifteenth century illuminators and painters elaborated this basic design to illustrate prayer-book manuscripts and allegorical poetry and love stories in which scenes took place in symbolic pleasure gardens such as those described in the *Roman de la Rose* in the thirteenth century and by Geoffrey Chaucer in the fourteenth. Happily much of this evidence survives to bring gardens and plants alive. Details in the background of great religious paintings show the ideal *hortus conclusus*, in which flowers are identified to become symbols illustrating Old and New Testament scenes and increasingly elaborate garden structures are featured. A greater number of plants will have steadily become available; those portrayed in these paintings and in the illuminated borders of delicately painted Books of Hours sometimes give an indication of dates of introduction. Plants known to have been grown in the thirteenth century have been planted in the 'period' garden recently constructed under the walls of the Great Hall of Winchester Castle.

THE IDEAL OF THE GARDEN AND PARADISE PARK

To understand the medieval garden, it is not enough to know how gardens were laid out or which plants were grown in them; it is also necessary to grasp some ideas implicit in their conception. The pleasure garden was more than a physical entity, a luxury partner to the medicinal and food gardens which were commonplace essentials for living. These gardens embodied a rich symbolic significance in religious terms as well as representing the pagan 'lovely place' – both fertile themes that inspired the imagination of poets and, towards the end of the period, of artists.

For Muslims and Christians alike, the origins of the idealized garden are encapsulated by the Old Testament Song of Solomon: 'A garden enclosed is my sister, my spouse: a spring shut up, a fountain sealed.' For the Christians the enclosed Persian garden of the desert representing the innermost joys of paradise became, in New Testament terms, a symbol of Christ and the Holy Church, bearing 'fruits of the spirit'. The enclosed garden, seemingly a place of luxury and ease and containing beds and pathways in disciplined shapes, became translated by the new Christian symbolism. In it the *hortus conclusus* represented the purity of the Virgin Mary. Roses, once sacred to Venus, become Mary's special flowers

Pleasure Gardens) of his *Liber ruralium commodorum*; running into many manuscript copies and printed editions, this work bridged the period between the Middle Ages and the new era of Renaissance garden making.

For the first time since Europe descended into chaos as the *pax romana* collapsed during the sixth century, gardening was once more described in aesthetic rather than purely useful terms. Trees and flowers chosen for their decorative qualities were to be planted in gardens.

The Albertus description contains many of the basic ingredients of a typical enclosed medieval garden which would have been attached to a castle or manor house. Such gardens may also have existed within walled monastic establishments, playing a luxury role separate from the infirmary and kitchen gardens. The open sunlit central lawn containing a clear fountain was surrounded by scented herbs and flowers; there were raised turf benches and shade was provided by fruit trees or vines (presumably growing over some sort of pergola). Although no portrayals even of typical

and red roses the blood of martyrs; white Madonna lilies became symbols of the Annunciation with the Virgin Mary identified as the 'beloved' of Solomon as well as the new Christian church, the modest violet reflecting her humility.

Besides the Christian symbolism involved in the *hortus conclusus* of the early Middle Ages, the ideal pleasure garden had its derivation in the Garden of Eden of the Old Testament in which the season was always spring – as late as the seventeenth century it was represented as a garden where trees bore blossom and fruit simultaneously – and there were gentle breezes and woodland glades; meadows were alive with flowers and birdsong. With rose- and vine-covered bowers, these gardens were of secular significance as the magical settings for courtly romance and dalliance, the *loci amoeni* described in poetry (see pp. 90–91) and illustrated by painters.

In the most famous literary celebration of gardens, the *Roman de la Rose*, the Lover wanders in the outer garden until the door is opened by Idleness; then he enters the inner garden, to find himself in a place which belonged to the spirit to make him 'happy and gay and full of joy'. The *Roman* was translated (as *The Romaunt of the Rose*) in the time of Chaucer, and Geoffrey Chaucer in his own writings included many references to gardens and plants – mentioning homely natives as well as the more exotic sweet bay ('the laurer alway grene'), linden or lime, 'firre' (probably the Norway spruce, *Picea abies*) and oriental plane. In *The Frankeleyns Tale* a May garden 'ful of leves and of floures; And craft of mannes hand so curiously arrayed hadde this gardin, trewely, That never was ther gardin of swich prys, But-if it were the verray paradys' is praised.

These gardens of the imagination also reflected reality. Although for many years the layout of a medieval pleasure garden was thought to be typified by the enclosed garden, placed for safety and privacy inside the confines of castle or abbey, contemporary records reveal that the much larger 'pleasance', a man-made park of trees and orchards, often lay beyond the inner walls. Enclosed

The Visitation by the Master of the Retablo of the Reyes Católicos in Valladolid in Spain, a fifteenth-century panel painting, shows a setting for the meeting of Mary and Elizabeth. Flowers associated with healing, including violets, daisies and dandelions, grow luxuriantly in the grass, and climbing roses grow on the walls. Clipped and shaped plants grow in three pots on a ledge on brackets under a window. One is in the shape of a sphere; the central pot has a topiary estrade, while the third pot contains what looks like carnations, grown and trained on a wicker frame.

on a grand scale by another wall or hedge, this garden area, often established for profit from both timber and fruit as well as for pleasure, more nearly approached the more pagan 'lovely place'. Recent research has revealed that these orchards and woods were laid out on a considerable scale. Castles, manors and great monastic establishments would have both small herbers for useful and decorative plants and also grander enclosed areas in which walks could be shaded by trees and where there were artificial pools for fish as well as natural streams; sometimes there were other features such as aviaries and menageries. Bishop Geoffrey de Montbray of Coutances visited his relatives in southern Italy before William's conquest of England and came back to Normandy to sow acorns and grow oaks, beeches and other forest trees inside a park enclosed by a double ditch and a palisade. He will have made this 'wilderness' in the manner described by Columella in Book XI of *De Re Rustica*: 'to loosened soil we have these seeds entrusted with fond care and culture'. After 1066, with large grants of land in Somerset in England from William the Conqueror, the Bishop of Coutances was able to fill the park with English deer, and planted a garden, the *virgultum*, and vineyard; he also expanded two pools with water mills to make a sort of early *ferme ornée*. After the beginning of the twelfth century Henry I enclosed a large park at Woodstock with a stone wall and stocked it with exotic animals, including a porcupine. Part of this area was further enclosed by Henry II in 1165 to make Rosamund's Bower and maze – although the actual maze is not mentioned until the fourteenth century, and does not appear in any documentary record – and in it in 1264 Henry III planted a hundred pear saplings for their decorative effect. The park seems to have become the material fulfilment of Hildebert de Laverdin's poem *De ornatu mundi*, written in 1099:

> There every tree a double honour shares;
> Its boughs bear fruit, its shadow cloaks the soil:
> Both are enjoyed by men, its fruit and grateful shade.
> . . . The apple, olive, pear-tree burgeon forth
> With apples, fresh green leaves, and ripening pears.
> The chants of bird, odour of spice, and flowers' hue
> Fill air with song, with scent the nostrils, and adorn the soil.
> Soft zephyrs waft, not harsh east wind; perfumes transpire,
> Not ice; there spring not winter reigns.[4]

Hildebert's imagery derives partly from the more southern paradise parks of Islam, but also echoes mythological descriptions of the Garden of Eden.

By 1190 at Noyers on the border of Burgundy the Bishop of Auxerre 'provided every pleasure and improvement that the industry of man could accomplish. The woods, beset with briars and undergrowth and thus of little value, he cleared and brought into cultivation. There he made gardens and planted trees of different sorts so that apart from deriving pleasure from them, he also got great quantities of fruit. He surrounded a large part of the woods with a ring fence carried from the gate at the near end of the dam of the third pool, and enclosed within a pretty quantity of wild beastes. These might be seen grazing in their herds by those in the palace, a pleasing sight.'[5] In 1150 the Bishop of Le Mans had planted so many lovely trees in his *viridarium* that 'those looking out of the hall windows to admire the beauty of trees and others in the garden looking at the fair show of the windows, could both delight in what they saw'.[6]

GARDENING PRACTICES

The works of both Albertus Magnus and the slightly older Bartholomew de Glanville are today worth consulting to obtain an idea of how thirteenth-century gardens looked and of some of the contemporary horticultural practices; from them we learn what features were commonplace and how the available plants were arranged in the different and distinct sections of a garden. They, and Pietro de' Crescenzi in the early 1300s, base their descriptions of gardens, the plants grown in them and how they were enjoyed on their knowledge of existing gardens. These writers were neither innovators nor teachers but observers; much of their own background knowledge of horticulture (and agriculture) still came from the handful of classical authors, but they were beginning to feel their way towards a more scientific attitude. Bartholomew spelt out the difference between trees and animals: 'For trees meve [move] not wylfully from place to place as beestes doo: nother [neither] change appettite and lykynge, nother felyth sorowe . . . in tres is soul of lyfe . . . but therein no soule of felynge'[7] and Albertus Magnus still wondered whether or not the souls of ivy and the tree with which it was intertwined were united. But they also tell us something of contemporary methods of cultivation (and

of horticultural aids such the wheelbarrow, see p. 75) which were practised, perhaps even for generations, before the written word established their existence. For their age these two writers were much-travelled cosmopolitans; they wrote mainly about the gardens of the great, those of important churchmen, royal princes or nobility, which they either saw as they moved round Europe or received reports about from others.

The value of decorative plants and ways of using them in the garden began to be more frequently considered during the fourteenth century. Trees, including forest and fruit trees (both native and introduced), were not only listed but specifically described as being grown and trained in particular ways. This was an important theme of Pietro de' Crescenzi's book on husbandry, *Liber ruralium commodorum*, completed in 1305 (see pp. 94–95). Crescenzi, although writing in Bologna in the early 1300s, was studied and interpreted during the next two hundred years, and became an important link between the medieval agricultural and gardening world and the new Renaissance gardening styles developing from the fifteenth century. Important as a farming manual in Italy at a time when changes were taking place in land tenure, his work was translated from Latin into French in 1373 and into Italian before the end of the century. It was also an early printed book, appearing in Latin in 1471, Italian in 1478, French in 1486 and German in 1493, and continuing to be read all through the Renaissance. A French manuscript edition of 1485 was illustrated and provides a contemporary vision of his teachings. Charles V of France had commissioned the translation of Crescenzi's work into French in 1373, seeing it as a useful agricultural manual, but it is likely that many of the contemporary royal gardens, especially that of the king's 8-hectare/20-acre garden of the Hôtel de Saint Pol in Paris, incorporated features from the book such as the interwoven tree arbours, *tonnelles*, and the living topiary walls[8] to supplement the meadows and vineyards. At Saint-Pol each garden space was surrounded by hedges supported with trelliswork, through which other plants were twined; lozenge-shaped arbours terminated each end. Inside these the seats were made of turf raised up on steps. There was also a labyrinth – as there was at Hesdin in Artois, laid

out a hundred years earlier – but we do not know how it was planted. Flower-beds were filled with roses, rosemary, lavender, wallflowers, marjoram and sage as well as strawberries. After the king's death in 1380 the garden at Saint-Pol deteriorated but was 'restored' and replanted by Charles VI in 1398 before finally being destroyed by the English Duke of Bedford in 1431. Fortunately there is a complete inventory for the trees and flowers planted in 1398; grape vines were bought to train over arbours, and pear and apple trees, cherries and plums as well as eight 'green bay trees', bought for 2 *sous parisis* (each worth between 2*d.* and 3*d.* of contemporary English money), were all new acquisitions, probably replacements. Perhaps the thousand cherry trees had limbs interwoven to make a shady arbour. There were 300 bundles of white and red roses (probably *Rosa gallica officinalis* and *R. alba*) at 20*s.p.* each, 300 lily bulbs at 6*s.p.* a bundle of *gerbe* (presumably *Lilium candidum*), and 300 flag irises (*flambes*) at 9*s.p.*; these may have been the purple *Iris x germanica* or white *I. florentina*, both of which would have been more desirable than the common 'flag' (*I. pseudacorus*). The eight Saint-Pol gardens, designed together, probably owing much to Crescenzi's influence, are among the most interesting of those recorded as being laid out in the last quarter of the century.

At almost the same date, towards the end of the fourteenth century, but in quite a different social sphere, a Parisian householder – Le Ménager de Paris – wrote a treatise for his young wife giving her instructions on how to run her house and garden. It was a useful manual describing the growing, harvesting and preserving of fruit, nuts, flowers and herbs. Athough nothing was said about how the plants were arranged in the garden, it is clear which plants were most popular with the husband; the management advice for individual plants was given in considerable detail. Violets needed to be kept indoors in pots during the winter and gradually hardened off again in spring. He described the method of rooting cuttings of rosemary, an especially valuable evergreen from the Mediterranean shores, and how best to send them on long journeys 'wrapped in waxed cloth sewn up, smeared with honey and powdered with wheaten flour'; roses were to be grafted, pruned and clipped, hyssop should be sown in August.[9] A contemporary in England, Jon the Gardener, wrote a poem in English before 1400; in its horticultural practicalities it closely parallels the Parisian's instructive list but adds little to our knowledge of the art of gardening.

A list of plants being grown in a garden in London in the fourteenth century puts plant collecting and identification on a more scientific basis. In Stepney, beside the City of London, Friar Henry Daniel, a Dominican monk and doctor living between *c.* 1315 and 1385, established an early botanic garden, almost the first in Europe. (The eleventh-century Huerta del Rey at Toledo established by Ibn Wafid and Ibn Bassal predates it by 300 years.) Daniel grew 252 different kinds of plants, all of which he observed carefully. He was remarkable both for his practical knowledge of plant behaviour and for his scholarly knowledge of plant drugs (as well as those from other substances); he was responsible for an

Above left: A fifteenth-century manuscript copy of Pliny the Elder's *Historia Naturalis* illustrates Book XXII, 'On the importance of herbs', with a painting of an enclosed garden. The master seated on a bench sniffs aromatic leaves while being presented with another herb. In the background there are fruiting trees and stylized umbrella pines. Written in the first century AD, Pliny's encyclopaedic work remained the great repository of knowledge throughout the Middle Ages and Giuliano Amedei's picture-book illustrations dating to the 1460s show typical incidents of contemporary Italian life.

Right: The Unicorn Tapestries, woven in about 1500, depicting episodes in the hunt of the legendary unicorn, show very accurate portrayals of many trees and flowers, about a hundred in all, as well as animals. The final tapestry shows the captured unicorn chained to a pomegranate tree – its fruit the symbol of fertility. In the flower-studded grass can be seen campion, bistort, orchis (*Orchis mascula*), lords and ladies (*Arum maculatum*), violas, sweet rocket, carnations, white lilies, holy thistle (*Silybum marianum*), leopard's bane (*Doronicum pardalianches*), stock and lady's mantle (*Alchemilla vulgaris*). Nearly all these plants are identified in medieval plant symbolism and could be found wild in the northern French countryside for artists to copy.

almost complete translation of Platearius's *Circa instans*, as well as frequently quoting works by all the major classical herbalists and medieval plant encyclopaedists. His English herbal was arranged under Latin plant names; in it he gave attention to the habitat of plants, indicating how and where natives were grown, and he also distinguished between methods of cultivation for indigenous plants and those introduced, such as cypress (presumably the Italian *Cupressus sempervirens*), germander, sweet marjoram, pomegranate

Benozzo Gozzoli's wall paintings (1459-63) in the Palazzo Riccardi in Florence, although intended to represent the landscapes through which the Magi travelled to Bethlehem, are actually of the fifteenth-century Tuscan countryside. Far from seeming an 'untamed' wilderness, its trees, including pines and cypresses, were planted in organized rows with scattered fruit orchards and patterns of flowering hedges. Records reveal that much useful tree planting took place in Europe during the Middle Ages, with specimen forests for timber as well as fruit and nut orchards. Most planting was of indigenous varieties or of trees introduced in Hellenic or Roman times and improved over the centuries.

and rosemary. Pomegranate grew but did not bear fruit. Rosemary, newly introduced to England by Queen Philippa, wife of Edward III, he grew in his garden with special care, stating that it needed copious watering and protection from black frosts and cold north winds. In her royal herbers Queen Philippa grew many unusual plants, including rosemary given her by her mother, the Countess of Hainault. Daniel translated the treatise on the virtues of rosemary, compiled at Salerno between 1338 and 1342.

THE DAWN OF RENAISSANCE ATTITUDES

In the *Decameron* Boccaccio's description of the gardens his aristocratic Florentines encounter shows a taste for and appreciation of gardening and the countryside (see pp. 92–93). These he shared with his contemporary Petrarch, who astonished people by climbing Mont Ventoux in Provence just for the view; Petrarch also had a vine-entwined garden in the Vaucluse and, in 1348, one near Parma, with fruit trees, rosemary and hyssop. His copy of Palladius, which he used as an instructive text, still exists with his annotations. Later he retired to another garden in the Euganean Hills just south of Padua, seeking peace for the contemplation of nature as well as time for scholarship, very much in the style of the Roman patricians escaping from pressures and frivolities of imperial life. Here he sowed seeds and transplanted plants according to the phases of the moon; it seems with little success. He died there in 1374. Petrarch's attitude to and love for nature anticipates views expressed by the Piccolomini pope, Pius II, a hundred years later in his *Commentaries*.

By the middle of the fourteenth century, encouraged by popular works such as that of Crescenzi with its distinction between the gardens of the great and more modest useful herbers, the richer Italian nobles began to turn their fortified castles into pleasure palaces, laying out new ornamental gardens and collecting plants – Boccaccio emphasizes plant collecting in the *Decameron*: 'It would take long to tell how many plants there were and of what sorts and how they were arranged but there was an abundance of every pleasant plant which grows in our climate'. Galeazzo Visconti, friend and patron to Petrarch, from whom he obtained plants, established an extensive garden and park around the castle of Pavia. A prosperous merchant class also became patrons of the arts and vied with the nobility in building and garden construction.

Albrecht Altdorfer's painting of Susanna bathing while being watched by the Elders, from the early sixteenth century, shows a contemporary view of a garden, in which numerous wild flowers bloom between meadow grasses. Poppies, daisies, lilies-of-the-valley, cowslips, with a tall verbascum at the far right, are all readily identifiable in this northern European version of a flowery mead. By this date pleasure gardens with decorative fountains and balustrading were accepted features of both town and country life.

Boccaccio's tale reflects the more luxurious attitudes which had existed a thousand years earlier in Roman times. But pleasure is combined with reading and improvement. His lords and ladies, although indulging in much singing and dancing in the garden, also strike a more serious note with readings from *The Lives of the Romans*, expressing the poet's own passion for classical literature. In all this Boccaccio anticipates Renaissance thought.

THE *CAPITULARE DE VILLIS*

The fruit trees enumerated in Charlemagne's decree concerning towns, the *Capitulare de Villis* of *c.* AD 800, are fewer than in Pliny's day, but the list includes other plants not mentioned in classical literature, all of which grew in some part of the new empire. The flower list, although primarily intended to ensure that herbs for diet and medicine were available, is headed by *lilium* and roses (probably the red *Rosa gallica officinalis* and white *R. alba*), undoubtedly grown for their beauty and religious symbolism as well as for their usefulness. Other herbs in the *Capitulare* which today we would consider sufficiently ornamental for a flower garden included clary (*Salvia viridis*), fennel, German flag iris (*Iris x germanica*), mallow (*Malva sylvestris*), rosemary, rue, sage, southernwood, tansy and the evergreen sweet bay. Some plants that we know from other contemporary sources were grown at the time were omitted; among the most

obvious are violets (*Viola odorata*), grown for scent and beauty (also symbolizing the humility of the Virgin Mary) as well as having medicinal virtues, stickadove (the desirable French lavender, *Lavandula stoechas*), balm, ordinary lavender and hyssop. Fortunately, to supplement the *Capitulare*, we have a plan for an ideal monastery garden which was drawn up within a few years of Charlemagne's decree. Preserved in the library in the great

Abbey of St Gall in Switzerland, it was addressed to the abbot there between 816 and 836. The details of narrow rectangular 'strip' beds, each filled with only one sort of herb or vegetable and allowing access in between, are typical of horticultural practices in the period; later illustrations show ornamental flowers grown in exactly similar ways. These beds almost certainly had raised edges made of board or woven willow.

A group of five illuminated manuscripts, represented by different *Tacuinum Sanitatis* originating in regions of Italy, and today held in the Casanatense Library in Rome, in Liège, Paris, Rouen and Vienna, have texts derived from Arab botanical and medical treatises such as those produced by the botanist Ibn Botlan in the eleventh century. Known as the medieval health handbooks, they date from the late fourteenth to the early fifteenth centuries. Plants depicted so beautifully throughout the series all have useful medicinal properties or fragrance. Shown in the smaller illustrations (from left to right,

on the top line) are rue, sour cherries, the dangerous mandrake and sage. Below these (also from left to right) are a bush of fruiting pomegranate and one of bitter oranges, succeeded by Walafrid Strabo's desirable water melons. Strabo, a ninth-century monk at Reichenau on Lake Constance, not far from St Gall, expressed evocative delight in both gardens and garden work in his poem *Hortulus*. He praised the ornamental plants such as sage, flag iris (*I. germanica*), lily and rose, 'the Queen of Flowers', and spoke of their beauty and fragrance. In one passage he described

cutting melons in summer: 'When the iron blade strikes to its guts, the melon throws out gushing streams of juice and many seeds, The cheerful guest then divides its bent back into many slices.' Walafrid's poem is a paean to gardening in a practical and ornamental sense. He encouraged the gardener to spread manure, tear up weeds and rout moles; he attacked nettles armed with 'mattock and rake'.

The large rose bushes (above) with red and white flowers were praised for their usefulness for inflamed brains. Many of the herbs, such as sage and rue, were grown as crops.

ALBERTUS MAGNUS

A chapter in the *De Vegetabilibus et Plantis* of Albertus Magnus, written in about 1260, first describes a medieval pleasure garden. Containing practical advice, mainly culled from the classical agricultural treatises, as well as giving an observer's account of what constitutes a garden of delight, it is well worth quoting from a translation made by John Harvey: 'There are, however, some places of no great utility or fruitfulness ... these are what are called pleasure gardens. They are in fact mainly designed for the delight of the two senses, viz. sight and smell.' About the lawn 'may be planted every sweet-smelling herb such as rue, and sage and basil, and likewise all sorts of flowers, as the violet, columbine, lily, rose, iris and the like. So that between these herbs and the turf, at the edge of the lawn set square, let there be a higher bench of turf flowering and lovely; and somewhere in the middle provide seats so that men may sit down there to take their repose pleasurably when their senses need refreshment. Upon the lawn, too, against the heat of the sun, trees should be planted or vines trained, so that the lawn may have a delightful and cooling shade, sheltered by their leaves. For from these trees shade is more sought after than fruit, so that

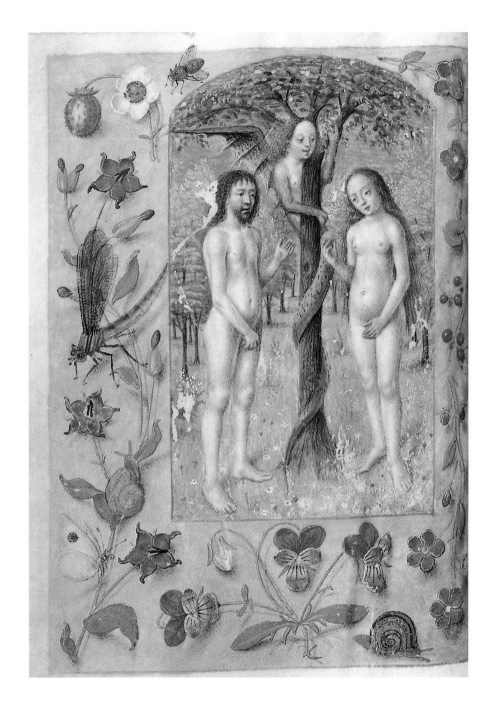

not much trouble should be taken to dig about to manure them, for this might cause great damage to the turf. Care should also be taken that the trees are not too close together or too numerous, for cutting off the breeze may do harm to health ... the trees should not be bitter ones whose shade gives rise to diseases, such as the walnut and some others; but let them be sweet trees, with perfumed flowers and agreeable shade, like grape-vines, pears, pomegranates, sweet bay trees, cypresses and such like.'

Far left: The man shown beating turf to make a lawn appears in an illustration in an Italian manuscript copy of 1450 of Pietro de' Crescenzi's *Liber Ruralium Commodorum*. Albertus Magnus describes the process: 'For the sight is in no way so pleasantly refreshed as by fine and close grass kept short . . . so it behoves the man who would prepare the site for a pleasure garden, first to clear it well from the roots of weeds, which can scarcely be done unless the roots are first dug out and the site levelled, and the whole well flooded with boiling water . . . then . . . to be covered with rich turf of flourishing grass, the turves beaten down with broad wooden mallets.'

Left: The illustration of Adam and Eve, standing in a flowery mead surrounded by trees, is taken from the *Warburg Hours*, produced in Flanders in the late fifteenth century. The border is filled with realistically painted flowers set on a background of gold. All were known to both Bartholomew de Glanville and Albertus Magnus (the latter mentions 270 species) 200 years earlier. They include violets, strawberries (in flower and fruit), borage, and daisies. As suggested by Albertus, these might 'refresh the sight with the variety of their flowers, and . . . cause admiration at their many forms in those who look at them.'

Right: The central panel of the Portinari altarpiece, commissioned for the Medicis in Bruges in 1475, shows vases containing purple and white irises, a lily (*Lilium bulbiferum*), a columbine and three carnations, with sweet violets strewn on the ground beside them. The purple or 'blue' iris here symbolizes the royal blue of the Virgin Mary, Queen of Heaven. The columbine with petals shaped like a dove symbolizes the Holy Ghost. Carnations, introduced from Spain into northern Europe only in the fifteenth century, are not in Albertus Magnus's list. They represent the Incarnation, while violets are for humility. The white iris is probably *Iris florentina*, traditionally brought to Europe from the east as a source of orris root, the dry and powdered rhizome. *Iris germanica* has a complicated and still confused history and in Albertus's day was already a hybrid.

A tos sont apres bien approuue
De en pres bien troue aperms
De actone one et non; maouble
A ne cru pas sauues alobco
A meone desoopt la bson
Un amm mepyl dpnon
A menquies cud nepn de
Que soit follom ne mesendie
De conte que soupt auceune
A mene buldar pour foul metielame
Ar endroit moy ay pe sance
Que songes sont surmsance
Des biens auv peno; des amus
Que les plusenrs songent de nme
manntes chose convettement

pines mome dient que saune
na sefolle non; mesounes
ar il on puet leu uesouevsour
Qu ne sot me mesoup et

THE GARDEN IN LITERATURE

Themes of courtly love proliferated in both prose and poetry, with the conception of the 'inner' and 'outer' spaces of medieval gardens often combined in one tale so that imaginary adventures took place both in the enclosed secret garden and in woods and meadows. After 1400 characters are portrayed in romantic garden settings where nature and art intermingle, preparing the way for new Renaissance interpretations of their interrelationship.

The most famous medieval love story is the French thirteenth-century *Roman de la Rose*, a poem begun by Guillaume de Lorris in 1237 and finished by Jean de Meun 40 years later. Translated into English in the time of Geoffrey Chaucer, poet and king's forester, it was illustrated in successive periods between 1400 and 1500. As in the Persian literature of the same period, much of the action takes place in an allegorical garden setting, with individuals personified as Love, Idleness, Mirth, etc. In the *Roman* the walled garden represents the Garden of Eden, a most pleasant place (*amoenissimus locus*) and one that is firmly rooted in Christian imagery. The Lover, in search of the desirable symbolic rose, is allowed to enter by Lady Idleness who leads him along a path 'Of myntes ful, and fenell greene'. The trees, set at exactly equal distances, have their tops so interwoven that the sun's rays cannot penetrate. Chaucer translated many of the fruit trees as natives, but others were exotics from hotter climates bearing sought-after eastern spices. Pines and cypresses, laurels (bay) and olives and taller forest trees are those laid out 'in assyse' – spaced in rows – and arched across. Many other medieval works describe rather similar adventures in imaginary settings, all of which harp on trees in perpetual flower and fruit, and meadows sprinkled with flowers, to illustrate an idea of paradise.

Opposite: In about 1400 the *Roman de la Rose* was illustrated by French miniatures, in one of which a circular walled garden – earlier 'images' of the garden are square, as suggested in the text – shows animals and birds among the trees and flowers. Amant, the Lover, is being let into the garden by Idleness, and Narcissus is studying his reflection in the well. In the poem, the Garden of the Rose can be reached only after first wandering along flowery paths in open meadows. On a practical level the illustrations convey informative images of contemporary gardens and the planting in them.

Not all the real gardens of the period were small enclosed spaces. The imagery of literature evokes outer gardens in which, as in real life, woods and orchards are successfully managed for profit as well as making a desirable pleasance. In the tapestry woven at Tournai in the early sixteenth century (*above*), woodcutters are clearing the forest to make a garden in which trees are laden with fruit. The presence of deer suggests the garden was also a park for hunting, the *paradeisos* of the Persians. Tapestries insulated rooms in winter and recalled the pleasures of the summer garden.

The garden described by Boccaccio is associated with the Villa Palmieri at Fiesole, although today the existing garden (*left*) is mainly seventeenth- and nineteenth-century in origin. Nevertheless the association in the mind and the villa's situation together convey some of the atmosphere of the poet's story. In the walled garden, which at first glance the storytellers found so beautiful, there were 'wide walks as straight as arrows, covered with pergolas of vines . . . the sides of these walks were almost closed with jasmine and red and white roses so it was possible to walk in the garden in a perfumed and delicious shade'.

The Cocharelli manuscript of the late fourteenth century (*right*) shows members of the nobility standing beside a marble fountain in a garden planted with figs, oranges, pomegranates and grape vines, much resembling that described by Boccaccio. 'And in the midst of this lawn was a fountain of very white marble most marvellously carved. A figure standing on a column in the midst of this fountain threw water high up in the air, which fell back into a crystal-clear basin with a delicious sound; . . . the water which overflowed . . . ran out of the lawn by some hidden way where it reappeared again in cunningly made little channels which surrounded the lawn.'

BOCCACCIO AND THE *DECAMERON*

The Italian poet Boccaccio, in his *Decameron* (written in 1348), gives a vivid picture of what the fourteenth-century villa and garden of any wealthy Florentine would have been like. He tells how a group of aristocratic Florentines escapes from the plague to find sanctuary in the gardens of a villa on the slopes of the Fiesole hills above the city.

As Boccaccio says: 'The sight of this garden, its form and contrivance, with the fountain and the spring proceeding from it, pleased the gentles and ladies so much, that they spared not to say, if there was a paradise on earth, it could be in no other form, nor was it possible to add anything to it'. In layout it still has all the characteristics of the medieval garden – a fountain stands in the centre of a flower-studded lawn, surrounded by vine pergolas with walks shaded by citrus trees and hedges of jasmine and roses; however, the conception of beauty strikes a Renaissance note almost echoed by Alberti in his *De re aedificatoria*, written in 1452.

Boccaccio is the first to mention terraced gardens, later to become such an important feature in Italy: 'On the fourth day the company finds itself in a valley surrounded by six hills, with sides terraced as if in a theatre, not by nature but by an artist's hand.' On the southern side are vines, olives, almonds, cherries, figs and other fruits and to the north a wood. At the bottom of the valley the garden opens out to become a gentle landscape, a *locus amoenus* of meadows, fruit trees and woodland, which surprised the poet because it was so nearly as good as art.

The flowery mead is one of the essential components in our perception of a medieval garden. Boccaccio's description of the flower-studded lawn in the gardens of the villa at Fiesole enlarges on the theme: 'In the midst of the garden a lawn of very fine grass, so green it seemed nearly black, coloured with perhaps a thousand kinds of flowers . . . shut in with very green citrus and orange trees bearing at the same time both ripe fruit and young fruit and flowers so that they pleased the sense of smell as well as charmed the eyes with shade.' The illustrations (*above*), part of an address to Robert of Anjou by the town of Prato (near Florence) completed in about 1335, show, lilies, dwarf iris and red and white roses among a wealth of stylized flowers.

The illustration (c. 1485) (*left*) from a French translation of Crescenzi, *Livres des proffits ruraux*, Book VIII, shows an enclosed garden in which an elaborate topiary estrade, grown on its supporting frame, is being tended by a lady. Carnations grow on supports – the single pink form had been earlier in cultivation but this double form was first recorded in France in the 1470s.

Below: Fruit trees and flowers being tended in a country orchard in a late fifteenth-century French miniature illustrating a translation of Crescenzi's work. In the foreground a lattice-work tunnel is draped with vines. Crescenzi suggests that around a summer pavilion vines could be planted to cover the whole edifice and that elsewhere there might be arbours of wood or trees all covered with vines.

PIETRO DE' CRESCENZI AND THE LIBER RURALIUM COMMODORUM

Pietro de' Crescenzi's *Liber ruralium commodorum* produced early in the fourteenth century was in format almost identical with Columella's twelve books of *De Re Rustica* (though it omitted Columella's poetic rendering of the garden intended as a supplement to Virgil's *Georgics*, see p. 25). Crescenzi provided practical information on plants and planting, including his own list of non-fruit-bearing trees – box, broom, cypress, dogwood, laburnum, rosemary, euonymus or spindle and tamarisk – considered for their decorative qualities. He also discussed gardens in categories of different sizes. Book VIII 'Of Gardens' opens with a description of a small garden of herbs; this is almost an exact word-by-word copy of the description of the pleasure garden by Albertus Magnus. Crescenzi's own sections described medium-sized gardens for the middle class and larger layouts – more than 4.8 hectares/12 acres, but including orchards – for kings and princes. The middle-sized garden could be 'surrounded by ditches and hedges of thorns or roses . . . in warm places make a hedge of pomegranates and in cold places of nuts or plums and quinces . . .'. Vines could be set between the rows of trees and 'constantly . . . weeded from every base and worthless plant. The meadows should be mown twice a year, so that they may be more beautiful and permanent.' The third category of garden contained arbours which predate those described in early Renaissance gardens. They could be made with thin wooden laths covered with vegetation, or they could be formed by living plants with limbs intertwined. Some of these with walks and bowers made entirely of leafy trees could provide 'cover without rain' for the king and queen. In another chapter Crescenzi suggests that willow and poplar trees, 'wrapped with vines and other plants densely intermingled', could be cut out in the shape of towers and crenellations.[10]

In the Flemish miniature by the Master of Margaret of York in a 1460 copy of Crescenzi's work there is a large courtyard herber showing raised beds with gardeners at work with spades and wooden rakes. Crescenzi recommended that 'trees are to be planted in their rows, pears, apples, and palms, and, in warm places lemons. Again mulberries, cherries, plums, and such noble trees as figs, nuts, almonds, quinces, and such-like, each according to their kinds, but spaced twenty feet apart more or less, according to the pleasure of the master.' Obviously in this interpretation trees are of dwarf forms, suitable to the restricted space.

CHAPTER FOUR

BOTANISTS, PLANTSMEN AND GARDENERS OF RENAISSANCE EUROPE

From 1554 the Emperor Ferdinand I's ambassador to the Ottoman Sultan in Constantinople was the cultured Fleming, Ogier Ghiselin de Busbecq. On the road from Adrianople the ambassador, to his astonishment as it was in the middle of winter, saw great expanses of flowers – narcissi, hyacinths and what the Turks described as *tulipand*. Admiring their splendour and perhaps dizzied by the unexpected beauty of the winter flowers, Busbecq got the name wrong; the guide was comparing the shape of the tulip's flower to that of a turban – in Persia and central Asia as well as in Constantinople tulips were always called *lalé*. Later Busbecq paid a considerable sum for bulbs and seeds and had them sent to the imperial court in Vienna, where they were received by the great botanist Carolus Clusius. In 1594 Clusius took his own tulip collection into the Low Countries when he went as Praefectus to the Hortus Academicus, the botanic garden in Leiden. During the first winter many of them were stolen by the avaricious Dutchmen, who were keen gardeners; three decades later the Dutch recklessly gambled huge sums on tulip bulbs losing and gaining fortunes in this speculation.

Of course, there are other stories of the tulip's arrival in Europe. It is said that a cargo of bulbs was brought by ship to Antwerp in 1562; some were eaten as food with oil or vinegar, others died, but part of the consignment was rescued by the merchant George van Rye, an amateur botanist – perhaps he could be called an experimental gardener – who cosseted the bulbs to good effect so that even before the arrival of Clusius, one John Hogeland was growing them in his garden in Leiden. Nor was it only tulips. In his Masters Memorial Lecture in 1965 Professor William Stearn summed up the revolutionary effect on western European gardens of these contacts with the Turkish empire:

'Never before or since has there been such an astonishing influx of colourful strange plants into European gardens, as when in the second half of the sixteenth century, importations of unpromising onion-like bulbs and knobbly tubers from Constantinople brought forth tulips, crown imperials, irises, hyacinths, anemones, turban ranunculi, narcissi and lilies.'

These introductions, many of which came originally from western Asia as wild species, were already cultivated as garden flowers in Constantinople showing a high degree of sophistication progressed through centuries of Islamic garden development. There, in fifteenth-century frescoes, single tulips with pointed petals were portrayed at the sultan's court and in 1561 tulip motifs decorated the Rustem Pasha Mosque. The new introductions from the east combined with plants coming from the New World to revolutionize gardening possibilities and fashions in Renaissance Europe.

Until the 1560s most plants used in western medicine and grown in both 'useful' and ornamental gardens had been species indigenous to Europe. Those which came from farther afield were native to the countries of the Mediterranean basin; a few had trickled into Europe from as far as the outer perimeters of both the Hellenistic world and the Roman Empire; some of these, lost to northern Europe in the Dark Ages, had returned to gardens

The crown imperial (*Fritillaria imperialis*), probably native to Persia, was introduced to European gardens from Constantinople towards the end of the sixteenth century, and was at first known as '*Corona imperialis*'. Its 'stately beautifulness' led John Parkinson to give it first place in the plant catalogue of his *Paradisus* of 1629 – 'to be here entreated of before all other Lillies'. In about this year the fritillary shown here was painted by Pieter van Kouwenhoorn in Holland for his manuscript florilegium.

De Bol Gewooge
410 A aze
658 —

Verkogt
f 3000 —
. 4200 —

This original painting from a Dutch manuscript catalogue of 1637 is of the tulip 'Viceroy', its bulb advertised for 3,000 florins (worth about £1,500 today). The 'Viceroy' is also known to have changed hands for goods including two loads of wheat, four loads of rye, four fat oxen, eight fat pigs, twelve fat sheep, two hogsheads of wine, four barrels of beer, two barrels of butter, 1,000 pounds of cheese, a bed, a suit of clothes and a silver beaker. 'Tulipomania' had very little to do with actual gardening, but was a speculative trade in buying and selling 'breeder' bulbs (see p. 119).

north of the Alps through the Muslims in Spain, with additions from the Persian boundaries of the Arab world. The 'explosive' arrival of plants from the Levant was made possible by the new political contacts established with the Ottoman sultans twenty years after the Turks had been at the gates of Vienna in 1529 – the first diplomatic exchange since Constantinople fell to the Turks in 1453. The exploitation of the exotic flora as it arrived gave new impetus to the study of medicine by physicians and to its logical offshoot, the development of a new botanical science. The exciting flora – within a hundred years twenty times as many plants entered Europe as in the preceding two thousand – also transformed the potential of ornamental gardening. At first the new plants, distributed through a network of physicians, botanists, royal patrons and rich merchants as well as the powerful princes of the church, were mainly available to augment the new botanical gardens and private garden collections, but gradually became more widely disseminated, sometimes through theft – as in the case of the tulips stolen from Clusius in Leiden.

During his time in Constantinople the ambassador Busbecq was also responsible for sending the lilac and the horse-chestnut to Europe. But he made another find; perhaps for posterity his most important, as plants would have come sooner or later without his agency. In 1569 he finally managed to purchase for the Emperor Maximilian II the finest illustrated copy of *De Materia Medica*, Dioscorides's famous first-century herbal, to date the most important source of plant identification in Europe. Originally made in AD 512 for the daughter of one of the last Byzantine emperors, this manuscript, now known as the *Codex Vindobonensis*, is still in the National Library in Vienna (see pp. 36–37).

PLANT PORTRAYALS

In the early years of the Renaissance the reawakened interest in the natural world, already explicit in the fourteenth century in works by Petrarch and Boccaccio, was complemented by a more scholarly approach to the study of herbalism and plants in general. Reflecting the general interest in landscape and nature, more naturalistic paintings of flowers began to appear in the borders of prayer books and in the detail of religious paintings; in these, flowers actually growing in gardens can be identified. Leonardo da Vinci's flower drawings and, by the early 1500s, Albrecht Dürer's more botanically accurate watercolours further demonstrate new attitudes to precise portrayals. Dürer recommended studying nature diligently: 'Be guided by nature and do not depart from it, thinking that you can do better yourself. You will be misguided, for truly art is hidden in nature and he who can draw it out possesses it.'

The invention of printing in the middle of the fifteenth century

had revolutionized the spread of 'shared' knowledge. The old herbals, laboriously copied and recopied by hand from ancient Greek and Latin texts, with stylized plant paintings depicting medicinal plants, were superseded by printed books, often illustrated with decorative woodcuts. Printed herbals became more freely accessible to those studying medicine as well as plants, and, of course, to laymen interested in plant collecting for their gardens. Botany as a science began to develop as a study of plants themselves rather than as a consideration of their usefulness in providing cures for illness. Printing made it possible to reproduce black and white illustrations of plants, set up side by side with the original text; the woodcuts, and the etchings and engravings used by the 1600s, could be hand-coloured later.

Printing gave a new impetus to re-issuing and re-editing classical texts of basic medical and botanic works such as Pliny the

Left: In this detail from Leonardo da Vinci's *Annunciation* in the Uffizi Gallery in Florence, painted in the 1470s when he was still in his twenties, the Madonna lily, which symbolized the Virgin Mary and often featured in Annunciation paintings, is depicted with great realism and botanical accuracy. In the background trees are stratified in estrade style as if in a formal garden instead of representing a country landscape. Both Leonardo and, later, Albrecht Dürer achieved a new realism in representing flowers which anticipated botanical illustrators such as Hans Weiditz who painted 'living portraits of plants' straight from nature to use as illustrations, printed as woodcuts, for Brunfels's *Herbarum Vivae Eicones* of 1530–6.

Above: By the first decade of the sixteenth century Albrecht Dürer had introduced a new note of botanical accuracy in his watercolours of flowers, intended as paintings in their own right. Only about ten of his flower studies survive, among which is the columbine (*Aquilegia vulgaris*) illustrated here. Unlike Hans Weiditz, who must have been influenced by Dürer's realism but was painting to illustrate a book about plants, Dürer himself painted plants in the natural groups he saw growing in the field and not as individual specimens. With the columbine are a meadow grass (*Poa trivialis*) and leaves of the creeping buttercup (*Ranunculus repens*).

Elder's *Naturalis Historia* and Dioscorides in both Greek and Latin (and in Italian in 1516), as well as those on farming and gardening typified by the *Liber ruralium commodorum* of Crescenzi, produced in French and Italian by the end of the fifteenth century. In the old herbals the plant drawings, laboriously copied by hand from other older manuscripts over centuries – although often beautiful – had become less and less accurate representations; on their own, without the accompanying text which was still usually based on Dioscorides's original, these would have done little to enlighten physicians seeking positive plant identification. Nor, of course, had these valuable hand-illustrated herbals been readily accessible to most doctors or horticulturists. Now in a new atmosphere of scholarship the printed texts, at last available to teachers and students and to gardening laymen, were studied critically.

The new science of botany throve not only on the interest in the flood of plant introductions which followed in the sixteenth century but also on the 'discovery' of more northern and localized flora, all of which, as plants unknown to the Greek and Roman encyclopaedists, needed listing and classifying. An additional challenge was to identify the 700 plants recorded by Dioscorides in the second century, many of which were native to the south-eastern parts of the Mediterranean and were known to herbalists north of the Alps only through descriptions in the old manuscripts.

In the 1530s and 1540s, just pre-dating the first wave of bulbs and tubers from the Levant, two printed herbals were issued in which paintings of plants from living flowers, rather than the old stylized copies, were transferred to woodcuts for printing. *Herbarum Vivae Eicones*, with Dioscorides-based text by Otto Brunfels (1488–1534) and woodcuts of plant drawings by Hans Weiditz, and *De Historia Stirpium* by Leonhard Fuchs (1501–56), a field botanist with a more genuine interest in living and 'growing' plants, both with accurate representations from nature, revolutionized not only the quality of botanical illustration but the information obtainable from the printed herbal (see pp. 116–17). They were the forerunners of a series of fine woodcut herbals among which one of the most beautiful was that of Pierandrea Mattioli, published in different forms and languages between 1544 and the 1560s, as well as in later editions until 1744. In his work Mattioli not only commented on Dioscorides but identified his plants through his own knowledge and botanical contacts; he also added a considerable number of 'new' ornamentals.

THE SEARCH FOR THE PLANTS OF DIOSCORIDES

Clearly the highly readable Brunfels and Fuchs herbals and Mattioli's *Commentarii* as well as other printed works re-stimulated a search for identification of Dioscorides's plants in the regions where he found his originals. The Greek herbalist's influence remained extraordinary; for another two centuries botanists and physicians still worked within the confines of classical procedures and knowledge, constantly making reference to the precedents set by Dioscorides. Busbecq and his physician Quackelbeen were by no means the first to notice the exciting flora of the eastern Mediterranean. As a symptom of the new Renaissance spirit of enquiry, Pierre Belon (1518–63), a Frenchman already interested in trees and medicinal plants and the acclimatization of 'foreign' introductions in France, was one of the earliest travellers to undertake serious botanical exploration. Sponsored by a wealthy patron, he journeyed in the Levant for three years between 1546 and 1549, calling at occasional Greek islands, with the primary purpose of identifying the plants described by Dioscorides rather than of collecting new plants. He too saw what he called '*lis rouges*' – the lyre-shaped tulips later gathered by Busbecq – as well as many other interesting plants, including the lilac that was cultivated by the Turks. He was the first to describe *Prunus laurocerasus*, later called by Clusius the 'cherry laurel' for its red fruit and for the glossy leaves which resembled those of the familiar bay tree. During his travels he saw in Crete a white oleander, the beautiful *Paeonia clusii* and *Cistus ladanifer*. He also reported seeing flowers from Persia and the east already long cultivated in the gardens of the Ottoman Empire. On Cos he admired the plane tree of Hippocrates and in Egypt he found papyrus and saw cultivated bananas (*Musa sapientum*), sugar cane (*Saccharum aegyptiacum*), and the 'exquisite greenery' of the sycomore fig. Most of the plants Belon collected were lost when the ship on which they were being sent home was attacked by pirates. But Belon's interest in new plants went beyond mere acquisitiveness.

Belon understood better than many of the more casual plant explorers, who until this period had discovered plants almost by chance, the difficulties of successfully cultivating exotics brought from different habitats. On his own return to France, he formulated ambitious plans to acclimatize both the cork and holm oaks (*Quercus suber* and *Q. ilex*), the spruce (*Picea abies*), the European strawberry tree (*Arbutus unedo*), as well as the sumach (*Rhus coriaria*), which coloured hills in Italy scarlet in autumn. He hoped to obtain a pension of 600 *livres* towards this object. By 1558 he was back in Italy furthering his study of 'taming' plants to French soil. He reported on rare trees and plants seen growing in some of the

The Solomon's seal (*Polygonatum odoratum*) and *Rosa gallica* are an illustration from an early sixteenth-century manuscript copy made in Paris of Platearius's *Livre des Simples Medicines*. These plants, associated with the Virgin Mary, are often shown together – another name for Solomon's seal was '*Sigillum benedictae virginis*', the seal of the Blessed Virgin. The original *Liber de Simplici Medicina* was compiled in the thirteenth century by Platearius at Salerno, the first medical school in Europe (founded at the end of the eleventh century), as a dictionary of drug synonyms drawing on both Latin and Arabic material. It was known as *Circa instans*.

Medici villa gardens around Florence, including the cherry laurel and the exotic banyan tree (*Ficus benghalensis*), the latter, as was customary also for most citrus fruit, probably covered in winter, or grown in movable containers. Today the banyan (or an acclimatized form) thrives only in the warmer climate of Palermo in southern Italy. The practice of covering exotics with a wooden frame was customary around Lake Como and found satisfactory in the temperate Atlantic English climate where Sir Francis Carew's famous oranges at Beddington in Surrey, reputedly the first to have been grown in England, were in open ground but covered in winter by a 'wooden tabernacle' and warmed by stoves. In 1658 John Evelyn found the same trees much overgrown but still being covered and accompanied by pomegranates bearing fruit; they survived until the bitter winter of 1739–40. Inventive gardeners like Sir Francis also defied the climate: for Queen Elizabeth's visit to Beddington in August 1599 Carew held back the ripening of black cherries by erecting a large canvas tent, cooled with water, over the tree, so that he could present her with a dish of fresh fruit.

Belon was not the only sixteenth-century Dioscoridean pilgrim to travel to Greece and the Levant in search of the 'plants of the ancients'. In 1573 the German physician Leonhardt Rauwolf (d. 1596) left Augsburg 'chiefly to gain a clear and distinct knowledge of these delicate herbs . . . by viewing them in their native places'.[1] He may have already seen flowering tulips in his home town: it was at the house of a merchant in Augsburg that, in 1559, the Swiss naturalist Conrad Gesner (1516–65) of Zurich had seen for the first time a tulip flowering in a garden belonging to 'the ingenius and learned Councillor Herwart . . . growing with a single, large reddish flower, like a red lily, with a pleasant smell, soothing and delicate, which soon leaves it'. The Augsburg tulips are reputedly the first to have flowered in the west after seed was received by Clusius. On his travels Rauwolf saw a 'pretty sort of tulip with yellow stripes' and also reported on a 'a kind of mandrake with blew flowers in great quantity' – *Mandragora autumnale*. On Mount Lebanon he saw the remaining grove of cedars, 26 aged trees, where none survives today. He noted that the Turks 'love to raise all sorts of flowers, in which they take great delight, and use to put them on their turban, so I could see the fine plants that blow one after another dailly'. Near Aleppo, Rauwolf found the wild hyacinth, already known in Europe as a cultivated plant. He also found the elusive rhubarb (*Rheum ribes*),

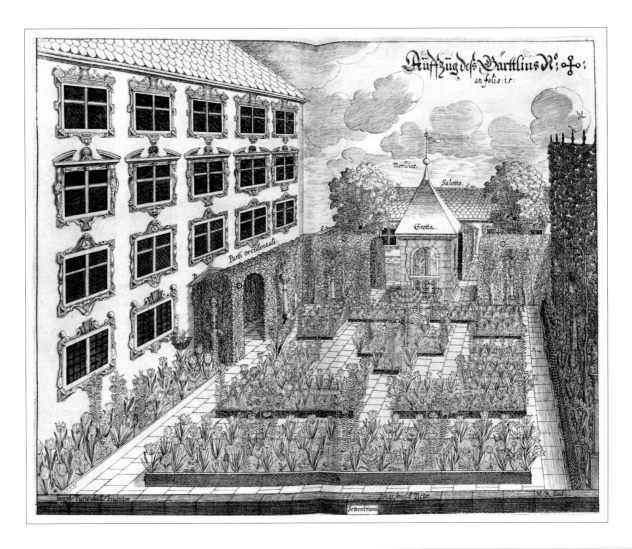

with stalks 'full of pleasant sourish juice', the true rhubarb of the Arabians. Rauwolf was primarily a botanist and not a collector, although he is reputed to have brought back seeds of a thorny shrub – which did not survive in Augsburg.

In 1700 Louis XIV dispatched Joseph Pitton de Tournefort (1656–1708) on a similar mission and the Dioscorides thread was followed through right up to the beginning of the nineteenth century; even by the second half of the eighteenth century still only 400 out of Dioscorides's 700 herbs had been identified. John Sibthorp (1758–96), Professor of Botany at Oxford, planned to scour Greece to complete the score, an attempt abandoned because of the disturbed state of many parts of the country under Turkish rule, and outbreaks of plague. On setting out, Sibthorp

Joseph Furttenbach in *Architectura Privata*, bound together with *Architectura Recreationis* and published in 1640, illustrates a town-lover's small garden filled with many of the new bulbous plants introduced from the Middle East only half a century earlier. Tulips, lilies and crown imperials growing in the flower-beds are immediately identifiable. Grape vines grow on shady arbours by the house. Furttenbach's brother Abraham provides a list of some forty plant species suitable for such a garden and presumably already available. In other plates Furttenbach proposes strongly architectural Italian-style gardens – he had spent some ten years in Italy – containing geometric flower plots.

travelled first to Vienna to view the famous illustrated *Codex Vindobonensis* of AD 512; in Vienna he collected Ferdinand Bauer who accompanied him as draughtsman. Although not achieving their original objective, Sibthorp and Bauer returned with some 2,000 species, about 300 of which were new. They also left a superb legacy; the ten-volume *Flora Graeca*, with Bauer's plates, was published after Sibthorp's death (with his bequest of £30,000) between 1806 and 1840, in a tiny edition of less than 30 copies.

A SCIENTIFIC APPROACH TO COLLECTING AND CATALOGUING

Fortunately the study and classification of 'nature' was an essential part of the Renaissance in Europe. The rebirth of interest in learning was allied to classical ideals of beauty and a love of nature. Although primarily believing that all natural products were created for the use of man, people also believed that 'usefulness' was implicit in delight in flowers and gardens. Renaissance Europe provided a setting in which doctors, scholars and gardeners could together experiment with and communicate about growing and acclimatizing new plants.

In the sixteenth century, as in the previous fifteen, the herbalists, who studied and grew plants and wrote the herbals, were trained as physicians. Many of the more familiar ones, such as Clusius and L'Obel, were pupils under Rondelet at the Medical School in Montpellier; others such as Mattioli studied at Padua; Brunfels, Fuchs, Dodoens and Besler were all practising doctors. The 'father of English botany', the naturalist William Turner, learned medicine in Italy; the first part of his *A New Herball* of 1551, written in English and illustrated by woodcuts taken from Leonhard Fuchs's work, was an important landmark in the development of English botanical scholarship, and Gerard and Parkinson were respectively barber-surgeon and apothecary. Like Clusius all three Englishmen were also practical gardeners, cultivating many of the plants they described.

Leon Battista Alberti had suggested in the fifteenth century that gardens should be encyclopaedic collections in which 'every known fruit that exists in any country' should be planted. By the sixteenth century this theme expanded so that gardens were intended to be representative of *all* nature; collecting and cataloguing old and new products of nature (not only plants but fossils, animals and minerals) became a Renaissance pastime that was by no means left to physicians in the newly founded teaching botanic gardens nor to the scholarly botanists expanding their new science by creating herbaria of dried specimens.

Collections of dried plants which were at first appropriately called *hortus hyemalis*, the winter garden, or *hortus siccus*, the dried garden, supplemented live ones. The first recorded herbarium may have been that of Luca Ghini, who besides sending dried plants glued on to sheets of paper to Mattioli in 1551, reputedly had assembled 300 specimens of his own. He may have inspired an early collection of dried plants in England; one belonging to John Falconer was known by William Turner in 1562. In 1645 John Evelyn was able to ask Dr Veslingius, Praefectus of the Padua Botanic Garden, to allow a gardener to make a collection of 'simples' for Evelyn's *hortus hyemalis*. An early herbarium to survive is that of Felix Platter, a physician at Basle, which was admired by Montaigne as he passed through in 1580:[2] 'Amongst his other work he was preparing a book of simels . . . and it was his practice, instead of painting like other botanists the plants according to their natural colours, to glue the same upon paper with so great care and dexterity that the smallest leaves and fibres should be visible, exactly as in nature . . . he showed us certain simples which had been fastened therein more than twenty years ago.' Platter, who had studied at Montpellier in 1554, used pieces of larkspur petal to record the blue of campanulas, since the corollas of these turn brown when dried. Platter's herbarium was rediscovered in Bern in 1930, together with some 80 of Weiditz's original watercolours for Brunfels's herbal; these include the common comfrey (*Symphytum officinale*), and the tall silver-leaved cotton or leaved thistle (*Onopordon acanthium*), both of which are still commonly found in gardens.

BOTANICAL PERSONALITIES

In northern Europe the three most important botanical figures of the second half of the sixteenth century were Dodoens, Clusius and L'Obel, all of whom published herbals or floras using woodcuts, many made from paintings by Pierre van der Borcht (1545–1608), collected by their printer Christopher Plantin in Antwerp. Their contribution to contemporary botany lies in their direct observations of plants, including assessing native habitats as a guide to required cultivation conditions. The Flemish Rembert Dodoens (1517–85) worked with his younger contemporaries Clusius and L'Obel, his collected botanical works being published as *Stirpium Historiae Pemptades Sex* in 1583. The Frenchman Matthias de L'Obel (1538–1616) – his name is commemorated in the genus

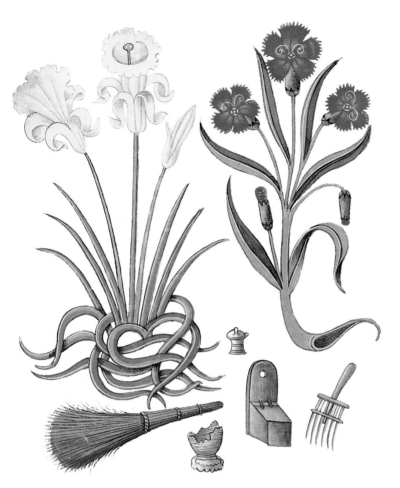

Lobelia – spent much of his working life in England; the manuscripts for his publications were acquired by John Parkinson, the English author of *Paradisi in Sole: Paradisus Terrestris* or 'A Garden of Pleasant Flowers', published in 1629 – the first English work to consider flowers for their beauty rather than their use as herbs.

The most intriguing of the three is the Flemish doctor Charles de L'Ecluse or Carolus Clusius (1526–1609), described as '*le père de tous les beaux jardins*', who cultivated rare plants from southern Europe, the Iberian peninsula and from Austria and Hungary and was among the first to grow the tulips sent to Vienna from Constantinople. Clusius compiled and translated many treatises during his life; his comprehensive *Opera Omnia Rariorum Plantarum Historia*, with its appreciation of the beauty of individual plants, confirmed new attitudes to serious botanical study. Clusius was also a practical gardener, by no means only a remote scholar. At the Leiden Botanic Garden, from 1592, Clusius was able to grow

The illustrations above are from a Tudor herbal picture book (an Ashmole manuscript in the Bodleian Library in Oxford). One shows daffodils paired with carnations together with a besom, wooden fork and saltbox, the other 'strawberries', in fruit and flower, growing over a wattle fence beside a tree. Many of the Tudor illustrators were copying earlier pictures or drawing from memory; the 'strawberry' is captioned 'blackberry' and the tree a 'birch', neither of which identifications seem very realistic. At the bottom of this second picture the charming blue-flowered plant looks like a periwinkle (*Vinca minor*).

ornamental plants rather than those that were purely useful in medicine, to make a true *hortus botanicus* rather than a *hortus medicus* (see pp. 118–19). During his years in Austria between 1573 and 1587, he explored peaks in the Tyrol and Styria in search of mountain flowers. At Leiden he grew the fragrant yellow auricula which he had found in the woods near Vienna, irises from Spain, carnations, African marigolds (*Tagetes erecta*), introduced to Europe from Mexico in the early 1500s but 'collected' near Tunis, the Jacobean lily (*Sprekelia formosissima*) also from Central America, in

1593, and the American agave – he failed to flower the latter, in spite of hearing reports of it in Rome with 'a stem like a pine tree twenty feet from the apex of which a mass of flowers originated'.[3] Seeds included many from the eastern Mediterranean, sent by his friend Joost Goedenhuyze (later in Italy known as Casabuona or Benincasa); at first, with no provision of hot-houses or frames, few germinated or survived. In 1592 Casabuona established the Pisa Botanic Garden, in its third and final site near the university, for the Medici Grand Duke Francesca I.

A host of lesser names became well-known on a local level. The naturalist William Turner supplied comments on plants already known and grown in English gardens although his writings were of little practical use to gardeners. The old mulberries at Syon House in Middlesex are reputed to have been planted by Turner when he was physician there to the Protector, Lord Somerset. From him we know that almonds, apricots, pomegranates, figs as well as black mulberries were commonly grown, probably against reflecting brick walls or even in front of earthed-up banks which provided extra heat. He and L'Obel discussed which introduced trees could supplement native species in gardens; some of them had been in the country already for many years. Oriental planes, umbrella or stone pines, spruce fir, the tender Italian cypress (*Cupressus sempervirens*) and the walnut had all been introduced before the middle of the century. In 1581 an evergreen oak (*Quercus ilex*) is recorded as growing in Whitehall. Shrubs such as *Cistus salvifolius*, white jasmine, Spanish broom (*Spartium junceum*), sweet bay, lavender, santolina and rue – with rosemary, grown since the fifteenth century – were all ingredients of the flower-garden.

John Gerard has assumed an importance in England beyond his true significance. In his *Herball*, published in London in 1597 (see pp. 120–21), Gerard listed plants already growing in gardens, with the result that the years of 1596 and 1597 are often given as the first recorded dates for plants whose actual date of introduction remains uncertain. Although still concerned with the 'virtues' of plants, Gerard described them with an intimate knowledge which touched on their ornamental qualities; he was certainly a practical gardener himself, head gardener to Lord Burghley at Theobalds, and with his own garden in Holborn, from which he compiled a list in 1596. Among his trees was the white mulberry, although James I is usually credited with introducing this for developing the silk trade at much the same time as Henri IV of France was

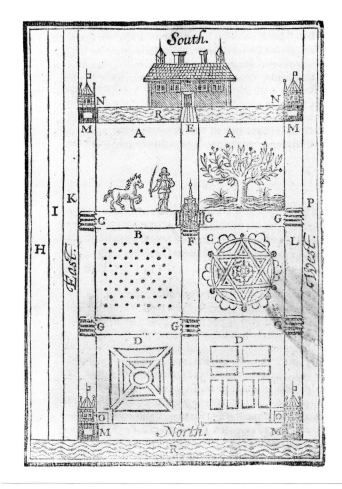

This plan for a typical manor-house garden in England is from William Lawson's *New Orchard and Garden* published in 1618. It shows a garden, with moat and river, divided into six sections, each of which is for separate garden themes and features. In two there are topiary pieces and espalier fruit trees, in another trees, probably fruit, are set in a quincunx 'twenty yards asunder'. Another area is set aside for knots, and the remaining two sections are for vegetables. Earth mounds are edged with quick thorn. Lawson also appreciated 'comely borders to the beds, with Roses, lavender and the like'.

establishing it in large numbers in his royal gardens – 20,000 at Fontainebleau and more at the Tuileries. In England Gerard is the first to mention the evergreen phillyreas – distinguishing twelve differing sorts already growing – which were frequently used for topiary during the following hundred years. He recorded planting one for the Earl of Essex at Barn Elms. Gerard remained as superstitious as many medieval chroniclers; although scoffing at the fearsome mandrake tales, he still quoted as genuine the fable of the barnacle tree from which geese were hatched (even Albertus

Magnus had disposed of this myth). Gerard's *Herball* described plants with a special charm which makes his work eminently readable even today, although many of his plant descriptions were plagiarized from Dodoens's previously published work in Latin and few of the woodcuts were original.

By 1629, for the first time in England – Clusius had already done this in Europe, but in Latin – plant interpretation emphasized not function but beauty as a desirable quality. Parkinson's 'Garden of Pleasant Flowers' published in that year marks the turning point (see pp. 120–21). Parkinson opened with an introduction to 'the ordering of the Garden of Pleasure' in which he revealed much about contemporary practice in England, often by setting the plants in particular gardens. At Cobham in Kent he saw a linden (lime) tree trained into a banqueting house, grander than the shady tree house at Villa Castello (see p. 155). Branches were pleached to make a low arbour; a further 2.4 metres/8 feet higher, branches were pleached again to make a 'house' with boards to walk upon: 'the goodliest spectacle mine eyes euer beheld for one tree to carry'. Yews were to be 'planted both in the corners of Orchards, and against the windowes of houses, to be both a shadow and an ornament, in being always greene'; cypresses to be planted 'in rows on both sides of some spacious walk', 'privet [buckthorn, or sometimes the desirable phillyrea] for no other purpose but to make hedges or arbours in the garden' and 'to bee cut, lead, and drawne into what forme one will either of beasts, birds, or men armed'. He had already seen Mattioli's lilac (*Syringa vulgaris*) as large as an apple tree, and grew the prized cherry laurel (*Prunus laurocerasus*) which produced ripe seeds in James Cole's garden in Highgate. Parkinson first drew attention to native wildflowers such as the yellow Welsh poppy (*Meconopsis cambrica*) and the now almost extinct lady's slipper (*Cypripedium calceolus*), the latter a much desired and protected rarity both in Great Britain and the U.S.A. Parkinson studied Gaspard Bauhin's *Pinax theatrici botanici*, published in 1623, the first attempt to coordinate the names of all known plants in a systematic concordance; thus his naming of plants is at least methodical, if still confusing to the modern reader. Both lilac (*Syringa*) and *Philadelphus*, having hollow stems, were classified under the heading of *Syringa*; the lilac was the 'blew Pipetree' (now *Syringa vulgaris*), the philadelphus was the 'single white Pipetree' (now *Philadelphus coronarius*), the scented mock-orange. This early nomenclature, with philadelphus often given the common name 'syringa', has led to a confusion which pertains even today. Like all his contemporaries Parkinson loved and praised all the new bulbs; but, in spite of instructions about sowing, planting, choosing and 'ordering' as well as drying them off in the dormant season, we do not know to what extent he and his readers grew them successfully. He had contacts with 'my very loving good friend John Tradescant'[4] as well as with collectors abroad such as Jean and Vespasian Robin in Paris. Both Thomas Johnson's edition of Gerard (1633) and Parkinson's *Theatrum Botanicum* of 1640 contain many useful references to the plants grown by the Tradescants. In 1632 Johnson paid a visit to the Tradescants' Lambeth garden and saw there young oriental plane trees, a horse-chestnut which four years earlier had been 'noursed up from the nuts sent us from Turkey', besides a 'Spring large floured Gentian' (*Gentiana acaulis*) with flowers of 'an exquisite blew'.

PLANT COLLECTING IN GARDENS

By the seventeenth century amateur gardeners and plant lovers were quite serious botanists: Besler's patron, the Prince-Bishop of Eichstätt, Francesco Caetani in Italy and Sir Thomas Hanmer in England were all collecting new plants in their gardens. If not botanists themselves, those that could afford it – such as Pope Paul III and the Medici Grand Dukes in Tuscany – employed experts to stock their gardens and became patrons of botanic garden collections. By the end of the sixteenth century botanists such as Clusius in northern Europe clearly differentiated between 'flowers' and the 'simples' grown in physic gardens. In Italy Agostino del Riccio's treatise on agriculture, published in the 1590s, was written in the style of the old classical treatises, with many similarities to the fourteenth-century Crescenzi, but he was already explicit about the difference between ornamentals and ordinary plants for physic. Even by 1559 Bartolomeo Taegio had included descriptions of ornamental gardens for delight in a book, *La Villa*, which is virtually a tract on life in the country. Writers such as Riccio recommended the new exotic bulbs, including scarlet lilies (*Lilium chalcedonicum*), tazetta narcissus, hyacinths and the much prized tulips, as well as scented jasmines such as the *Jasminum grandiflorum* which came from Spain, although originally from Asia, and, of course, New World flowers such as African marigolds, sunflowers, Indian shot (species of *Canna*) and trailing nasturtiums (*Tropaeolum majus*),

known as Indian cress, all of which would flower after the bulbs were over. In 1577 Thomas Hill in England wrote a general gardening manual of practical advice in which the familiar voices of Cato, Pliny, Columella and Palladius are still echoed. *The Gardener's Labyrinth* (published first under the pseudonym of Didymus Mountain – a shorter version, *The Proffitable Arte of*

The Stoke Edith needlework tapestries, showing formal gardens in the sixteenth century, hang at Montacute House in Somerset. An unidentified garden inspired this embroidery; later garden designs were influenced by elaborate needlework patterns. Here fruit trees, underplanted with Madonna lilies, grow against brick walls; tulips are lined up in the narrow beds surrounding the pools and what appears to be carnations stretch in a row to edge square lawn areas. Bushes are clipped in geometric shapes and citrus fruit grow in decorative vases.

Gardening, had appeared in 1563 – mentioned the newly arrived tulip but, in general, the main influx of exotic species and varieties had not yet crossed the channel and were first described in Gerard at the end of the century. One wonders how quickly botanists and horticulturists coped with the demands of acclimatization and specific growing conditions? Perhaps in a warm summer climate such as that of Italy, bulbs which require baking with hot sun during dormancy would be left in the ground, while in gardens such as the Hortus Academicus in Leiden these would be lifted, dried and stored until the autumn, leaving flower-bed spaces for American and tropical annuals including the by now familiar amaranthus. In *Paradisis in Sole: Paradisus Terrestris* Parkinson detailed the cultivation of tulips from the sowing of seed to bringing them to flower, and 'drying off' of the older established plants.[5]

The floral treasures flooding into Europe from both east and west could be portrayed in contemporary herbals with fine lifelike plant illustrations: by the early 1600s etched or engraved copper plates allowed more precise details of plants to emerge than the coarser woodcuts could show. Although botanical illustration is primarily concerned with accuracy for identification purposes, the beauty of many of the paintings and drawings of individual plants and flowers stimulated gardeners to acquire plants for their collections, giving an impetus to ornamental horticulture as well as providing instruction to students of medicine and botany. Then, as the science of botany emerged for the first time as distinct from the study of medicine, the herbals, describing 'useful' plants, were also superseded by modern florilegia in which plants were studied and illustrated purely for their beauty and desirability as ornamentals. By the early seventeenth century the new florilegia were diffusing ideas of gardening possibilities all over western Europe.

The tradition of the florilegium, technically a book describing a collection of living ornamental garden plants, originated with the publication of Pierre Vallet's *Jardin du Roy très Chrestien Henry IV* in 1608, in which 75 etchings were made from drawings of plants actually growing in the French royal gardens. Dedicated to Marie de Medici, who was responsible for laying out the gardens of the Luxembourg Palace after she was widowed, Vallet's embellishments, regarded as patterns for needlework, influenced the developing patterns of box parterres. Many of the plants illustrated were in the Paris garden of Jean Robin (1550–1629), the director of the king's gardens and a foremost plant collector. In Emmanuel Sweert's *Florilegium*, first published in Frankfurt in 1612 but compiled while he was in Prague in charge of Rudolph II's gardens, 250 plants were described as being purely for ornament; it was a sort of catalogue of the plants he had for sale at the annual fair at Frankfurt and subsequently at Amsterdam.

The *Hortus Floridus* of Crispin van de Passe, in four books with engravings of spring, summer, autumn and winter flowers, was published in Latin in 1614; a Dutch and an English text, issued at Utrecht, followed almost immediately in 1615. The book's frontispiece of the Spring Garden shows tulips, crown imperials and hyacinths planted in beds in the sparse fashion of the time, when these new rarities were on display. Arranged in the same way in seasonal chronology to help gardeners was the most impressive of the great florilegia, that of Basil Besler, *Hortus Eystettensis*, first published in 1613 with engraved copper plates, which catalogued all the plants in the garden at Eichstätt (see p. 122–23). Although more than 150 of the 580 species described came from the Mediterranean area they did apparently grow outdoors at Eichstätt. Many plants only recently introduced to Europe were included. A facsimile edition published in 1987 as *L'Herbier des Quatre Saisons* and translated from the French into English in 1989 now provides the most complete record of plants in garden cultivation at the beginning of the seventeenth century and is a useful aide to interpretation of nomenclature.

The establishment of botanic gardens, in later years developing as general collections, marked a new stage in the study of plants as a botanical science, as well as furnishing live plants for medical students to recognize and study. Plants were searched for and collected by both botanists – for use as dried specimens for study in herbaria as well as for growing 'live' in the botanic gardens – and by plant explorers who supplied plant collectors who wanted

The knot garden, an adaptation of Colonna's flower-bed patterns taken from his *Dream of Poliphilus*, was a characteristic feature of both French and English sixteenth-century gardens. In England the scale was more intimate, with a single knot pattern lying near the house windows rather than a series being arranged in a grand progression. Sometimes the patterns were marked out in a continuous weaving thread, with sand or gravel in between; at others edging plants such as hyssop and thyme enclosed beds where flowering herbs increased the display. At Rosemary Verey's modern garden in Gloucestershire, seventeenth-century knot patterns have been adapted with interlacing patterns of box surrounding clipped phillyreas.

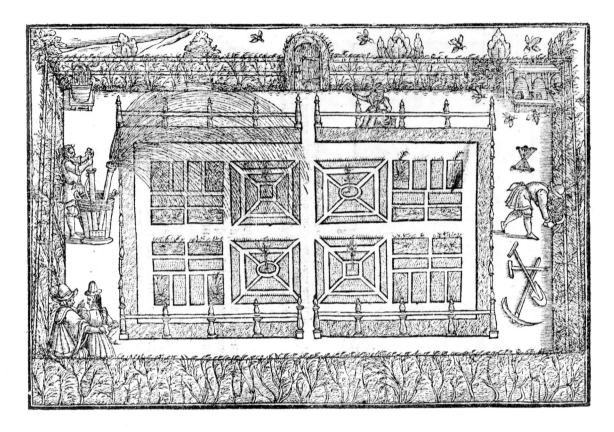

One of the most useful practical gardening manuals was that published in England as *The Gardener's Labyrinth* by Thomas Hill in 1577 (under the pseudonym of Didymus Mountain). Containing little new information about plants (although the tulip had arrived in time to get a mention), and in style and content still strongly reminiscent of the familiar Roman texts on husbandry, Hill's writing has a down-to-earth quality which speaks of his own experience in plant management. Suggestions for how to prepare and dung the soil, how and when to sow, and ingenious devices for watering the complicated beds (as shown here) were all included.

new exotics in their gardens. In design the new teaching botanic gardens had much in common with many of the large contemporary gardens being laid out throughout western Europe. Those belonging to royalty and princes of the church rivalled them in size and importance. Luca Ghini (1490–1556) had established a small garden of 'simples' in Bologna in 1528, but the two earliest botanic gardens established in Europe were those at Pisa and Padua, both founded in 1545, primarily as collections of plants for education in the University medical schools. Montpellier in France (1593) and Leiden in Holland (1587) were followed by Oxford in England in 1621 and that of the Jardin du Roy in Paris (1625–36) (see

pp. 124–25). In 1549 the catalogue of plants grown at Pisa, written in the hand of Ulisse Aldrovandi, contained only 620 plants, most of which were European natives. Within a generation all this changed with the flow of plants from the eastern Mediterranean and the New World; the gardens also contained 'cabinets of curiosities', museum collections of all sorts of thing's of natural origin.

The encyclopaedic attitude to collecting also had an effect on layout, with plants' positions carefully recorded. The most usual scheme was based on dividing a square garden area into four to represent the four corners of the earth. Now, with plants streaming into European gardens from four continents – Europe, Asia, Africa and America (fortunately few people dreamed of the fifth continent, Australia) – this pattern assumed a greater and almost biblically inspired significance. In *L'Horto de i semplice di Padova*, Porro mentioned that plants which came from the east such as cedar, laurel and myrtle were planted in the eastern section of the Padua Botanic Garden in 1591, and at Oxford there was a confused attempt at geographical planting during the eighteenth century. Each of the main quarters was then further subdivided in various practical ways for ease of codifying each plant's position. At this stage with systematic botany still embryonic – Bauhin's *Pinax* of 1623, listing 6,000 plants, was the earliest work to have attempted to coordinate all plant names and their synonyms in a methodical concordance – flowers were not planted in families, which were still unknown, but in groups of recognized species.

PLANTSMEN GARDENERS

In England the famous garden of John Tradescant the Elder and his son John Tradescant the Younger, established in Lambeth, was so comprehensive that the lists of plants grown in it provide a record of most plants known at the time, which could be grown successfully in northern Europe. England, in fact, had a particularly favourable temperate climate. Both Tradescants not only found and introduced plants themselves but obtained them through contacts in Europe and through the Virginia Company; they also grew for the first time actually in a garden, many plants already known about, and they kept lists and records (see pp. 126–27). Surplus plants were almost certainly for sale, which meant that those new in cultivation got around quite quickly – this also happened with plants from the Oxford Botanic Garden after its foundation in 1621, and more so after its published list of 1648. At first working for others, including the Cecils at newly built Hatfield and later the royal family, the Tradescants probably did more for the development of English horticulture than anyone else in the first half of the century. From 1630 Tradescant was Keeper of the Royal Gardens at Oatlands Palace for Queen Henrietta Maria (this at a time when André Mollet was laying out the gardens at St James's Palace for the queen), and in 1636, the year before he died, was advising about the laying out of the new Botanic Garden at Oxford. John the Younger worked with his father and 'inherited' his Oatlands job. His greatest contribution was plants from Virginia, although his father had already received several through the Virginia Company. The contents of their museum at Lambeth, Tradescant's Ark (listed as *Musaeum Tradescantianum* in 1656), became the nucleus of the Ashmolean Museum in Oxford. The formation of the Tradescant Society and the restoration of St Mary's Church at Lambeth where their tomb lies in the graveyard (together with the establishment of a Museum of Garden History there) has done much to emphasize their importance.

Pierre Vallet, painter to the French court, produced one of the first important florilegia, originally intended as a pattern book for embroidery (and as such dedicated to the queen, Marie de Medici). In *Le Jardin du Roy très Chrestien Henry IV* (1608) the flowers he painted included rare specimens grown in the king's Paris garden of the Louvre by Jean Robin, *arboriste* to the king, and in his own garden on the Ile de la Cité. The exotic *Canna indica* (as shown here), with both red and yellow flowers, was probably first introduced to Europe from the West Indies, although today it is recognized as common to all tropical zones; many hybrids are grown in gardens.

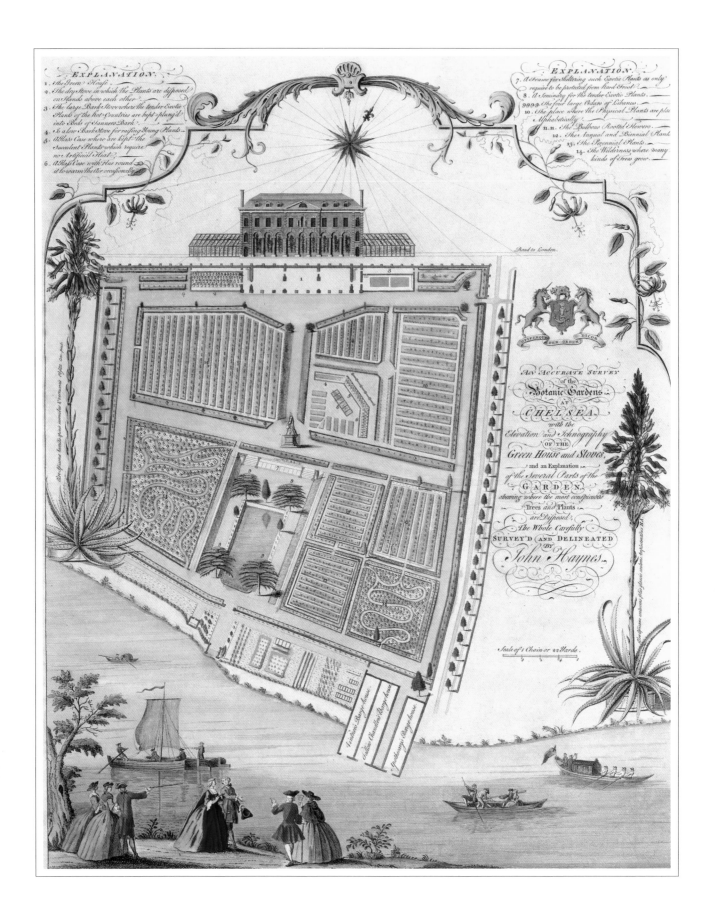

Road to London.

An Accurate Survey
of the
Botanic Gardens
AT
CHELSEA
with the
Elevation and Ichnography
OF THE
Green House and Stoves
and an Explanation
of the Several Parts of the
GARDEN
shewing where the most conspicuous
Trees and Plants
are Disposed.
The Whole Carefully
SURVEY'D AND DELINEATED
BY
John Haynes.

Scale of 1 Chain or 22 Yards.

In spite of the influx of plants during the sixteenth and seventeenth centuries, Renaissance garden styles remained strictly architectural with an emphasis on layout, perspective, balance and symmetry (see Chapters Five and Six); traditional plants of known hardiness and behaviour retained their roles in the execution of the stylized schemes. But side by side with the development of gardening styles, individual plant collectors working in widely different climates concentrated on specialist flowers. In a sense, the seventeenth-century plant specialists, although often richly endowed grand landowners, were the forerunners of the more humble Florists' Societies. These developed during the succeeding centuries and concentrated on a limited range of flowers chosen from eight kinds: anemones, auriculas and primroses, carnations and pinks, hyacinths, ranunculus and tulips, all cultivated to a state of 'perfection'. In Italy Francesco Caetani, Duke of Sermoneta, gardening at Cisterna south of Rome, collected 'double velvet anemones' as well as other new-fangled rarities (see pp. 128–29), while in England John Rea, Samuel Gilbert and Sir Thomas Hanmer had proud collections of tulips and double carnations.

Sir Thomas Hanmer (1612–78) who lived at Bettisfield in Shropshire on the Welsh border, was a friend and neighbour of John Rea, whose book *Flora* (1665) was dedicated to Sir Thomas, and also of John Evelyn; during the Civil War he retired to the country and continued to develop his garden. The Revd Samuel Gilbert was John Rea's son-in-law and published *The Florist's Vade Mecum* in 1682, in which he gave a garden calendar of flowers for each month as well as some nice gardening detail. John Rea was a nurseryman and was reputed to have the largest stock of tulips in England; in the second edition of his *Flora* (see pp. 130–31) he mentioned more than 200 named varieties, including the famous 'Semper Augustus' and 'Agot Hanmer', described by Samuel Gilbert as having three fine 'setting off' colours: pale 'gredeline', or flax-grey, rich scarlet and pure white. Hanmer's gardening

philosophies are expressed in his *Garden Book* which, although completed in 1659, remained unpublished until 1933. As well as information on pears and vines, it contains descriptive and cultural notes favouring his specialist interests, which centred around tulips, anemones, auriculas, daffodils, primroses and cowslips. In

The Chelsea Physic Garden was established in London in 1673 on the banks of the Thames by the Society of Apothecaries for the purpose of demonstrating medicinal plants. Van Huysum's painting of the survey by John Haynes in 1751 is framed by a pair of African aloes. The illustration shows 'where the most conspicuous trees and plants are disposed', as well as greenhouses, stove houses and frames for housing many of the tender exotics and succulents. Four Lebanon cedars, among the first to be planted in England in the last quarter of the seventeenth century, are depicted on the corners of the large water basin near the river. Two of these survived until the nineteenth century.

A watercolour drawing of violets and a red admiral butterfly by the French Protestant painter Jacques Le Moyne de Morgues (1530–88) is in the Victoria and Albert Museum, London. Although as recording artist and cartographer Le Moyne accompanied Laudonnière's disastrous expedition to Florida in 1564, no paintings of North American flowers survive. His later work, in France and when a refugee in England after 1572, depicting flowers already common in European gardens, owes much to the French miniature painting style of Jean Bourdichon. Many of the watercolours were utilized for the woodcuts in Le Moyne's *Clef des Champs*, published in Blackfriars in 1586.

The Duchess of Beaufort was an expert on exotic flowers and had all the latest rarities besides a large number of tender plants in her greenhouses at Badminton in the early years of the eighteenth century. She hired the Dutch artist Everhard Kick, known to her through Sir Hans Sloane, to draw plants in the collection. Among the paintings was one of a red-flowered polyanthus, a cross between a primrose and a cowslip, one of the plants later prized by florists.

an aside on the difficulties of collectors in faraway countries in getting seeds and roots home, he advised: 'The fibrous sorts must bee made up alone by themselves, with moist mosse or grasse about them tyed fast, which is better than earth, which will dry and fall away, unless the voyage be short but all the other kinds must bee packt up dry without earth in papers, and soe boxt up that they shake not . . . so that they may bee convey'd safely very farr.' In another manuscript, possibly intended as a preface to his garden book,[6] he recorded not only what plants were grown in each flower-bed but also the changes in garden style which had occurred in one generation.

The original version of Hanmer's manuscript gives a picture of how a contemporary fashionable garden should look: 'The knotts or quarters are not hedg'd about with privet, rosemary or other tall hearbs which hide the prospect of the worke and nourish hurtful worms and flys, nor [are] our standard fruit trees suffer'd to grow soe high or thick as to shadow the wyndowes or cumber and barren the soyle; but all is now commonly neere the house

layd open and exposed to the view of the chambers and the knotts and borders upheld only with very low colour'd boards, stone or tile. If the ground be spacious the next adjacent quarters of Parterre as the french call them, are often of fine turf, kept low as any greens to bowle on – cut out curiously into Embroidery of flowers, beasts, birds or feuillages and small alleys and intervals filled with severall coloured sands and dust with much art, with but few flowers . . . least they debase the beauty of the embroidery.' Farther away from the house were more knot compartments with borders for flowers intermixed with grasswork, and placed at regular intervals on the outside either flowers in pots or dwarf cypresses, firs or other evergreens, kept clipped into topiary globes or pyramids. Farther still there would be labyrinths with hedges cut out to a man's height with 'severall straight or gravelly winding walks'. Other alleys might be of 'high trees such as elms, limes, abells [poplars], firrs, pines or others' as well as more architectural features such as fountains, statues, arbours, cabinets and seats. The 'grounds are commonly a third part longer than broad'. Besides describing his own garden beds, Hanmer gave descriptive and cultural notes which speak of his experience and skill in acclimatizing the exotic bulbs as well as in keeping tender 'greens' such as the orange in a 'winter house'. Other shrubby plants that he overwintered were phillyreas, arbutus, the coral tree (*Erythrina crista-galli*), the pepper tree (*Schinus molle*), myrtle and oleander.

His interest in trees paralleled that of his better known friend John Evelyn, whose *Sylva* was published in 1664; Hanmer was particularly keen on evergreens such as the cedar of Lebanon and evergreen oak. He also recommended that all 'florists' should keep a private piece of ground as a nursery area to sow and raise plants and trees in, and 'keepe such treasures as are not to bee exposed to everyone's view and adjoining to which they have a wynter house for shelter of tender plants in cold weather'. Hanmer's personal garden was a collector's piece, probably with no pretensions to following a 'style', but organized to provide the best sort of growing conditions for his much-loved plants. Even so, by this time – as recommended by Leonard Meager in *The English Gardener* in 1670 – the 'new' exciting flowers were to be arranged in separate areas from the 'herbs for setting knots', which were of the more traditional type. By 1677 William Lucas's nursery list had 75 flower seeds and about 40 bulbs and rhizomes all as 'named' varieties.

THE TREE PLANTERS

In England both individuals growing for pleasure and nurserymen growing plants for sale were beginning to discern the advantages their climate could offer. Some seeds of plants from countries with hotter summers might fail to ripen, and certain plants such as the tender evergreens so popular in the sixteenth century might need winter protection (John Evelyn coined the term 'greenhouse' to describe such protective devices, and also used 'conservatory' in this sense). However, the temperate climate – without extremes of cold or heat – allowed many plants from very diverse habitats to thrive without special protection or culture. Perennials, woody plants and climbers were discovered to be especially successful.

By the second half of the seventeenth century the flow of new plants was transforming gardening possibilities. Plants were being grown experimentally by collectors such as Henry Compton, Bishop of London (1632–1713) (see pp. 134–35). He not only introduced a considerable number of new hardy plants, many from North America, to his 13-hectare/32-acre garden at Fulham Palace, but then – by making them available to the famous Brompton Park Nursery – ensured their relatively swift distribution around various important estates. The bishop also grew plants which came through Holland from the Cape of Good Hope, and which needed winter protection: one was *Pelargonium inquinans*, a parent of our modern bedding pelargonium (the other, *P. zonale*, was being grown by the Duchess of Beaufort in her greenhouses at Badminton by the turn of the century). The Fulham Palace garden was neglected and trees cut down after the bishop's death, but not before the nurserymen Robert Furber of Kensington and Christopher Gray of Fulham were able to augment their own plant collections.

George London (fl. 1681–1714) and Henry Wise (1653–1738), joint proprietors of the Brompton Park Nursery, were the most important garden advisers and nurserymen of the day. London had worked at Fulham as a young man and part of his developing success as designer and adviser was due to Compton's patronage, as well as that of John Evelyn and Queen Anne. The nursery was a rich source of plants of various kinds, although the London and Wise partnership designed strictly in the grand French style (see Chapter Six), which was adopted in England after the Restoration of 1660. After 1688 William and Mary brought with them a

John Evelyn, the celebrated connoisseur of trees and gardens, recorded an after-dinner walk in the garden at Ham in August 1678: 'the House and Garden of the Duke of Lauderdale, which is indeed inferior to few of the best Villas in Italy itselfe. The house furnished like a great Princes: the parterrs, flo: Gardens, orangeries, Groves, Avenues, Courts, Statues, perspectives, Fountains, Aviaries, and all this at the banks of the sweetest river in the World, must needes be surprizing'. Many of the flowers at Ham were painted by the florist Alexander Marshall, who also painted Bishop Compton's plants at Fulham Palace. The carnations are from Marshall's florilegium.

distinct and more intimate Dutch nuance, better suited both to the English temperament and to the unforested countryside.

The diarist and writer John Evelyn (see pp. 132–33) adopted an economic and scientific approach to forestry and gardening and made fashionable tree planting, both in woodland and to implement the schemes of London and Wise with their tailored outlines. But Evelyn had also studied the development of gardening styles in Europe. His dissemination of knowledge of both plants and design precepts provided the background against which trees and shrubs grown experimentally as natural specimens rather than used as architectural features could emerge into the English Landscape style of the eighteenth century (see Chapter Seven).

But this is to run too far ahead, beyond the period of the Renaissance and the scope of this chapter with its focus on key figures. We must first trace the patterns of formal garden design in which Italy and France excelled.

THE WOODCUT HERBALS OF BRUNFELS, FUCHS AND MATTIOLI

The earliest of a series of illustrated herbals establishing a new style in botanical illustration, in which plants were accurately portrayed from nature rather than being stylized copies from earlier manuscripts, was published in Strasbourg in three parts in 1530, 1532 and 1536: the *Herbarum Vivae Eicones*, with text by Otto Brunfels (1488–1534) and plant illustrations by Hans Weiditz. Brunfels's herbal was followed in 1542 by *De Historia Stirpium* with text by Leonhard Fuchs (1501–56), published in Basle, in which 400 German plants and 100 foreign ones were also drawn from nature.

To gardeners the woodcut herbal of the greatest interest is by Pierandrea Mattioli (1501–77), the Italian botanist and physician, who spent 20 years in Prague in the service first of the Archduke Ferdinand and then of the Emperor Maximilian II. His commentaries on Dioscorides, eventually illustrated with remarkably beautiful large woodcuts, became the standard work on medical botany for European physicians during the second half of the sixteenth century, going into over 60 editions in Latin, Italian, French, German and even Czech. Besides identifying many of Dioscorides's original herbs, which he was able to do through his own travels and by correspondence with a wide circle of botanist plantsmen, in the *Commentarii*, Mattioli

Mattioli's *Commentarii*, with a Latin text, was first published without pictures in 1544: small illustrations were added in the 1550s, while the most beautiful edition, with large pictures, was printed in Venice in 1565. The white jasmine or gelsiminum (*Jasminum officinale*), no 85, is from that 1565 edition, in which elaborately shaded flowers and foliage filled the whole space available in each woodcut. Some of Mattioli's pearwood blocks from the 1560s are still preserved.

incorporated observations and descriptions of new plants which he had either seen or received. Willem Quackelbeen (1527–61), ambassador Busbecq's doctor in Constantinople, sent Mattioli accounts of at least ten new plant species, including the lilac and horse-chestnut, which Mattioli was able to include in his book. Among other new plants Mattioli portrayed were grape hyacinths, sea holly, datura, auricula, *Arum italicum* and four different pines.

Hans Weiditz, who drew the plants for the *Herbarum Vivae Eicones* of Otto Brunfels, produced between 1530 and 1536, was almost certainly a pupil of Albrecht Dürer. He painted 'lifelike' plants drawn directly from living specimens; his daffodil (*Narcissus pseudonarcissus*) and spring snowflake (*Leucojum vernum*) are shown here. Although as a traditional physician Brunfels was only interested in Dioscorides's original herbs from a more southerly Mediterranean region, and his text remains medieval in content, Weiditz added northern plants found in the Strasbourg locality. These plants had to be given appropriate Latin names as they would not have been known to early herbalists.

The drawings for Leonhard Fuchs's *De Historia Stirpium* were by Heinrich Füllmaurer and Albrecht Meyer, and the woodcuts were made by Veit Rudolph Speckle. The large woodcuts were intended for later colouring. The winter cherry (*Physalis alkekengi*) is a native of eastern Europe – water distilled from the berries was said to cure stone in the bladder. Fuchs (after whom the genus *Fuchsia* was named), besides being a physician, was also a field botanist with a real interest in observing and identifying flora.

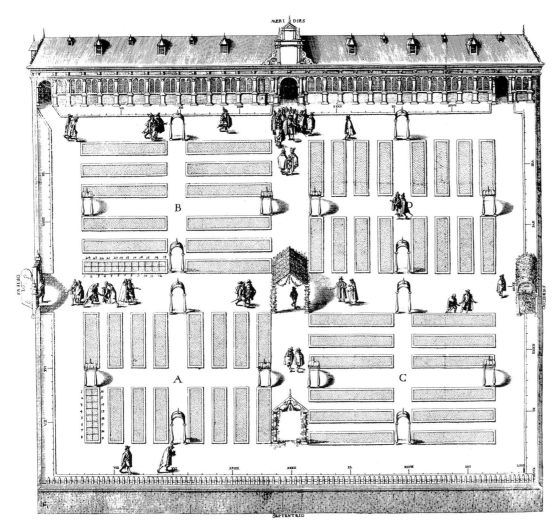

the duties of director of the botanic garden. Two years later Dirck Outgaertszoon Cluyt was appointed superintendent of the gardens; it was Cluyt who had to supervise the laying out and planting of the garden which took place in September of that year. Plants growing in the garden were listed in catalogues issued in the 1600s. They include a number of those only recently introduced: *Argemone mexicana, Canna indica*, nasturtium, *Tagetes patula, Zea mays* as well as mandrake, the Italian cypress, *Ricinus communis*, the Indian fig (*Opuntia ficus-indica*), the Judas tree, lilac (*Syringa vulgaris*), *Philadelphus coronarius*, tobacco and the true ginger (*Zingiber officinale*) from the East Indies. By 1608 there were 600 tulip bulbs, including early and late, rare and common varieties. The Florentine plant collector Matteo Caccini gave Clusius bulbs of the pink-flowered species, *Tulipa clusiana*, in 1607.

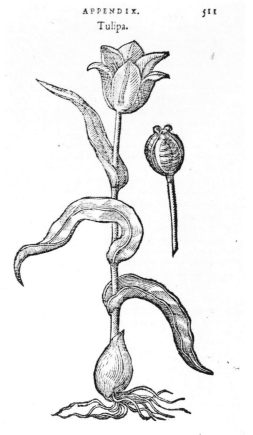

CLUSIUS AND THE LEIDEN BOTANIC GARDEN

Born at Artois in 1526, Carolus Clusius (Charles de L'Ecluse) first studied law but later went as a pupil of Rondelet to the Medical School at Montpellier, where he was able to see many new plants growing in the warmer south. His first academic publication, in 1557, was a translation into French of Rembert Dodoens's newly published *Crŭÿdeboeck* (later Gerard borrowed this to compile his *Herball* of 1597). In 1571 Clusius visited London, where he acquired some of the recently introduced American plants and became acquainted with Nicolas Monardes' book on American plants – which he later translated from Spanish to Latin – which includes descriptions of sunflowers and tobacco. (Its English translation with the picturesque title *Joyfull news out of the newe founde worlde* was completed in 1577.) Clusius's final work, published in 1601, *Opera Omnia Rariorum Plantarum Historia* emphasized the distinctive beauty of individual plants, predating Parkinson's *Paradisus* or flowers of delight by 28 years.

In 1592 the Curatores at Leiden were able to persuade Clusius, by then living in Frankfurt and already in his sixties, to undertake

Clusius received his first tulips while he was in Vienna in 1574 and took his collection, built up from bulbs and seeds, with him to Leiden in 1592. The woodcut of a tulip (left) is from his Rariorum Plantarum Historia. It was noticed that some of the self-coloured tulips, later known as 'breeders', would 'break' to produce a flower striped or splashed with another colour. Caused, as we know now, by a virus transmitted by aphids, this phenomenon led to an outbreak of speculative 'tulipomania', in which, especially in Holland, bulbs fetched huge prices; the craze reached a peak in 1634 before the market collapsed, plunging speculators and merchants into debt.

Although the size and shape of the site are changed, the restored Hortus Academicus at Leiden has most of the original characteristics shown in the engraving of 1601 (far left) from Christopher Plantin, which depicts students with a teacher, possibly Clusius, taking a class. The garden was divided into four quadrangles by two intersecting paths; each quadrangle was divided into two halves containing a number of beds called in Latin pulvilli, meaning small cushions or parcels. Each pulvillus, 40 x 31 metres/133 x 103 feet, was in turn subdivided into smaller numbered units for different plant families, each long 'parcel' for plant references measuring 53 centimetres/21 inches

along its short side. These beds are clearly visible in the photograph of the garden as it is today (above). A printed catalogue of the gardens appeared in 1601, giving a complete inventory and the exact location of the thousand different species and varieties. There were also pot plants, including oranges and lemons; together with other plants that did not fit into the narrow beds, these were 'planted in the surrounding plots for the decoration of the garden'. An inscription in stone on the north façade (today restored) gave regulations for visitors in Latin – jumping over beds, picking or breaking flowers or branches, and tearing out bulbs and roots were all strictly forbidden.

Gerard's *Herball*, published in 1597, is much more of a gardening treatise than William Turner's *New Herball* of 1551–62, but it is still a catalogue of plants considered for their 'vertues'. Parkinson, in writing his best-selling florilegium, *Paradisi in Sole: Paradisus Terrestris*, and his herbal (the *Theatrum Botanicum* of 1640), emphasizes the garden of pleasure and its 'ordering'.

Although assembled in part from the works of the Flemish herbalist Rembert Dodoens, Gerard's main work, including notes on cultivation of plants new and old, still holds interest. He had his own plot in Holborn in London where he grew more than a thousand plants: 'all the rare simples' and 'all manner of strange trees, herbes, rootes, plants, flowers, and other such rare things' which he listed in his 1596 catalogue, along with the first printed reference to the potato. Among these

GERARD AND PARKINSON

were many of the latest exotic bulbs, a few American plants and other new trees and shrubs.

Parkinson also grew many of the plants he writes about in his own garden, which was in Long Acre in London; plants from the New World (mainly obtained through Spain) included four-o'clocks or marvels of Peru, tobacco (he grew two kinds for the pleasure of the flowers), 'Indian cress' (*Tropaeolum majus* – the common nasturtium) and canna (already seen, he comments, by Clusius growing by the wayside in Spain and Portugal); *Aster tradescantii*, African marigolds originally from Mexico (but found growing near Carthage), blue passion flower or maracoc (*Passiflora caerulea*, listed in the *Horto Farnesiano* of 1625),

Smilacina racemosa, and *Tradescantia virginiana*. He treasured a yucca (*Yucca filamentosa*) as it was a lineal descendant of Gerard's plant, a piece of which went first to Robin in Paris and in due course came back to Long Acre.[7] In the *Paradisus* he listed many anemones, auriculas, 'gilliflowers' (carnations and pinks), hyacinths, ranunculus and tulips, which had been much developed in the short period since their introduction. There were lilies and 'martagons' (still classified separately), narcissus, iris, and the beautiful *Ornithogalum arabicum*. He opened his plant catalogue with the great 'Crowne Imperiall', then called 'Corona Imperialis': 'for its stately beautifulness it deserveth the first place in this our Garden of delight'. Other 'outlandish flowers' he recommended to 'give such grace to the garden, that the place will seem like a piece of tapestry of many glorious colours'.

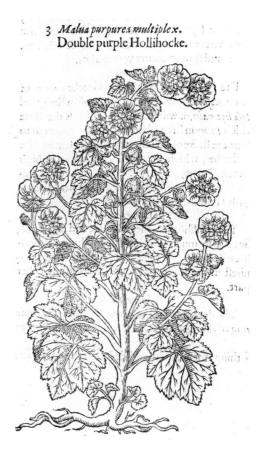

Far left: The title-page of Gerard's *Herball* of 1597, in which the plants are illustrated with woodcuts, was designed and engraved by William Rogers. The strapwork and cartouche design, typical of those with 'emblematical' motifs, is dominated by the goddess Flora holding 'White Mountaine Pinke', 'Lillie of the valley' and the common American sunflower, with other flowers grouped around her and framing the title. One male figure holds the 'Purple Passe flower' (*Anemone pulsatilla*), another holds the crown imperial, a third the Madonna lily and the fourth the 'Changeable checkered Daffodil' (*Fritillaria meleagris*) and 'Turkie Wheat' (*Zea mays*). The garden shown in the cartouche is probably Lord Burghley's Theobalds, where Gerard worked.

Left: Amaranths are divided by Gerard into 'Purple Floure gentle' (*Celosia cristata*) and 'Floramor'. Two woodcuts from the 1597 edition show – the true *Amaranthus tricolor* – and Gerard's 'Double purple Hollihocke', known as 'the tame or garden mallow'. Gerard's work was revised by Thomas Johnson in 1633 and it is this amended version, illustrated with 2,766 wood blocks from the Antwerp printer Plantin's collection, which is most familiarly quoted. Among the foreign trees and shrubs Gerard grew in his own garden, many of which were described in the *Herball*, were laburnum, the Judas tree, the persimmon (*Diospyros lotus*), white mulberry, the hackberry or nettle tree (*Celtis australis* from southern Europe), pinaster, *Lavatera olbia* and laurustinus, as well as arbor-vitae (*Thuja occidentalis*) and *Yucca americana* from America.

Right: The title page to Parkinson's florilegium, *Paradisi in Sole: Paradisus Terrestris* of 1629 – a pun on 'paradise' and 'park' . The *Paradisus* is illustrated with wood engravings described by Agnes Arber as of no particular merit, but the plant group on each page have considerable charm. The title page shows the Garden of Eden, in which it was assumed before The Fall all plants created by God were grown. Adam is shown plucking the forbidden fruit, while Eve fingers an unidentifiable flower. Among date palms, tulips, the crown imperial and the exotic pineapple is the 'plant animal', the notorious vegetable lamb of Tartary which was supposed to grow from a stalk out of the ground.

Basil Besler (1561–1629) was in charge of the gardens of Johann Konrad von Gemmingen, Prince-Bishop of Eichstätt, from 1595 to 1612. The bishop was a plant lover and botanizer, surrounding his palace, high on the hill of Willibaldsburg above the city, with luxuriant terraced gardens. There were 'three greatly celebrated ornamental gardens, all presently on view' at the time that the catalogue of the garden was published. One section was laid out as a shrubbery and there were specialist areas for different sorts of plants. Sadly the garden declined after the bishop's death, just before final publication of the catalogue, and was almost totally destroyed by the Swedes during the Thirty

BESLER AND THE EICHSTÄTT GARDEN

Years War. Attempts were made at the end of the nineteenth century to effect a restoration, but today only a wild shrubbery covers the slopes and frames the remaining castle walls with a garland of foliage.

Besler was both apothecary and botanist at Nuremberg and not only compiled and published the great *Hortus Eystettensis* in 1613, which catalogued all the plants in the garden at Eichstätt, but was also responsible for some of the planting. It seems that the Prince-Bishop, who in about 1600 commissioned Besler to prepare the illustrated work por-

traying the botanical richness of the garden – the projected cost was 3,000 florins – had a collector's instinct and wished to grow every plant known at the time in his garden. Besler himself probably made some of the original drawings and the 400 plates were prepared by a team of engravers. Each plate shows several plants, sometimes ill-assorted in type, but specially arranged so that each group portrayal, besides being botanically more or less accurate, looked decorative on the page. In the two volumes Besler showed more than 660 botanical species and more than 400 varieties differing from the type, with double flowers or some colour variant, to make a total of over a thousand plants.

Ficus Indica Eystetten, sis ex uno folio enata lu, xurians.

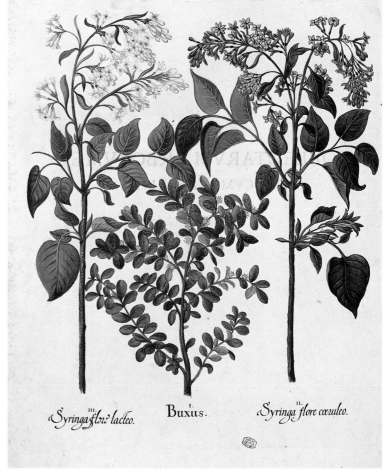

Syringa flore lacteo.   Buxus.   Syringa flore cœruleo.

Far left: As some plants portrayed and listed in the florilegium are unlikely to have been hardy in southern Germany, it seems certain that, as in common contemporary practice, specially prepared wooden frames would have sheltered the plants during the winter. The painting of the Indian fig (*Opuntia ficus-indica*), a tender cactus of unknown but tropical origin, shows the plant in a pot sunk in the ground and the framework of carpentry to which the winter frame would be attached.

Left: The plants in the *Hortus Eystettensis* are arranged in four seasonal sections, with trees and shrubs preceding non-woody plants; these are organized by Besler into several different categories, often with unrelated species appearing on the same plate. Plate I shows both the purple- and white-flowered forms of *Syringa vulgaris*, introduced from the Balkans in the sixteenth century, as well as the common box (*Buxus sempervirens*), native to Europe, northern Africa and western Asia. Lilacs had been grown by the Arabs in Spain for centuries, hence Besler calling it '*lusitanica*' and '*Spanischer Springebaum*'.

Right: Paeonia mascula, a native European plant, shown in flower and fruit, has sadly almost disappeared in the wild; other species shown are today unknown in their wild state and some horticultural varieties no longer exist. Besler described 250 plants as being in the garden purely for ornament; among these he included many plants only recently introduced to Europe.

Sanicula. III.

Pæonia mas flore purpureo. I.

Alchimilla. II

The earliest official botanic gardens in Europe were established in Italy in the sixteenth century. Attached to a chair of botany and the schools of medicine at Pisa and Padua, they were in a clear line of descent from the physic gardens looked after by monks during the Middle Ages as part of their 'licence' to practise medicine. The garden at Pisa has been moved twice, in 1563 and in 1591, when it was given its permanent site close to the cathedral and university. Plans for parterre layouts for use in botanical gardens, some of which distinctly resembled those published by the architect Serlio in 1537, have

THE EARLY BOTANIC GARDENS

been discovered in the archives at Pisa. At Padua the designs have been gradually altered.

In Paris in 1626 Jean Robin drew up plans for the Jardin du Roi (the Jardin des Plantes after the revolution of 1789), a project which was not finally realized until 1636. From the beginning the idea of having a fine plant collection and acclimatizing plants seems to have been of more importance than using the garden for teaching the use of drugs. Many of Robin's own plants were transferred to it and

his son Vespasian Robin was appointed lecturer under the direction of Guy de la Brosse, the king's physician. The latter published a description of the garden and a catalogue of its 2,500 plants in 1636. A south-facing terrace in the Paris gardens supported evergreens such as pine, fir, yew, holly, evergreen oak, cork oak, junipers, phillyreas and pyracanthas, and even more tender Mediterranean shrubs and herbs such as lentiscus, terebinth, and various cistus – plants especially noted by Pierre Belon in his travels a hundred years before and which he had tried to acclimatize – as well as rosemary, sages and thyme.

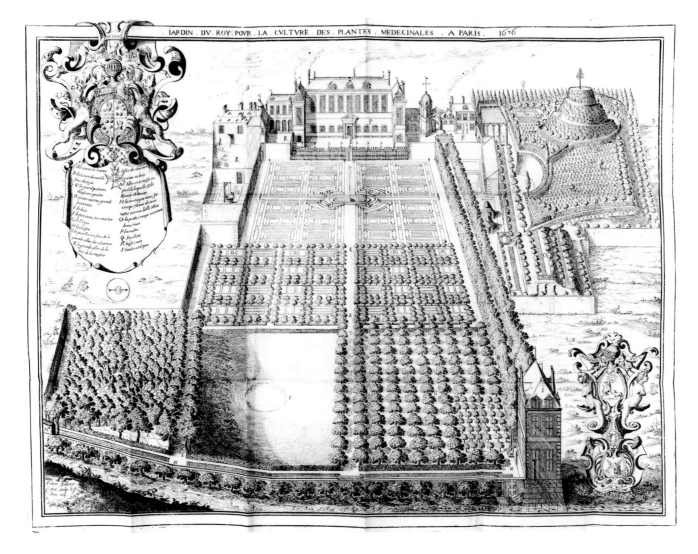

IARDIN · DV · ROY · POVR · LA · CVLTVRE · DES · PLANTES · MEDECINALES · A · PARIS · 1636

RARIORUM PLANTARUM
HORTI MEDICI
AMSTELODAMENSIS
HISTORIA.

Above: The merchant Jan Commelin (d. 1692) who was in charge of the Amsterdam Physic Garden made it into one of the most interesting in Europe. His catalogue of the garden of 1697–1701, listed many new plants introduced through East India Company merchants and brought from the Cape of Good Hope, a Dutch colony since 1652. The title-page shows glasshouses in the background. The watercolours for this work were by Johann and Maria Moninckx.

Left: The Jardin du Roi was laid out with two main parterre areas. One was flat with simple rectangular beds, in which plants were arranged in some sort of methodical order based on known and named species; the adjacent parterres were traversed by tree-lined *allées*. On its north side an avenue of hornbeam and lime stretched east towards the Seine; to the south a shorter alley of hornbeam shut off a woodland area. A small walled enclosure was the *jardin à tulipes* in which precious bulbs could be protected from robbers. Other features included a mount where vines were grown, which sheltered a crescent-shaped bed for tender citrus fruit, myrtles, palms and sugar cane, all of which were covered with a wooden frame in winter.

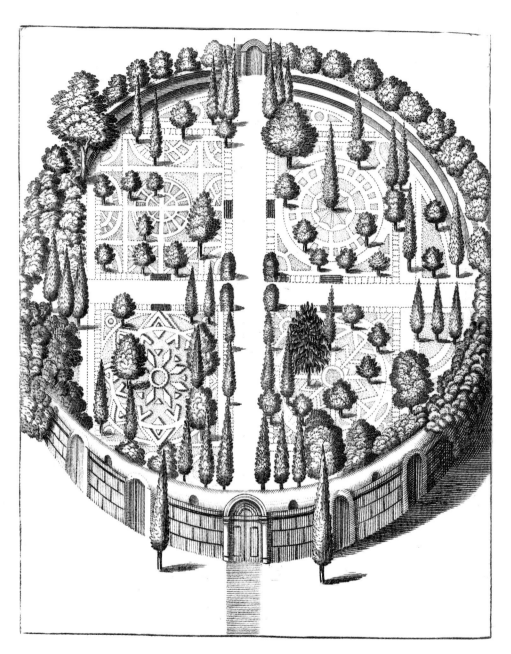

Above: At the Padua Botanic Garden, established by Francesco Bonafede, who had set up the first *Lectura Simplicium* Venetian decree in 1545, a circular layout was subdivided into ornate and complicated squares and further circles, patterns reproduced and used again in public and private gardens during the next two centuries. An earlier plan had proposed an even more complicated arrangement. Padua has the oldest printed catalogue, that of 1591 by Cortuso, enumerating 1,168 plants. The European fan palm or Goethe's palm (*Chamaerops humilis*), seen on his visit in 1786 and which influenced his views on the origin of man, was brought to Padua by Prospero Alpini, the author of *De Plantis Aegypti*, in 1581, together with other Egyptian plants. It and a chaste tree (*Vitex agnuscastus*), planted in 1550 and now 20 metres/60 feet high, can be seen today.

THE TRADESCANTS

John Parkinson's contemporaries, the two John Tradescants, father and son, played an important role in introducing and growing many new plants. John the Elder found plants in Europe, North Africa and Russia, as well as obtaining them through the Virginia Company in North America, while John the Younger brought back trees, shrubs and perennials collected on his three trips to Virginia.[8] Between 1610 and 1615 the first John travelled to the Low Countries, where he obtained cherries, quince, medlars and Provins roses for the gardens at Hatfield (still in construction); many of the bills for his purchases still exist. At Leiden he found several new varieties of 'gilliflowers' and 'fortye frittelaries' at 3*d*. each, and in Haarlem 800 tulip bulbs for 10*s*. per hundred as well as arborvitae (*Thuja occidentalis*), which had come from the French colonies in Canada as early as 1536. In Russia he found *Rosa acicularis*, 'the wild bryer of Muscovia'; in North Africa purple clover (*Trifolium*) and cistus, and he brought back more treasures acquired from the Robins and others in Paris.

Listed inside the Tradescants' own copy of Parkinson's *Paradisus* are the plants grown in their own garden at Lambeth, first planted in 1629, and their date of acquisition. John the Younger brought from North America the American plane (*Platanus occidentalis*, still colloquially called a sycamore in the United States), the tulip poplar or tulip tree (*Liriodendron tulipifera*), the black locust or false acacia (*Robinia pseudoacacia*), swamp cypress or bald cypress (*Taxodium distichum*) and Canadian red maple (*Acer rubrum*). The Tradescants were also responsible for the smoke bush (*Cotinus coggygria*), silver-leaved *Teucrium fruticans*, *Atriplex halimus* and the oleaster or Russian olive (*Elaeagnus angustifolia*), as well as *Aeonium arborescens* from Madeira, already illustrated and described by sixteenth-century writers.

The portraits of the Tradescants, father and son, were painted by Emmanuel de Critz. The likeness of John Tradescant the Elder is also carved on a newel post on the Grand Staircase at Hatfield, and a mulberry tree which may have been planted by him still survives in the garden there.

The listed contents of the Tradescants' garden at Lambeth was astonishing and showed what a wide range of plants could be obtained by a dedicated plant-searcher before the middle of the seventeenth century. The plant collection was probably also a nursery.

Bottom left: This nineteenth-century illustration, an unsigned lithograph by Gottlieb Prestele (1827–92), is entitled 'The Tradescant Black Heart Cherry'. This was the cherry brought back by John Tradescant the Elder from his first expedition to Holland when collecting for Robert Cecil's new garden at Hatfield, where he was gardener.

Besides many trees including the tulip tree *Liriodendran tulipifera* – shown below in a hand-coloured engraving after a painting by Ehret, John the Younger brought shrubs, climbers and perennials from the New World. Among them were *Rhododendron hirsutum, Rosa virginiana, Yucca filamentosa.* Herbaceous plants and bulbs included the foam flower (*Tiarella cordifolia*), the maidenhair fern (*Adiantum pedatum*), *Aquilegia canadensis* with striking yellow petals and red spurs, *Aster novi-belgii*, the false spikenard (*Smilacina racemosa*, at the time thought of as a form of Solomon's seal), the Atamasco lily (*Zephyranthes atamasco*), *Solidago canadensis, Erythronium americanum*, the American agave and the red-flowered evergreen honeysuckle (*Lonicera sempervirens*).

LIRIODENDRVM foliis angulatis truncatis.

Liriodendron: tulipifera.
Sp. pl. 2. 755.

THE HORTI
FARNESIANI AND
FRANCESCO
CAETANI'S FLOWER
COLLECTION

The Horti Farnesiani were laid out by Vignola at the instigation of Pope Paul III in the middle of the sixteenth century, their terraces descending to the Forum from the top of the Palatine Hill. Today, although Vignola's aviaries remain, all the lower part has disappeared, excavated to reveal classical ruins, and nothing remains of the planting of 'rarities' which gave it renown in the 1620s. The rich collection of plants was catalogued in the *Horto Farnesiano Rariores Plantae Exactissime Descriptae* written by Pietro Castelli in 1625. In it many of the latest exotics to have reached Italy were described, including the tropical *Acacia farnesiana* introduced in 1611. Yuccas and agaves from America; passion flower, called *Maracot indicum*; the cinnamon tree from the east, called *Laurus indicum*; castor-oil plants from the tropics; narcissus and 'lilio-narcissus' (probably *Sprekelia formosissima*); convolvulus from Peru and Mattioli's lilac. Both *Yucca aloifolia* and *Agave americana* flowered for the first time in Europe in Rome. Many of the new bulbs were classified under

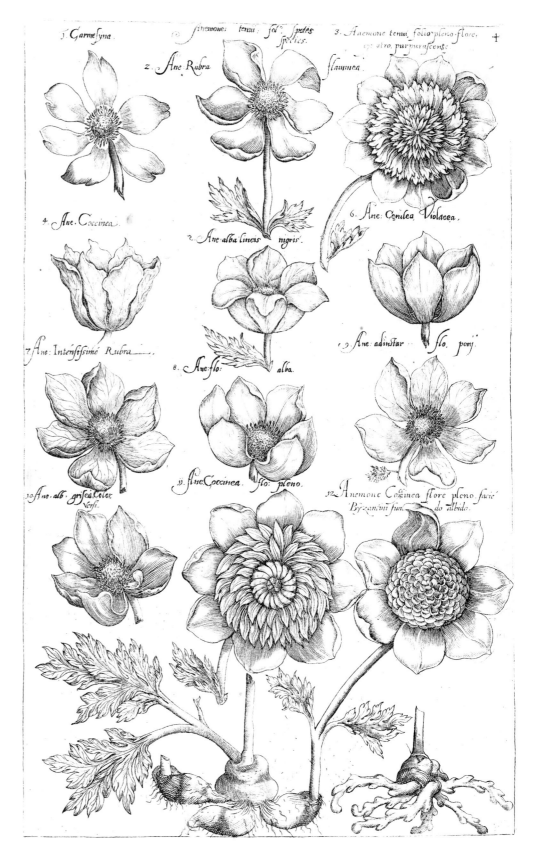

inclusive names such as 'hyacinths' (the tuberose from Mexico, *Polianthes tuberosa*, was regarded as a hyacinth) and 'narcissus' (amaryllis, *Brunsvigia*, *Sprekelia formosissima* and the Atamasco lily, *Zephyranthes atamasco*, were all classified as 'narcissi').

The most enthusiastic amateur plant collector was Francesco Caetani, Duke of Sermoneta, whose garden near Cisterna south of Rome became famous for the numbers of flowers and exotic bulbs grown there. Two manuscript books in the Caetani archives list all the plants growing in the garden in 1625 (when Caetani was only 31 – he lived until 1683). Plants were obtained from Constantinople, Paris, Avignon, Brussels, Amsterdam, Vienna and Frankfurt.

The design for the flower-beds at Cisterna (far left) is reproduced in *Flore overo cultura di fiori distinto in quattro libri* (Rome, 1638) by Giovanni Battista Ferrari 'who singled it out as a perfect example of contemporary planting'. Ferrari described how the Cisterna beds were edged with small bricks – *pianelle* – and planted in a mixture of two or three kinds of flowers to give, with one colour predominating, the effect of an 'orderly carpet of flowers'. Dwarf orange trees and white-flowered broom provided vertical accents in beds predominately of low-growing bulbs. Tuberoses were sunk in flower pots in the beds so that they could be given extra water.

Caetani's own plant lists show detailed plans to match the design. The names written in his own hand include white narcissi from Constantinople, Brancion tulips and tulips from the garden of Giulio Altovili. The duke grew 15,000 tulips but his greatest interest was in anemones, of which, by the middle of the century, he had 29,000 of 230 different kinds; one called 'Sermoneta' was grown by Sir Thomas Hanmer in his garden at Bettisfield in 1659 (see p. 130) and others were included in Pierre Morin's nursery *Catalogue de Quelques Plantes*, published in Paris in 1651. The most sought-after was the plush anemone, '*de veluto*' in Italian. Many of them seem to have been obtained through Matteo Caccini, but others came from Emmanuel Sweert, whose own *Florilegium*, from which the illustrations of the scilla (*left*) – then known as 'hyacinth' – and the anemones (*opposite*) are taken, was first published in 1612.

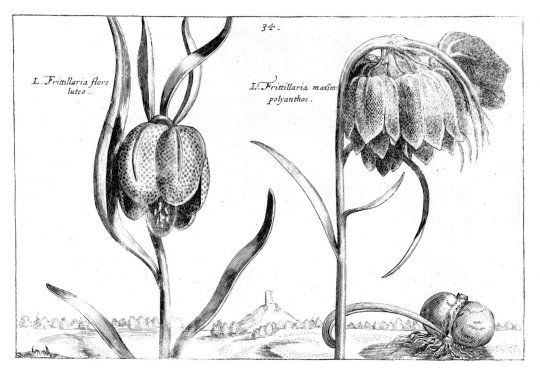

34.

L. Frittillaria flore luteo.

L. Frittillaria maxim: polyanthos.

JOHN REA AND SIR THOMAS HANMER

In Sir Thomas Hanmer's garden at Bettisfield, wall-trained fruit trees stood in flower borders round the perimeter of the walled Great Garden and his flower-beds were rectangular. The four main beds, about 1.2 metres/4 feet wide, all edged with boards (as were the outer borders) and with earth sloping up towards the middle, each had twelve or thirteen ranks of plants along the edge of the bed and four across the width. The first bed on the right near the house had thirteen ranks of four tulips – for Hanmer, 'the Queene of Bulbous plants whose Flower is so beautiful in its figure and most rich and admirable in colours and wonderfull in variety of markings'; the bulbs were to be lifted every third year and offsets grown on elsewhere.

John Rea, in his *Flora* of 1665, gave explicit directions for laying out a garden. Two garden areas should be divided by a wall with fruit and ordinary flowers on one side and the rarer plants in the real Flower Garden. To the Revd Samuel Gilbert, his son-in-law, the term 'ordinary' signified the 'trifles adored by country women ... but of no esteem to a florist who is taken up with things of most value'. In the next area, 'to keep Nature's choicest jewels' alleys and paths were to be exact widths and edged with ornamental lattice, on which roses could be trained, and soil would be kept in with boards 10 centimetres/4 inches high. The 'fret', as Rea called it, was divided up into a collection of flower-beds, very similar in design to those of the Duke of Sermoneta at Cisterna in Italy, and planted with bulbs. To a collection of perennials he recommended the addition of some annuals such as amaranthus and marvels of Peru. Gilbert, who inherited his collection, went further and suggested planting these as well as African and French marigolds and Indian cress to take the place of tulips, ranunculus and anemones until their time of replanting. 'Transplant these [the annuals] in June from off your hot-beds into good rich soil ... where they may stand and bear flowers' for the summer months.

The second bed in Hanmer's flower garden had double-flowered crown imperials in the centre and six rows of iris raised from seed supplied by John Rea. Four central beds bordered with anemones had 'tulips and narcissus in the midst with some gilliflowers ... and cyclamens at the four corners'. Hyacinths, *Scilla peruviana*, erythroniums, 'one gray fritilary' narcissus and jonquils grew in other beds. Hanmer's 'gray fritilary' (*Fritillaria persica*) is probably the '*Fritillaria maxima*' (*left*) illustrated in the English version of the *Hortus Floridus* of Crispin van de Passe (published in 1614), the flowers of which had a network of purple 'in a pleasing depth'. A nursery plant list found among Sir Thomas's papers priced gilliflowers at 1s. 6d. a root, 11 anemone roots at 8s., and 6 kinds of auricula, with a double at as much as 4s.

The title-page of John Rea's *Flora* (*right*) depicts urns containing many of the flowers which were being grown in contemporary enthusiasts' gardens. Hanmer, Rea and his son-in-law Gilbert grew all the new bulbs in their flower gardens, taking a lot of trouble to do it well. For protecting tulips Rea suggested a series of canvas tilts to keep off wind, hot sun or showers of rain (as Gilbert said later, 'prejudicial to their different yet admirable complexions'), which could be erected or removed with the vagaries of the weather. Rea recommended lifting tulips with a long hollow trowel to dry off in some boarded store, and wrapping them up to keep well until the end of September.

John Rea was one of the advocates for the fashionable phillyreas. In his plant catalogue he specially recommended the striped phillyrea (sometimes called mock privet) 'to stand amongst the fairest evergreens . . . and may be fashioned into what form you effect'. The engraving depicting variegated forms of phillyrea is by Abraham Munting. Rea also listed plants in their order of flowering and provided lists of hardy perennials to give summer colour, hollyhocks, globe thistles, foxgloves, French honeysuckle (*Hedysarum coccineum*) and everlasting pea. In the wall borders in Rea's special flower garden he recommended planting auriculas, primroses, hepaticas, 'double rose champion [*Lychnis coronaria*], or double non-such, double dame's violet [the prized double form of *Hesperis matronalis*], the best wallflowers and double stock gilliflowers [double carnations – *Dianthus caryophyllus*]'.

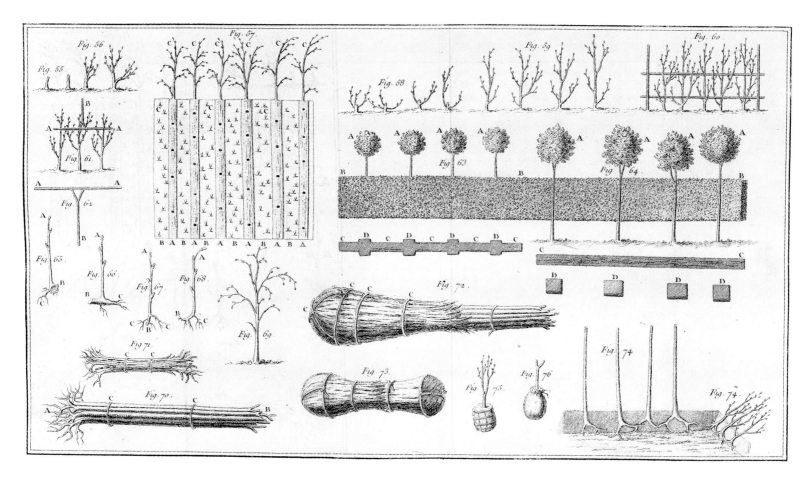

JOHN EVELYN

John Evelyn's *Sylva or a Discourse on Forest Trees* was published in 1664; thanks to an eighteenth-century edition by Alexander Hunter, it remained the standard English work on trees for over a century. Evelyn's knowledge of every aspect of forestry and arboriculture included the use of trees both in existing gardens and in garden design projects. Much impressed by gardens in Europe, Evelyn acquainted an English audience with Italian and French contemporary garden design philosophy, influencing the taste of the whole nation. After his return from his Continental tour in 1653, Evelyn continued to visit and describe gardens throughout England and is a major source of contemporary information.

He was also a gardener. In the *Kalendarium Hortense*, a gardener's almanac, he gave monthly duties as well as listing the flowers and fruit in season.[9] In January, flowers 'in prime or lasting' were laurustinus, mezereon, praecox tulips, hyacinths and winter cyclamen. In February 'sow alaternus seeds in cases, or open beds; cover them with thorns that the poultry scratch them not out'. In March 'sow pinks, sweet william and Carnations also seed of trees Alaternus and Philyrea and most perennial Greens'; and 'Now do the Farewell-frosts and Easterly-winds prejudice your choicest Tulips . . . therefore cover such with mats or canvas to prevent freckles and some times destruction'. The oranges and lemons for the portico would need repotting in May 'using natural-earth (such as is taken the first half spit from just under the turf of

the best pasture ground), mixing it with one part of rotten cow-dung or very mellow Soil screen'd and prepared some time before . . . then cutting the roots a little set your plant; but not too deep'. In June 'take up yor rarest Anemones and Ranunculus after rain (if it come seasonable) the stalk withered and dry the roots well'.

Top left: In Henri Louis Duhamel de Monceau's *Des Semis et Plantations* (the sixth volume of his *Traité complet des Bois et des Forets*, a comprehensive work describing all aspects of trees and their cultivation) of 1760, Plate VI shows methods of packing and planting young trees. Like Evelyn a hundred years earlier, Duhamel's own practical experience provided the core of his material on climate, soil, tree propagation and planting, which made his books so valuable.

Left: Evelyn was almost the first writer – Parkinson had previously recommended them for decorative use – to encourage the use of yew trees for woods, for hedging and for clipping into topiary shapes in the garden as 'standards, knobs . . . pyramids, conic spires, bowls or what other shapes'. The engraving is from the 1776 Hunter edition of Evelyn's *Sylva*. Taking stock of the tree situation in England in the second half of the seventeenth century, Evelyn found that since the middle of the sixteenth century 'newcomers' for general use were evergreen phillyreas, cork and evergreen oaks (*Quercus suber* and *Q. ilex*), cypress (*Cupressus sempervirens*), cedar of Lebanon (mid-seventeenth century), and umbrella or stone pine (*Pinus pinea*) from the Mediterranean regions – many of which were killed in the disastrously cold winter of 1683–4 – and flowering or manna ash (*Fraxinus ornus*) from Asia Minor. Common spruce (*Picea abies*), silver fir (*Abies alba*) and larch (*Larix decidua*) had come from

colder European regions. New trees after 1600 included *Robinia pseudoacacia*, hackberry (*Celtis occidentalis*), honey locust (*Gleditsia triacanthos*), *Liriodendron tulipifera*, *Thuja occidentalis* and Weymouth or white pine (*Pinus strobus*), so desirable for masts, all from the east coast of North America.

A painting by Johannes Vorsterman (1643–99) shows the elm avenue at Greenwich Park noted by Evelyn in 1664; the design owed everything to French influence. Evelyn encouraged intensive tree planting, primarily intended at providing supplies of timber for the British navy following depredations of forests and parks during the Commonwealth, but he was also insistent on the merits of great avenues of elms, linden or limes and walnuts, such as he had seen during his tour of northern France. He is said to have introduced the word 'avenue' into the English language.

An engraving of the American black walnut (*Juglans nigra*) at Fulham Palace; John Claudius Loudon reported it still surviving in 1834 with a height of 21 metres/70 feet, as well as a box elder 13.7 metres/45 feet high, the old cork oak (*Quercus suber*) at 15 metres/50 feet and some flourishing robinias. The bishop grew other trees introduced earlier in the century: tulip trees, sassafras, hickory (a species of *Carya*), the 'Constantinople nut' – or horse-chestnut (*Aesculus hippocastanum*), and various crataegus and cornus. The bishop himself planted a fashionable linden (lime) tree avenue during his 35 years at the palace.

The charming native American *Comptonia peregrina*, named for Henry Compton was painted by Redouté at the end of the eighteenth century. Related to the European native bog myrtle or sweet gale (*Myrica gale*), it was not introduced by the bishop but seems to have been grown somewhere near or in London by about 1700. It is the 'sweet fern' of Whittier's poem (1884), with a pleasant bay laurel aroma to the fern-like leaves.

BISHOP COMPTON AND THE BROMPTON PARK NURSERY

As the see of London, Compton's bishopric extended to Virginia; there he appointed an able botanist, the Revd John Banister, as one of his ministers. Banister's duties included sending new plant species to Fulham, the Chelsea Physic Garden (the Society of Apothecaries' garden on the Thames founded in 1673), and the Oxford Botanic Garden. Among the trees and shrubs consigned to the bishop and which have become important additions to our gardens are the sweet bay (*Magnolia virginiana*), the box elder (*Acer negundo*), the devil's walking stick or Hercules' club (*Aralia spinosa*), *Liquidambar styraciflua*, the balsam fir (*Abies balsamea*) and *Rhododendron viscosum*. Smaller plants included the Indian physic or ipecacuanha (*Gillenia trifoliata*), *Dicentra cucullaria*, the red-flowered *Trillium sessile* and *Viola pedata*. Aiton's *Hortus*

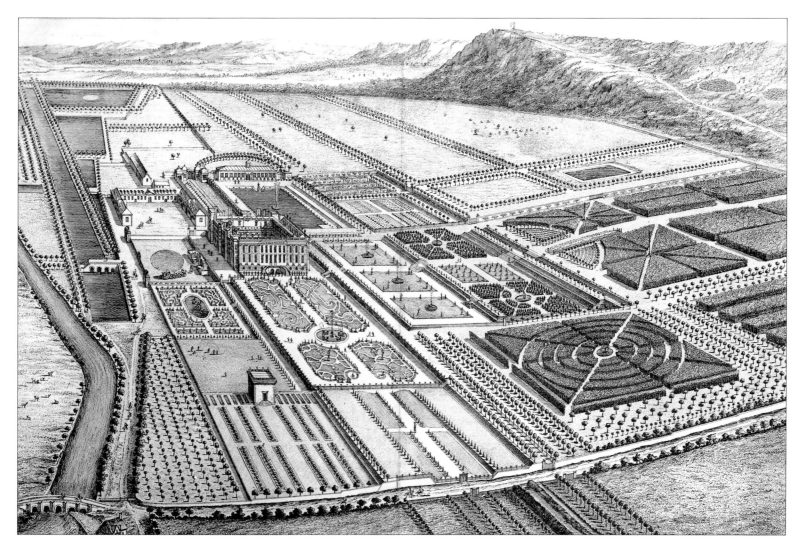

Kewensis (1789) credits Compton with over forty new introductions.

The Brompton Park Nursery, extending to 40.5 hectares/100 acres (roughly occupying the museum area between Hyde Park and South Kensington), employed twenty men and two women and held a stock of 40,000 plants. It was the foremost of its period, reaching its peak in reputation after 1693–4 when George London took Henry Wise as his partner. London travelled giving advice to the great estates, while Wise, as well as having commitments to the royal gardens (he became Master Gardener to Queen Anne) at Kensington, Windsor, St James's and Hampton Court, managed the nursery. Lindens (lime), elms and chestnut trees were for avenues, standard elms, hornbeams and yews for alleys, yews and hollies for clipped specimens, and box was supplied to edge the flower-beds and mark out the patterns (but not for Queen Anne, who had it all removed from Kensington Palace). The nursery also had 'greens' and exotics (they had plentiful and choice collections of oranges, lemons, myrtles, bays, jasmines and other tender plants), for growing formally in pots, and Wise was 'perfectly well skill'd in Fruit'.

The gardens of Chatsworth, perhaps the grandest in England, but with many changes and additions in their style during three centuries, were first landscaped by London and Wise between 1687 and 1706. The above engraving by Kip and Knyff shows the layout in 1707. George London had acquired a knowledge of the French formal style and a taste for clipped trees and shrubs which personified his work. He gave advice at the great estates which, remodelled in the French style as depicted by Kip and Knyff at the beginning of the eighteenth century, required vast numbers of trees – radial avenues and stars pierced the landscape – as well as clipped specimens for alleys and flowers for the extensive parterres.

CHAPTER FIVE

THE GARDENS OF THE ITALIAN RENAISSANCE

I t was the Grand Duke Francesco I's pleasure to have transformed a 'bare mountain slope' at Pratolino in the second half of the sixteenth century into the greatest of all the Medici gardens. It was known as *il giardino delle meraviglie* and was a place of pure delight. There meadows were strewn 'with thousands of varieties of colourful flowers', and there were all the other marvels of nature, with nature itself imitated by man's ingenuity. When he visited a beautiful garden, the Grand Duke, 'took a flower in his hand and contemplated it in all its exquisite colour and beauty with great delight and contentment.'[1]

It may come as a surprise to many, seduced and charmed by the green architectural gardens which remain from Renaissance days, relatively austere and flowerless today, to learn that during their period of greatest opulence, these gardens were colourful with the exciting exotic flowers recently introduced to western Europe. Most of these flowers had vanished by the time the gardens were 'discovered' by young Englishmen on their eighteenth-century grand tours; such travellers saw these gardens, already in relative decay, dominated by light and shade and green and grey textured foliage, and gained a lasting impression of romantic grandeur.

Far from being flowerless, the gardens of the aristocracy, of the leaders of the church and of private botanists and collectors grew all the rare and exotic plants possible – including flowers. Agostino del Riccio was one of the contemporary writers who emphasized the importance of flowers. Writing at the end of the sixteenth century, Riccio clearly differentiated between ornamental flowers and the ordinary simples and herbs traditionally grown in flower-beds. He disparaged spending money on planting a garden with common flowers of the fields. Instead of the customary planting of single types of flower together, he suggested making flower-beds interesting by filling them with combinations that would perform at different times, and to help the garden planner he supplied a list of plants that bloomed in each successive month.

Planting in the fifteenth-century garden of Lorenzo de' Medici at Careggi bears witness to an enthusiasm for exotics. He grew trees from southern Italy, which would have been rare enough around Florence, including hornbeam, the Turkey and cork oaks (*Quercus cerris* and *Q. suber*) and an 'incense tree' – a species of juniper (*Juniperus thurifera*) rather than the incense tree of Egyptian times, the Ethiopian *Boswellia serrata*. Among his 'foreigners' was an 'ebony tree' of uncertain identity: this may have been the golden chain or false ebony (*Laburnum anagyroides*) from the Balkans, but could conceivably have been the *guaiacana* – the date plum or false lote tree (*Diospyros lotus*) later portrayed in Besler's *Hortus Eystettensis* as a sort of ebony, although this is not thought to have arrived in Europe from Asia until the end of the sixteenth century.

Almost certainly many of the Levant exotics, described as arriving in Vienna and northern Europe in the second half of the sixteenth century, will already have been grown in Italy, probably obtained through the Venetian Republic; others arrived through far-flung contacts established by missionaries, especially Jesuits in the Far East. Whether growing in the botanic gardens established during the sixteenth and seventeenth centuries, in the flower-beds

In Fra Angelico's fifteenth-century painting of the *Annunciation*, Adam and Eve are shown being driven out of the Garden of Eden, a garden depicted with all the flowers and fruit trees known in Angelico's Renaissance world. It was assumed that the legendary biblical garden would have contained all plants that existed; a place where 'every tree that is pleasant to the sight and good for food' (from *Genesis* 2:9) would be grown. Animals wandered freely through the trees and over the flowery mead, in which grew recently introduced carnations as well as more commonplace medieval plants.

Although stylistically in keeping with sixteenth- and seventeenth-century geometric layouts, the planting of many of the early twentieth-century restorations of Italian villas and their gardens, often undertaken by foreigners, was far from authentic. Nevertheless, with shapely green hedges and elegant stonework, backed by cypresses, pines and evergreen oaks, and decorated with vases of lemon trees, the gardens of villas such as Gamberaia (shown here), Cappone and I Tatti in Florence convey a sense of Renaissance symmetry. In the flower-beds it would be possible to substitute, for the more recently introduced annuals and cultivars, some of the collectors' flowers so popular after their introduction in the sixteenth and seventeenth centuries.

laid out in ordered patterns inside a grander architectural unit, or in orchards, *boschi* and meadows, these plants became the foundation of encyclopaedic collections which reflected contemporary notions of the original Garden of Eden in which all God's plants, flowering and fruiting at the same time in a sort of perpetual spring, were gathered together. In Italy there was great enthusiasm for acquiring these new rarities, much as we have seen in northern Europe, with encouragement and advice given by the more professional botanists such as Ulisse Aldrovandi, Luca Ghini and Andrea Cesalpino, who were also instrumental in collecting for the newly established botanic gardens. All the new plants would have been not only expensive and difficult to acquire in good condition but would have needed skilled transplanting and acclimatization; many could have been obtainable only through a sort of old boys' network between European botanists and the affluent collectors who had the essential facilities for experimental growing. In Italy

the botanic gardens founded at Pisa, Padua, Bologna and Florence and the famous Horti Farnesiani in Rome, as well as those of great princes such as the Medici and church magnates, grew many of the rarest introductions.

Paintings executed by Jacopo Ligozzi for the Medici and for Ulisse Aldrovandi at Bologna in the last few decades of the sixteenth century show plants which were grown at Pisa and Bologna and in the gardens of the Medici grand dukes. These include flowers from the New World such as *Agave americana*, morning glory and four-o'clocks or marvels of Peru as well as *Muscari macrocarpa* from the Levant. From Aldrovandi's notebooks in the University of Bologna we know that he corresponded with botanists and noblemen all over Europe, and that he received seeds from the young Prince Count Charles d'Arenberg (who later laid out the famous gardens of Enghien), and sent seeds to Jean Robin, director of Henri IV's garden at the Louvre.

EARLY RENAISSANCE GARDEN DESIGN

In Renaissance Italy we are on relatively firm ground with documentation of the gardens in which the new exotics were grown. From the fifteenth century onwards written and pictorial evidence abounds, giving precise details of the evolving garden style. By the 1580s and '90s, with contemporary writers providing lists of plants which had become available only recently, gardens began to incorporate different areas for their use in the overall design. In Tuscany alone it is possible to trace, in the lunettes painted by Giusto Utens for the Villa di Artimino in 1599, the architectural development of the villa garden in a chronological sequence from the mid-fifteenth-century fortress-castles of the Medicis in the Mugello Hills above Florence to the pleasure palaces and villas, central dwellings for surrounding farmland, being made for the same family at the end of the sixteenth century.

The fifteenth-century Italian gardens with architectural layouts were symptomatic of early Renaissance ideals. Inspired by classical formulae of symmetry and proportion, gardens laid out as a sequence of geometric divisions linked by a common axis portrayed a grasp of linear perspective, which could be interpreted in gardening with double lines of trees, bushes, pergolas and 'living' tunnels, as well as with vases and statues. At first the gardens could be to the side of and unconnected with the architec-

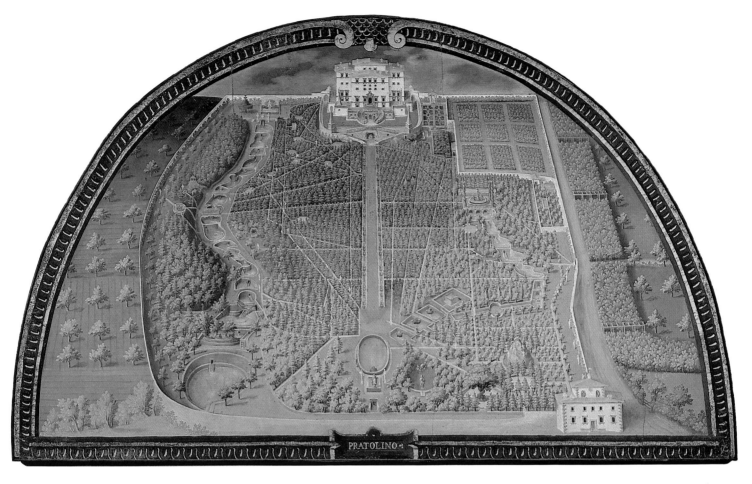

The Utens lunette of the Villa Pratolino was painted in 1599; the gardens, laid out for the Grand Duke Francesco I after 1569 by Bernardo Buontalenti, were famous for their complicated waterworks. Utens shows a thickly wooded park on what had been a barren slope. Native evergreen trees were planted both in natural groups and in ordered rows, with the addition of horse-chestnuts and fruit trees, the latter in quincunx pattern. A symmetrical circle of fir trees can be identified on the lower right beside the tree house, and reports speak of labyrinths of bay laurel and meadows thick with thousands of varieties of colourful flowers.

ture of the villa, as they had been during the Middle Ages, remaining separate but enclosed units like the garden at the fortress of the Medici, Il Trebbio, where Michelozzi's vine-covered pergola dating from the 1450s still survives. The planting, with every species of sweet-scented herb in the beds, probably owed much to Pietro de' Crescenzi's *Liber ruralium commodorum*, long read in manuscript form but actually printed in Italian only in 1471. In the same century more philosophical writers developed themes, often based on the works of Roman architects (and on Pliny the

Younger's detailed description of his own two gardens), which set out principles of garden design, in much the same way as Roman textbooks on husbandry had been a fundamental source for the medieval farmer and gardener.

As it evolved, the designed Renaissance garden, based on those of ancient Rome, developed an axial unity with the villa it framed, marking a break with medieval practice and allowing the gardens to appear to be a series of interconnecting spaces as an extension of the house. In 1460 Bartolomeo Pagello of Vicenza, although modestly not requiring a villa layout as grand as those of Pliny, wished to have a library and portico running into the garden where he could grow 'many apples, pears and pomegranates, damascene plums and generous vines; many plane trees near the house, clipped box and beautiful bays; and a fountain more clear than crystal, dedicated to the muses like the Castalian spring at the foot of Parnassus'.[2] A further link could be established, especially when country villas were built on steep sites, with the landscape beyond the garden perimeter; views out of the garden and over distant hills and valleys, such as those from the Piccolomini Palace at Pienza, built between 1459 and 1463 by Bernard Rossellino for Pope Pius II, were part of the formula. This new garden recipe, also inspired by humanist attitudes seeking to re-establish a relationship between art and nature already hinted at by Petrarch and Boccaccio, was superimposed on the essentially geometric medieval enclosed garden to give emphasis to classical proportions. All the raw materials of a garden, the terrain and stonework and water features with trees, shrubs and flowers, were organized by man's art so that the living plant's form, colour and texture became an integral part of the whole. Not only was nature itself seen as cosmically ordered so that the art of gardening required its imitation; it was also seen that nature could be improved upon if planted and cultivated in an ordered way.

An architectural book evoking the villa ideal, quoting almost directly from Pliny the Younger's letters and the works of Vitruvius, was mainly theoretical. Leon Battista Alberti, in his *De re aedificatoria* of 1452 (see pp. 92–93), above all recommended the architect's role in extending the layout of the house into the garden, a maxim to become a *sine qua non* in the development of the Italian garden. Some of his more detailed gardening advice was also taken from Pliny; it emerged in passages concerning the setting for and adornment of houses.[3] Alberti recommended that the symmetrical pattern of gardens should be accentuated by 'Laurels, Cedars and Junipers with their branches intermixed and twining one into another' and stated that 'trees ought to be planted in rows exactly even and answering to one another exactly in straight lines . . . let the walks be lined by evergreens. And on that side which is best sheltered, a box hedge (which can suffer injury from strong winds and especially from the least spray of the sea) should be planted. In open places, most exposed to the sun, some people plant myrtles, because, they say, these flourish extremely well in the summer heat. And Theophrastus affirms that the myrtle, the laurel and the ivy are desirable.' Porticos and vine-covered arbours also offered appropriate Plinyesque sun and shade. Cypress trees – rather than Pliny's planes – could be draped with ivy. The gardens could be enriched with rare plants and others which were highly esteemed by physicians. They could be further adorned, as Alberti quoted almost verbatim from Pliny, if 'gardeners traced their master's names in box or sweet smelling

herbs', with rose trees intermixed with pomegranates and cornels making a beautiful hedge. Alberti quoted too from Horace: 'Your hedge of oak with plums and cornel made, To yield the cattle food, the master shade' – but remarked that this kind of thing was better suited to a farm intended for profit than to a garden.[9]

Alberti's book urged, in theoretical terms, a return to the classical concept of the architectural garden. The influential *Hypnerotomachia Poliphili* (see pp. 150–51) by Francesco Colonna, written by 1467 but not printed until 1499 in Venice, used woodcuts to illustrate imaginary garden themes, in which buildings were derived from recognizably classical ruins and roses and vines clambered over arbours and pergolas. Alberti's theories permeate Colonna's romance, an allegory of Love's dream inside a dream (thought to be based on a true story with known participants). The descriptions of planting which accompany the woodcuts were obviously based on contemporary gardening practice and were portrayed in enough detail to provide patterns for European gardeners to copy for the next hundred years or more and to expand further as new plants became available. Colonna's allegorical work inspired new mannerist gardens in the sixteenth century in which mythological and classical statues, together with fountains and grottoes and living plant features such as groves of trees and labyrinths, defined iconographical programmes to stimulate intellectual as well as purely sensuous appreciation. To grasp their meaning in full it was necessary to have a thorough literary background. Colonna's influence can also be seen in the early seventeenth century, when traditional hunting parks were transformed into allegorical pleasure parks.

Fortunately we have a description written by the owner himself of one of the earliest Renaissance gardens in Florence. The Quaracchi gardens in Florence were laid out for Giovanni Rucellai, an intimate of Alberti, from 1459. The garden was distinguished by a main axis which extended from the villa through the whole garden. For the first 90 metres/100 yards this was merely a path sheltered by a barrel-shaped pergola 2.4 metres/8 feet wide – Rucellai's *con archie di quercie* probably meant a framework of oak

Sandro Botticelli's *La Primavera* was painted in 1478 and later hung in the Medici villa of Castello. The flowers portrayed on the dress of the goddess Flora include carnations, cornflowers and roses, with another 37 species portrayed in the garlands and scattered in the grass and on other figures, all plants with some symbolic or allegorical significance in Florence at the time.

and *not* a growing tunnel of evergreen oak, which is called *lecce* in Italy; it finally emerged as a tree-lined avenue which stretched some 550 metres/600 yards to descend to the banks of the river so that 'if I stand in [the] middle I can see boats passing in the Arno'. Four openings along the axial pergola were framed by tall trees with vines trained over them. This pergola linked all the separate and different enclosed garden areas which lay as lateral compartments, hedged or walled or separated by further walks, on either side. There were topiary shapes cut out in box, a square 'hut' of intertwined fir and poplar and a smaller edifice of textured junipers, besides a rose garden and an exedra framed in clipped bay. Borders of boxwood on either side of the upper loggia were almost head high and a foot or so wide. One hedge was 366 metres/400 yards long and seats shaded by bay were set along it. Rucellai spoke of the 'heads of Damascus violets and of dark

The gardens of the Villa d'Este at Tivoli were created for Cardinal Ippolito d'Este after 1559 by the architect and archaeologist Pirro Ligorio. The scheme of waterfalls and fountains was laid out on the steep slopes, with ramps and steps lined by low hedges of ilex, bay and box to join the levels. In the lowest part of the garden there were orchards and covered pergolas in a formal pattern aligned on the centre of the villa. The painting by Gerolamo Muziano shows the garden at this time. By 1611 Antonio Del Re described the replacement of the elaborate cross pergola, which had also been illustrated by Etienne Du Pérac in 1573, by compartments of fruit trees and simples; within a few years this was in turn replaced by a rondel of cypress trees.

In the Renaissance garden the maze or labyrinth developed as an extension of Serlio-like flower-bed patterns to become a dramatic feature; examples are seen in Du Pérac's engraving of the Villa d'Este, at the Villa Lante, and in de Caus's *Hortus Palatinus* of 1618 – as well as in many later gardens. In this painting (*right*) from the school of Jacopo Tintoretto – set in some luxurious court garden in Italy – the 'labyrinth of love' consists of concentric alleys lined with hedges composed of trellis on which plants have been trained and symbolized the fortune and misfortune, joy and suffering that were a part of life's journey.

brown or purple marjoram and basil, and many other odoriferous herbs which are exquisite to the human sense'. The topiary collection alone was amazing; ships and temples, wild animals and philosophers, giants, men and women were all executed in box or other plants such as myrtle, bay, jasmine and roses, all of which were familiar topiary subjects for gardens in fifteenth- and sixteenth-century Florence.[4]

The pergola at Quaracchi stretched for some distance but in small areas a pergola was also used either as a central feature or to cover a pathway that went around the inside of the garden (see pp. 152–53). Sometimes the structure of the tunnel itself was of a sophisticated pattern. Jacopo de' Barbari's view of Venice of about 1500 shows a series of town gardens behind the houses on the Giudecca from the largest of which, beyond an enclosed patterned garden, a centrally positioned pergola stretches to the end of the garden.[5] In Nanna's fictional garden in Pietro Aretino's *Pagionamenti*, written before 1536, vine-covered pergolas shaded the two main pathways which cross at the centre, dividing flower-beds edged with clipped rosemary in which figs (the prized black *Brogiotti*) and scarlet-flowered pomegranates bore fruit. Scented jasmine grew against the walls and sweet rocket, stocks and roses bloomed nearby to charm Nanna's friends. Pliny's Paestum rose (*Rosa bifera*) flowered for the second time in September.

All illustrations of fifteenth- and sixteenth-century Italian gardens show the garden perimeters enclosed by walls covered with trellised vegetation (ivy and vines or even trained trees were shaped on to frames made of thin laths) to create the 'architecture of nature'; if not walled, the garden was surrounded with quite tall hedges *tre a quatro braccia* (about 1.5–2 metres/5–7 feet) high. Fruit trees, thorns, evergreen oak (*Quercus ilex*), Italian buckthorn (*Rhamnus alaternus*) and dogwood (probably *Cornus sanguinea*), bay, jasmine, ivy, holly, honeysuckle, cherry laurel (*Prunus laurocerasus*), pistachio (*Pistacia lentiscus*), yew and juniper were all used. Further hedges of lower-growing myrtles (both *Myrtus communis* and the smaller *M.c. tarentina*), lavender, box, rosemary, brooms (*Genista germanica* and *Spartium junceum* from Spain), pomegranate, sage (*Salvia officinalis*) and cotton lavender (*Santolina*) were planted, not as single-specimen hedges but in a 'mixed' combination to surround the inner flower-bed areas, where familiar herbs still grew until such time as some of the new bulbs from the Levant became available. Around 1590 Soderini recommended laurustinus for hedges of various heights.[6] Although it seems almost certain that box is being portrayed as hedging in the contemporary paintings by Utens of some of the Medici villas round Florence (see pp. 154–55), Soderini disparaged its use as a hedging material on its own because of its unpleasant odour and suggested combining it with other shrubs such as myrtle. Often a plot of grass was edged with a rhythm of broad-headed fruit trees and some low hedging.

As terracing on the steep slopes developed, so more and more trees and bushes, especially citrus types and pomegranates needing sun for ripening fruit, were skilfully espaliered against the retaining walls as well as on the outer boundaries. Architectural wooden pergolas, clothed with living green, seldom survived; by the seventeenth century tall wall-like hedges of bay laurel, myrtle, evergreen oak and laurustinus took the place of the architectural tunnels and, with rows of pencil-slim cypresses, were used to flank the important axial pathways and to line slightly grander *viali*. These features are to us more evocative and 'typical' of the classic Italian garden. By the 1640s John Evelyn, visiting Roman gardens, described the head- and breast-high hedges surrounding flower-bed compartments in the Villa Medici garden in Rome, and others, double that

height but pierced by central lateral views, which lined the main garden divisions. Venturini's view of steps at the Villa d'Este in 1691 reveals French-style wall hedges which appear to be 6 metres/20 feet or more in height, but it seems most likely that many of these 'new-style' hedges are probably composed of the original plants grown to a great height after a hundred years. In France they would be *charmilles* of clipped hornbeam or sometimes elm or other dense-growing deciduous woody plants; in Italy evergreens were commonly used.

FLOWERS FOR DISPLAY

The differing patterns of the flower-beds, seldom linked as a theme with those in adjacent garden 'rooms', were visible only from the villa windows or from higher terraces. Nor from inside each area were further axial views opened up to reveal the designs in an adjacent area. These flower-beds with their geometric design (see pp. 156–57) were a very different conception from the flatter parterre effects developed in sixteenth-century France (as seen in du Cerceau) or the swirling patterns of box used by Mollet and Le Nôtre in the latter part of the seventeenth century (see Chapter Six). In Italy later French-style designs were often later used to modify earlier flower-beds. The box parterres at the Villa Lante are an example of the adaptation of the original geometric Italian pattern to a more curvilinear theme.

Georgio Vasari's recommendations for princely country palaces (in *La città ideale*) included separate planting areas for flowers and simples. Writing in northern Italy in 1559, Bartolomeo Taegio described ornamental gardens in *La Villa*, a book which is virtually a tract on life in the country. Writers such as these were able to recommend some of the new plants from the Levant, including the scarlet Turk's cap lily (*Lilium chalcedonicum*) – the red lily of the Santorini frescoes – tazetta narcissus, as well as new species of scented jasmine. They also recommended plants from the New World such as the African marigold (*Tagetes erecta*) and nasturtium (*Tropaeolum majus*), from Mexico but introduced via Spain and northern Africa, and Indian shot (species of *Canna*) from the West Indies.

In writing his description of an imaginary 'ideal' garden, *Del Giardino di un Re*, at the end of the sixteenth century, Agostino del Riccio was fully aware of contemporary garden fashions, knowing

PROSPETTIVA DEL GIARDINO PONTIFICIO SVL QVIRINALE. *Architettura di Ottauio Mascarini.*

1. Palazzo Pontificio che guarda uerso il Giardino.　4. Parte del Palazzo dou' e' la Cappella Papale.　7. Organo hidraulico.　10. Fontana dell' Ombrella.　13. Palazzo Mazzarini.
2. Cortile grande del Palazzo Pontificio.　5. Fabbrica nuoua della famiglia uerso la strada delle 4 fontane.　8. Fontana del Bicchiere a capo il Viale principale.　11. Fontana del Sole.　14. Basilica di S.ta Maria Maggiore.
3. Orologio del Palazzo.　6. Piazza della Cisterna uerso il Giardino.　9. Fontana di porfido del Padiglione.　12. Colossi su' la Piazza di Monte Cauallo.　15. Veduta di Roma.
Gio. Bata Falda del et inc.　G. Iac Rossi le stampa in Roma alla pace con Priu del S. Pont.

Giovanni Battista Falda's etchings in *Li Giardini di Roma* published in 1683 are a rich source for research into the seventeenth-century gardens of Rome. In the perspective view of the Pope's garden on the Quirinale Hill, the *viali* of cypresses and the square gardens – each bordered with a hedge almost certainly of trimmed box – trace contemporary styles. The enclosed parterres visible are all of French-inspired curvilinear scrollwork and no longer of the more geometric layout typical of the early Renaissance. By 1726 Paolo Bartolomeo Clarici, in *Istoria e coltura delle piante*, is distinguishing between these new French patterns and gardens in which flowers played a more significant role.

most of the layouts of the grand villa gardens in central Italy. His recommendations of plants for the king's garden will have been inspired by those he had actually seen growing (see pp. 158–59). His extensive catalogue confirms the 'explosive' arrival of 'foreign' trees, shrubs, plants and bulbs which must have effectively revolutionized the appearance of gardens, at least those belonging to the aristocracy who would have been able to augment their collections. His planting suggestions for the imaginary garden gave quite detailed and elaborate lists of plants, although unfortunately his use of vernacular names makes certain identification of individual plants, described nearly two hundred years before Linnaeus simplified classification with his binomial system, not always possible. Some comparisons between Riccio and the Florentine Giovanvittorio Soderini's work and Girolamo Fiorenzuola's contemporary lists have helped to resolve some of the nomenclature problems, but dates of introduction remain uncertain.

Matteo Caccini (*c.* 1573–1640), a Florentine botanist and dealer in rare plants and a collector of tulips, narcissi, ranunculus and anemones sent plants – including *Tulipa clusiana*, some strange forms of hyacinth (the *Curae Posteriores* of 1639, a volume of flower paintings sent as portraits by Caccini, named '*Hyacinthus asiaticus foliato caule*' and '*Hyacinthus orientalis subvirescente*'), *Tulipa saxatilis* from Crete and *T. stellata chrysantha* from Afghanistan – to Clusius after he became Praefectus of the garden at Leiden. In 1608 Caccini received a letter from d'Aremberg requesting seeds of *Impatiens balsamifera*, four-o'clocks (*Mirabilis jalapa*) and nasturtium, all of which as summer-flowering annuals could be planted in bare earth with amaranthus to decorate the beds after the bulbs had been lifted. Later he asked for the Spanish jasmine (the Indian *Jasminium grandiflorum* illustrated in Besler in 1613) introduced to Italy by Alamanno Salviati from Spain in the middle of the previous century but actually obtained by Caccini in a double form (*J. sambac*) from Alexandria. The extra double form known as 'Mogherina del Granduca di Toscana' was not introduced to Italy, by another Salviati, until 1689.

THE WOODS AND ORCHARDS

The design of concentric circles in Cythera's island garden in the *Hypnerotomachia Poliphili*, with an outer screen of cypresses and another of myrtle, recalls Dante's hierarchy in the *Divine Comedy*, and in addition stresses the categorization of plant types for different areas of a large garden, which had existed since the early Middle Ages. This attitude continued to dominate early Renaissance planting, and influenced both contemporary perceptions, and hence descriptions of gardens, on which modern interpretations have to be based, for another two centuries. The actual flower-beds, fruit orchards or woodland areas, although essentially 'compartmentalized' into regularly shaped units to allow vistas and linear perspective, might be anywhere that fitted satisfactorily into the whole domain. Thick woods would give wind protection; orchards throve best and bore most fruit if exposed on southern slopes, and flower and vegetable areas were placed where the terrain was flat enough to provide easily workable surfaces; fruit trees might also line the larger flower-beds. Rare and exotic trees were planted in ordered rows 'so that one could see and admire them with ease',[7] much as Cyrus the Younger had laid out his park in the fifth century BC. Giorgio Vasari described the thick woods above the upper terrace at Villa Castello in the second half of the fifteenth century as composed of cypresses, firs, evergreen oaks and bay laurel and other evergreens *con bel' ordine partite*, while fruit trees had already been grown in ordered quincunx patterns for centuries. Level planting spaces were provided by the steep terraces made necessary by hilly terrains. On Cythera's island flower and herb gardens are nearest the centre; the inner three circles contain segments for flower-beds designed in elaborate patterns. These are encircled by fruit orchards in meadows strewn with

The arcade of oranges growing under a protective roof in Cardinal Pio's garden in Rome comes from Giovanni Battista Ferrari's *Hesperides*, published in 1646 – the first book devoted to oranges, lemons, citrons and limes and their varieties. Citrus fruits probably originated in tropical east Asia but had been cultivated in the Mediterranean basin for centuries. Alexander the Great introduced the Seville orange to Greece and lemons (*Citrus limon*) were grown by the Arabs in Seville before the twelfth century. Both the Greeks and Romans had grown citrons (*Citrus medica*) and even possibly lemons at Pompeii; the sweet orange (*C. sinensis*) was introduced from China in the fifteenth century. These trees fruited south of the Alps, with or without protection, but farther north, in spite of heated houses, 'the orange', reported Parkinson in 1629, 'could seldom be coaxed into fruit'; a problem soon solved by better heating techniques.

low-growing herbs, the *prati*, which resemble the flowery meads portrayed in paintings and illuminations during the fifteenth century but described in literature much earlier. The outer ring of woodland, the *bosco*, would be planted with native trees and undergrowth, its contents varying with climatic regions.

All through the sixteenth century there are examples of man-made landscapes in which plant categories, arranged in an ordered geometric way, continue to define separate garden areas as in Cythera's circular garden – although not, of course, in concentric circles. Sangallo's drawing in 1525 for the unexecuted gardens of the Villa Madama in Rome shows the vast upper terrace in the shape of a hippodrome as a 'place for fir and chestnut trees' with an intermediate level for oranges and a lower terrace for more intimate garden beds. The fir might be either the 'habeti rossi' (*Picea abies*) or 'habeti bianchi' (*Abies alba*); the chestnut would mean the European or sweet chestnut (*Castanea sativa*). In a letter written in 1542 to the humanist philosopher Agostino Brenzone, who had laid out a compartmental garden of classical themes illustrated by Latin inscriptions on the shores of Lake Garda, Pietro Aretino spoke of the essential elements of a garden near Verona: 'I . . . gaze upon the various flowers and diverse flowers, the ancient and beloved trees, and the numerous and lifegiving orchards.'

Often, of course, as villas developed, sometimes from being more humble farmhouses, gardens were made in the land taken from the surrounding vineyards and orchards, and new and more unusual fruits were grown around the edges of flower-beds either in tubs to be moved to sheds (*stanzone limonaie*) in the winter, or, if sufficiently hardy, planted in the soil. The rarer and more difficult fruits, especially citrus and pomegranates, would often succeed when grown against garden walls.

The more useful orchards or *orti* were planted with fruit trees such as almonds, apricots, cherries, peaches, pears and plums as well as figs. Among the citrus fruit grown were varieties of the sweet orange (*Citrus sinensis*) from China and of the bitter orange (*C. aurantium*), as well as many different kinds of lemons (*C. limon*) developed since early times. Adam's apple or citron (*C. medica*, but then called '*poma Adami*'), believed to be the forbidden fruit plucked by Eve in the Garden of Eden, were introduced to Italy via Portugal in the sixteenth century. There are other interesting asides which show horticultural experiments in action: Duke Cosimo grew dwarf fruit trees – grafted on quince root stock – in an

orchard of the Boboli gardens (both in Jupiter's Orchard and in the adjacent nursery area known later as the Giardino di Madama); at the Villa d'Este at Tivoli oleanders and *cedri*, Riccio's name for citron (*Citrus medica*), were trained like espalier fruit on the walls. Grafting was common practice, especially for fruit.

By the middle of the sixteenth century the *boschi*, the woodland groves sometimes arranged as a labyrinth or wilderness (see p. 143) and transversed by axial paths, were not always on the outer edge of a large garden but became a feature inside it with quite formal planting; tall cypresses, edged with a hedge of laurustinus, could be adjacent to little woods of arbutus, and clumps of fir arranged in regular patterns. At the Villa Lante (see pp. 160–61) orchards of quince, pomegranate, peaches and even figs alternated with groves of olive and holm oak and shady woodland, the fruit occupying the more southern-facing slopes and even lining some of the broad woodland rides.

The *boschi* included in parts of the gardens would have been composed mainly of natives such as the evergreen holm oak, cypress, fir, juniper, arbutus and bay as well as deciduous sweet chestnuts, walnuts, oak, maple and elm, all of which are mentioned in Virgil's *Georgics*. Trees were under-planted with scented box and myrtle, dogwood, laurustinus, mastic and terebinth. Both natives, the umbrella or stone pine (*Pinus pinea*) and Scots pine (*P. sylvestris*) were omnipresent; the shade-giving oriental plane tree with peeling bark, often associated with water and grottoes (to this day groves of plane surround fountains and grottoes at the Villa d'Este and at the Villa Lante), had been in Italy since before Pliny the Elder's time. By the end of the sixteenth century exotic trees became available and were avidly collected. It is uncertain exactly how they were planted. Although the *boschi* were usually at the perimeter of a garden or villa estate, pines and cypresses would have shaded the terraces nearest the house and in all probability the much prized new trees will have been given important positions, although from contemporary paintings and engravings it seems unlikely that single specimen trees were planted on their own. The Indian banyan tree (*Ficus benghalensis*) from India – not to be confused with the Indian fig (*Opuntia ficus-indica*) from the West Indies, illustrated in Besler's *Hortus Eystettensis* of 1613 – was seen and described by Pierre Belon in 1558 in the gardens of the villa at Castello recently laid out for Duke Cosimo de' Medici; it also grew close by in the Petraia gardens, where it was seen by Riccio later in the century. Another much prized tender exotic was the Chinaberry or bead tree (*Melia azedarach*), often in early documentation confusingly referred to as a Persian lilac because of its lilac-coloured sweetly fragrant flowers.

The earliest horse-chestnuts recorded in Italy were those in the 'Garden of Simples' founded in 1545 in Pisa and they were soon brought to the Grand Duke Francesco I de' Medici's *giardino delle meraviglie* at Pratolino. The true lilac (*Syringa vulgaris*), from the Levant but already grown for centuries in the Iberian peninsula, was in the botanic garden of Padua; it was also grown at Pratolino, observed there 'besides hollyhocks and other rare plants' by Ulisse Aldrovandi in the 1570s. In 1578 he sent Francesco a drawing of the newly arrived crown imperial (*Fritillaria imperialis*). The glossy-leaved cherry laurel (*Prunus laurocerasus*) – known in Italy as '*lauro regia*' as opposed to '*lauro silvestro*', which designated the native laurustinus (*Viburnum tinus*) – was also a sixteenth-century arrival and was certainly planted generally by the end of the century. Belon, having seen it during his travels in the Levant, mentioned it as having arrived in Italy, in *Les Observations* published in 1558; he described it as a tree from Trebizond '*qui porte des cerises*'; in Italy he was offered two fine cuttings of it, and we hope they survived. The all-embracing word '*lauro*' or '*alloro*' is usually translated quite correctly to mean the indigenous sweet bay or bay laurel (*Laurus nobilis*) of classical times. In the garden of the Villa Lante a level terrace shaded by plane trees was called the '*Piazza dell' auro regia*' – probably an incorrect transcription of '*lauro regio*' – and may indicate plantings of the new cherry laurel which must have needed shade to survive summers in central Italy.

The study of flowers was painted by Girolamo Pini in 1614. The bulbous and perennial plants are all identified – though without any attempt to use contemporary botanical names – in the key on the left. Easily recognized are red and green tulips, narcissus, snowdrops, red anemones, scillas, *Paeonia mascula*, *Lychnis coronaria*, iris, scabious, sweet rocket, red valerian, nigella, white asphodel, crocus and lily-of-the-valley.

THE DREAM OF
POLIPHILUS

Colonna's *Hypnerotomachia Poliphili* (1499) buildings resemble classical ruins, and roses and vines clamber over arbours and pergolas. The dream traces the love of Poliphilus for the nymph Polia through a series of scenes beginning in Queen Eleuterilyda's palace, its approach lined with stately cypresses, and culminating in the circular island of Cythera, a garden area also bordered by cypresses and divided into 20 equal sections with arbours and porticos draped with climbing roses, jasmine, honeysuckle, convolvulus and other vines. The banks of the encircling canal are fragrant with bowers of orange and lemon trees. A rose garden is planted with the roses named and described by Pliny in his *Naturalis Historia*; the scented Damascene, Prenestine (Provins roses), Milesian (Gallica roses), centifolias (with more than a hundred 'petals') and the famous roses of Paestum in the Campania which bear twice in the year. Although many of the 'gardens' described are fantasies with compositions of glass and silk flowers, there are architectural features clearly inspired by Roman ruins and practical details which must have been copied from contemporary Italian designs and planting. In some beds cypress and box are planted alternately and pillars are intertwined with convolvulus. Inside rectangular compartments a 'parterre' is laid out with an intricate knot pattern, there is a complicated water labyrinth, trees are grown in tubs, 'simulated' roses grow over arbours. On the island a colonnade is decorated with elaborate topiary of humans, animals, vases and urns cut in box. These designs were later almost exactly reproduced in French pattern books at the time Versailles was being laid out in the second half of the seventeenth century. Flower-strewn orchards, fragrant with fruit blossom and luxuriant with fruit, give an atmosphere reminiscent of a medieval romance.

At the Villa Salviatino outside Florence, the modern pergola resembles the wooden frames illustrated by woodcuts in Francesco Colonna's work. At Salviatino a yellow-flowered Lady Banks rose (the banksian rose – *Rosa banksiae*), introduced from China in the early years of the nineteenth century, and named for the wife of Sir Joseph Banks, covers the pergola in clouds of fragment blossom.

Above: Unlike the by now familiar regularity of flower-beds defined and separated by readily accessible pathways which, in most fifteenth-century garden representations, were enclosed by surrounding trellis-work palisades, Colonna's figured patterns were ornate and complicated, with plants tracing out eagles and capital letters. Nor do the interlacing geometric curves and loops, making self-contained representations, resemble Serlio's more austere patterns or the late sixteenth-century flower-bed layouts depicted by Utens *c.* 1599 in the lunettes of the Medici villa gardens. Colonna's designs were more frequently adopted in France – the Dream was translated into French by Jacques Gohorry and Jean Martin between 1544 and 1546 as *Le Songe de Poliphile* – and are much more like the open or closed knots, derived from France, but particularly associated with gardening in Tudor England. Gardening precepts might be new but plants implementing the flower patterns were from the familiar repertoire of the late Middle Ages. Those used for edging and suggested by Colonna included evergreens such as lavender, rue, cotton lavender, pennyroyal (*Mentha pulegium*) and thyme, which would give a textured pattern in winter, but he also recommended basil, costmary, lemon balm, marjoram and southernwood. The plants which composed the solid massed ground-planting were asarabaca (*Asarum europaeum*), bugle, camomile, house-leek, lily-of-the-valley, marigold, mint, orache (*Atriplex hortensis*), pansy, periwinkle, stocks or wallflower, tarragon and violets, while clipped balls of hyssop, juniper, myrtle and rosemary and taller hollyhocks and mallow were 'features'. In the French version of the *Hypnerotomachia* planting was less diverse.

Top centre: A scene from an imaginary garden in the Dream showing a simple timber-framed pergola and timber fence backed by a tall row of cypresses and a shallow fountain. Many of the themes in the Dream are still reproduced as decorative features in gardens, as at the Villa Salviatino.

Above: A scene showing a flower-covered pergola and meadow flowers, from Francesco Colonna's *Hypnerotomachia Poliphili*. The printed work, illustrated with attractive woodcuts, provided models for seventeenth-century Renaissance garden features in Italy and, after translation into French in the 1540s, in France.

PLANT ARCHITECTURE: TUNNELS AND PERGOLAS

From the terrace or entrance gate of a villa pergolas of living plants, made with pleached or intertwined branches or constructed of thin lattice woodwork draped with vines or other climbers, would provide the shady walks essential for hot summers. The prototypes of these, with interlocking branches of fruit or willows, elms or poplars or vines covering frameworks, were recommended by Crescenzi for shade and shelter as early as 1309; the *Hypnerotomachia Poliphili*, with explicit woodcuts as illustrations, further stressed their importance as garden features. Often they linked garden areas, forming cross-walks or providing a shady tunnel around the inner paths of flower gardens in which beds were laid out in patterns.

Pergolas of living plants growing on strong frames are important architectural features in many of the sixteenth-century Medici villas so beautifully illustrated in the Utens lunettes painted for the Villa di Artimino in 1599. At Ambrogiana the arched pergolas enclose three sides of four inner patterned gardens. Each garden area is framed by small fruit trees, and low-growing herbs on the outer edge mark out letters displaying, amongst others, the name 'Ferdinandus'.

By the last two decades of the sixteenth century Soderini recommended using bay, laurustinus and even myrtle so that no sun could penetrate the dense leafy tunnel. The carpentry frames gave opportunity for more architectural detailing such as raised domes at intersections and classically shaped doorways and 'cut out' windows which, as Riccio said, provided views to the flower-beds. These architectural and living edifices seldom survived in the following centuries; within a hundred years tall wall-like hedges of bay laurel, myrtle, evergreen oak and laurustinus took the place of the architectural tunnels

and, with rows of pencil-slim cypresses, flanked the important axial pathways and lined the fashionable *viali*. These are to us more evocative and 'typical' features of the classic Italian garden.

The lunette painting of the Villa Petraia, a garden renovated by Ferdinando de'Medici between 1591 and 1597, shows two almost circular 'green' tunnels which enclose symmetrical orchard planting, while flower-beds, their corners accented by orange or lemon trees in pots, lie closer to the villa under the newly terraced walls. Any trees with branches sufficiently flexible for pleaching might be used; willows and mulberries were popular later, to be superseded by evergreen oak or bay which provide almost rain-proof shelter in gardens today. Lattice-work frameworks were clothed with grape vines and evergreen ivy as well as with more flowery plants such as roses and jasmine.

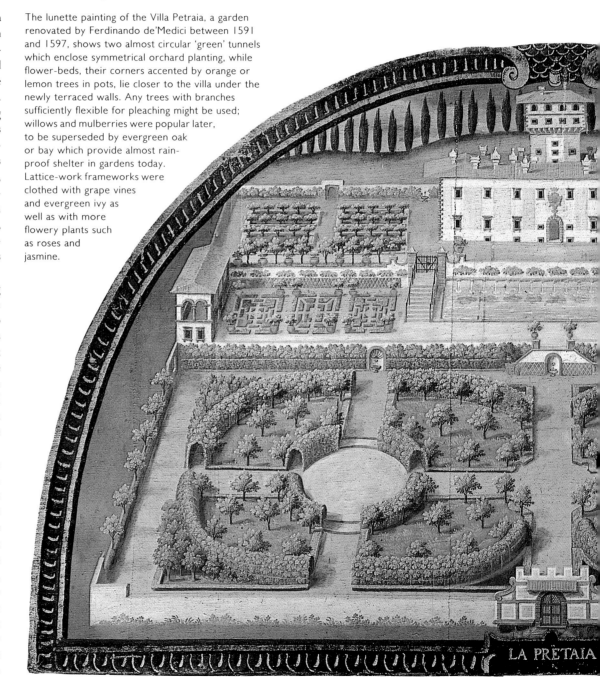

LA PRETAIA

In 1576 Ferdinando de'Medici, Cardinal in Rome before becoming Grand Duke, had purchased the Villa Medici on the Pincian Hill, near the site of the garden of Lucullus. He levelled the ground and hedged in a series of garden compartments with transverse pergolas with low hedges set between them (shown in the detail here). Later engravings show the pergolas mostly gone and hedges of bay, cypress, evergreen oak and laurustinus allowed to grow tall. In the 1640s John Evelyn described them as of head- and breast-height, surrounding the flower-bed compartments. Others double that height, but pierced by central lateral views, lined the main garden divisions.

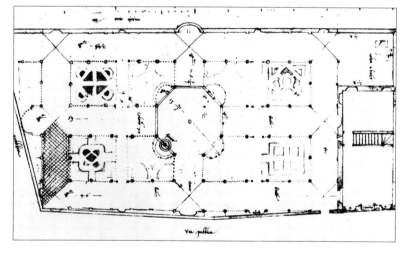

One of the earliest extant designs for a garden project is Baldassare Peruzzi's drawing of 1527, now in the Uffizi Museum. It shows an almost rectangular garden with a *casino* at one end, two sides flanked by public streets, and the third side an orchard. A pergola, almost certainly formed by a pattern of thin carpentry laths, covers the path running round the outer edge. Eight square compartments have four identical layouts surrounding the octagonally shaped feature at the centre of the garden. The flower-bed patterns are all of segments of squares or circles, with two of a different design at either end.

The famous lunettes of the Medici gardens, all near Florence, were painted by the Flemish Giusto Utens for the Villa di Artimino in about 1599. They were commissioned by the Grand Duke Ferdinando I and show the gardens as they looked through the sixteenth century, a sequential portrayal of design and plant detail. All the fourteen surviving paintings, done with oil on wood and now in the Topographical Museum in Florence – known as 'Firenze com'era' – show gardens firmly divided up into spatial units, most of which, although having separate identities, are linked by some sort of axial organization. This is increasingly evident as the century proceeds, developing from the original fortress-like Cafaggiolo, with a medieval-style garden, into sophisticated garden

THE UTENS LUNETTES

schemes, in which allegorical sequences designed by Niccolò Tribolo and Buontalenti, record the importance of the Medici family. The garden of the Villa Castello was laid out for Grand Duke Cosimo, and the Boboli Gardens for Cosimo and his wife Eleonora of Toledo. Villa Petraia was restored for Grand Duke Ferdinando after 1575. The most spectacular was Francesco I's Villa Pratolino, although little remains today except the giant figure of 'Appennino' sculpted by Giambologna. Contemporary travellers such as

Montaigne described many of its marvels, including complicated hydraulic systems, grottoes and statues, at the time the place was still being developed.

In the fifteenth century Lorenzo de' Medici had planted hornbeam, Turkey and cork oak, and the 'incense' tree (probably *Juniperus thurifera*) at Careggi. The Grand Dukes Cosimo, Ferdinando and Francesco planted exotic trees such as the Indian banyan, horse-chestnut and the date plum or lotus (*Diospyros lotus*) at Castello, Petraia and Pratolino as well as oleanders, then called 'rododafne' (sometimes confusingly translated as rhododendron). Visiting Pratolino in 1577 Aldrovandi was able to observe horse-chestnuts, which he called 'callix praecox', conifers, 'xilobalsamum', and a type of hibiscus – 'altea flore magno'.

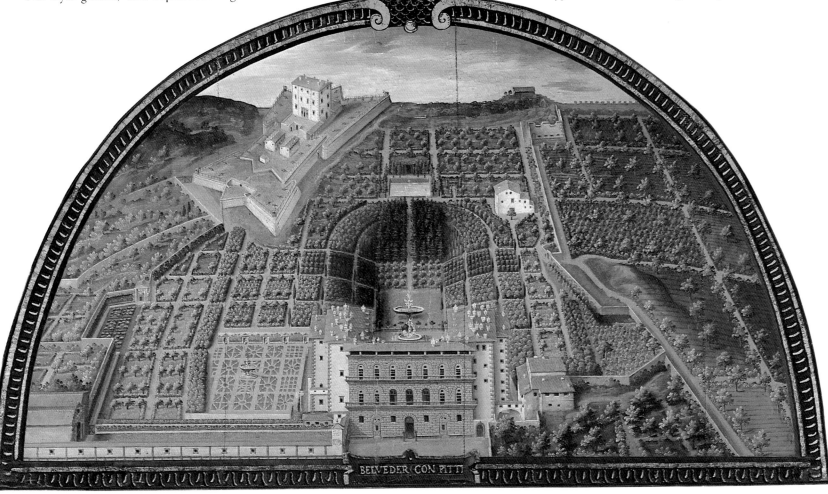

BELVEDER CON PITTI

Left: The vast Boboli Gardens laid out behind the Pitti Palace in Florence for the Grand Duke Cosimo de' Medici and his wife Eleonora of Toledo were begun in 1550. The ground, originally olive groves and vineyards, was first flattened and manured for planting with firs, cypresses, evergreen oaks and bay laurels in the spring. Vines, the *vigne di moscadello*, had already been planted in the previous year. The horseshoe-shaped amphitheatre, an imitation of an ancient Roman circus and perhaps inspired by Pliny the Younger's garden in the upper valley of the Tiber, was thickly wooded in the steepest part, and closed in the view behind the palace. Cosimo also had an orchard of dwarf fruit trees and by 1563 had established a nursery for citrus fruits. The central grass of the amphitheatre was kept as a meadow until about 1740, when parterres of flowers accented with small cypresses and boxwood and with ornamental vases of citrus fruit were introduced. It may well be that box was already used for low hedging in Italian gardens in Utens's day.

Below: Begun in 1537 for Cosimo de' Medici, Tribolo's garden project at Castello was realized on a south sloping site. The lunette shows conventional separate enclosed garden spaces surrounding a central 'wilderness' – a labyrinth of cypress trees, myrtle and bay laurel. Georgio Vasari described the garden in 1580, calling the garden compartments, surrounded by rows of small fruit trees and alternating topiary, *orticini*. The practice of cutting quite ordinary bushes and flowers was explained at length in Soderini's *Il trattato degli arbori*, written in the 1580s or '90s. Vasari also noted a tree house made in a vast *lecce* (*Quercus ilex*).

Other contemporary visitors described trellised citrus fruit: oranges, lemons and Clusius's *Adami mali* or *pomadami*. Botticelli's *Primavera* (shown on p. 141) originally hung at Castello; the flowers depicted in it, none of them exotic newcomers, would all have been grown in the garden. The lunette shows an extension to the house itself, which was never completed, thus leaving the garden with its axis off-centre.

FLOWER-BED
PATTERNS

To match the 'green' pergolas of early Renaissance gardens, which made strong architectural statements as well as channelling and obscuring views, flower-bed areas were also surrounded by inner hedges. It seems certain that basic 'recipes' for these patterns existed in manuscript form in Italy from the early sixteenth century onwards; certainly similar designs recur in different gardens which are portrayed in paintings and later engravings. Within the next 150 years pattern books were commonplace.

The earliest designs were of simple geometry, flower-beds separated by sand or gravel paths, often arranged in compartmental squares backed by the arching tunnels or pergolas as in Peruzzi's drawing. By the 1530s and the 1540s these could be complex but simplified versions are recognizable both in the 1590s layout depicted by Utens at Villa Petraia and in G. Lauro's engraving of the Villa Medici on the Pincian hill in Rome, published in *Antiquae urbis splendor* (1612–14).

By the second half of the century garden areas became more adventurous in shape, with circles or ovals, sometimes contained within square-shaped enclosures, but still geometrically inspired by classical writers such as Vitruvius, providing settings for the new bulbs and flowers. As in Islamic architecture, they also represented the circle and square as the image of a divinely inspired cosmos. In the 1560s Giovanvittorio Soderini drew a circular garden inside a square frame, a project which may have been intended for his own garden; almond-shaped beds, overlooked by raised platforms for vases, are for flowers. In these, as he recommended in a related passage in his treatise *Trattato degli arbori*, he would have planted hyacinths, grape hyacinths, lily-of-the-valley, sweet-scented violets and roses. In small beds in corner niches he advises compact herbs such as scented marjoram and basil and little salads.

Top row: Designs for parterres by the Flemish Hans Vredeman de Vries (1527–1606) were published in *Hortorum viridariorumque elegantes et multiplicis formae* in 1583 and adopted in many northern European capitals. He worked for the Emperor Rudolph II in Prague where he introduced a distinctively Flemish–Italian style fifty years before pattern books published in France by both Claude Mollet and his son André became available. One of his most significant contributions was his design for *parterres de pièces coupées*, also called in France *parterres fleuristes*, in which the flower-beds, raised a few inches above surrounding levels, were specifically intended for the display of exotic plants.

Far left: Serlio's designs for geometric flower-beds published in the fourth volume of *De Architetture Libri Quinque* in 1569, but available in 1537, were actually illustrated by the author; they may well have been an early source of inspiration for parterres – Porro's engraving of the Padua botanic gardens in 1591, Parkinson's patterns in 1629, and many French parterre designs seem Serlio-based. The designs for 'frets' in John Rea's *Flora* in 1665 are also similar. Illustrated here from his *Tutte l'opere d'architettura et prospettiva*, published in Venice in 1619, Serlio's are complicated versions of simple triangles and semi-circles. Planted up with flowers and straggling herbs, they must have entailed considerable maintenance.

Left: One of the oldest layouts still extant is at the Villa Ruspoli near Viterbo, where box plants mark out an early-seventeenth-century pattern. In the original planting schemes herbs such as rosemary or sage may well have been used in place of box, and almost certainly the new bulbs from the Middle East would have been grown in the beds.

Writing in Florence in 1552, in *La grande arte della agricultura*, Girolamo Fiorenzuola recommended plants which could be used as *spalliere* to make hedges growing against the low lattice fences. These included citrus fruit, pomegranate, almonds, apricots and quince, as well as laurustinus, jasmine, myrtles and red roses, with other plants such as thyme, hyssop, ranunculus and hyacinths between them. Fio-

TWO GARDEN WRITERS: FIORENZUOLA AND RICCIO

renzuola also recommended planting the dwarf fruit trees, grafted on to quince stock, which became so popular in garden layouts towards the end of the sixteenth century.

In Agostino del Riccio's treatise on agriculture, published in 1597, *Del Giardino di un Re*, his planting suggestions for an imaginary garden were detailed. For ornamenting the entrance courtyard he recommended many different citrus fruits. There were fourteen sorts of lemons, new types of orange – the sweet orange from China had reached Italy in the middle of the sixteenth century – and what he called '*cedri*' (*Citrus medica* or *Mala*

medica), as well as many sorts of dwarf fruit trees including apples, two sorts of palm, three sorts of peach and *fichi d'India tenuta nani* – this might be the banyan or Besler's *Ficus indica*, the opuntia.

As well as the fruit, Riccio's courtyard list included native oaks, myrtles, rosemary, ten sorts of rose, *Colutea arborescens*, with bulbous plants and some summer-flowering perennials. Among the bulbs were eleven sorts of anemone, twelve different lilies, four hyacinths, five narcissus, six varieties of tulip; the perennials included sixteen sorts of *Dianthus* (probably both clove carnation and pinks), eight aquilegias, three sorts of campanula, five different knapweeds known as cornflower or sweet sultan (*Centaurea*), four delphiniums, phyteumas, hollyhocks, daisies (known as *margheritine*), peonies, nine sorts of poppy called by him *Papaver pellegrini*, stocks and various violas. For the king's flower garden he recommended peonies, hyacinths, narcissi, primroses and tulips, while for the *bosco regio* he suggested cypresses, '*lauri regio di Trebisonda*' – almost certainly the cherry laurel – pines, junipers, oleanders and box.

The artist Jacopo Ligozzi (1547–1626) became court painter to the Grand Duke of Tuscany, Francesco de' Medici, in 1577 and, in watercolour and gouache, portrayed plants, and in particular some of those recently introduced, in accurate and refined life-sized paintings. Many of his paintings were also completed for the scientist Ulisse Aldrovandi, who described Ligozzi as 'A most excellent artist who has no other care day or night but to paint plants and animals of every kind'. His plant portraits, mostly collected in the Uffizi and the University of Bologna, include dittany (*Dictamnus albus*), known today as the burning bush (*far left*), and *Doronicum*. From the New World are *Agave americana* (*left*), a morning glory (*Ipomoea quamoclit*) and four-o'clock or marvel of Peru (*Mirabilis jalapa*) (*right*), while mourning iris (*Iris susiana*) and *Muscari* are from eastern Europe and the Levant and the cashew tree (*Anacardium oxydentale*) is from Africa. Aldrovandi, the superintendent of the 'garden of simples' at Bologna, also worked for Francesco I de' Medici and 'studied' the rare plants being introduced – some of which came through the botanic garden at Pisa, for the Grand Duke at the Villa Castello and Pratolino.

Mirabilis jalapa

A rare inventory, taken at the Villa Lante at Bagnaia north of Rome after the death of Cardinal Gambara in 1587, provides a list of trees, fruit and shrubs which were in the garden and park. Without giving all the topographical details, the inventory can be used as a source list for plants actually grown. It speaks of all twelve flower-bed squares, having eight different fruit trees besides a central fountain in the form of a spire, hedged around by tall evergreen laurustinus; box surrounds the almond-shaped slope above the main parterre area. In the inventory the terms used were those common in the sixteenth century. The plants are

SIXTEENTH-CENTURY PLANTING AT THE VILLA LANTE

described as suitable for different areas of the garden; the *boschetto*, the *prato* and the *spalliera*. Elms, in rows with seven a side, were planted outside the gates. On an upper level called the *Piazza dell'auro regia* – probably meaning a planting of cherry laurel – and a fountain shaded by plane trees. Higher up on a lawn there are five plane trees on either side, while to the left is a grove of arbutus, known at the time as '*cerase marine*', and evergreen oaks. Farther up still are *boschetti* of fir trees,

surrounding juniper, arbutus and myrtle, and higher still another little wood of pomegranates and quinces, above which are oak woods and olive trees with a sunny slope planted with peaches. Walls are covered with fruit: plum, medlar, pomegranate and quince, with vines beyond and a row of figs. Above the aviary there is an olive grove surrounded by a hedge of roses. On either side of the avenue leading into the park are various fruit trees on wooden trellises as well as elms and unstaked grape vines. There are European or sweet chestnuts, and orchards of apricots and the fashionable dwarf fruit trees grafted on quince.[8]

The Villa Lante, designed by Vignola for Cardinal Gambara, probably from 1573, remains almost as it was originally intended, although modern plantings of azaleas, camellias, hydrangeas and rhododendrons strike a discordant note. The cardinal wrote to his relative Ottavio Farnese, Duke of Parma, in 1576: 'I am levelling my garden and planting a grove of plane trees in the *parco* [the park outside the garden area]'. Plane trees still remain as a feature of the garden, sheltering the grotto (*left*) on the upper level. The formal garden at the Villa Lante is strictly architectural in nature, with terraces, stairways and pools on many different levels, reminiscent of the Villa d'Este at Tivoli. The original park to the side was also laid out with axial alleys, groves of dark trees and orchards on the slopes. Perhaps the most memorable change since the garden's laying out is in the organization of the lower parterres, which replaced the flower-bed patterns at the end of the seventeenth century. A French gardener, later tragically drowned in the pool, was employed by Cardinal Montalto after he took over the villa; his distinctive French-style scroll parterres executed in box and gravel survive today.

The engraving by Tarquinio Ligustri of 1596 shows the gardens after they were acquired by the Montalto family but before the parterres had been altered. The hillside, partly planted with evergreen oaks – Ovid's oaks 'which ran with honey' – represented Mount Parnassus, the home of the Greek muses. Avenues, squares and circles, and groves of fruit and olive trees, mark out patterns between fountains along directional pathways. Although plants are not specifically identifiable it is possible to follow some of the planting itinerary in the inventory made in 1587.

The fresco of the Villa Lante executed for the Palazzina Gambara (1574–78), one of a pair of casinos in the garden, shows the lower garden, projected in 1568, as being divided into equal squares, each subdivided by cross paths and planted with a variety of plants, differentiated in the painting by various shades of green, surrounding the fishponds and main fountain. The flower-beds were in simple geometric shapes, either large rectangles or small segments, surrounded by some sort of edging plant; by the beginning of the sixteenth century this 'living' edge was replaced by baked bricks, called *pianelle*.

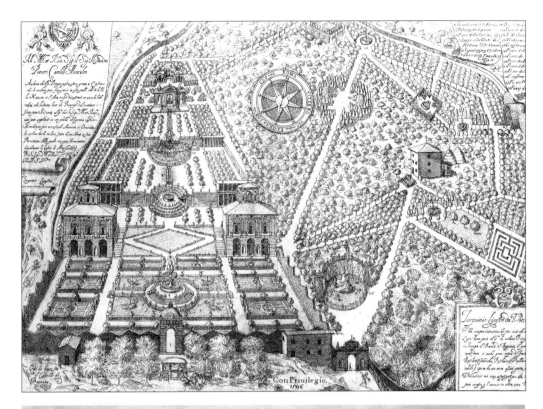

CHAPTER SIX

THE ORIGIN AND DEVELOPMENT OF FRENCH FORMALITY

The Sun King's monumental garden at Versailles, its vistas stretching to the horizon to demonstrate man's – or the king's – power and control over nature, was the ultimate expression of the gardening style that developed in seventeenth-century France, and remains the world's most cogent image of French gardening (see pp. 178–79). But far more than that; the style spread through the courts of northern Europe and ultimately returned to Italy to extend the simpler classical gardening concepts, thus becoming a dominant influence in all formal garden themes. Architectural theories – culminating in Le Nôtre's masterly exploitation of linear perspective – played a dominating role in French gardening; the practical realization of the gardens, however, depended on the exploitation of living plants, controlled by a series of explicit rules. Low-growing plants in parterres made patterns to be seen from above; taller shrubs and trees were clipped into 'walls' or topiary, trained into formal 'green' structures, or, growing freely, were planted in regimented lines to impose geometry on the landscape. At Versailles even the clipped orange trees in tubs were arranged in parade-ground fashion. In La Quintinie's famous Potager du Roi, new espalier patterns set standards of fruit pruning, a peak of ordered perfection which has not been surpassed; three hundred years later we still look to France for guidance on fruit-tree pruning and shapes.

Pierre Patel's overview of Versailles painted in 1688 demonstrates the power and glory of the French gardening style as exemplified by Louis XIV and Le Nôtre. In the perspective, avenues stretch into the distance, while nearer the château ordered and disciplined plants line expanses of green and the wide alleys through which the king makes his tour. Tall hornbeams are clipped and trained to make vertical screens – the charmilles lastingly associated with French formal gardening – and the bosquets make a dense screen around their inner features and planting.

Like so much in garden design theory, many of the new ideas were inspired by Italian writers and architects; this time not those of ancient Rome but the great Renaissance men who recognized that villas, their gardens and the farther landscape should be linked as one unit. In the hills of Tuscany and Latium terraced gardens looked out over the countryside rather than to distant horizons, but farther north in the flatter plains of the Veneto Andrea Palladio (1508–80) could have a wider vision, and axial vistas stretched on both sides of a villa. At the Villa Emo views from the house itself, built by Palladio in 1560, are carried today by lines of poplars into distant fields to both north and south. Ideas derived from Italy were expounded by André Mollet and expressed in *Le Jardin de Plaisir* in 1651. Mollet recommended that main routes might be wide and beautified by planting trees on one or both sides or perhaps in four rows. Mollet spoke of planting 'a big avenue with a double or triple row of female elms, or lime trees (which are the two species of tree which we esteem most suited to this effect) which must be planted in line at right angles to the front of the château . . . and be of convenient and proportionable breadth. Then, facing the rear of the house must be constructed the *parterres en broderie*, near to it so as to be easily seen from the windows, and gazed upon without obstacles such as trees, *palissades* or any other elevated thing which can prevent the eye from embracing its full extent. Following the said *parterres en broderie* will be placed the parterre or compartments of turf, as well as the *bosquets, allées* and high and low *palissades* in their proper place; made in such a way that most of the said *allées* lead to something and always terminate in a statue or the centre of a fountain.'

Wherever they appear, the elaborately patterned and *soigné* box and gravel parterres, essentially relieved and set off by adjacent

alleys of soaring 'green' walls, 'green' cabinets and *berceaux*, with avenues thrusting into vast forests and stretching to the horizon, remain quintessentially French. These garden features are so fundamental to the designs that, in spite of the French development of their own picturesque version of the English landscape in the second half of the eighteenth century – a form of *jardin anglo-chinois* in emulation of the simpler English landscape ethic – it is Mollet's box parterres and Le Nôtre's *allées* and avenues which express the idea of this style, a 'Frenchness' rapidly adopted in suitable terrains all over Europe in the early eighteenth century.

By the middle of the seventeenth century the French garden had developed its own characteristic formal planting and with it a new language to define gardening terms. André Mollet, who worked in Sweden, Holland and England besides his native France, set out the main concepts of classical French garden design in his *Jardin de Plaisir*; we can trace its evolution through other writers and artists including André's own father Claude, who first popularized box as the fundamental ingredient of the 'Groundworks'. Before the end of the century André Le Nôtre had extended the basic ingredients of avenues, *allées, bosquets* and *parterres de broderie*, used by the whole Mollet family, in developing his own wider theories of perspective and proportion. Except in the

Above: The illustration by Israel Silvestre shows the Tuileries newly planted after Le Nôtre's renovation between 1665 and 1672. Today the Arc de Triomphe stands on the distant horizon. Arranged as a set piece, the gardens almost completely conformed to Dezallier d'Argenville's recommendations set down nearly forty years later in *La Théorie et la Pratique du Jardinage*, in which he summed up the theories of Le Nôtre for future generations. Some features such as the white mulberries on the northern Terrasse de Feuillant remained, but most of both Catherine de Medici's layout and Henri IV's restoration after the civil war (including trellised arbours and flower-beds edged in jasmine, quinces and pomegranates planted later, in 1618, by Le Nôtre's father) made way for grander Mollet-style patterns, and the central elm avenue was felled to broaden the view.

Right: One of the first box parterres with flowing lines rather than old-fashioned contained patterns was made in the Luxembourg gardens in about 1619. Evelyn visited in 1644 (by then the palace was owned by Gaston d'Orléans, Nicolas Robert's patron at Blois) and described the parterre as 'so rarely designed and accurately kept cut, that the embroidery makes a wonderful effect'. Evelyn also mentions allées and trees, including 2,000 elms, planted 13 years earlier: 'The walks are exactly fair, long and variously descending, and so justly planted with limes, elms and other trees that nothing can be more delicious, especially that of the hornbeam hedge, which being high and stately, buts full on the fountain.' The engraving is by Gabriel Perrelle.

form of letters and reports, Le Nôtre himself committed none of his theories to paper, but his 'rules' were retrospectively set out for practical interpretation in *La Théorie et la Pratique du Jardinage*, published by his former student Antoine-Joseph Dezallier

d'Argenville (1680–1765) in 1709 and first translated into English by John James in 1712. It is the theorists's implicit instructions on the rules of formality and how the plants were to be used that should be studied first in order to grasp the true complexity of the garden and how each separate part related to the whole (see pp. 174–75 and 180–81).

THE EVOLUTION OF THE FRENCH STYLE

Jacques Androuet du Cerceau's drawings and his later engravings (the latter published in the 1570s) gave the first indications of differences between the basic style of Renaissance gardens as they developed in Italy and those in France after Charles VIII's return from Italy in 1495. The earliest du Cerceaus show a series of flat parterres, each with a separate knot or geometric pattern, with no direct axial alignment with the main building. At Amboise these flat but decorative patterns were surrounded by galleries; at Blois they were laid out about a central pathway, and at Gaillon they were arranged on a vast new terrace adjoining the château court-yard. Unlike the Italian flower-bed compartments, in which each parterre pattern was given height and interest with flanking fruit trees and hedges, these French parterres, as portrayed by du

Cerceau, appear to have been edged only with low railings so that adjacent flat patterns succeeded each other in an almost mono-tonous progression. Fortunately both the Mantuan envoy in 1510 and Don Antonio de Beatis in 1517 gave a more colourful report of planting at Gaillon to prove that the relatively lifeless du Cerceau engravings were intended only as a guide to the essentials of theoretical planning. Besides being surrounded by wrought timber, painted green, each square compartment was differently planted; some with flowers or fruit trees, including peach, apple, pear and cherry; others had box and rosemary cut into forms of horses, ships and birds or more low-growing patterns tracing out coats of arms or mottos or labyrinths.

Working for François I after 1526, designers such as Primaticcio, Vignola and Serlio from Italy clearly influenced basic garden concepts and in particular established the axial relationship, a style only recently adopted in Italy, for a château and its garden. The flat garden compartments, in future to be called *parterres* and to take on a distinctive French connotation in the next 200 years, were now aligned to centre on the main façade of a château, and lay directly under the windows. Tradition has it that it was Henri II's wife Catherine de Medici, daughter of Lorenzo the Magnificent and daughter-in-law to François, who first introduced flower parterres to the French court in the gardens of the Tuileries after her husband became Dauphin in 1536; certainly in her time not only did Sebastiano Serlio actually work in France but his first drawings, almost the earliest in Europe for cut-out flower-bed patterns, became available in 1537. It may well be true that the very word *parterre* is coined from the Italian *partire* – to divide – rather than from the more obvious French *par terre* – on the ground. The French box and gravel *broderies* introduced at the turn of the sixteenth century seem to derive their inspiration more from the complicated knot or *entrelac* patterns proposed in Colonna's *Hypnerotomachia Poliphili* (translated into French in 1546 as *Le Songe de Poliphile*), in which there are continuous lines of one plant, than from other Italian sources in which flower-beds are separate units inside a design. French adaptations of these complicated knot patterns were recommended in treatises such as *L'Agriculture et Maison Rustique* by Charles Estienne and Jean Liébault (first published in French in 1564 and in English in 1600, after which one of its knot designs replaced an earlier 'proper knot' in a new 1608 edition of Thomas Hill's *The Gardener's Labyrinth*). Olivier de Serres's *Théâtre d'Agriculture et Mesnage des Champs* published in 1600 also shows some of Claude Mollet's early parterre layouts, specifically for Saint-Germain-en-Laye in 1595 and later for both the Fontainebleau and Tuileries gardens.

In the 1582 edition of Liébault's book a whole chapter with illustrations indicated how to lay out herbs and flowers. The word 'parterre' was used to indicate the flower garden as a whole; each part of it was a *compartiment*, whether a unit designed as a linking knot or *entrelac* (as advocated in *Le Songe*) or visualized as made up of separate *carreaux* (literally 'tiles', equivalent to the 'pillows' recommended in botanic gardens such as Leiden), and as shown in Serlio's drawings for flower patterns. The French *compartiment simple* would be a square occupied by a continuous knot pattern or labyrinth; a *parterre de carreaux rompus* would be a design of separate flower-beds linked by an overall pattern. Yet more complicated designs included a combination of both separate *carreaux* and *entrelac* compartments. In planting up the compartments, as well as stressing uniformity and balance, de Serres proposed some interesting variations, including suggestions that plants be placed sufficiently far apart in the compartments to ensure that earth or some substitute 'coloured' material be visible, in this way setting off the plants. Within half a century, in the 'ideal' *parterres de broderie*

illustrated by Claude Mollet and André Mollet, lines of box were so finely tuned with adjacent chipped marble, coloured gravels and trimmed grass that other living flowers – tending by their exuberance to blur the essential perfection of the design – were confined to outer borders or planted in adjacent *compartiments*.

THE INFLUENCE OF THE MOLLET FAMILY

The Mollet dynasty, each member working at first as head gardener rather than as designer, is particularly associated with developments of parterre styles. There were three generations; by the third, the Mollets proliferated to provide gardeners in many of the royal properties in Paris. Jacques Mollet first worked at Anet after 1576 for the Duc d'Aumale; his son Claude, the author of *Le Théâtre des Plans et Jardinages* (published posthumously in 1652) worked principally for Henri IV; his sons were André, author of *Le Jardin de Plaisir*, Jacques II and Claude II, all of whom were involved in making designs for and maintaining parterres. By about 1600 the increasing use of boxwood to mark out the dominant pattern of the design (from 1595 Claude Mollet used mainly box for his *broderies*) facilitated the development of more sophisticated and complicated patterns of box arabesques, scrolls and palmettes.

In 1593 Henri IV commissioned Etienne du Pérac to build the new château at Saint-Germain-en-Laye, incorporating a project already outlined by Philibert de l'Orme for Henri II. Du Pérac's vision extended to using water devices inspired by the marvels of the Villa d'Este, but Claude Mollet's new parterres, planted only with box, set a new style. By using the dense foliage of box, tightly clipped, the embroidered parterre could depict finer patterns more clearly than was possible with traditional mixed herbs. Later Mollet made living green walls from taller box plants, although he found their rate of growth almost unacceptably slow. After 1600 he was given the task of planting Le Jardin Neuf, a new garden east of the Tuileries buildings; at first he surrounded the garden with Italian cypress as a clipped *palissade*, but a severe winter in 1608 killed the lot. Until then Mollet had reinforced double hedges with an inner framework of woodwork. 'Therefore,' he wrote 'I resolved never to plant palisades of cypress, but to use box; as I did when I began to represent works of architecture made only with the shears, without any dead wood or ties. But it needs patience; ten or twelve years for something fine of

The painting by J. Fouquières shows the Renaissance garden of the Hortus Palatinus at Heidelberg, laid out between 1613 and 1618 by Salomon de Caus for the Elector Frederick and his bride Elizabeth Stuart, who had been de Caus's pupil in England. De Caus laid out five narrow terraces, each of which was divided up by hedges and pergolas with further areas of enclosed box-patterned parterres and a maze, all in a mixture of French and Italian styles. Although influenced by his years in Italy, de Caus – grandson of J. A. du Cerceau – was also inspired by contemporary French garden development, in particular the use of continuous low box hedging for parterres.

any height.' After 1608 Henri IV and Sully re-drew the compartments of Le Jardin Neuf, surrounding designs of low-growing box and rue with *palissades* of juniper.

From now on the finest parterre design work was to be dominated by the dwarf smaller-leaved box (*Buxus sempervirens* 'Suffruticosa'), known to both Gerard and Parkinson in England as Dutch or French, but originating in Holland. The taller native species, *B. sempervirens*, was and is used for hedges designed to reach knee height and over. Even then André Mollet recognized the limitations of European box in harsh climates and recommended the use of deciduous whortleberry or bilberry (*Vaccinium myrtillus*) in Sweden. Today cultivars of cold-hardy Korean box (*Buxus microphylla*), introduced to Europe and America only in the nineteenth century, make box-style designs feasible in New England and Canadian gardens, while a dwarf form of the American yaupon holly (*Ilex vomitoria*) or the taller dahoon, *I. cassine*, is

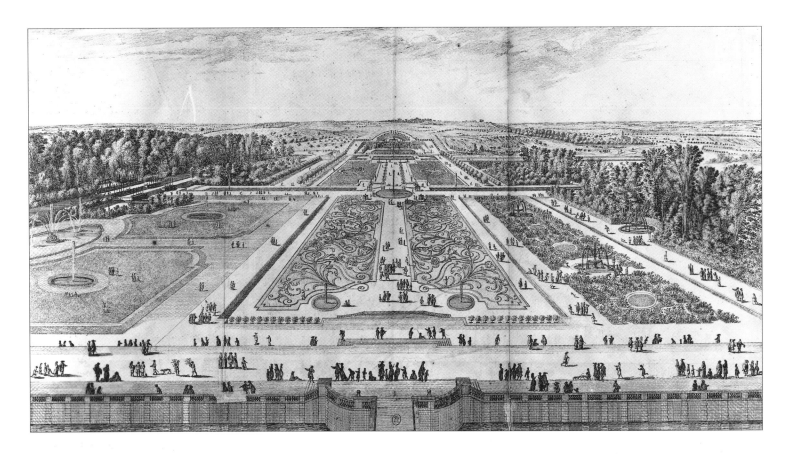

suitable in the Mediterranean region or southern states of America.

Claude Mollet remained essentially interested in the detail of gardening rather than in the grand overview of garden style. His *Théâtre des Plans et Jardinages* is a practical book; he discusses the laying out of parterres, the spacing of *allées*, the maintenance and methods of making 'walls' and *palissades* of both beech and hornbeam. Besides first advocating box as a fundamental ingredient of the embroidered parterre, perhaps his most useful contribution to the development of the French style lies in his stress on the 'relief' effects of tall *allées*, rows of trees, arching *berceaux* and sharply cut hedges and *bosquets*, when set to act as backdrops to the flat parterres. Some of his advice for preparing flower-beds, although essentially tied to his own type of gardening, seems remarkably apt even today and indicates the use of flowering plants. For a parterre, 'after squaring up the garden which you want to make in the form of *compartiments* (either *en broderie* or otherwise) it is necessary to make a border six feet wide . . . all round your square so that the gardener can plant all the tall

The engraving of Vaux-le-Vicomte by Israel Silvestre shows how the main and sunken embroidery parterres lie directly centred under the windows of the château. It also shows the more relaxed flower garden lying to the west where beds, some of which seem to be circular, are overflowing with bloom. Even before laying out Vaux, Fouquet had been a plant collector; in his far from modest 12.5-hectare/30-acre garden at Saint-Mande, which adjoined the park at Vincennes, he employed a German gardener, Besseman, who built up a collection of rare shrubs and flowers, among which were two hundred orange trees. Although the more elaborate new *parterres de broderie* allowed little space for flowing plant forms, the great gardens laid out by the Mollet family and Le Nôtre always contained flower-beds. Besides the main *parterres* the adjacent beds or *compartiments* were for flowering shrubs, bulbs and summer flowers.

flowers there, making a belt spaced in an orderly way all round the four squares. Also it is necessary to intermix them, so that when one flower is over, the place will not be left empty, and one may always be able to see there all sorts of colours of flowers on one side of the compartment as much as the other; by this means the tall flowers will add greatly to the ornament of the compartments.'[1]

In his *Jardin de Plaisir* André Mollet defined the scope of pleasure grounds, going beyond the 'growing' components with which we are concerned: 'The Garden of Pleasure consists in Ground-works, Wildernesses, choice Trees, Palissades and Alleys or Walks; as also in Fountains, Grotto's and Statues, Perspectives, and other such like Ornaments; without which it cannot be perfect . . .' In the French formal garden water features, stonework and statuary were part of the organization designed to present unforgettable monumental effects. 'Let us come to the inner embellishments which we commonly call Garden; which ought to be composed of Imbroider'd Ground-works, knots of grass, Wildernesses, fine Alleys in Terraces, and flat walks, so ordered that they may still end at some Fountain or Statue . . . also ought to be set up some fine Perspectives painted on Cloth . . . All these so-called ground-works to be visible from the house without being concealed by any Trees, Palissades or other high Work.' Mollet also stressed that those most remote from the eye 'ought to be drawn of a larger Proportion than those that are nearer' (an important point especi-

A watercolour of the *berceaux* in the garden at Heemstede in the province of Utrecht is by Isaac de Moucheron. The garden, possibly inspired by the layout of the Tuileries gardens in Paris, with separate garden sections arranged around a central axis, was separated from the countryside by protective screens of trees and dykes and laid out after 1680. The picture shows the view along the main *allée* back to the house with tall vertical hedges, probably of hornbeam, with architectural motifs, and trellis-work, from which further walks stretched into lateral woodland of ash, oak, elm, beech, linden (lime), trimmed yew and junipers to make a star-shaped pattern.

ally to be remembered in reconstructions and restorations) so that 'they will thereby appear more beautiful' and that in general these inner embellishments should occupy a flat area at 'the backside of some great palace about a third longer than it is broad'. The knots in embroidery could be made with box or with turf. 'Those of Box are more fit for the neat and small embroidery partly because it can be clipped in any shape and is less pain to preserve and keep than turf which has to be mown and rolled. Turfs are more fit for great works and for knots than embroidery.'

The embroidery was enlivened by cypresses used as feature plants in half-ovals around plots of grass or placed in a regular progression along the flower-bed edges or actually standing in them, on plinths raised a hand's breadth above the ground. Mollet condemned the practice of tying in the branches of cypress to make them grow taller so that 'being without Air within-side, they wither and become full of dead wood'. Instead he recommended clipping them twice a year so that 'they will strengthen themselves towards the roots and better resist bad weather.' (By 1709 Dezallier d'Argenville's preference was for using yew, *Taxus baccata*, obviously a more reliable and hardy plant in northern climates.)

André Mollet also suggested that areas at the side of the house could be reserved for rarer trees and shrubs, most of which would be overwintered in orangeries. Oranges and other citrus fruit, jasmines and 'other choice Trees, and evergreen dwarf Trees' were all grown in vases or boxes, soon to be known as Versailles tubs.

THE OUTER GARDEN: THE WILDERNESS AND AVENUES

For the whole garden a basic rectangle should be divided by *allées* and walks into a regular grid pattern with all the parts, including what Mollet called the 'Ground-works', arranged symmetrically about a central axis. Avenues should be extended beyond the façade of the house as 'a great Walk of double or treble rank', the walk to be drawn as a perpendicular line to the façade and be 'of convenient and proportionable breadth to the house'. Given space, there might also be 'drawn large Walks on the Right and on the Left . . . which must be parallel to the said House . . . One ought to begin to Plant even before the beginning of the House, that the Trees may be come to half-growth when the House shall be built.'

After the knots of embroidery and the compartments of turf 'follow the Wilderness, Plants of Trees, Ponds and grass plots, in

Although the house in W. Schellinks's painting of a garden by a river near Haarlem in the Netherlands cannot be identified, the scene presents a fine example of Dutch gardening between 1660 and 1670, an extension of the French style in more intimate circumstances. Set in the flat landscape, the garden is enclosed by high hedges and white-painted fences with topiary trees lining the flower-beds. To the right, shaped bushes sit in tubs and an orchard area, more utilitarian in mood, has trees in beds trimmed with wood.

the midst of which may be erected arbours'. For this area Mollet recommended planting limes rather than elms with their spreading roots. Round the outer edge of the parterre area Mollet would use *palissades* of beech cut quite low, to about 60–90 centimetres/2–3 feet, in order to preserve the proportions and to allow views out to the rest of the garden. He described how the wildernesses (*bosquets* in French) were laid out beyond the parterres. The wilderness, far from being untamed forest as its name implies, was essentially formal and geometric, with tall hedges flanking open pathways of grass or sand, marking out a geometric pattern. 'At the end of the Grand Parterre there are to be three alleys issuing forth from the same centre' – to be known as a *patte d'oie* or goosefoot – 'and these should be planted with rows of Beech which serve for high Palissados and within the space of six foot are marked the places where to put Cyprus Trees, which must be kept always cropt neatly in a Pyramidal form (not allowed to grow more than six or seven feet at the most). Instead of beech the said palissado's could be planted with Alaternus's [probably *Phillyrea* and not a buckthorn], holly, or Cherry-Laurel which would produce a far more

pleasing effect.' In this outer area the double palisades, two rows of plants trained head-high on to a central framework of thin laths, framed wide walks in different radiating patterns, sometimes marking out labyrinths tall enough to be deliberately confusing.

Within angles made by the palisades there could be hidden orchards of dwarf fruit trees or a kitchen garden: 'For we do not allow that the Garden of Pleasure should admit of common herbs; nor yet of Fruit-Trees, except that they be planted as wall trees.'

These inner wildernesses could also be planted with native trees or with more choice evergreens; arbours could be made at the corners of the timber which joined with the framework. Here it would be possible to have 'the enjoyment of society with two or three friends, a Bottle of wine and a Collation'.

In the wilderness areas directly beyond the ground-work parterres tall *allées* were made either by trees, grown on a framework and worked into an elaborate screen, or by tightly clipped hedges. The hornbeam *charmilles* which were to become features of many French-style gardens throughout Europe in the following years were sometimes grown on frames and sometimes in freestanding lines.

Dezallier d'Argenville described how the 'wilderness' walks and *allées* were created (see pp. 176–77). Some were open to the sky; others, slightly narrower, were closed overhead with arching branches. In walks flanked by a single pair of *palissades* with trees growing on a frame or with free-standing hedges, clipping was carried out to a specified height, sometimes with trees allowed to branch out overhead. In double walks or avenues single isolated specimens flanked the main pathway, but in the outer row trees were linked together and tied in to a frame. Unlike the low beech hedges surrounding parterre areas, these flat walls of living green were intended to prevent farther views, and were encouraged to grow as perpendicularly as possible, but fully clothed to the ground, against the laths. If the lower part became thin it could be thickened by adding box or yew or some of the original hedging plants. The vertical 'walls' were clipped by means of double ladders and 'rolling carriages' – a sort of scaffolding on wheels. Further decorative effects could be achieved by allowing shoots of hornbeam to rise above the palisade and then clipping them into balls and vases to make a 'green' architecture. Using a close-knit plant such as hornbeam made it possible to design niches and close arbours without the usual lattice-work. Often the grandest bowers and *cabinets* were of trees such as (female) elms and Dutch linden (lime) 'artfully interwoven', with hornbeam used to fill up the lower part. The young saplings had to be grown for two or three years before being bent across while still supple.

Trees both from southern Europe and from farther afield had been regularly introduced to the northern regions since Roman times, but in a more scientific manner since Pierre Belon's early attempts at acclimatization in the middle of the sixteenth century. Already in 1558, on his return to France from Italy and other countries, he had offered to 'tame' holm oak, cork oak, spruce, strawberry tree, *Pistacia terebinthus* and Sicilian sumach (*Cotinus coriaria*) for Henri II if he could be guaranteed an annual pension – Belon even formulated proposals to introduce the culture of opium poppy for pharmaceutical purposes. Nothing much came of this, but Belon did introduce his favourite plane tree, imploring it to survive from a seedling: 'And so Platanus, you who chose for your wild habitat the valleys of Asia, a colder climate than ours, why should we not be able to have you here? . . . For since you have grown from seed up to the fifth leaf, we hope that you will not slip away from us in the winter . . . if once we have a dozen of you, we will one day have a thousand.'[2] We do not know in what period the shade-giving plane trees became such a common feature in the southern parts of France.

Little is heard of avenue planting until the early seventeenth century. Then most of the newly planted avenues will have been either of elm or of the European broad-leaved lime (*Tilia platyphyllos*), commonly found in France and Germany. The small-leaved *T. cordata* was rarely employed, but the new lime, *T. × europaea*, a natural hybrid between the two, was being propagated in vast numbers in Holland. Its use rapidly spread to France and England. The English elm (*Ulmus procera*) could be increased only by suckers, and the French mainly used what was called the French elm (*U. carpinifolia*). The Dutch elm (*U. × hollandica*, probably a hybrid of *U. carpinifolia* and *U. glabra*), was available by the second half of the seventeenth century. By 1669 the nurseryman Jan van der Groen, who had been a gardener at Honselaarsdijk where André Mollet had also worked in 1633, was listing elm and Dutch elm, birch, English oak (still used extensively in Holland), ash, European or sweet chestnut, sycamore, lime, beech, larch, spruce fir, Scots pine, both abele and black poplar, all recommended for avenues. Mollet had found an avenue at Honselaarsdijk planted in 1625 in

Cultivating rare plants, and in particular tender citrus and evergreens which needed to be moved into orangeries for the winter, became a favourite pastime throughout Europe during the seventeenth century. Jan Commelin, the Amsterdam merchant who had access to rare seeds and plants from the East and West Indies and the Cape of Good Hope, became an expert on growing tender exotics. His book, *De Nederlandze Hesperides*, published in 1676, gave advice on how to set up an orangery and open court for summer display. The garden of Magdalen Poule, mistress at Gunterstein, constructed in the 1680s, followed his precepts. In it she successfully grew oranges, limes, myrtle, jasmine, camphor and double oleander trees besides other rare exotic trees and bulbs.

eight rows stretching 773 metres/845 yards, but we do not know which tree was used. Horse-chestnut, although introduced only in the sixteenth century, soon became popular.

Jan van der Groen's *Den Nederlandtsen Hovenier* was published in Amsterdam in 1669, three years before the author's death. He believed above all that the garden should be laid out in the architectural French manner with 'geometry and uniformity' (see pp. 184–85). In the flat Dutch landscape gardens, often limited in size and scope by existing drainage dykes, van der Groen advised that tall avenues of oaks, poplars or elms would not only provide a design with a sense of enclosure and an 'inward-looking orientation', but also protect against wind and provide shade in the heat of summer. Unlike France, with its extensive forests, Holland by the seventeenth century had little surviving native woodland. By the end of the century Dutch tree nurseries were well established as to supply owners of country estates as far away as Russia.

NEW PLANT COLLECTING

Although when Henri IV first came to the throne there was no official botanic garden in Paris, Jean Robin (1550–1629) had already established his own collection of plants on the Ile de la Cité by 1598. Before this he had been appointed as *arboriste et simpliciste du roi* to Henri III as well as director of the gardens at the Louvre. Robin became responsible for the introduction of many new plants, 'dealing' and exchanging with plant collectors from Holland, England, Switzerland and Italy. Robin's garden became famous for its rarities, many of which were portrayed by Pierre Vallet in *Le Jardin du Roy très Chrestien Henry IV*, published in 1608. His son Vespasian Robin (1597–1662) travelled widely throughout Europe and north Africa, bringing new plants to Paris for acclimatization, many of them found through contacts with travellers rather than actually collected in the wild. Among seeds obtained from Virginia, possibly coming through England, were those of the black locust or false acacia (*Robinia pseudoacacia*), which was named in Jean Robin's honour. The first tree was planted in Robin's garden in 1601, the same year as he published his *Catalogus stirpium* showing the wide range of plants he already owned; tuberoses, double-flowered anemones, tulips, hyacinths and other exotic bulbs as well as small local plants such as European ginger (*Asarum europaeum*). John Tradescant, travelling from the Low Countries, probably first met the Robins at the end of November 1611; from them he bought a pomegranate, Spanish broom (*Spartium junceum*), eight pots of oranges, oleanders, a fig, myrtles, as well as pears, plums and cherries; he was also given a pot full of carnations. Many other plants arrived from the French colonies in North America, collected by missionary fathers who went out not to collect plants but to convert the Indians; those with the epithet *canadensis* usually date to this period. Maidenhair ferns came to Vespasian Robin from Father du Tertre in the West Indies.

By Le Nôtre's time there was no shortage of ornamental flowers or of new exotic trees and shrubs to decorate the royal gardens for Louis XIV, with more arriving annually from both Canada and the Far East (see pp. 182–83). From an expedition in 1687 came the first Chinese wisteria (*Wisteria sinensis*), the China aster (*Callistephus chinensis*) and pink (*Dianthus chinensis*), soon to be followed by delphiniums (*Delphinium grandiflorum*). The first Chinese rhododendrons were received for the Jardin du Roi.

FLOWERS IN THE FORMAL SETTING

Contemporary paintings and engravings and written descriptions of these ordered gardens are sufficiently detailed to present clear-cut images. In spite of these the French formal garden, with its elaborately controlled *parterres de broderie* based on low-growing clipped box and its axial *allées* and *berceaux*, has acquired an unjustified reputation for being almost inhumanly 'flowerless', with nature, in the shape of trees and shrubs, clipped into subjection and arranged only in parade-ground patterns (see pp. 186–89).

Neither of the Mollets ever neglected flowers. André Mollet stated that low-growing flowers should be grown in 'lifts' – presumably raised beds – 1.8 metres/6 feet in breadth. For the alleys between the flower-beds 'in which England excels – choose a firm gravelly sand without the least mixture of earth, except clay – coarser than fine and even small shells – the Master-stroke which forms the design to be of box, and clipped square, flower-beds set 3″ or 4″ above ground level camomile and matted Pinks observing symmetry'.

After the ground-works in embroidery came *compartiments* of 'Turff-work and of Flowers, which being kept as they ought to be will make a glorious shew'; in achieving good results with flowers the French were said by Mollet to be the best in the world. 'For Turf choose that grazed by sheep with no weed except camomile' and move it in after Michaelmas, or 'with drought in spring nothing will remain but base herbs and Weeds'. It had to be rolled with wooden and then stone rollers and mown at least twice a week so that the grass would grow thick.

Le Nôtre's employer and patron Louis XIV was an avid plant collector, and new trees and flowers, brought back by his botanizing explorers and first cultivated in the Jardin du Roi, established in 1635, were used extensively in the flower-beds of his royal gardens. Other trees and flowers were 'tamed' at Montpellier. Although Le Nôtre was mainly concerned with controlling the components of huge garden compositions, since he was also in overall charge of the detail of each of the king's gardens, it was his specific duty to see that the gardens of the Tuileries should be stocked with flowers 'even in the winter'.

Flowers were always in great demand and not easily found in the quantities needed to satisfy the king. The main varieties used were those from the Mediterranean and those long grown in

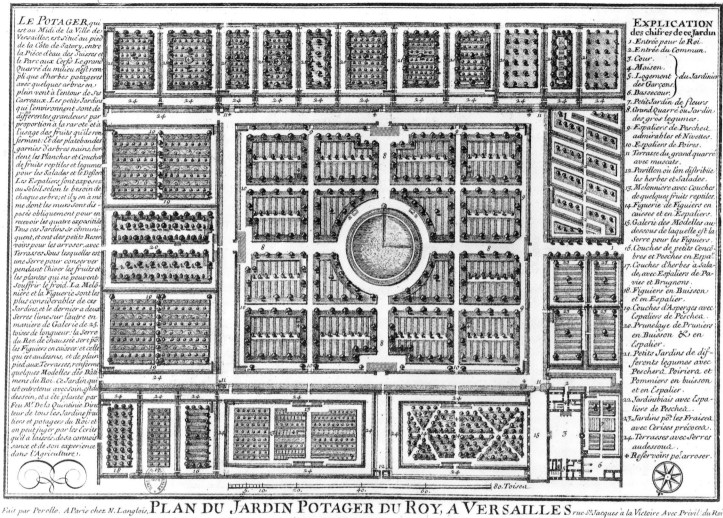

PLAN DU JARDIN POTAGER DU ROY, A VERSAILLES

Europe: anemones, columbines, carnations and pinks, iris, lilies and peonies and, of course, bulbs such as tulips and fritillaries. Others came from America – Canadian lilies, rudbeckia, helianthus and tropical canna, besides the desirable tender tuberoses (*Polianthes tuberosa*) from Mexico, introduced to Paris in 1629. For Versailles many, including daffodils and tuberoses, were grown and brought from Provence. In one season of 1672 10,000 tuberoses were specially grown in Avignon and transported to Versailles. Some of the other flowers, quite tender ones from the West Indies, were cultivated in pots under glass, and, as an early form of bedding out, were used for decorating the garden during summer;

The royal fruit and vegetable garden, the Potager du Roi, at Versailles was laid out by Jean de La Quintinie between 1677 and 1683 on a plot of land southeast of the château. When completed, the unit covered 8 hectares/20 acres and had 29 separate walled enclosures for all kinds of fruit, including the exotic sago palm (*Cycas revoluta*). The central area was sunken, with 16 raised beds, and surrounding walls espaliered with pears and peaches. La Quintinie's book, *Instructions pour les jardins fruitiers*, was published in 1690, two years after his death. It contained instructions for fruit pruning and descriptions of his preferred varieties; in various editions and translations, it became a classic reference for his successors.

sometimes they had to be ready for 'instant' effects for balls, dinners and fêtes held in the *bosquets*.

THE FRENCH PARTERRE

In *La Théorie et la Pratique du Jardinage*, published anonymously in 1709, Dezallier d'Argenville summed up Le Nôtre's principles of ordered gardening and set out definitions of the different types of parterre which, under the influence of the Mollet family, had emerged during the last 50 years. These were characterized by five different kinds: the *parterre de broderie; parterre de compartiment: parterre 'à l'Angloise'* (or after the English manner); *parterre de pièces coupées pour les fleurs* (cutwork parterres for flowers, also called *parterres fleuristes*), and parterres of water; there were also *parterres d'orangerie*.

Dezallier started by saying that a parterre was the first thing that should present itself to sight and should 'possess' the ground next to the main building, 'low and flat with groves and palisades raised to set it off' as contrast.[3] The oldest form was the *parterre de compartiment*, to be seen only from one direction; from this the *parterre de broderie* had developed sym-metrically on both axes. *Parterres de broderie* had flowing plant lines which joined different areas or compartments together into one pattern. As developed by the Mollets, in the first half of the seventeenth century, the continuous lines were of box, making elegant arabesques in flower and leaf motifs to be seen against a relief of coloured earth or sand; the finer lines of the motifs could be laid out with marble or stone chippings giving an even more precise delineation. Bands of grass were incorporated to unite the whole design. These parterres were by no means devoid of living plants, but the plants had to contribute to a recognized art form and worked best when uncluttered by flowers. However, flower-borders, planted with small trees at regular intervals, often marked the edges. *Parterres à l'anglaise* were laid out with the main background as cut turf, with a box-edged bed for flowers, usually embellished with strips of pale sand. The English, in fact, preferred simpler grass *plats* adorned with statues and fountains, rather than more elaborate patterns of the low-growing box.

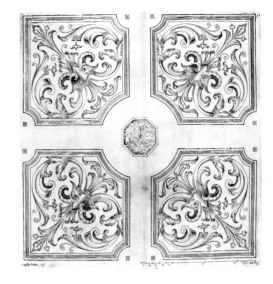

A design from *The Garden of Pleasure*, the 1670 translation of André Mollet. By the middle of the sixteenth century both Mollets, Claude and his son André, had developed the *parterre de broderie* using continuous flowing lines of box. Both the design treatment and the employment of box as foundation planting was innovatory: the elegant scrollwork gave an almost three-dimensional sense of raised embroidery, while winter-hardy box, planted instead of the assorted 'green' herbs, was neater as well as proving very practical in the French climate. Narrow *plates-bandes* edging the parterres, with accent planting of small evergreens such as juniper, fir or yew, provided space for flowers.

Parterre a l'Angloise

Parterre de pieces coupées pour des fleurs

Parterre d'Orangerie

In *La Théorie et la Pratique du Jardinage* by Dezallier d'Argenville, translated into English by John James in 1712, there are illustrations of the different parterres. The pattern in the English manner, with its surrounding bed for flowers usually edged with low-growing box, is of cut turf with gravel walks marking out an elegant pattern. In the centre the cutwork provides more planting space. The third illustration shows a suggested pattern for a parterre of orange trees, for summer display.

The classical *parterres de broderie* at the château of
Vaux-le-Vicomte, first developed in the seventeenth
century, have been restored to their original
patterns. Vaux was the first great work by André
Le Nôtre, executed between 1656 and 1661, and
remains one of the most notable of his grand linear
concepts, with intricate schemes of dwarf box
scrollwork, framed by clipped trees and elegant
statues, and amazing perspective views
incorporating broad grassy walks and cascades.

PLANT ARCHITECTURE: PALISADES AND ARBOURS

In the seventh chapter of *La Théorie et la Pratique du Jardinage* Dezallier d'Argenville wrote that 'Arcades and Arbours of greenery are really "fragments of architecture" which … have a special beauty and magnificence that greatly enhances the natural beauty of the garden'. What he was

saying, in effect, was that in French formal gardening all of the taller woody plants became architecture and were used as essential but controlled elements in the design. The most fundamental feature was the *palissade*, which was wall-like in its construction, composed of plants either used as hedging or trained against a framework of laths – usually made of European or sweet chestnut, pine or fir.[4] It was in his words 'entirely smooth and even, well filled up from the very bottom [and] clipped on both sides as perpendicularly as possible'. When composed of hornbeam

The *charmilles* at Beloeil in Belgium are made with hornbeam grown on frames. The gardens in French style were laid out in the first part of the eighteenth century with the help of the French architect Jean-Baptiste Bergé.

(*Carpinus betulus*) – *charme* in French – these 'barricades' were called *charmilles*. Solid palisades were designed to stop views beyond, but sometimes had windows cut in them; they could be further embellished with a kind of rural architecture – vases formed by shoots of hornbeam rising above the palisade and 'clipped with art to bring them to a proper shape'. *Berceaux* and *cabinets* were vaulted arbours composed either of intertwined branches or of trellis work on which trees such as hornbeam and elm were trained so that the structure was entirely covered with foliage. The *bosquet* remained something peculiar to French gardens, attaining a rather specific interpretation at Versailles, as an ornamental grove, thicket or shrubbery pierced by walks. In England it was commonly translated as 'wilderness' – a confusing term except to garden historians, as there was nothing 'wild' about it. Usually occupying a geometric section of the garden, probably adjacent to the flatter parterres, the walks and *allées* were generally aligned in a formal intersecting pattern. In the early eighteenth century these rigid patterns were superseded by winding paths introducing a slightly more naturalistic element.

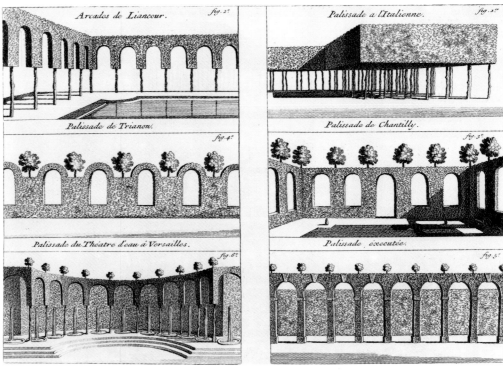

The illustrations (*above right*), taken from Dezallier d'Argenville, show several different ways of making a decorative palisade. If a frame was used, trees such as elm and hornbeam – and others – were chosen in two sizes. The taller ones 2.4–3 metres/8–10 feet high were planted 90 centimetres/3 feet apart, with smaller trees half that height planted between. The trees had to be bushy from top to bottom and were then pruned so that the side boughs were spread out and fastened on the frames. If no frame was used the trees had to be smaller at the start, probably at most 1.8 metres/6 feet, as they had to be tightly clipped to make a wall.

Right: At Zorgvliet in Holland the tunnel arbours or *berceaux* were laid out on Italian lines in the sixteenth century. Much rougher and less tailored than the French palisades as they later developed, a mixture of plants was often used. Hazel, honeysuckle, ivy, viburnum, holly, elder and whitethorn, as well as fruit trees – all plants hardy in the northern climate – were recommended by Jean Liébault.

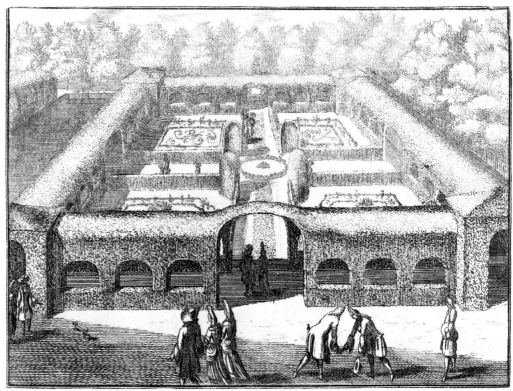

PLANTING AT VERSAILLES

Each part of the garden at Versailles – the Orangerie, the flower-garden parterres, the Petit Parc and the *bosquets*, the Grand Parc and the Potager – had individual head gardeners and teams; their duties were to obey the wishes of the king and, above all, despite a continual shortage of water, to keep the thousands of plants alive and growing. The growing plants, used as architectural features, nevertheless had to be clipped at least once a year; box for *broderies* and for hedges, yews as pyramids and cones, and palisades and *charmilles* of hornbeam and other trees all needed skilled cutting by hand. Even the main trees for the avenue alignments needed pruning at least every three years.

At Versailles, besides trees and shrubs moved wholesale from Vaux-le-Vicomte during the early 1670s, there were walks and cross walks of linden (lime) and maple (sycamore, *Acer pseudoplatanus*, and Norway maple, *A. platanoides*), planted from saplings found in forests all over France. For other avenues there were elms, including some from Flanders and a large-leaved form – '*ypreau*' – from Ypres and, by the early 1670s, horse-chestnuts. The new hedges, which stretched for miles lining the *allées* and enclosing the *bosquets*, making architectural walls of smooth green 6 or 7 metres/20 odd feet high, were mostly of hornbeam; in 1685 nearly three million of these came from the forest of Lyons and others from Picardy. The hornbeams were clipped to form palisades, shutting out the woods, while specimen trees of spruce, fir, beech, linden (lime) and evergreen oak were planted within the *allées*.

Besides all the hardy species, there were many rare and tender trees and shrubs, including citrus fruit, which were grown in tubs and had to be sheltered in the Orangerie in winter.

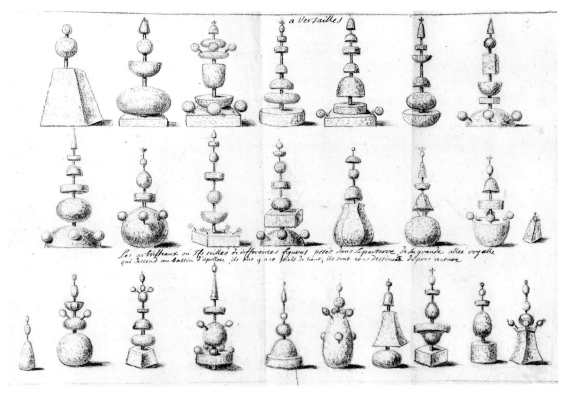

Opposite: Jean-Baptiste Martin's painting of Versailles, of 1688, showing the *bosquets* of the Arc de Triomphe and that of Trois Fontaines, both completed in 1677 is taken from a view to the north above the Bassin de Neptune and does not emphasize the architectural treatment of the trees. For laying out the *bosquets*, the *charmilles* were reinforced by a palisade of yews and box set back 3 metres/9 feet from the line of hornbeam; this, by leaving both vertical faces freestanding, facilitated clipping.

Seventeenth-century topiary patterns in the museum at Versailles bear a distinct resemblance to the original woodcuts used to show topiary framed by columns on the island of Cythera in the illustrations for the *Hypnerotomachia Poliphili*, first published in 1499 and translated into French in 1546 by Jean Martin – with rearrangements and insertions – as *Le Songe de Poliphile*. Many contemporary views of the gardens of Versailles reveal plants clipped into obelisks, pyramids, globes and more complicated fancy layered shapes.

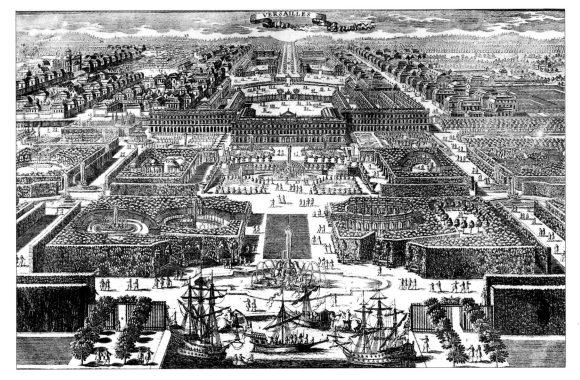

The view of Versailles by Aveline in 1710 shows the regular geometry in design and planting which called for a very high standard of execution and maintenance; trees had to be exactly in line, tall clipped hedges had to have smooth and sheer 'green' walls, and any irregularity in the laying out would be immediately noticed and not tolerated. In the illustration the palisades are of hornbeam and the main avenue trees, replaced by Lemoine in 1776 by horse-chestnuts, were probably elms or linden (lime). Directions to gardeners and bills for plants running into thousands of *livres* reveal the scale of planting operations and the work involved in the skilled trimming and cutting.

THE GRAND TRIANON

Set in a garden already completed in 1667, the Trianon de Porcelaine, its roof decorated with ceramic tiles, was built in 1671 for Madame de Montespan, the royal favourite; by 1687 it was destroyed to give place to the Trianon de Marbre – known as the Grand Trianon – around which gardens to the north were further developed. Already by 1671 there was an upper garden with elaborately scrolled cut box parterres in front of the pavilion; the lower four box-edged *compartiments* were hemmed in at the side by two decorative *berceaux* made in traditional trellis, probably with laths of painted European or sweet chestnut; orange trees and jasmine grew in the inner beds and were protected *in situ* by wooden frames in winter. In the same year 60 horse-chestnuts were planted in rows between the two *berceaux*, the first of these trees to be introduced into the royal gardens. Horse-chestnuts had been planted by Fouquet at Vaux-le-Vicomte and ten of these, together with 2,500 obtained elsewhere, were brought in the 1690s to implement a scheme to the north of the new Trianon de Marbre; a scheme later to be known as the Jardin des Marronniers.

At the Trianon de Porcelaine flowers were grown in pots in tiers to ornament the sloping banks which led down to the branch of the canal completed in 1679 and to the grand point of arrival for the king by boat. Among them were tender tuberoses which perfumed the garden air so strongly that on one occasion the king and court could not stay. By the 1680s plants would have been supplied, at least for the Trianon gardens, by the royal nurseries at La Roule, from where the new 'head gardener', Antoine Trumel, came in 1682, having previously worked at Vaux. The new garden, in which planting was recorded, was made to the north in the 1690s.

The painting by Jean Cotelle (*right*) shows the flower gardens of the Grand Trianon in the summer of 1693 with the planting as described in the plan shown here (*below left*). Although the king was insistent about having flowers in all his royal gardens, there is a ring of triumph in a note sent to William III of England in 1698 by Hans Willem Bentinck, Earl of Portland and ambassador to Louis XIV. As head steward of all William III's properties in Holland, he enjoyed criticizing the gardens of Versailles: 'Of all the thousands of flowers of which Your Majesty has heard so much, that the flower gardens were full of them at all seasons, I have not seen a single one, not even a snowdrop.' Plants specified for the scheme were planted in a quite firm design with symmetrical repetitions of the main blocks; each bed was surrounded with box. Tulips, white narcissi and hyacinths were the main spring bulbs; they were followed by double sweet rocket, large speedwells (*Veronica*), sweet william, 'Hiacinthes orangères' (?), cornflowers, pasque flowers, carnations from Spain, and violets. Larger perennials and later-flowering bulbs included campanula, large wallflowers, Greek valerian or Jacob's ladder (*Polemonium*) and white lilies.

A painting of the Grand Trianon by Jean Rigaud (*above left*), completed in 1738, shows that the gardens were still kept up, with tender trees and shrubs in tubs, possibly citrus fruit from the Orangerie. Perhaps the pots were among the 250,000 ordered for Versailles in 1686 and 1687. Jacques-François Blondel, the successor to Dezallier d'Argenville, described the Trianon as 'a happy invention and treated in the best manner'. He was replying to criticism from England that French gardening expressed too great a love of symmetry and ignored 'the genius of the place'.

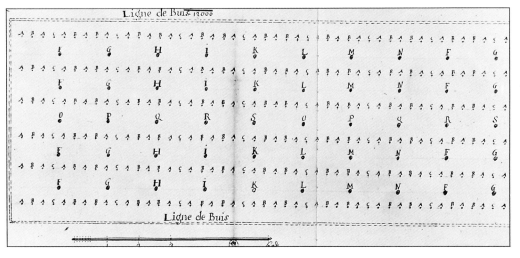

PLANTS IN THE MORIN NURSERY

Although Jean Robin's plant collection, made in the early years of the century, may have provided plants for the royal gardens, these were not always available to the public. René Morin (died *c.* 1657/8), the first in the family line of Parisian nurserymen, produced his *Catalogus plantarum horti Renati Morini*, one of the earliest trade lists, in 1621. In it were exotics from North America including the persimmon (*Diospyros virginiana*) and sumach (*Rhus typhina*). He had the new *Pelargonium triste* from the West Indies, which he gave to the Tradescants in 1631, and in 1633 he also gave them the 'great whyte Ranunculus' (*Ranunculus asiaticus*), a 'Duble Greene' anemone with a little leaf and other double anemones. Of course he specialized in 'new' bulbs – anemones, colchicums, crocuses, cyclamen, dog's-tooth violets', fritillaries and crown imperials, irises, lilies – as well as tulips. John Evelyn visited Pierre Morin's garden in April 1644, the day after he had admired the gardens at the Luxembourg Palace: 'I was had by a friend to Monsieur Morines garden; a person who from an ordinary Gardner, is arriv'd to be one of the most skilled & Curious Persons of France for his rare collection of Shells, Flowers & Insects: His garden is of an exact Oval figure planted with Cypresses, cutt flat & set as even as a Wall could have formed it: The Tulips, Anemones, Ranunculus's, Crocus's &c being of the most exquisite; were held for the rarest in the World, which constantly drew all the Virtuosi of that kind to his house, during the season; even persons of the most illustrious quality.' Pierre, married to a cousin of Guy de la Brosse, the director of the king's new Jardin du Roi, went on to write *Remarques necessaires pour la culture des fleurs* (Paris, 1658) as well as a catalogue of plants present in his garden in the 1650s. *Morina longifolia* from Nepal was named in his honour.

Clematis quinquefolia Americana siueFlos.
Passionis.
Clematitis d'Amerique à cinq feuilles ou Fleur de la Paſſion.

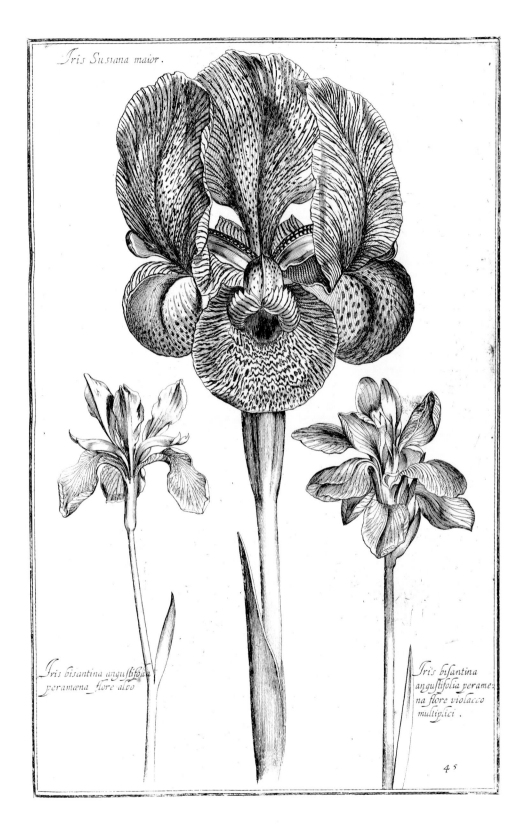

Iris Susiana maior.

Iris bisantina angustifolia peramœna flore albo

Iris bisantina angustifolia peramœna flore violaceo multiplici.

4⁵

In the first half of the seventeenth century many newly collected plants went first to the garden at Blois of Louis XIII's brother Gaston, Duc d'Orléans (who by the 1640s also owned the plant collections at the Luxembourg Palace noticed by John Evelyn). There they were portrayed in bloom in meticulous detail by artists such as Nicolas Robert (1614–85), who painted the sunflower (*Helianthus annuus*) shown above. Robert worked with watercolours on a special vellum prepared from calfskin; many of his works are found among *Les Velins du Roy* in the Musée National d'Histoire in Paris. The nurseryman Morin received the American yucca, the rare Jacobean lily (*Sprekelia formosissima*), the Persian lilac and the guelder rose or snowball tree (*Viburnum opulus* 'Sterile') in an exchange with the Tradescants.

Nicolas Robert's interest in scientific botanical illustration was fostered by the Scottish botanist Robert Morison, later to supervise the Oxford Botanic Garden. Robert worked for Louis XIV after the death of Gaston d'Orléans in 1660. The American passion flower (*far left*) was painted by Nicolas Robert life-size in 1676 for Dionys Dodart's *Mémoires pour servir à l'Histoire des Plantes*, published by the royal press. The original of the blue-flowered *Iris susiana* (*left*), painted by Daniel Rabel (1578–1637), the court painter, and published in his *Theatrum Florae* in 1624, is also in the Musée National d'Histoire Naturelle in Paris.

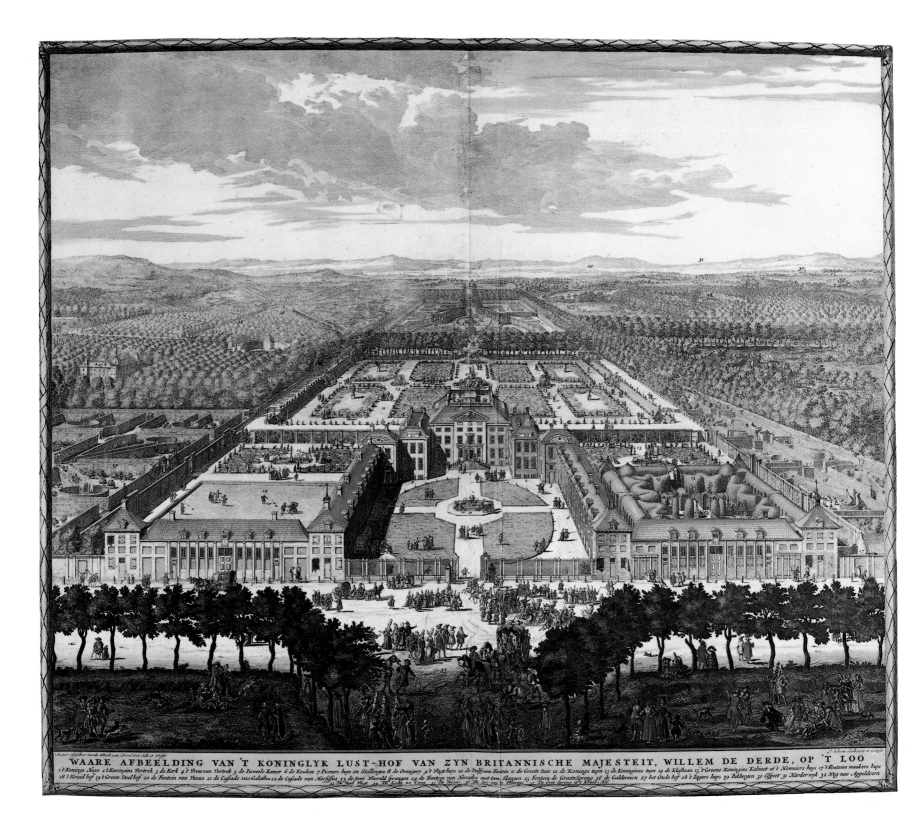

WAARE AFBEELDING VAN 'T KONINGLYK LUST-HOF VAN ZYN BRITANNISCHE MAJESTEIT, WILLEM DE DERDE, OP 'T LOO

THE FORMAL
GARDEN AT HET LOO

The baroque gardens at the palace of Het Loo in Holland were constructed for William of Orange (1650–1702) and Mary Stuart (1662–94) from 1685 to accompany the palatial hunting lodge built by the Dutch architect Jacob Roman (1640–1716) with decorations by the French Huguenot Daniel Marot.

By 1687 the Lower Garden, its size and site delineated by the transverse avenue of oaks to the north and the raised terraces surrounding it to the south, east and west, consisted of a lavish *salle de dehors* of eight square beds, of which the middle ones were elaborate *parterres de broderie* designed by Daniel Marot. The King's Garden to the west of the palace was in two sections; that nearest the palace was planted with clipped topiary box; two beds had plants and flowers as well as regularly placed pyramid-shaped junipers. The second part, a sunken mall, originally connected the garden

with a maze and menageries to the west. The Queen's Garden on the east side was also divided into two parts, with that to the north having three beds, two of which were surrounded by flower borders edged with clipped box and junipers. Exotic plants overwintered in hot-houses were an extra feature. The second part was raised and was mainly composed of trellised arbours of hornbeam with cut-out alcoves.

In the modern restoration Christmas roses, aquilegia, dittany, *Iris florentina*, Madonna lilies, peonies and *Malva moschata* are in the beds. Peaches, apricots and nectarines grow and ripen on the sunniest walls, while apples, crabs and pears occupy less favoured sites. In the King's Garden – the garden of William of Orange – there were always orange and blue flowers, like the tropaeolum, nigellas and pansies which grow in the garden today.

After 1689 the gardens were expanded to the north beyond the oak avenue, which remained as a colonnade between the two areas.

The coloured engraving of the palace of Het Loo (*opposite*) was published by Petrus Schenk (1660–1719) in about 1700 and shows the layout of the garden at the time the English physician Walter Harris described it. The engraving shows the forecourt and oak avenues at the front of the palace. The sunken garden and two side gardens – the King's Garden to the west and the Queen's to the east of the main axis – were destroyed by Louis Napoleon between 1807 and 1809.

In the restoration two main sources for contemporary seventeenth-century plants have been used: Jan van der Groen's *Den Nederlandtsen Hovenier* ('The Dutch Gardener') of 1669, and a manuscript held in Florence (Codex *Hortus Regius Honselaerdicensis*) in which plants grown in the orangery at Honselaarsdijk, during the time van der Groen was gardener there, are illustrated. The painting of nasturtiums (*Tropaeolum majus*) (*left*) from South America is from the Codex.

In the Lower Garden the intricate parterre patterns (*above*) in box and gravel have been authentically restored. In the flower-beds around the main parterres, plants, including bulbs, perennials and annuals, grow as single specimens for museum-like display between regularly spaced conifers – originally these were junipers (either *Juniperus communis* or *J.c. suecica*), not yews.

THE FRENCH INFLUENCE IN EUROPE

For the rest of the world Mollet's plans and Le Nôtre's Vaux-le-Vicomte and Versailles express the epitome of baroque 'Frenchness', an ordered style of planting and a control of natural plant shapes which was to be copied in suitable terrains by all the princes of Europe. In England under the Stuarts, particularly after the Restoration of Charles II, the French style predominated; it was extensively illustrated by the drawings and engravings of the Dutchmen Leonard

Knyff and Johannes Kip, which show regularity and order and avenues stretching across the countryside. In Holland, the style, adapted to the unforested canal-cut flat countryside and small estates, developed its own characteristics with views of distant avenue-lined prospects and in detail, more plants in pots, ornaments and topiary: in the more restricted spaces, features included mazes, arbours, hedges, *bosquets* and, when possible, avenues in a wood radiating from a central point. The elaborate decorative embroideries and flower-beds, laid out by the Huguenot refuge Daniel Marot (1671–1752) under William of Orange, were essentially French in origin. Earlier in the century

parterre patterns had been lifted wholesale from French gardens for adaptation in the smaller Dutch layouts, which although enclosed by hedges and moats, had already developed with symmetrical divisions placed on a central axis.

Dezallier d'Argenville's *La Théorie et la Pratique du jardinage* was soon translated into other languages (a German edition came out in 1731), and remained an important gardening text throughout Europe until the fashion for the English landscape became a popular novelty. On the Continent the French 'idea', modified by other influences already received from Italy or Holland, was interpreted to suit national characteristics. Much of all of this

At Fertőd in Hungary, formerly the palace of the Esterházy family, the 1760 garden design rivalled that of Versailles in its conception of linear perspective. This eighteenth-century plan shows three linden (lime) avenues, flanked by hedges of box, radiating out from the façade of the palace, stretching beyond *parterres de broderie* and water basins deep into the surrounding forests.

At Herrenhausen near Hanover the engraving of *c.* 1720 shows the Garden Theatre with trees rising above the tightly clipped hedges as suggested by both the Mollets and by Dezallier d'Argenville. Small clipped pyramids are of yew. After 1750 the garden developed as a botanical collection. Restorations of the garden, carried out after 1945, have retained the original baroque outlines of the box patterns and reinstated original plantings.

La Granja, built for Louis XIV's grandson Philip V in the 1720s, is on a precipitous slope near Segovia. It was described by Lady Holland when she visited in 1811: 'The gardens are reckoned among the finest in Europe; they are in the old French style of high clipped hedges, *salons de verdures*, alleys etc: that is the style I prefer beyond any other.' There were eight radiating avenues; lime trees brought from Holland, chestnuts, hornbeams and yews from France, all of which had to be planted in specially prepared pockets excavated with gunpowder.

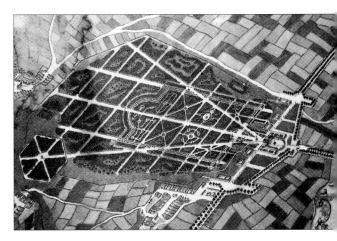

grandeur was swept away during the eighteenth and nineteenth centuries when newly discovered trees and shrubs were given space to develop as specimens. English-style landscape parks were readily adaptable to house tree and shrub collections, in which the plants, previously clipped into stylized shapes, were allowed to grow with freedom.

Above left: The gardens of the Palace of Schönbrunn in Vienna as painted by Bellotto *c.* 1750 show all the characteristics of French planting style, with parterres, trees in vases and slim-line topiary. Laid out for Franz I, by J. B. Fischer von Erlach after the Turkish defeat of 1699 the gardens were intended to imitate Versailles, with *parterres de broderie* designed by a Frenchman, Jean Trehet.

Above: The garden made at the Palace of Fronteira at Benfica in Lisbon in about 1668, dominated by the glowing blue-greens of the *azulejo* tiles, has parterres of intricate geometry based on the drawings of J. A. du Cerceau published in 1576. In J. Pillement's illustration of 1785, in which tree-covered archways frame the receding view, raised beds overflow with flowers.

Right: At Hampton Court the *patte d'oie* of radiating linden (lime) trees – imported from Holland – was introduced by Charles II after the Restoration in 1660. By 1662 Evelyn visited to admire the 'sweet rows of lime trees, and the canal water now nearly perfected'. But the most important period in the history of the gardens was during the reign of William III who, after 1689, imported a new French–Dutch style of intricate box-scrolled parterres, probably designed by Daniel Marot, to fill in the semi-circle of the goose's foot. Yew trees trimmed as obelisks, and 'white hollies' – presumably silver-variegated varieties – were trained as globes to edge the beds. Leonard Knyff's painting dates from the reign of George I.

CHAPTER SEVEN

THE EIGHTEENTH~CENTURY ENGLISH LANDSCAPE

By the end of the eighteenth century the English landscape or 'natural style' was to mature and spread its influence as far as the ordered perspectives of Le Nôtre's Versailles had reached in the preceding hundred years. In the 1770s the English landscape park was introduced to Russia: as Catherine the Great said, 'I passionately love gardens in the English style, the curved lines, the gentle slopes, the ponds pretending to be lakes . . . and I deeply disdain straight lines . . . I should say my anglomania gets the better of planimetry.'[1] Yet in England the early years of the century seemed remarkably inauspicious and still firmly geared to French formality. Kip and Knyff in *Britannia Illustrata*, published between 1707 and 1715, show English estates wearing a distinctly French look, with avenues reaching unhindered into the open countryside and parterres and wildernesses stocked with clipped and regimented trees and flowers – probably provided by the Brompton Park Nursery. A few estates, influenced by Dutch William, have more complex topiary and 'greens' in tubs as well as canal systems lined with hedges, lifted seemingly straight from the flat dyke-lands of Holland – demonstrated today by the restoration at Westbury Court in Gloucestershire, with its finials and spirals of individual hollies and yews rising above hedge-lines as extra 'Dutch' decoration. In all, as Pope wrote later to Lord Burlington:

'Grove nods at grove, each alley has a brother,
And half the Platform just reflects the other.'[2]

Changes were, however, already in train. Batty Langley (1696–1751) wrote in the introduction to *New Principles of Gardening* in 1728: 'Nor is there anything more shocking than a stiff regular garden; where after we have seen one quarter thereof, the very same is repeated in all the remaining parts' which are 'fluffed up with trifling flower Knots, parterres of Cut-work, Embroidery, Wildernesses of Ever-Greens and sometimes of Forest Trees.' The subtitle to his book – *The Laying Out and Planting Parterres, Groves, Wildernesses, Labyrinths, Avenues, Parks & After a more Grand and Rural Manner, than has been done before* – nevertheless reveals that, at first, the novel cult of an irregular style of gardening still presupposed a formal framework; it was only the 'infilling' which was irregular in detail. Serpentine and meandering paths, 'green openings like meadows' and less regularly shaped 'groves' and shrubberies (in which flowers were also found) began to take the place of the stereotyped wildernesses; they were no longer to be planted like orchards, 'with their trees in straight lines ranging every way, but in a rural manner, as if they had receiv'd their situation from nature itself'.

Rather than being clipped into regimented shapes, trees 'that cause fine shade such as planes, English elm, horse-chestnut and lime instead of regular yews and holly' were encouraged. Addison had already complained in 1712 of the contemporary fashions in tree-clipping: 'for my own part I would rather look upon a Tree in all its Luxuriancy and Diffusion of Boughs and Branches, than when it is thus cut and trimmed into a mathematical Figure: and cannot but fancy that an orchard in Flower looks infinitely more

The painting completed in 1799/1800 by Johann Erdmann Hummel shows some of the exotic-looking planting in the romantic landscape park at Wilhelmshöhe near Kassel, completed after 1785 by Wilhelm IX and the architect Heinrich Christian Jussow, an enthusiastic follower of 'Capability' Brown. The park extended the original baroque garden of 1700, with its grand cascade modelled on the Villa Aldobrandini, and in part replaced the episodic rococo *anglochinois* layout of the 1760s and '70s, attempted by Landgrave Friedrich II (married to Mary, daughter of the Hanoverian George II of England) and his gardener Daniel Schwarzkopf, a former pupil of Philip Miller.

delightful, than all the little labyrinths of the most finished Parter-res.' In fact, as Mark Laird has pointed out,[3] in spite of both Addison's and Langley's appreciation of nature, trees in the early eighteenth century were often planted as standards with trunks cleared of branches up to 6 or 9 metres/20 or 30 feet, to resemble architectural columns – Thomas Whately in 1770 called them 'poles'. They thus continued to give a 'formal' air to irregularly shaped groves. Only the more 'picturesque' taste developing towards the end of the century encouraged 'crooked' and gnarled specimens resembling those found in unimproved natural circum-stances, the method and style of planting and type of tree chosen very much affecting 'mood'. A mature chestnut implied a savage grandeur reminiscent of Salvator Rosa's paintings; a cypress was still given funereal associations as well as reminding travellers of the eighteenth-century grand tour of Italy. By the early nineteenth century Repton was even encouraging planting more than one tree in each hole to simulate native multi-stemmed birch and alder, and his theories of complementing architecture with suitable trees is well known.

But to return to the early years of the eighteenth century. Alexander Pope was already satirizing excessive artificiality in his 'Catalogue of Greens to be disposed of by an eminent Town Gardener', written in the *Guardian* in 1713. There were 'Adam and Eve in Yew; Adam a little shatter'd by the fall of the Tree of Knowledge in the great storm . . . St George in Box; his arm scarce long enough, but will be in a Condition to stick the Dragon by next April . . . A pair of Giants, stunted, to be sold cheap . . . a Quick-set Hog shot up into a Porcupine, by its being forgot one Week in rainy weather . . . Noah's Ark in Holly . . . the ribs a little damaged for want of Water'. Yet Pope's own garden at Twicken-ham, where Langley was a close neighbour, retained elements of formality in spite of his friendship with Charles Bridgeman and William Kent and his own written incentives to changing garden taste. Although woods crammed with pools, temples, and statues, all with literary allusions, were also labyrinthine, with winding walks in the new landscape style, the garden was still dominated by an axial alignment centred around an open glade, the Bowling Alley. The layout bore a strong resemblance to Robert Castell's imaginative reconstruction of Pliny the Younger's first-century villa garden at Tusci, drawn for *Villas of the Ancients* in 1728, in which Castell, reflecting elements of his own contemporary

fashion, portrayed 'naturalism' in the garden areas flanking the central 'hippodrome'.

A NEW IRREGULARITY

Ideas on beautifying rural estates had been propounded earlier by Joseph Addison. In the *Spectator* of 1712 he suggested that parks and all rural scenery could be successfully integrated (this was topical at a time when landlords were concerned with enclosures and agricultural improvement): 'Why may not a whole estate be thrown into a kind of garden by frequent plantations, that may turn as much to profit, as the pleasure of the owner? . . . if the natural embroidery of the meadows were helped and improved by some small additions of Art, and the several rows of hedges set off by trees and flowers, that the soil might be capable of, a man might make a pretty landskip of his own possessions.' In this he perhaps anticipated Southcote's *ferme ornée* of the 1730s, in combining functional use with beauty of trees, flowers and hedgerow walks.

But even Addison and Pope were not the first to describe the possibilities of natural or irregular gardens. If Sir William Temple's *Sharawadgi*, in his *Garden of Epicurus* (published 1692) dealt more with winding paths and wild, shady gardens adorned with rough rock work than with plants, Timothy Nourse in *Campania Foelix* (1700) was explicit about planting naturalism in the third of his series of terraced gardens. There the evergreens were to be planted 'in some negligent Order' and 'up and down let there be little Banks or Hillocks, planted with wild Thyme, Violets, Primroses, Cowslips, Daffadille, Lillies of the Valley, Blew-Bottles [*Centaurea cyanus*], Daisies, with all kinds of Flowers which grow wild in the Fields and Woods . . . in a word let this be . . . a real wilderness or Thicket . . . to represent a perpetual Spring.' It all sounds remark-ably like some of Joseph Spence's mid-eighteenth-century planting schemes, and the 'real wilderness' bears no relation to Le Nôtre's ordered alleys.

Stephen Switzer (1682–1745) in 1718, in *Ichnographia Rustica*, and Batty Langley in 1728 were recommending an 'irregularity' in garden layouts. They were the theorists of the 'new' style pro-pounded by satirists such as Addison and Pope, while practitioners – led by Charles Bridgeman (d. 1738) and William Kent (*c.* 1685–1748) in the 1720s and '30s as well as 'amateur' estate owners – executed more relaxed designs in which geometry, both

In 1728 *The New Principles of Gardening* by Batty Langley, a neighbour of Alexander Pope's, provided readers with an alternative to strict French practice, signalling a departure from 'mirror-image' gardening to a more natural approach. In fact, although deploring 'a stiff regular garden . . . fluffed up with trifling flower Knots', Langley's informality in design extended only to the introduction of serpentine and sometimes meandering paths inside a structured frame, although he did recommend that beyond the hedge lines several 'Kinds of Jessemines and Honeysuckles' should be encouraged to twine about other shrubs 'in a wild and rural manner'.

needed no longer to plant in regimented standard patterns but introduced informally planted woodland groves where specimens could develop into natural shapes. They also re-introduced the time element into gardening, it being necessary to wait many years before knowing how the new plants would 'do' – a time span extending over more than two centuries as today we assess some of Brown's mid-century planting.

Charles Bridgeman had been, like Switzer, a pupil of London and Wise at the Brompton Park Nursery and was the immediate inheritor of their controlled style. Horace Walpole, looking back from the middle of the century, nevertheless credited Bridgeman with 'many detached thoughts that strongly indicate the dawn of modern taste'. His chief contribution to the development of the landscape style was the use of the 'simple enchantment' of the ha-ha, or sunken boundary wall, laying open to the garden unimpeded views into the gentle English countryside. Thus both he and William Kent are credited with a share in the popularization of this hidden 'fence', of which Langley also approved as allowing views as 'extensive as possible into a landscape'. In fact it was Kent who imposed the new irregularity, often as an overlay on traditional formal plans originated by Bridgeman, in somewhat modified form anticipating Lancelot Brown's mid-century landscape which transformed English parkland. Kent, a painter by training, reduced the regularity of Bridgeman's axial plans at Stowe, Claremont and Rousham, by deftly softening the linear approach, thinning back the edges of thick woods and opening views. As Horace Walpole wrote between 1750 and 1770 in his essay 'On Modern Gardening' published in 1770: 'He leaped the fence, and saw all nature was a garden.' To get his effects Kent used his painter's eye to create three-dimensional pictures with contrasts of light and shade; he liked to lay out gardens without assistance of line or level, using unmethodical but effective means described by Joseph Spence: 'Mr Kent always used to stake out his grovettes before planting, and to view the askews everyway to make sure that no three were in a straight line.'[4] In fact Kent, although even recommending enlivening the evergreen screens at Rousham with flowery underplantings, had as little interest in individual trees or flowers as had Lancelot Brown in his later park planting; plants were merely tools of the trade which, like a painter's pigments, would give shape and colouring to a composition, and these visual values mattered more than rarity or specific genera to the land-

in layout and in plant clipping, was gradually abandoned in favour of natural contours and free-growing untortured shapes. On estates such as Thorndon, Whitton, Goodwood and Painshill, owners, stimulated by plant introductions and seeking to establish their patterns of hardiness and acclimatization to English soil,

scapist. Instead of harsh outlines of clipped trees, smooth-sided hedges, straight alleys and parterres, there were soft tree plantings in all their 'luxuriance' of growth, as if in a painting by Claude. Avenues gave way to clumps, solid woods gradually dissolved into open sunlit glades carpeted with undulating lawn, all of which merged together as one landscape with curving paths inviting exploration as they revealed passing views. At Chiswick, for his patron Lord Burlington, Kent's irregular style was superimposed on the radiating *patte d'oie* of tightly trimmed hedged alleys, each focusing on a garden building, reflecting earlier modes.

Between 1753 and 1777 Copleston Warre Bampfylde painted various water-colours of the Stourhead gardens; these still hang in the library at Stourhead next to copies of Virgil and Horace, whose works may have inspired Henry Hoare in his creation of the garden from 1745. The view of the Pantheon (*above*) seen beyond the Palladian bridge and the Temple of Apollo, its slopes almost bare of planting in 1775, was described by Horace Walpole as 'one of the most picturesque scenes in the world'. Much of the intensive tree planting was underplanted with cherry laurel (*Prunus laurocerasus*), already becoming an important ingredient and cohesive feature of eighteenth-century woodland.

Many of the trees for laying out the park at Stowe (*left*) were obtained locally. Sixty to seventy thousand trees were obtained as 'sets', grown from seed or literally gathered as suckers from the woods and hedgerows. In 1722 4,500 privet and 1,200 field maple together cost £1 0s. 7d. Most seeds were grown in the estate nursery, but two and a half hogsheads of acorns of evergreen oak were sent from Minorca in 1723. Larger trees had to be bought and a Mr Parker provided 37 cartloads of yew in the autumn of 1723, with sycamores, Scots pines and elms. For the more regular avenues and quincunxes of elms, horse-chestnuts, silver firs and linden (limes), trees of uniform height were essential and cost more – £10 for 400 Dutch elms during 1721/2. The painting by Jean Rigaud shows the Queen's theatre from the Rotunda.

At Claremont Kent introduced irregularity in form and plant-ing, using groups of beeches to blur Bridgeman's formal lines; at Stowe Kent followed Bridgeman to plant groves of trees in naturalistic style on the valley slopes, thinning out foreground woods; later, after 1742, during Brown's time, more beech, elm

and Scots pine as well as exotics such as cedars, and the American *Taxodium distichum* and *Robinia pseudoacacia* were introduced.[5]

Other landscapes with Arcadian evocations of Elysium followed on from Kent. Studley Royal in Yorkshire, Painshill in Surrey and Stourhead in Wiltshire were all planned and executed by the owners. Perhaps none of this would have been acceptable without an alteration in attitude to nature, anticipating Rousseau-like romanticism; in the eighteenth century it was seen that by taming nature to be 'improved' for man's delight, man also achieved a new liberty of thought and conscience. The effect of the garden view on man's mood – nature improved and made pleasing to the eye could generate distinct feelings and sensations – became a further ingredient of landscaping. Gaiety, grandeur, tranquillity and, above all, melancholy and 'sublimity' were all to be evoked by various devices such as breaking the lawn's edge with clumps of trees and turning straight canals into winding streams or placid lakes.

THE NEW NURSERY TRADE

All these ideas were given incentive by the arrival of plants in greater and greater numbers, all waiting to be assessed, categorized and cultivated in 'natural' ways. Pope's 'Catalogue of Greens' seems a world apart from the serious nurseryman and plant collector Thomas Fairchild, whose *The City Gardener* (1722) advised quite another sort of town gardening and opened visions to the scientific world of botany, plant collecting and cultivation.

From the early years of the century many plants were first introduced or first cultivated by nurserymen. The nursery at Brompton Park declined after 1714 but others developed in its stead. The fifteen or so London nurseries existing in 1700 had increased to almost double by 1730, with regional nurseries being established throughout the country by 1800. The nurseries met the expanding demand for 'different' trees, a demand accelerated by the gradually changing fashion towards the new irregularity in garden design. Whereas a formal layout required huge numbers of standardized trees and hedge shrubs, often already trained into prescribed shapes, the evolving landscape style could incorporate more specimen and naturally grown trees. In 1728 Batty Langley warned against the 'nurseryman who for his own interest advises . . . such forms and trees as will make the greatest Draught out of his Nursery, without regard to anything more'. This may be seen as a condemnation of the Brompton Park-style nursery which excelled in providing clipped and trained trees and shrubs as essential ingredients of garden artistry. In fact friction between designer and nurseryman was a common problem. In the 1730s Stephen Switzer wrote angrily to his client Henry Ellison about the nurseryman Henry Woodham, respected in London and one of the subscribers to Miller's *Gardeners Dictionary*, whom he accused of cheating Ellison by striking some sort of bargain with the latter's steward; Switzer complained that the plants 'were all pretty small tho: I daresay the price will be large enough'.[6]

Robert Furber (1674–1756), nurseryman in Kensington Gore from about 1700, is celebrated for the series of plates entitled *Twelve Months of Flowers* and *Twelve Plates of Fruit* which he issued in the form of nursery catalogues between 1730 and 1732. Each month of the year was illustrated by an appropriate arrangement, with individual flowers numbered to a corresponding key so that customers could make an order. Furber's nursery was the first known source for a moss rose. The originals, painted by Peter Casteels, were engraved by Henry Fletcher and others, and hand coloured later.

The new nurserymen who especially featured the specimen trees and shrubs lately introduced from foreign parts seem to have been as much interested in growing (usually from seed) and acclimatization as in selling. The specialists in exotics, both for open ground and for heated houses or 'stoves', were influential in encouraging experimental planting in large estates as well as in smaller city and country gardens. By listing plants available to

In 1771 George III appointed Sir Joseph Banks, scientific patron and plant collector, as unofficial director of the gardens at Kew – later to become the Royal Botanic Gardens – developed by the Dowager Princess of Wales on some 4 hectares/9 acres of sand and gravel near the Thames. From the time of Banks's appointment, plant hunters were given special assignments abroad. Few plants found on Banks's own voyage with Captain Cook to Australia (1768/71) could thrive in the English climate – except in subtropical gardens such as Tresco Abbey in the Scilly Isles – but the Australian honeysuckle, forms of the genus *Banksia*, have since flourished in gardens in Florida and other suitable regions. *Banksia integrifolia* was painted by Sydney Parkinson during the voyage.

would-be gardeners, the *Catalogus Plantarum* published by the Society of Gardeners in 1730 (guided by Philip Miller) gave an impetus to experimental planting (see pp. 206–7). From the early years of the century the lists of trees, shrubs and flowers offered from North America alone make exciting reading. Christopher

Gray's bilingual catalogue of 1737, compiled to sell American plants found by Mark Catesby on his travels, was aimed at customers in France and the rest of Europe, as well as in England. Peter Collinson's introductions from John Bartram in Philadelphia, over a thirty-year period from the 1730s, were offered to good nurseries as soon as possible; sometimes Collinson even used nurserymen to germinate the seeds. He found that James Gordon (*c.* 1708–80) of the Mile End Nursery was adept at germinating difficult ones such as 'the dusty seeds of Kalmia's, Rhododendrons, or Azalea's from North America' and *Arbutus andrachne*, sent from the slopes above Aleppo, which flowered in Fothergill's garden in 1765. The famous Lee and Kennedy Vineyard Nursery at Hammersmith, developed after 1745, was by 1760 using Linnaeus's new binomial system for naming plants. By the end of the century more plants flooding in from oriental trading posts in India and the Far East (particularly those of the East India Company), from South Africa and South America led to an expanding nursery trade throughout the country. Aiton's *Hortus Kewensis* of 1789 gave brief descriptions not only of plants actually being grown at Kew at the time but also of almost all the species then being cultivated in England, while the *Botanical Magazine* founded by William Curtis in 1787 recorded and published drawings of flowers from all the most prominent nurserymen around the country who were able to offer the rarities.

In the 1770s plants from Australia began to appear. Although most of the thousand or so new plants discovered by Joseph Banks on Cook's voyage with the *Endeavour* between 1768 and 1771 were introduced to Europe as dried specimens, some seeds survived the journey. The first New Zealand and Australian plants were offered by nurseries soon after; these included *Sophora microphylla* as well as *Leptospermum scoparium* (1772) and *L. lanigerum* (1774) at Malcolm's nursery. In practice many of the Australasian plants proved to survive only in areas with a comparable climate, such as California, parts of South Africa, and Mediterranean regions; plants from the windswept South Island in New Zealand and from Tasmania had a wider range of viability.

During the last quarter of the eighteenth century and until his death the wealthy Sir Joseph Banks (1743–1820), a brilliant man who became President of the Royal Society and *ex officio* director of Kew Gardens (later to become the Royal Botanic Gardens) under George III, proved an influential patron to gardeners, plant collectors and the expanding science of botany. In 1804 Banks was one of seven men who met at John Hatchard's book shop in Piccadilly to found what is now the Royal Horticultural Society. He himself accompanied the *Endeavour* round the world in 1768–71, bringing back the first callistemons from Australia and the parrot's bill (*Clianthus puniceus*) from New Zealand. Later *Banksia*, a genus of tender plants from the same family as the African proteas, and found only in Australia, was named in his honour.

Fortunately records survive of the experimental tree and shrub planting carried out at many large estates in the first half of the eighteenth century. One of Peter Collinson's most enthusiastic friends was young Lord Petre, who laid out extensive gardens and stoves at Thorndon Hall in Essex as well as elsewhere (see pp. 208–9). His plans for Thorndon, executed after 1732 but not completed before his premature death from smallpox in 1742, show an intermediate style between regularity and the natural landscaping which developed as the century proceeded. Notes of Lord Petre's planting were made by Collinson and early editions of Miller's *Dictionary* include comments on it. Miller also prepared a catalogue of the contents of the garden in 1736. The first major planting at Thorndon was an avenue of elms, transplanted when already 15 to 20 years old and some 12–18 metres/40–60 feet tall, and 'each requiring 20 strong horses to draw them'. In the Octagon Plantation Petre grew the American plants received as seed from Bartram through Collinson, germinated and grown in the extensive nurseries. In 1740–2 more than 60,000 trees were planted, among which were cedars, larch, pines, Swedish junipers and silver firs, as well as cherry laurels, both Spanish and horse-chestnuts, Dutch elms and many others. Collinson made notes (in his own copy of Evelyn's *Sylva*) of the trees planted at the Upper End of the Park and on the two mounts by May 1740. In a letter to Bartram he mentioned that 10,000 'Americans' were included. Among these were 70 'pensilvania Cherrys', 107 black walnuts,

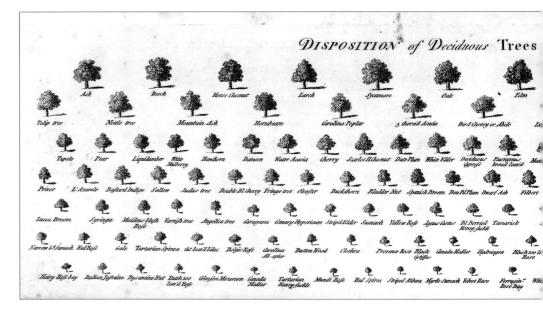

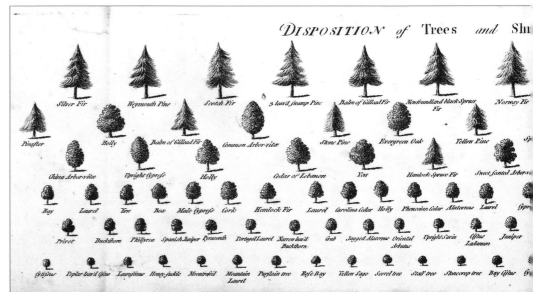

109 cockspur thorns (his name for *Crataegus crus-galli*), 69 tulip trees, 76 Virginian flowering maples, 59 Virginia acacias (his name for *Gleditsia triacanthos* the honey locust), 230 Carolina oaks, 124 occidental planes, 10 balsam fir or balm of Gilead (*Abies balsamea*) and altogether over 1,000 red cedars (*Juniperus virginiana*).

After Lord Petre's death the Duke of Bedford employed Philip Miller to value the thousands of trees and to purchase those suitable for planting at Woburn. In 1737 the duke had agreed to

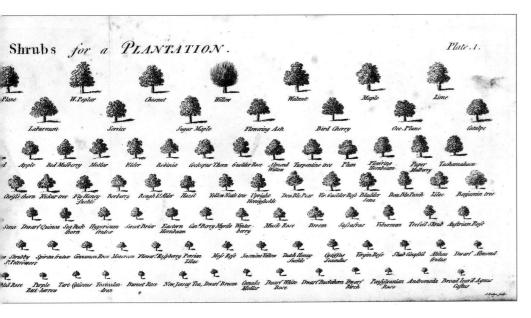

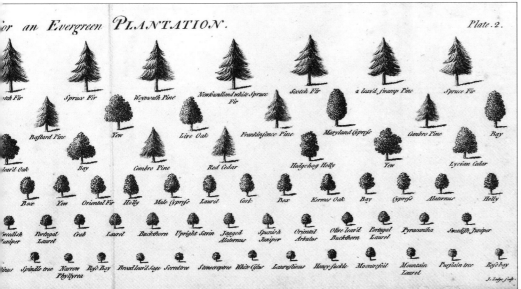

Before 1779 James Meader was gardener to the Duke of Northumberland at Syon House near Kew, where the tree collection was already well established (William Turner first planted there in the sixteenth century for Protector Somerset), until he left England to work for Catherine the Great at the Peterhof Palace near St Petersburg. Meader's *The Planter's Guide* was published in 1779. Plate I shows the disposition of deciduous trees and shrubs for a plantation; Plate 2 shows the disposition of evergreens. Meader advised planting to avoid an 'improper mixture' so that trees 'would be covered with verdure down to the very front, in an easy theatrical manner, and in summer scarce a stem visible'.

pay Miller '20 guineas a year for inspecting my Gardens, hot house, pruning the Trees, etc and to come to Woburn at least twice a year, and oftner if wanted.' His tasks included advising the duke's agent about putting up a moveable roof over the orange trees each autumn. The duke had a special interest in American evergreens, which grew well in his acid soil. Many of these, among which were the balsam fir – 'the only place they have made any figure is at Woburn' – and the Virginian pitch pine (*Pinus rigida*, 1739), were grown from Bartram's seed (although the former had already been in Bishop Compton's Fulham garden in 1686).

At Goodwood the second and third Dukes of Richmond were both avid collectors, using a copy of the third edition of Philip Miller's *Gardeners Dictionary* (see pp. 210–11) for noting planting dates. Among new American trees grown by the second duke (1701–50) – until they were killed in the cold winter of 1740 – were the frost-susceptible cedar of Goa *Cupressus lusitanicus* from Mexico and the evergreen *Magnolia grandiflora*. They may have been in his collection of evergreens on the Bowling Green or in the Arbor-Vitae Grove with the tender American live oak (*Quercus virginiana*). At Longleat Lord Weymouth planted such a vast number of the American white pine (*Pinus strobus*) that to this day it is called the Weymouth pine. Acclimatization problems and suitability of soil made all the 'new' planting hazardous and pleasure grounds were backed by private nurseries where trees and shrubs grown from seed led protected lives. Peter Collinson wrote of 1,000 five-year-old cedars of Lebanon (bought for a total of £79 1*s*.) planted in the park to be part of the evergreen wood with which the duke wished to clothe 'the naked hills' at Goodwood. Plants from north-east America, accustomed to much hotter summers and colder winters, and mostly calcifuge, were particularly hard to establish; by the end of the century designers such as Humphry Repton were making areas for special 'American Gardens', with bog-like conditions and acid soil provided, which became fashionable adjuncts to landscape parks.

In 1738–73 the Hon. Charles Hamilton created the landscape gardens at Painshill in Surrey – 'a fine place out of a cursed hill', according to Horace Walpole in 1748 – which today are in the process of restoration (see pp. 212–23). Both natural and picturesque in style, the gardens are centred round a lake; classical buildings invoke the literary spirit of Rome. Already aware of the evolution of Kent's more 'natural' style, which he had encountered at Chiswick and at Rousham, Hamilton studied paintings by Claude, Poussin and Salvator Rosa and sought to capture their image in his three-dimensional landscape. Thomas Whately described the richness of the planting in 1770: 'the thickets are of flowering shrubs; and the openings are embellished with little airy groupes of the most elegant trees, skirting or crossing the glades.' Many others testified to the beauty of the garden. The cedars of Lebanon which still remain are close cousins to those supplied for Goodwood and Whitton. Through Peter Collinson's agency Hamilton obtained many of his American seeds from John Bartram. Painshill was owned by Benjamin Bond Hopkins between 1773 and 1794, during which period he did a substantial amount of new planting including horse-chestnuts, cedars and copper beech (only just available from Europe) on the slopes below the house and south of the lake. He supplemented Hamilton's lime trees with planes, beech and oak, possibly adding newly introduced pines such as the Labrador or Jack pine (*Pinus banksiana*) and *P. nigra caramanica* to the conifer collection, respectively introduced in 1785 and 1790.

Although no actual lists survive of Hamilton's planting, his correspondence with the Abbé Nolin in Paris in 1755 reveals plants which were being grown. The Abbé was adviser to Louis XV and Louis XVI and inspector of the royal nurseries; like Hamilton, he was an avid collector, particularly of the American species, for which he established a commercial nursery in Paris. In 1756 Hamilton, who had his own nursery for growing on trees for Painshill, sent him seeds reminding him that some would not come up until the third year: '20 pinasters . . . 6 Weymouth pine, 6 balm of Gilead, 6 frankincense pine [the loblolly pine – *Pinus taeda*], 2 two-leaved American pine [*P. echinata*], 6 American spruce fir [*Picea glauca*], 20 red spruce [*P. rubens*], 6 white cedar or arbor-vitae [*Thuja occidentalis*], 3 China arbor-vitae [*T. orientalis*], 6 Virginia cedar [*Juniperus virginiana*], 6 wax candleberry myrtles [*Myrica cerifera*].' All these plants mentioned were growing at Painshill as well

as other American natives: robinias, andromedas, loblolly bay (*Gordonia lasianthus*), evening trumpet flower or *Bignonia capreolata*, Carolina yellow jessamine (*Gelsemium sempervirens*), rhododendrons and kalmias, clethra, liquidambar, willow-leaved oak (*Quercus phellos*), the Indian bean tree (*Catalpa bignonioides*), several forms of sumach, liriodendron and Carolina allspice (*Calycanthus floridus*).

SHRUBBERIES AND FLOWERS

Nor, in spite of the development of the new landscape style, were flowers neglected. Flowering shrubs, including many of the exciting new 'Americans', were used to introduce a 'wilder' note to what had been formal French-style wildernesses in which winding paths now replaced straight alignments. It is difficult to be quite certain at which period the shrubbery emerged as a planting style distinct from the more orderly wilderness of the French taste: William Shenstone's planting at the Leasowes in 1748 is the first known mention of a shrubbery. There was probably a quite gradual progression to more natural planting. 'At all the intersections of your walks should be made a fountain, or a little garden . . . these gardens will look as well a mile or two off, as just by the house,' wrote Stephen Switzer in 1715; 'such Gentlemen, as find little Hedge-rows, Coppices and lawns, mix'd one amongst another by nature; for there they may easily cut a Walk, of about six or eight Feet wide . . . and these Hedge-rows being mix'd with Primroses, Violets, and such natural, sweet and pleasant Flowers; the Walks that lead through afford as much Pleasure as . . . the most elaborate fine Garden.'[7] In 1728 Langley went further, saying that shady walks near the house should include 'groves planted with sweet brier, white jasmine, honeysuckle, environ'd at Bottom with a small Circle of Dwarf Stock, Candy-turf and Pinks', all to be arranged in graduated heights from front to back. Philip Miller, extending the theme in his *Dictionary* in 1731, specified similar planting to replace the firm hedge-line required to contain the formal wilderness areas of the earlier period. In the outer garden Miller advised that flowers, such as primroses, violets, daffodils and 'many other Sorts of Wood flowers' should be planted 'not in a strait line but rather to appear accidental as in a natural wood', and should be 'backed' by rows of flowering shrubs such as philadelphus, cytisus, lavatera, daphnes and in successive height 'laburnum, lilacs, water-elder or guelder roses, and other flowering shrubs of large growth . . . back'd with many sorts of trees'.

We are already far away from the Brompton Park Nursery's interpretation of a wilderness, although Miller at first continued to recommend keeping evergreen and deciduous shrubs in separate groves, later modifying this to separate parts of a plantation. In a later edition of his *Dictionary*, Miller explicitly mentioned 'Gardeners . . . making borders along the sidewalks for their choicest flowers', and again: 'where flowers are desired, there may be borders continued round the extent of the lawn, immediately before the plantation of shrubs, which if properly planted with hardy flowers to succeed each other will afford a more pleasing prospect.' Although written in the middle of the century, this seems to be more in the spirit of self-conscious flower-gardening such as that realized at Nuneham in the 1770s and Repton's 'separate' flower-garden spaces a little later, both anticipating nineteenth-century styles. At the same time Miller's evergreen plantations are both reminiscent of Evelyn's planting and a foretaste of the gloomy Victorian shrubbery. This tradition of keeping evergreens separate was obviously not universal; as early as 1750 the planting at Rousham was enlivened by roses growing out of laurels, syringas (*Philadelphus*) out of holly, a lilac out of a yew, so that 'every leafe of the Evergreens, produced one flower or another',[8] a descriptive passage enlarged upon as late as 1823 by Henry Phillips in his *Sylva Florifera* 1823.

Joseph Spence (1699–1768), designing in about 1736–66, mainly with smaller layouts and *always* a strong advocate for flowers, recommended quite familiar plants for borders: 'stocks, double and single pinks, pheasant eyes and double rocket, Sweet Williams, Fetherfew, Roses, India pinks of different colours, honeysuckles, larkspur, some asters, some auriculas good, carnations ditto, some nasturtiums'. In his shrubbery planting he was hardly more adventurous, seldom recommending any of the recently introduced exotics. For a client he planted thickly near the house with 'the lowest and best evergreens, laburnums, 3 sorts of lilac, water-elder or guelder roses, double-blossom peach and cherry trees, intermix't, mountain ash, laurustinus, arbutus, Portugal laurels, cytisus, Phillyreas, and the furthest part with acacias, larches, almond trees, wild cherries, Weymouth, Scotch, silver and spruce firs . . . the best and lowest things should be scattered near the margins, the most pleasing wild flowers to be supplied

Napoleon's sister Elisa Baciocchi was anxious to convert the elegant seventeenth-century garden of her summer residence, the Villa Marlia, into a *giardino pittoresco* in imitation of the park at Malmaison: she sought advice from Josephine's designer, Louis Berthault. Weeping willows, acacias, ginkgos as well as American tulip trees and thujas were all planted, and today fine specimen trees frame the view from the villa across the Arno valley to Monte Pisano.

everywhere largely in the grove but particularly towards the walks and margins: primroses, violets, cowslips, wood-strawberries'. In another garden he advised that 'at two points on the edge of a round of gravel and on a gravel path beds of 3 feet [were] to be sow'd with grass seed . . . intermix't with the seed of violets, cowslips, primroses and wild strawberries', a conceit which suggests modern 'meadow' gardening. In his early career Spence held a respect for symmetry in placing flower-beds and shrubbery areas, but by 1765, in Dean Paul's garden in Ireland, he was adventurously using irregular fluid shapes, thickening the edges of groves with both evergreen and deciduous shrubs.[9]

With 'his little clumps of flowering shrubs', Spence admitted being much influenced by Philip Southcote's informal hedgerow planting at Wooburn Farm (see pp. 214–15). Southcote (1699–1768) was somewhat of a pioneer in his transformation during the 1730s of his rural working farm into a landscape where buildings occurred at prescribed intervals and both herbaceous flowers and flowering shrubs were used to decorate the most distant walks and plantations and to edge the hedgerows. In his *ferme ornée* he created an original garden around the buildings much as he would paint a picture, with foreground, middle ground and background effects, using plants to create patterns of light and shade – 'the evergreens which are the shades in summer are the lights in winter' – and to control distance and dimensions. The various walks were especially designed to carry a visitor around the perimeter (it is even said that 'Capability' Brown's trademark, an outer ring of screening trees, originated with Southcote) through improved pasture and ordinary fields of tillage. Southcote's relative Lord Petre advised about planting and perhaps introduced Southcote to some of the newer plants.

Spence advised Sir William Chambers on his garden and probably considerably influenced Chambers in his *Dissertation on Oriental Gardening* of 1772, published while William Mason and George Harcourt were beginning the Flower Garden at Nuneham. Although mostly an exaggerated polemic aimed at discrediting 'Capability' Brown, it encouraged more natural-style flower planting, attributing this to the Chinese taste. Groves of trees might be surrounded with 'rose trees, sweet brier, honey-suckles, scarlet beans, nasturtiums, everlasting and sweet-scented peas [*Lathyrus odoratus*, the parent of our modern sweet pea, had recently arrived from Sicily], double-blossomed brier, and other odoriferous shrubs, which beautify the barren parts of the plant, and perfume the air'.

By the 1770s William Mason was helping to lay out the Flower Garden at Nuneham in a separate irregularly shaped enclosure where assorted flower-beds, temples and grottoes lent a charming picturesque air. Nuneham has been considered as the pre-eminent eighteenth-century flower garden. For both Repton (in his *Observations on the Theory and Practice of Landscape Gardening* in 1803) and Loudon, in presaging his gardenesque style, it played a model role. 'Without being formal', Repton described it as 'highly enriched, but not too much crowded with seats, temples, statues, vases, or other ornaments, which, being works of art, beautifully harmonize with that profusion of flowers and luxurious plants which distinguish the flower garden from natural landscape, although the walks are not in straight lines.' For many years Nuneham's innovatory role was an accepted view, but research shows that there was nothing totally new even about the informality of the layout. Without denying its potent influence as well as its 'sensibility' and charm, its irregular structure, with beds scattered seemingly aimlessly around in the open glades and grass, was nevertheless anticipated in gardens forty years earlier. Thomas Robins's painting of the Hon. Richard Bateman's Grove House at Old Windsor, completed before 1751, shows a similarly asymmetrical enclosure, as at Nuneham separated from the rest of the garden, with arbitrarily placed (but formally shaped) beds with flowers and scattered pots of flowers. In 1765 Walpole described Bateman's garden as a 'kingdom of flowers' where could be found 'wagon loads of acacias, honeysuckles and seringas'.[10]

Repton was the most influential landscape gardener – he was the first to use this title – to bring back flowers into parts of the great gardens. He incorporated them in enclosed areas in which he might advise planting a rosary (as he did at Ashridge) or gardens specifically for American or Chinese plants such as hydrangeas, aucubas and *Camellia japonica* (recommended at Woburn for the Duke of Bedford with accompanying suitably styled buildings). In the 'Rosary' at Ashridge, garlanded roses on chains floated over lower-growing roses. In reality flowers had never disappeared. Even in 'Capability' Brown's more monotone green landscapes, flowers were grown in walled kitchen gardens placed at some distance from the house, and at the beginning of his career in the 1750s at Petworth and towards the end of it at Cadlands, Brown specified more flowery effects for suitable areas.

By the 1790s Charles Marshall (1747–1818) was recommending edging walks in the distant pleasure grounds with 'herbaceous flowery' plants as well as smaller shrubs; 'neat sheltered compartments of flowers (every now and then to be met with) have a pretty effect'.[11] More practical gardening manuals, including Nathaniel Swinden's, as well as nursery catalogues, provided the means of implementing these schemes.

William Cobbett's section on flowers in *The English Gardener* (1829) showed that their cultivation had never gone entirely out of fashion but had remained something taken for granted while grander schemes were talked about and implemented. 'Flowers,' wrote Cobbett, 'are cultivated in beds, where the whole bed consists of a mass of one sort of flower; or in borders, where an infinite variety of them are mingled together, but arranged so that they may blend with one another in colour as well as in stature.' Only florists currently favoured beds, 'but the fashion *has for some years* been in favour of borders, wherein flowers of the greatest brilliancy are planted, so disposed as to form a regular series higher and higher as they approach the back part, or the middle of the border; and so selected as to insure a succession of bloom from the earliest months of the spring until the coming of the frosts.' Cobbett also recommended leaving space between several plants, carefully

controlling those that strayed so that they did not look untidy ('a mat of the most beautiful flowers in the world, crowded up against each other, and out of all order, never can look like any other than a mass of brilliant weeds') and specified staking and tying 'to sticks of proper height and strength. Many do not want it at all but many do, and, if this be neglected or put off, a good high wind will tear up the high plants, such as hollyhocks, African marigolds, four-o'clocks [marvels of Peru], and make them the means of beating down and destroying the lesser and, perhaps choicer ones below them.' In all this Cobbett gives us an insight into eighteenth-century planting and a foretaste of nineteenth-century artifice. In his list of flowers which followed, Cobbett suggested using many of the more recently introduced flowers, even including Douglas's annual clarkias, newly arrived from California.

It is clear that flowers, both old and new, described in successive editions of Miller's *Dictionary*, were grown throughout the great landscaping era. Just as all through the nineteenth century both ordinary and botanist gardeners continued to grow flowering perennials in their quite modest gardens while grander estates set fashions by adopting monotonous annual bedding schemes and

The idea of having a separate area of the garden kept as an 'American Garden' became fashionable in England towards the end of the eighteenth century and thereafter. In them, calcifuge plants from North America (plants of similar requirements from any continent were later included) would be grown in a deep acid loam. Authors such as Uvedale Price encouraged the picturesque use in landscape of shrubs such as kalmias and rhododendrons; Humphry Repton incorporated suitable sites in overall plans. There were 'American Gardens' at William Beckford's Fonthill Abbey (shown here), at Milburn Tower near Edinburgh, and at Woburn Abbey, and in 1843 Loudon proposed an 'American Garden' as part of his schemes for Coleshill in Berkshire.

developing Victorian evergreen shrubberies, so in the previous century 'simple' gardening continued as an accepted mode although it was the ethic of Brownian 'naturalism' that was written about and eulogized. As Mark Laird suggests,[12] the tradition of borders and planting, real flower-garden planting, probably came from the baroque *plates-bandes* which surrounded *parterres de broderie* and *parterres à l'anglaise* before 1700, similar to those which at Het Loo outline the scrolled parterres in the Lower Garden (see pp. 184–85). Becoming progressively less formal and developing a much freer, less grid-like pattern of planting to match fashionable tastes, flower-beds were re-interpreted in a picturesque form by

Spence, Miller, Mason, Marshall and finally Repton and Loudon in the early years of the nineteenth century.

ENGLISH LANDSCAPE STYLE

By the 1750s serpentine lines and informal planting were all the vogue; it remained for Lancelot Brown (1715–83), a gardener of quite humble birth in Northumberland, to change the face of England with grander and more permanent schemes which involved widening rivers, creating lakes, moving earth to alter the contours of the parkland and planting groves, hanging woods and encircling belts of perimeter trees. In one Midlands estate Brown is said to have planted more than 100,000 trees, mainly oak. To some, Brown – who, in order to create these telling scenes with gentle groves and swelling hills, destroyed all remnants of French-style formality, including great avenues of elm and lime – is the great enemy of gardening. Others remember the thousands of native and exotic trees he planted, many of which reached maturity only after two hundred years, some to fall in the unusually fierce storms experienced in 1987 and 1989. Brown was not primarily involved in growing rare species, but in the effects plants could create. A letter

At Petworth Lancelot Brown's vision of the 1750s is portrayed in the park and lake views captured in oils by Turner in c. 1828. Turner's group of oaks still survives. Besides cedars, pines and clumps of beeches and chestnuts to make hanging woods on the farther hills, Brown's work at Petworth is given interest in his unusual provision of flowering trees and shrubs for the Pleasure Ground. The genera mentioned in a surviving nursery list are disappointing when so many new plants were then being described by Philip Miller. The exceptions are 8 candleberry trees (*Myrica pensylvanica*), 10 Virginia raspberry, 10 Virginia sumach and 4 trumpet flowers (*Campsis radicans*), all from North America.

written to the Revd Thomas Dyer in 1775, in answer to a request from a French friend seeking advice, suggests however that he was more interested than we suppose: to produce 'all the elegance and all the comforts which Mankind wants in the country . . . and, if right, be exactly fit for the owner, the Poet and the Painter . . . there wants a good plan, good execution, a perfect knowledge of the country . . . an infinite delicacy in the planting etc., so much Beauty depending on the size of trees and the colour of their leaves to produce the effect of light and shade so very essential to the perfecting [of] a good plan . . . getting shade from larger trees and sweets from the smaller sorts of shrubs etc.'[13]

By 1770 Thomas Whately was able to assemble his thoughts on

the new style in *Observations on Modern Gardening*: 'Gardening . . . being released now from the restraints of regularity . . . the most beautiful, the most simple, the most noble scenes of nature are all within its province.' A few months later Horace Walpole added, 'How rich, how gay, how picturesque is the face of the country . . . every journey made through a succession of pictures . . . what landscapes will dignify every quarter of our island when the daily plantations that have attained venerable maturity.'

Even at the time Brown had critics; strangely, more for his schemes of planting than for his overall influence in sweeping away time-honoured landscapes, and many of his 'followers' failed to understand the subtlety of his planting nuances. Unable to appreciate the time trees take to mature to create the desired effects, they questioned his 'belting, clumping and dotting' practices, explained later by Humphry Repton in defence of his admired predecessor.[14] Brown planted a number of 'nurse' trees calculated to shelter one another and to promote the growth of those few which might be ultimately destined to remain and form a group or even be retained as single specimens, a well recognized forestry practice. At the time of Brown's death, Walpole pasted into his notebook an anonymous obituary which sums up his greatness and the difficulty we have in understanding his vision: 'Such, however, was the effect of his genius that when he was the happiest man, he will be least remembered; so closely did he copy nature that his works will be mistaken.'

The English landscape garden as interpreted abroad has been at its most successful when, in suitable terrain, it has been combined with botanical collections such as those at Caserta and Malmaison (see pp. 216–17 and 218–20). The French version of the English style, the *jardin anglais* or *anglo-chinois*, later adopted in its more picturesque forms in the rest of Europe, has often seemed a travesty of the Brownian ideal, with little attention being paid to enhancing the landscape with fine trees. All over Europe a frenzy of winding paths, bridges, follies and temples proliferated. By the end of the eighteenth century and during the nineteenth, further 'English' interpretation influenced not only private landowners, many, throughout Europe, with a genuine interest in collections of fine trees, but also affected the development of public parks in both Europe and America. George Washington read Batty Langley and introduced curving lines at Mount Vernon by the close of the eighteenth century. Thomas Jefferson's tour of English gardens in

Redouté's drawing of *Stuartia ovata* (*S. pentagyna* at the time), a shrub native to Virginian woods and watersides, appeared as Plate 6 in Volume I of the *Nouveau Duhamel*, published first in seven volumes between 1800 and 1819 and reissued in 1825 and again in about 1852. Based on the *Traité des Arbres et Arbustes* by Duhamel de Monceau of 1755, it was expanded from the original two volumes with paintings by Pierre Joseph Redouté and Pancrace Bessa, the latter's mainly of fruit. Volumes I-V were dedicated to the ex-Empress Josephine at Malmaison, and it remained the standard account of trees growing in western Europe until Loudon's *Arboretum et Fruticetum Britannicum* of 1838.

1785 inspired adaptations at Monticello in Virginia, particularly, after his visit to Wooburn Farm, in relation to his flower-bed planting. Birkenhead Park in Liverpool, one the first public parks in England, was laid out by Joseph Paxton with the assistance of Edward Kemp in 1843. Its naturalistic style strongly influenced Frederick Law Olmsted in his schemes realized for Central Park in New York.

THE SOCIETY OF GARDENERS AND LONDON NURSERYMEN

From 1725 the Society of Gardeners, an association of twenty leading London gardeners and nurserymen, met monthly – not only to discuss plants, including those newly introduced, but also to attempt to clarify and regularize their names. Their *Catalogus Plantarum*, of which only Part I on trees and shrubs was actually published, came out in 1730. Jacob van Huysum contributed 21 water-colours depicting individual plants, seven of which are printed in colour with the further fourteen engravings coloured by hand. Some of these, such as a lily and a double nasturtium, were intended for use in the additional volumes projected, which were to include flowers, fruit and greenhouse plants. Plants of the various species described could be obtained by writing to the Society. Philip Miller (1691–1771), in charge of the Chelsea Physic Garden after 1722, was clerk to the Society of Gardeners and played a major role in recording the plant descriptions in the catalogue (the first edition of his *Gardeners Dictionary* was published in 1731).

Among the Society's members were Thomas Fairchild, Robert Furber and Christopher Gray. Thomas Fairchild (1667–1729), who combined practical knowledge with scientific interest (he was the first to make a planned hybrid, crossing a carnation with a sweet William to produce *Dianthus caryophyllus × barbatus*, known as 'Fairchild's mule') had established his nursery in 1690. His book *The City Gardener*, dealing with trees, fruit, vines and other plants which would grow in urban conditions, came out in 1722. It included designs for improving wasteland with evergreen holly, ivy, box, privet, ilex and bay as well as deciduous laburnum, lilac, philadelphus and viburnums; they should be of 'Wilderness-Work rather than in Grass Platts

The uncoloured frontispiece to Part I of the *Catalogus Plantarum* of 1730 was engraved and etched by Henry Fletcher in 1729. The catalogue was published by the Society of Gardeners and dedicated to the Earl of Pembroke, a contemporary patron of gardening. The frontispiece, giving little hint of the tree and shrub treasures listed inside, shows a perspective view of a narrow garden framed by tall clipped hedges, with groups of flowers and fruit in the bottom corners, reflecting the current taste for French-style gardening.

and Gravel Walks', with flower-beds edged with scarlet thrift, perennial sunflowers, sweet William and asters. Fairchild offered the then new (but now ubiquitous) London plane (*Platanus* × *hispanica* now *P.* × *acerifolia*, a hybrid between the oriental (*P. orientalis*) and American (*P. occidentalis*) planes, which

with its tolerance of pollution and severe pruning has proved an ideal city tree.

Robert Furber (1674–1756) and Christopher Gray (1694–1764), also members of the Society of Gardeners, had purchased part of Bishop Compton's collection after his death in 1713; both their nurseries became famous for

exotics. Gray's catalogue of American trees and shrubs 'that will endure the climate of England' was published *c.* 1737 in collaboration with Mark Catesby, predating the latter's own more elaborate account of some of these plants in his *Hortus Britanno-americanus* by nearly thirty years.

Robert Furber's hand-coloured engraving of 'a tulip tree, a magnolia and a silk cotton tree', all of which flowered in the Earl of Pembroke's garden at Wilton, is dated 1720. The tulip poplar or tulip tree (*Liriodendron tulipifera*) was about twenty years old and bore 500 flowers. The magnolia or American sweet bay – known then as the 'White Tulip'

(*Magnolia virginiana*) with almost evergreen leaves was introduced by John Banister to Bishop Compton's garden at Fulham; it flowered after nine years. The tender South American *Bombax ceiba* flowered in a stove house at eleven years old. All these new exotics were available in Furber and Gray's nurseries in the 1720s and '30s.

Plate 13 in the Society of Gardeners' *Catalogus Plantarum*, by Jacob van Huysum, is of two Virginian hawthorns (probably identifiable as *Crataegus phaenopyrum*, the Washington thorn, and *C. pedicellata*, the 'Virginian Azarol'); both had red fruits. The engraving was by Henry Fletcher and was coloured by hand.

THE GREAT EXCHANGE: PETER COLLINSON, LORD PETRE AND THEIR PLANTING

Peter Collinson, Quaker, horticulturist and friend of both Philip Miller and Carl Linnaeus, was an important plant collector and recorder of new plants. In *Hortus Kewensis* Aiton attributed 42 new introductions to Collinson, but his own *Hortus Collinsonianus*, not discovered and published until 1809, confirms that plants previously assigned to Sherard, Catesby and Miller were acknowledged to have been received through him, bringing the total number to about 170. Most came from the American colonies through his friend and collector John Bartram of Philadelphia – plants also travelled in exchange across the Atlantic to America. Collinson, and a list of distinguished subscribers including Miller, paid Bartram 5 guineas a box, 20 boxes to be sent each year. Collinson himself grew an extensive collection of the rarities in his own gardens, first at Peckham where he lived until 1749 – a letter to Linnaeus records his moving 40 large evergreens without loss – and then at Ridgway House at Mill Hill. His catalogue lists the plants he grew (not only his own introductions) and gives his comments on their performance in his two gardens and elsewhere, but particularly at Thorndon Hall in Essex, the estate of the great tree collector, Lord Petre.

Other plants came to Collinson from Asia: the tree of heaven (*Ailanthus glandulosa*, now *A. altissima*), grown from seeds sent by Père d'Incarville from Nankin in 1751; the paper mulberry (*Broussonetia papyrifera*), and the bushy *Carpinus orientalis*, grown from seed sent from Persia in 1735, as well as annuals such as gomphrena from India and zinnias from Mexico. Plants seemed to do well for Collinson: *Clematis cirrhosa* from 'this warm year of 1762' had a 'profusion of sweet flowers all November; the like I never saw before'. Both in his plant list and in his commonplace books[15] Collinson brings alive contemporary gardening scope and practice. He commented that Portugal laurel, when first grown, was 'kept in a greenhouse' but later 'exposed by degrees and since found to endure all weather'.

In a note written in his own copy of Miller's *Dictionary*, Collinson declared, in his sixty-eighth year, that the plants in his Mill Hill garden were his greatest source of happiness.

The stove houses at Thorndon, where different temperatures could be maintained, resembled those shown here. They grew and brought to fruiting novelties such as limes, bananas, guavas, papayas and passion fruit. In one, the camellia first flowered in England – Collinson described the two fine *Camellia japonica* as 'evergreen shrubs with bay-like leaves; the one bore white flowers the other red'; in August 1740 one bore a 'most delightful crimsonish double flower'. In 1742 Collinson estimated that the nurseries contained 219,925 plants, mostly exotics 'raised from seed and layering, budding, [and] grafting'.

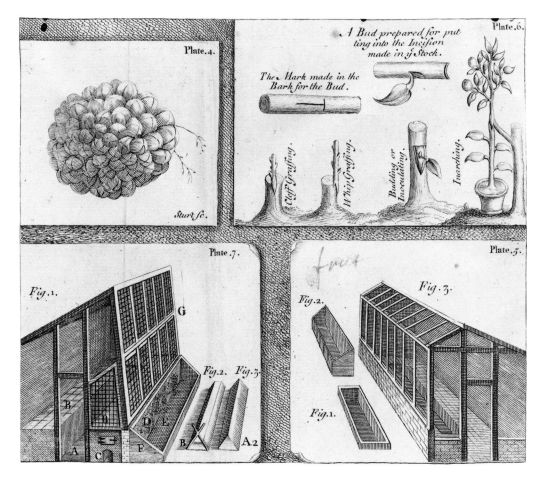

Above: The frontispiece to *New Improvements of Planting and Gardening* (1717) by Richard Bradley, later Professor of Botany at Cambridge, shows protective frames for wall fruit and two different types of cloches in use. Bradley made a practical study of glasshouses and in particular their glazing, publishing information for the use of gardeners. Among trees and shrubs received by Collinson from America were forms of amelanchier, *Rhododendron nudiflorum*, the old-man's-beard or Virginian fringe tree (*Chionanthus virginicus*) and Carolina allspice (*Calycanthus floridus*), flowering at Mill Hill every year from 1756. The mountain laurel or calico bush (*Kalmia latifolia*), introduced in 1734, produced a few flowers in July 1740. In 1759 Collinson saw the American dogwood (*Cornus florida*) flowering for the first time at Enfield.

Collinson also grew smaller North American plants successfully: shooting star (*Dodecatheon meadia*), shown here with American woodcock in Mark Catesby's painting; bee balm or bergamot (*Monarda didyma*) and *Phlox subulata* as well as cypripediums – 'perhaps the first with white flowers that ever flowered in England' – some of which were stolen from the garden in both 1762 and 1768. Also the unusual and difficult sarracenias and Atamasco lilies (*Zephyranthes atamasco*) – the latter sent by John Clayton from Virginia in pots to flower in April – and the sweet fern (*Comptonia peregrina*), re-introduced through Bartram but known earlier.

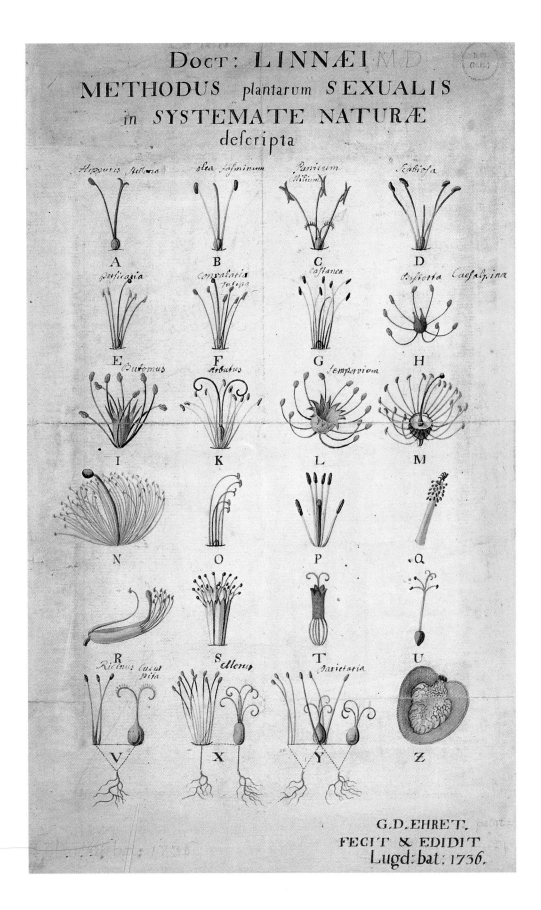

MILLER, LINNAEUS AND EHRET

In any study of plants used in landscapes and gardens in the eighteenth century three closely linked experts appear, each outstanding in his own field, and of immense importance in the history of horticulture. Philip Miller (1691–1771) of the Chelsea Physic Garden, writer, horticultural botanist, plant collector and advisor to the great; the Swedish naturalist Linnaeus (1707–78) later ennobled to Carl von Linné, who introduced the binomial system of botanical nomenclature; and the flower painter extraordinary, Georg Dionysius Ehret (1708–70), perhaps the greatest of all botanical illustrators.

Philip Miller's influence was felt far beyond the confines of his immediate work in administering the Chelsea Physic Garden, the botanical garden founded in 1673, from 1722 until 1770. The garden was rescued from decay in 1722 by Sir Hans Sloane, and during his period in office Miller contributed to making it the most richly stocked garden in the world. His famous *Gardeners Dictionary*, first published in 1731, ran into eight editions in his lifetime and eight more before 1830; in

Although by the early nineteenth century the 'sexual system' of classifying plants developed by Carl Linnaeus, based on the number of stamens and stigmas found in a flower, was made obsolete by the adoption of more natural systems of classification, his new binomial system, first published in full as *Species Plantarum* in 1753, is still accepted as the starting point for all botanical nomenclature. He first applied his method of specific names during preparation of the *Hortus Cliffortianus*, a systematic catalogue of the plants in the garden near Haarlem belonging to the Anglo-Dutch merchant George Clifford, in 1735–8. This was illustrated with drawings by Georg Dionysius Ehret, engraved by J. Wandelaar, who also did some of the drawings.

the eighth edition in 1768 Miller adopted the binomial system, by which plants had a one-word generic name and a single specific epithet, recommended by Carl Linnaeus in his *Species Plantarum* of 1753. Between the first and eighth editions of Miller's *Dictionary* the number of plants cultivated in England had multiplied five times; some of the credit for this must be ascribed to Miller's avid collecting. He received booty from America, the West Indies, the Cape of Good Hope and Europe. The *Dictionary* was not only a catalogue of all plants cultivated; together with the *Garden Kalendar*, published with the third edition, it was a comprehensive manual embracing most contemporary aspects of gardening.

Carl Linnaeus trained as a physician at Uppsala in his native Sweden and returned there as a teacher after introducing his binomial system to the world of European botany. Ehret, who married Miller's sister-in-law in 1738, remained in England with 'painting access' to a large supply of new plants which he continued to portray on paper and vellum as well as practising as an engraver for his own publication *Plantae et Papiliones Rariores* (1748–59).

A painting by Ehret of *Magnolia grandiflora*, the evergreen magnolia from America, was used in Mark Catesby's *Natural History of Carolina*, published from 1729 to 1747. The magnolia's white and fragrant flowers, together with the exciting red and green colouring of the seed vessel and its habit of keeping its glossy leaves in winter, made it among the most exciting acquisitions from the New World. Even before it was explained to him by Linnaeus, Ehret, through his patron Dr Christoph Jacob Trew at Nuremberg, had grasped the prime importance of detailed plant observation and which parts of a flower or fruit should be represented most clearly in order to understand its sexual character.

MAGNOLIA *altissima, Lauro-cerasi folie flore ingenti candido.*

William Aiton in *Hortus Kewensis* credited the Duke of Argyll with introducing various andromedas, paper birch (*Betula papyrifera*) and poplar-leaved birch (*B. populifolia*), the hardy bonduc or Kentucky coffee tree (*Gymnocladus dioica*, 1748), Carolina or American holly (*Ilex opaca*), *Itea virginica*, and snowy mespilus or shadbush (*Amelanchier canadensis*) to British gardens. He grew these plants and many others at Whitton, the gardens and vast 3.5-hectare/9-acre nursery established after 1725 on the wastelands of Hounslow Heath. The gardens were

PLANTING AT WHITTON AND PAINSHILL

in effect an experimental site for trees growing in the open air in England, many from different climatic regions. Miller often visited Whitton and described how the narrow-leaved *Kalmia angustifolia* was spreading rapidly to make a thicket. John Claudius Loudon remarked that although the estate was broken up into three parts after Argyll's

death, many fine cedars, Weymouth pines, silver firs, deciduous cypresses, walnuts, hickories and American oaks still grew there when he visited it in the 1830s.[16] A Lombardy poplar (*Populus nigra*), one of the first to be grown in England, measured 35 metres/115 feet in height and more than 5.8 metres/19 feet in girth in 1835.

Painshill, Charles Hamilton's estate in Surrey, its buildings and plantings now being restored, had many of its trees recorded by later garden visitors. Loudon described a visit he made to 'Pains Hill' in 1837: 'Among the trees ... are some remarkably fine silver cedars [Loudon here meant a form of *Cedrus libani* with leaves of a silvery hue.[17]], pinasters, and other pines, American oaks, cork trees, and ilices, a tupelo tree (*Nyssa sylvatica*), tulip trees, acacias, deciduous cypress, Lombardy and other poplars, etc. Here are some of the first rhododendrons and azaleas introduced into England.'[18]

Hamilton experimented with many exotics, both trees and shrubs, to help further his effects. Besides conifers, there were plants from North America (including rhododendrons and azaleas), which he found would thrive in his acid soil. Contrary to the normally preconceived notions of eighteenth-century fashion, he planted flowering shrubs in woodland areas and to frame his garden buildings. The gardens at Painshill have been recently restored: the photograph (*left*) shows a view of the Gothic Temple.

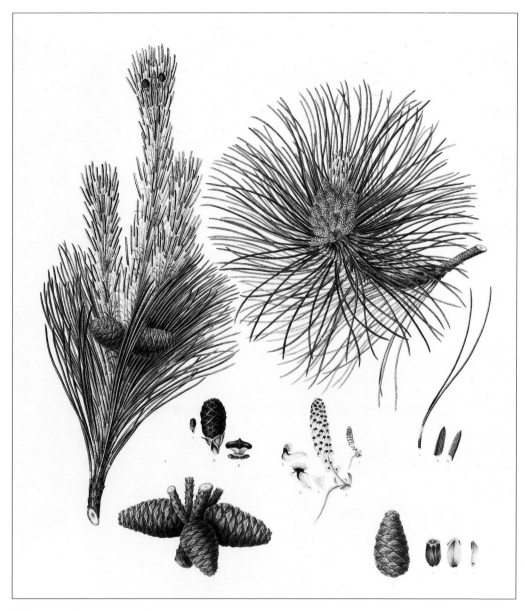

At Whitton American pines, firs and cypresses, an avenue of cedars of Lebanon, raised from seed in 1722, groves of deciduous cypress (*Taxodium distichum*), American bird cherries, and Swedish and scarlet-flowered maples from Virginia were all described by Joseph Spence on a visit in 1760. After the Duke's death in 1761, many plants were moved to Kew and became the core of its expanding collection under the Princess Dowager Augusta, mother of George III – a male maidenhair tree (*Ginkgo biloba*), (*left*) introduced to Europe in about 1730 and England in *c.* 1754, still survives.

Ferdinand Bauer's drawing of the cones of red pine (*Pinus resinosa*), used to illustrate *A Description of the Genus Pinus* by Aylmer Bourke Lambert, published in two volumes in 1803 and 1804 (in which all conifers were generically classified as *Pinus*). Lambert was a leading botanist with an outstanding botanical library and important herbarium of 30,000 specimens. Among the pines described by Lambert at Painshill and later seen by Loudon were the loblolly pine (*P. taeda*), Jersey pine (*P. virginiana*) and northern pitch pine (*P. rigida*) all introduced from North America.

EIGHTEENTH-CENTURY FLOWER PLANTING

In *Observations on Modern Gardening* (1770) Thomas Whately gave an account of Philip Southcote's *ferme ornée* at Wooburn Farm as he saw it when the garden was at its peak: 'The buildings are not ... the only ornament of the walk; it is shut out from the country ... by a thick and lofty hedgerow, which is enriched with woodbine, jessamine and every odoriferous plant ... a path, generally of sand and gravel, is conducted in a waving line ... and the turf on either hand is diversified with little groups of shrubs, or firs, or of the smallest trees, and often with beds of flowers ... in some parts ... carried between larger clumps of evergreens, thickets of deciduous shrubs or still more considerable open plantations ... and in every corner or vacant space is a rosary, a close or open clump, or a bed of flowers.' Detail of the flower planting in one border is supplied by Joseph Spence, who even made a rough sketch plan. The planting is interesting for its conventionality, and few of the shrubs or flowers were novelties or recent introductions. The flowers are arranged in rows of successive height in a border 75 centimetres/$2\frac{1}{2}$ feet wide with trees and shrubs in a similar gradation at the back extending twice that distance again. At the front pinks serve as edging, behind which in the first rank are bulbs – crocus, snowdrops and jonquils (*Narcissus jonquillus*) – succeeded by primroses and something unidentifiable marked as 'hypia'. Stocks, sweet Williams, Canterbury bells, wallflowers, catchfly (*Silene*), carnations, lavender, scabious, marjoram and cotton lavender grow in the next line, all plants which will cover the fading leaves of the spring-flowers. Lilies, hollyhocks, golden rod, columbine, starwort (probably one of the new American asters), honesty, crown imperials, sunflowers (presumably the perennial *Helianthus multiflorus*), peonies and evening primroses ('the primrose tree') will grow taller at the back: 'all replenished the air with their perfumes' and made 'every gale full of fragrancy'.[19]

Thomas Robins, whose painting career spanned the years between 1747 and 1766, portrayed gardens and flowers in his own particular rococo style. In this picture of Woodside House (*left*), paths wind through a wood while double rows of trees flank an open lawn on which gardeners are at work rolling and raking. A Chinese Chippendale kiosk has fret paling. Robins liked to frame his pictures with the flowers which might have been planted in the garden.

The Flower Garden at Nuneham (*right*) was made famous by the watercolour sketches of Paul Sandby (later widely distributed as engravings) portraying the garden beds and flowers in 1777. The separate and asymmetrical garden, enclosed with thick shrubberies, had an informal planting style, with irregular-shaped beds. Except for tall sunflowers in the beds and some specimen Swedish junipers (*Juniperus communis* var. *suecica*) dotted about the lawn, the flowers in the watercolours are not easy to identify. The miscellaneous groups are likely to have been arranged as recommended by the nurseryman Nathaniel Swinden, to give a mixture of colour and scent all through a season: the flower-beds 'by the colours being diversified will have a most agreeable and pleasing appearance'.

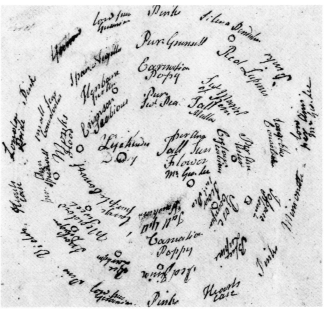

Detailed plans dated 1799 of flower-bed planting at Hartwell in Buckinghamshire were found in the Bodleian Library at Oxford. The beds are circular, oval or kidney-shaped and mainly planted with herbaceous perennials, some of which were gifts from Nuneham; they are graduated in height, with the tallest in the centre of the beds. In a round bed are candytuft, sweet mignonette, dwarf pinks backed by love-in-the-mist, lupins, poppies, four-o'clocks or marvels of Peru, mallows and sweet peas. In the centre are tall sunflowers, and 'lichnedeas' (*Phlox paniculata* or *P. maculata*) and the red-flowered annual persicaria (*Polygonum orientale*).

THE ENGLISH GARDEN IN EUROPE: CASERTA

The English Garden at the royal palace of La Reggia at Caserta, just north of Naples, was conceived and laid out during the last part of the 1780s. Adjacent to the baroque French-style gardens designed (but only partially realized) by the Vanvitellis, it was intended, with naturalistic lines, to be a complete contrast. The British envoy, Sir William Hamilton, was instrumental in encouraging the Austrian-born Queen Maria Carolina, wife of the reigning Ferdinand IV and sister of the ill-fated Marie Antoinette of France, to consider embellishing the landscape with an 'English' park emulating her sister's Petit Trianon at Versailles. The new garden was not only envisaged as a pleasure ground; exotic trees and other plants, some to be grown in glasshouses, were to be part of a scheme for experimental acclimatization which extended to agricultural corn and grasses for animal feeding.[20]

By 1786 20 hectares/50 acres of fertile land had been acquired and work could begin on building an encircling wall. Through Sir Joseph Banks at Kew, Hamilton found John Andrew Graefer, an Austrian gardener who had been a pupil of Philip Miller at the Chelsea Physic Garden, and had since worked at the Mile End Nursery of James Gordon in east London. The experienced Graefer arrived in Naples in 1786 to become the gardener in charge. By 1793, in spite of encountering many initial difficulties, Graefer had laid out the main lines of the garden, with groves of

Jacob Philipp Hackert's painting of La Reggia at Caserta shows the English Garden with the remarkable scenic backdrop of Vesuvius. The general aspect seemed likely to provide suitable open-air conditions for growing rare trees and shrubs from colder climates in both America and the Far East, as well as those from hotter tropical regions. The fertile plain of the Campania with its rich volcanic soil – so often praised by the classical authors – with its relatively mild winters and hot summers (including a damaging two months of scorching sun) and exceptionally abundant water supplies from the calcareous tufa hills just to the north-east, ensured a high rate of growth.

native and exotic trees and open areas of green lawn. As Hamilton had proposed in a letter to Banks in 1788, there was 'a specimen of an English pleasure garden – a compleat botanic garden – a good kitchen garden – and a sort of *ferme ornée*' for agricultural experiments with grasses to fatten cattle. To these were added a flower garden and a nursery as well as stove houses and greenhouses for tropical rarities and for overwintering semi-tropical plants. Today, two hundred years after its conception, the English Garden at Caserta awaits restoration.

In 1794 the Chinese parasol tree (*Firmiana simplex*) – known, at its introduction from China in the eighteenth century, as '*Sterculia platanifolia*' – flowered in the open for Graefer in the English Garden at Caserta. (By 1876 it had reached a height of 27 metres/88 feet.) With large maple-like leaves, it was rare and tender. Although suitable only for greenhouses in England, at Sir Joseph Banks's request Graefer sent a young plant to him at Kew. The tree is now often seen in the Southern states of North America. Graefer maintained his contacts with nurseries such as Gordon and Lee and Kennedy in London through the 1790s; through them and from Holland he obtained many newly introduced plants.

THE ENGLISH GARDEN IN EUROPE: MALMAISON

Marie Josèphe Rose Tascher de la Pagerie (1763–1814) from Martinique married Napoleon Bonaparte in 1796, acquiring the Château and park at Malmaison in 1798, before, in 1804, becoming empress. According to her contemporaries the Empress Josephine's taste for botany and for collecting plants was no mere caprice but a serious study. Josephine employed Etienne Pierre Ventenat (1757–1808) as her botanist and Pierre Joseph Redouté (1759–1840) as botanical artist to record her plant collection at Malmaison.

Redouté, a Belgian but working in France, was the most celebrated botanical painter of his day. In 1803 Josephine commissioned Ventenat to publish *Le Jardin de la Malmaison*, with 120 illustrations by Redouté. Thereafter a series of large folios, illustrated by Redouté in watercolours reproduced by stipple engraving and colour printing, came out under her patronage. Of these *Les Liliacées* (1802–16) in eight volumes with 508 magnificent plates, all of plants in the Malmaison gardens, is the most sumptuous, although owing to the frequent reproduction of pictures from his *Les Roses* (1817–24), in which he recorded the empress's rose collection, this later work is more familiar. Some of the Malmaison roses

The gardens at Malmaison were in romantic style, well embellished with rustic bridges and temples: the watercolour by Garneray shows the Temple of Love. Groves of tall trees were interspaced with luxuriant lawns, and exotic purple-necked black swans floated beside pleasure boats on the lakes and canals. Josephine's taste for the *jardin anglais* did not please Napoleon, but she insisted that if a Scotsman, Thomas Blaikie, could lay out Bagatelle for the Comte d'Artois before the Revolution, she also could have a garden in the fashionable style, eschewing the outmoded French formality. Louis Berthault, who later gave advice to Napoleon's sister Elisa Bacciochi at Marlia near Lucca, became her landscape adviser.

collected for Josephine came from the rose garden at Wilhelmshöhe in Kassel, where a rose nursery had been established as early as 1766 for the Landgraf Friedrich II during the period when the baroque garden there was being 'anglicized' with naturalistic planting. Redouté contributed drawings to many other publications, among which were those of succulents for A.P. de Candolle's monograph (1798–1829). Many of the original paintings, mainly on vellum, are in Paris.

Josephine spent vast sums of money on acquiring plants (as much as 3,000 francs on one bulb) for the garden and greenhouses, on laying out the grounds and on having her plants illustrated (a total of 42,862 francs was distributed between Ventenat and Redouté alone). She was instrumental in first introducing many new exotics to French soil; their cultivation and acclimatization was still experimental. Outside, beside robust European natives, she planted trees and shrubs from Asia and the Americas, including the Chinese *Magnolia denudata* (1789), and the American *M. macrophylla*, with its large tropical-looking leaves, and the sweet bay (*M. virginiana*). In her extensive glass and stove houses she cultivated acacias, boronias, casuarinas, grevilleas, eucalypts and melaleucas recently arrived from Australia and New Zealand (some of them through Commodore Baudin's expedition of 1800). From South Africa she cultivated as many as 50 species of pelargoniums and heaths, besides *Sparmannia africana* (1790) and a selection of bulbs such as ixias and the scarlet *Brunsvigia josephinae*, which she herself 'found' as a bulb in a Paris market and first brought to flower. She was one of the earliest to develop dahlias (already by 1789 cultivated as varieties in the botanic garden in Madrid), obtaining new seeds of species through the botanical explorers Aimé Bonpland and Friedrich Humboldt direct from Mexico.

Many of the plants, were obtained from the Vineyard Nursery (owned by James Lee and Lewis Kennedy) in Hammersmith in London.

Hemerocallis Cærulea   *Hemerocalle Bleue*

Kennedy, partner to the better known Lee (d. 1795, author of *An Introduction to Botany* in 1760), travelled often to Malmaison, taking plants and advising Josephine. During the war with France, Kennedy was even provided with a special passport, and careful instructions were issued by the admiralty to prevent plants being damaged if they were intercepted. James Lee met Redouté when the young painter came to London in 1786 and 1787, receiving a gift of a painting of a campanula from him. *Kennedia coccinea*, painted by Redouté for *Le Jardin de Malmaison*, was named for Lewis Kennedy, and James Lee's name is commemorated by *Cereus leeanus*, a Mexican cactus Kennedy raised from seed grown in the empress's garden. In 1803 the bill for plants from the Vineyard Nursery came to £2,600 and in 1811 another was for £700. After Josephine's divorce in 1809 it is said that Napoleon rooted up many of her 'English' plants – Josephine was at first banished to Navarre in Normandy, but died at Malmaison in 1814.

After Ventenat's death in 1808, Aimé Bonpland, botanist and plant explorer, grew rare plants – many from South America and Mexico, where he had been with Humboldt – in the fine neo-classical greenhouse at Malmaison, as well as experimenting with exotics outside; his *Description des Plantes Rares Cultivées à Malmaison et à Navarre* came out in 1812–17. Among Redouté's illustrations for Bonpland's work was the moutan peony (*right*). These shrubby peonies from China were planted outside but protected in winter with a glass frame packed with straw.

Left: One of the plants grown by the Empress Josephine at Malmaison was *Hosta ventricosa* (then named '*Hemerocallis caerulea*'). It was illustrated by Redouté in his *Les Liliacées* in 1805. Although many of the plants portrayed have been reclassified according to modern rules of nomenclature, the accuracy of Redouté's painting ensures precise identifications. Before being at Malmaison he had illustrated the books of the amateur botanist C. L. L'Héritier, a follower of Linnaeus, developing a scientific attitude to his plant portrayals.

CHAPTER EIGHT

EXPANSION AND EXPERIMENT IN THE NINETEENTH CENTURY

By the 1830s almost all identifiable garden 'styles' had already been tried in the gardens known to civilization. Even the apparently novel 'wild' or native plant garden had already been hinted at, first by Joseph Spence and then by John Claudius Loudon in 1803 when he suggested that the lawn at Scone Palace should be left unmown with white and yellow clover, patches of thyme, daisies and saxifrage. Since then it is variants of previous designs – in modified and extended forms – that have been adopted. Twentieth-century gardeners can find Victorians' 'historicist' schemes – whether inspired by Egypt, Italy, France or Tudor and Jacobean England – as inspirational and adaptable as authentic reconstructions of what are today known as 'period' gardens. Nineteenth-century planting is characterized by a general eclecticism, involving a great deal of trial and error, with gardeners tending to rush into exaggerated and dogmatic themes as more and more plants became available – their range soon vastly extended by hybridization and selective breeding, and their increase matched in scale by a growth in technological advances, horticultural skills and imaginative possibilities.

By the 1820s and '30s gardens were no longer idealizations of nature where artistry was disguised, but plots in which as many plants as possible should be grown as well as possible. In gardens contrived as works of art, not only were new and exotic plants displayed; the plants themselves were often deliberately chosen to demonstrate the considerable skill that it took to grow them successfully. During the rest of the century gardening tastes on the European Continent, in England and in America were accommodated to these two main interacting factors. Ideas of a gentle landscape emphasizing natural beauties or the more rugged 'patch of wild nature' advocated by exponents of the 'picturesque' were

swept aside to make way for scenes which confirmed the triumph of Art over Nature, a point of view already forcibly pronounced by Repton as early as 1808 (see pp. 240–41). In Prussia Prince Pückler-Muskau (1785–1871) began alterations and extensions to his park at Muskau in 1815 after a visit to England, during which he had come to admire examples of the English landscape style, particularly parks and gardens laid out by Humphry Repton, whose son John Adey Repton he employed after Repton's death in 1818. In his early life inspired by Goethe with an interest in nature – and its extension, the art of gardening – his aim at Muskau was to convert the park into the highest form of artistic achievement (see pp. 242–43). His book *Andeutungen über Landschaftsgärtnerei* (1834), with descriptions of practical applications of his theories, established the prince as an important figure in the history of German landscape development and led to his advice being sought for the Royal Park at Babelsberg near Potsdam. Both Karl Friedrich Schinkel (1781–1814), the German architect and town planner, and Peter Josef Lenné (1789–1866) were much influenced by Prince Pückler in their garden and park designs in Germany and Poland.

The more museum-like attitude to gardening, with an emphasis on plant collecting – sometimes carried to an extreme in recom-

A painting by Silvestro Lega, *Il Pergolato*, conveys the refreshing coolness experienced under a vine-covered pergola in gardens of the Brera in Milan. The pergola, a frame over which plants could be trained, is a well-established feature in western gardens. Originally intended to provide shady walks in hot climates, it was adopted as a useful architectural adjunct even in cooler gardens and, of course, provided plantsmen with an ideal structure for rambling and twining plants. Besides grape vines, Gertrude Jekyll recommended aristolochias, Virginia creeper or Boston ivy, Chinese gooseberry (*Actinidia chinensis*), wisteria, large-leaved *Vitis* and *Ampelopsis* and any number of roses and clematis.

In the garden of Thomas Fish's *cottage orné* at Sidmouth, basket flower-beds in the lawn were surrounded by wickerwork, painted turquoise to match the trim of the house, very much in the style of the *corbeilles* designed by John Adey Repton for gardens at Potsdam. (These were later called 'Hardenberg' baskets after the State Chancellor, Prince Pückler-Muskau's father-in-law, and used extensively by the German designer Peter Josef Lenné.) The design was originally proposed by Humphry Repton for the gardens of the Prince Regent's Pavilion at Brighton. On his tours reported in *The Gardener's Magazine* during the 1830s and '40s, J. C. Loudon saw basket beds of this kind in many quite modest villa gardens.

mending the use of exotic plants only – was further confirmed by the development of the 'gardenesque' style, in which plants were displayed to their best and sometimes individual advantage rather as if they were in a gallery. Trees and shrubs grew free-standing on lawns, to be admired from every angle, and irregularly placed flower-beds proliferated (see pp. 246–47). None of this was really stylistically innovative. From the end of the sixteenth century, and even before then, individuals had obtained exotics as soon as they were available and they had grown tulips in rows and trees and shrubs for individual assessment. What was new, and made possible by the expanding nursery trade and an increase in horticultural skills, was the more rapid availability of these introduced plants, augmented by new cultivars and selections, to a much wider public. This public was in the same period being horticulturally educated by gardening journals and books expressly written for this purpose. The nineteenth-century explosion of gardening periodicals was comparable to the seemingly almost miraculous availability of information in the vernacular after the invention of printing in the fifteenth century, only with greatly magnified effects. The new reading matter took every advantage of the scientific botany introduced by Linnaeus and expanded by the French in the Jussieus' 'natural' system of classification. In 1789 Antoine de Jussieu (1748–1836), nephew of Antoine and Bernard, published his *Genera Plantarum Secundum Ordines Naturalis Disposita*, which arranged plants according to natural affinities rather than sexual distinctions; this work formed the basis of modern botanical classification.

After Repton's death in 1818 until his own death in 1843, John Claudius Loudon towered above all his contemporaries throughout the horticultural world as garden journalist and historian, plant encyclopaedist and adviser on garden layouts and style, exponent of gardening techniques and general garden popularist. His most important books were the *Encyclopaedia of Gardening* (1822) in which he included histories of the development of Continental styles of gardening (including that of Russia) through the ages, an *Encyclopaedia of Plants* (1829), *The Suburban Gardener, and Villa Companion* (1836–8) and in 1838 his monumental work on trees and shrubs, *Arboretum et Fruticetum Britannicum* (which came out in parts to ensure wider circulation but was finally collected in eight volumes – four of text and four of plates). The latter is still a valuable reference for descriptions of all woody plants then in cultivation, besides containing useful historical assessments and dates of introduction. Perhaps Loudon's most useful legacy was his inauguration of a series of gardening periodicals. In 1826 he started *The Gardener's Magazine*, a topical journal which gave many descriptions of contemporary gardens, including lists of trees and flowers growing in them, both at home and abroad; in it new plants as well as layouts in gardens and 'style' in general were important issues. Through all his works there runs an 'improving' vein, as he sought to establish better methods of both farming and practical and ornamental horticulture for the good of mankind. Loudon travelled in Europe and his journalistic efforts extended to events on the Continent and in North American gardening, with correspondents reporting from the countries concerned. By the 1840s cheaper printing methods and more efficient distribution allowed for other journals such as the *Gardener's Chronicle*, the *Horticultural Magazine* and the *Cottage Gardener* (later the *Journal of Horticulture*) to reach a wider and humbler audience, thus fulfilling a need motivated by the general Victorian ethic, already expressed by Loudon, to educate and improve as well as to inform.

THE PROFESSIONAL PLANT HUNTERS

Plant collecting had hitherto been left to amateur enthusiasts; by the end of the eighteenth century it had become much more professional, with trained botanists given specific plant-hunting instructions and sent out by botanic gardens and by nurserymen – although right up to the end of the nineteenth century many missionaries and explorers were also naturalists.

Bodies such as the new Horticultural Society and the developing gardens at Kew sent or encouraged collectors to forage for exotics all round the world, for practical and scientific rather than for purely ornamental interest. Nurserymen, too, increasingly employed their own collectors to look for new plants to augment

The large-leaved maple, *Acer macrophyllum*, a native of the north-west coast of America – first discovered by Archibald Menzies but introduced to England in 1812 by Pursh – was already available in the Loddiges nursery in the 1830s, although (as Loudon remarks in his *Arboretum et Fruticetum Britannicum* of 1838) it still had not flowered and was propagated by layers. It was illustrated in Loudon, Volume 5, and the Plate is from one of the 25 copies issued with colour illustrations. David Douglas sent specimens of the dried leaf as well as the timber to England, describing the tree as likely in 'some future time, [to] constitute one of our most ornamental forest trees'.

their stock. David Douglas (1799–1834) was trained as a gardener and collector in Scotland. W. J. Hooker took him on botanizing trips in the Highlands – and Hooker's great *Flora Boreali* and *Americana* of 1833 was based largely on collections made by Archibald Menzies, Douglas and Thomas Drummond. In 1824–7 Douglas was engaged by the Horticultural Society to collect plants in the remote north-west of America. His three expeditions to this coast, regions of which had a climate very similar to the British Isles, yielded exciting new plants which still play major roles in British gardens. At the time they influenced the appearance and developing style of gardens as much as the increasingly vast flow of incoming plants from farthest Asia would do as the century advanced.

Douglas and his companions, in spite of considerable hardship, collected a wide range of plants, from sun-loving Californian natives to seeds of giant trees from the north-west rain forests. By 1827 he had introduced the Douglas fir (*Pseudotsuga menziesii*), now an important forestry tree in Europe, and by 1830 the noble fir (*Abies procera*); he had also brought back cones of the sugar pine (*Pinus lambertiana*), the largest of all pines. On his second expedition Douglas had seen 'the great beauty of Californian vegetation', the famous redwood forests dominated by *Sequoia sempervirens*, but many of the seeds and plants he collected were later lost in a hazardous journey down the Fraser river. From 1833, during his third and last expedition, Douglas searched mainly in California where the missions founded by the Spanish proved hospitable and helpful. He was able to introduce valuable plants (some already noted by Archibald Menzies in the 1790s), among which were the beautiful Monterey pine (*Pinus radiata*) from northern California, as well as evergreen shrubs such as the tender *Arbutus menziesii*, shade-tolerant *Garrya elliptica* and the Oregon grape (*Mahonia aquifolium*). The flowering currant (*Ribes sanguineum*) was considered so important a find as to be itself worth the cost of the whole expedition, a modest £400. Smaller plants included the bulbous *Camassia esculenta*, *Lupinus polyphyllus* and other woody lupins (*L. nootkatensis* was already in Europe and listed by the Loddiges nursery as early as 1823). Some of the annuals Douglas introduced from the west, like those introduced from South America with particularly vivid flower colouring, would become popular bedding plants later in the century. Besides the annual *Eschscholzia californica* which covers Californian hills with an orange haze in spring, he introduced

Clarkia elegans in multicoloured tints, red and yellow gaillardias, the poached-egg plant (*Limnanthes douglasii*), *Mimulus moschatus* and *Phacelia tanacetifolia* with blue bell-like flowers. In 1834 Douglas died tragically aged only thirty-five, having fallen into a bull pit trap in the Hawaiian Islands.

Within a decade Theodor Hartweg, a German also working for the Horticultural Society, who had been collecting in Central and South America, went to California to collect seed of the giant or evergreen chestnut (*Castanopsis chrysophylla*), the seed of which Douglas had first discovered in the crop of a bird he had shot. Hartweg is also credited with the introduction of the redwood (*Sequoia sempervirens*), the seed of which Douglas had lost, and was the first to find the impressive Monterey cypress (*Cupressus macrocarpa*). He retired to become Inspector of Gardens to the Duke of Baden at Schwetzingen, where Friedrich Ludwig von Sckell had after 1776 created an English-style garden separate from the baroque garden made earlier in the century. There Hartweg was able to experiment with some of his tree introductions. In 1850 a group of Scottish gentlemen who wanted new conifers for their northern estates formed an association in order to send John Jeffrey to collect seed of Douglas's trees. On this expedition Jeffrey collected seed of the western hemlock (*Tsuga heterophylla*), which proved another important garden conifer.

Other botanist-collectors explored in India and China, finding plants for European gardens. The Dane Nathaniel Wallich became Director of the Calcutta Botanic Garden, founded in 1786 with the support of the East India Company, taking over from William Roxburgh (1751–1815) whose *Flora Indica* was published posthumously in 1820–24. Wallich's collections went to Kew and included Nepalese seeds of *Rhododendron arboreum*, successfully packed in tins of brown sugar. One of his visitors in Calcutta was the French naturalist Jean-Baptiste Leschenault (1773–1826), who had gone with Captain Baudin's expedition to Australia in 1800, taking back seeds for the Empress Josephine to grow at Malmaison. In India he was to collect economic plants for the French government and establish a botanic garden at Pondicherry. Another Frenchman, Victor Jacquemont (1801–32), went to India in 1829. Although collecting for the Jardin des Plantes, he too was dependent on the English-based East India Company introducing him to governors of the British possessions. After visiting the Mughal gardens in Kashmir, he collected more than 600 items,

In 1824 David Douglas (1799–1834) was sent out by the Horticultural Society of London to collect plants in the north-west of America. Best remembered for the Douglas firs, which have influenced the development of whole landscapes in Europe, Douglas also helped introduce many smaller Californian plants. They include the perennial *Lupinus polyphyllus*, one of the parents of the modern lupin – painted by Miss Drake with *Cyclobothra pulchella* and *C. alba* (now in the genus *Calochortus*), and the annual *L. nanus*. Charles Sprague Sargent, the American botanist, said of him that no other collector reaped such a harvest in America or associated his name with so many useful plants.

including some Japanese hackberry or nettle trees (*Celtis sinensis*), a service tree 'with fruits the size of an apple', azaleas, rhododendrons and plenty of herbaceous plants. He died in India but his notebooks, with description of the localities and ecological conditions in which he found each of his plants – 4,700 in total – were returned to the herbarium of the Musée National d'Histoire Naturelle in Paris. To gardeners Jacquemont is best remembered for the white-stemmed Himalayan birch (*Betula utilis jacquemontii*),

named in his honour but introduced to Europe only in 1880.

There were plenty of other plant explorers: Robert Fortune worked in Japan and China; the nurseryman Veitch sent his collectors (including the Lobb brothers) all over the world; and explorers from European countries collected in South America, in states newly independent of Spanish and Portuguese control. By the end of the century subscribers could take shares in financing specific expeditions, sharing out the rich harvests of seeds or plants among the members.

THE NURSERIES

The proliferation of nursery gardens in the period around 1800 was considerable and made distribution of newly introduced plants speedy. Some 58 nurserymen and 35 seedsmen were recorded within a ten-mile radius of London in the last two decades of the eighteenth century; by 1822 Loudon regarded 36 firms in Greater London alone worthy of his mention, and by 1837, the year of Queen Victoria's accession, *The Floral Calendar* listed 11 principal seedsmen as well as 19 nurserymen 'whose gardens are within the distance of a convenient morning's drive'. Many of the 150 main businesses listed for the British Isles, and individual nurserymen, played an important role in the development of horticulture, not only making good plants available to the public, but investing time, money and knowledge in research on plants and their culture and acclimatization.

One of the most influential nurserymen before 1800 was Conrad Loddiges, a German with a nursery in Hackney in London; his nursery's first catalogue in 1777 was trilingual, issued in Latin, English and German, showing how important was the Continental as well as the home market. At this time the nursery was known especially for the American plants sent by John Bartram's son William, who carried on with plant exploration after his father's death. Between 1800 and 1818 the nursery supplied models for some 200 of the 1,500 new plants illustrated in Curtis's *Botanical Magazine*, many of them credited to the nursery's introduction. In the *Gardener's Magazine* in 1826 Loudon particularly praised all aspects of the Loddiges enterprise, including their extensive *Botanical Cabinet* published 1817–33 in 20 volumes. 'This catalogue exhibits such an assemblage of plants . . . The total number of species exceeds 8,000, all plants that may be purchased, and

The lithograph by Walter Fitch of *Rhododendron griffithianum* is Plate II from *The Rhododendrons of Sikkim-Himalaya* by Joseph Dalton Hooker (published 1849–51), taken from Hooker's own drawing completed on the site. At first identified and named by Hooker as *R. aucklandii*, its bell-flowers of ethereal whiteness are said to have a 'careless rapture of form . . . which defies description'. Too tender, except in favoured maritime gardens, in northern Europe, it is the parent of many desirable hybrids, in particular 'Pink Pearl', put out by Waterer of Bagshot in the 1890s. Hooker's expedition to Sikkim was an important landmark for rhododendron gardening.

exclusive of about 2,000 varieties.' In his *Arboretum et Fruticetum Britannicum* (1838) Loudon described the nursery arboretum, laid out in alphabetical order, as 'forming a scroll like the Ionic volute, extending over a space of upwards of seven acres, commencing with the letter A, at the outer circumference, and terminating with

Z (*Zizyphus*)'. In the centre ten concentric zones were laid out with special peat beds (for plants starting with *Andromeda* and ending with *Vaccinium*) – 'So spirited an undertaking cannot be sufficiently appreciated'. It certainly shows the trouble which nurserymen would take to introduce their customers not only to available plants, but also to the conditions in which they would grow successfully. In his *History of English Gardening* published in 1829 George Johnson considered that the extremely valuable nursery stock (estimated to be worth £200,000) of Loddiges in Hackney afforded 'a better criterion of the state of our Horticulture, and the efforts made to increase the number of our Garden Plants than any other I can make'.

Loddiges also obtained plants on an exchange basis from newly formed botanical societies overseas, thereby saving the risk and expense of sending out their own plant-hunting expeditions. At its peak in 1836 the Loddiges nursery list included 67 different species of oak, 29 of birch, 91 of thorns, 180 of willow and 1,549 different roses.

Some of the nineteenth-century tree discoveries ultimately changed whole landscapes rather than remaining specimens for garden ornament. Many of the conifers introduced in the nineteenth century, particularly those from north-west America, are used extensively in the twentieth century for forestry schemes. These include Douglas fir and Sitka spruce (*Picea sitchensis*), and many pines, such as the Monterey pine and the Bishop's pine (*Pinus muricata*), as well as the Monterey cypress, that have proved useful and decorative shelter-belt trees in coastal areas influenced by the Atlantic. The Monterey pine from coastal California, tender in most of Europe, naturalizes in Australia and New Zealand, just as eucalypts from Australia now dominate skylines in favoured coastal areas of Portugal and in Pacific Coast California. However, not all acclimatization and naturalization of foreign trees and plants is beneficial on either ecological or aesthetic grounds.

In gardens the innumerable forms of Lawson's cypress (*Chamaecyparis lawsoniana*) which have developed since the type plant was introduced as seed to Lawson's nursery in Edinburgh in 1854 are also important. Leyland's cypress (× *Cupressocyparis leylandii*), first originating in Wales in 1888 as a seedling between *Cupressus macrocarpa* and *Chamaecyparis nootkatensis*, and the fastest-growing conifer in the British Isles, is useful for screening if well pruned.

During the century the number of plants which easily

acclimatized to European conditions multiplied a thousand-fold. The influx of plants and the growth of competent nurseries to distribute them led to a huge expansion in popular and quite modest suburban gardening. However, as the century developed, the clients proved less selective and seemed content with quantities of 'improved' performance plants rather than experimenting with new species. The result, noted by horticultural writers and journalists at the time, as planting styles, and particularly schemes employing soft-stemmed perennials and annuals, evolved during the middle years of the century into a series of prescribed formulas, was that the actual range and availability of these same plants diminished. Nurseries came to offer *less* variety, reflecting the realities of contemporary demand.

NEW LAYOUTS FOR NEW PLANTS

As 'landscaping' in Brownian terms on the grand and 'natural' scale went out of fashion, an amazingly diverse range of gardening styles evolved to help display the new rarities.

Early in the century Repton re-introduced the flower garden either on terraces near the house or by devising separate flower-garden areas throughout the extended pleasure grounds – in particular making 'American Gardens' with soil specially prepared for the acid bog-loving eastern American plants and others with similar needs. This prepared the way for the implementation of further 'compartmentalization', based on historical precedent and styles as much as on particular plant themes. There were Dutch and French, Gothic and 'picturesque', Italianate and Elizabethan gardens – at Elvaston there was even an enclosed garden called the Alhambra in compliment to Islamic styles – none of them of great historical authenticity, but all containing elements of an earlier style which could be loosely adapted to growing a much wider plant range than when it first evolved. Loudon distinguished between these varying 'historicist' layouts as the geometric (exploiting French, Italian, Dutch and Tudor themes), the rustic (which evolved with no particular format but had a cottage-garden simplicity), the 'picturesque' (which imitated natural terrain but did not provide for appreciation of individual trees, new or old), and the 'gardenesque'; this last, although at first used in quite modest-sized suburban gardens, ultimately became the style most readily adopted by botanic gardens and by public parks – it was the

Veitch's Nurseries, run by succeeding generations of the Veitch family from 1808 until 1914, was one of the most important nurseries in the nineteenth century, responsible for sponsoring collecting of both hardy and tropical plants all over the world – their collectors included the Lobb brothers and E. H. Wilson – as well as making available many nursery hybrids. Over 400 of the Veitch introductions were illustrated in Curtis's *Botanical Magazine*, including *Caryopteris incana*, a small blue-flowered shrub from Asia, a parent of *C. x clandonensis*, which, although introduced by Robert Fortune as a greenhouse plant in 1844, was lost and reintroduced to Europe by Charles Maries in 1880.

antithesis of the contemporary 'picturesque' in which wild and gnarled plants twined in romantic painterly profusion (see pp. 246–47). Loudon himself designed one of the first public parks, the Derby Arboretum, in 1839, for education as well as recreation. With a peripheral walk and sinuous raised mounds, it expressed his version of the 'gardenesque' but, just as important to him, also furthered his schemes for creating 'breathing zones' for the people of the big cities. His plan for a type of green-belt system for London was never realized.

Nor, of course, were all gardens landscape parks. Most pleasure gardens would have contained shrubberies, backed by tall trees, with foreground planting of herbaceous plants, very much in the style of Wooburn Farm or the more precisely delineated island beds at Nuneham. In 1829 William Cobbett advised on how shrubberies should be laid out and deplored the recent fashion for establishing 'clumps of shrubs, or independent shrubs, upon grass plats', instead advocating 'a sweep of lawn surrounded with suitable shrubs and flowers separated from it by walks of beautiful gravel'. Cobbett sounds quite modern.

In the first half of the century some gardens became show-cases exemplifying several of Loudon's categories. Alton Towers, already begun in 1814, had a bewildering number of garden buildings and features; later Lord Shrewsbury's son added a box and gravel parterre in Italianate style designed in the form of a giant 'S' by W. A. Nesfield, the whole softened and 'improved' by an excess of trees, rhododendrons, heathers, rock and moss work which conveyed an exotic jungle effect. At Biddulph Grange there was an Egyptian garden with yew, flanked by stone sphinxes, clipped to resemble the pyramids; this hid a Dahlia Walk and the 'quiet green' of the Pinetum. Beyond it was 'China', reached through a rock tunnel, where Asiatic trees and shrubs framed a tea-house and red-painted bridge; elsewhere a French-style parterre was planted with low-growing monkey puzzles (*Araucaria araucana*, first introduced by Menzies in 1795 but only available in quantity from viable seed obtained by William Lobb in 1844 on his first expedition to Chile). An avenue of deodars (*Cedrus deodara* came from the Himalayas in 1831) and wellingtonias (*Sequoiadendron giganteum*, usually ascribed to William Lobb's collecting and offered by Veitch in 1853 at two guineas, reduced to one guinea if the client took twelve or more) stretched up a hill outlining the edges of a narrow path, the hill giving the illusion of a distant obelisk.

W. A. Nesfield, landscape painter and garden designer, is best remembered for the elaborate parterres in Italianate style with which he decorated the terraces of the great houses of England in the 1840s and '50s. Nesfield did not use only gravel to make the 'alleys' between his lines of box, but also brick dust, minerals, coals, chalk or coloured marble chips – he gave Lady Emily Foley at Stoke Edith a blue top dressing which contained lead and killed the box. One of the only surviving parterre layouts can be seen at Broughton Hall in Yorkshire, where Nesfield recommended allowing the box to grow only up to a height of some 10 centimetres/4 inches.

At Elvaston Castle the planting of conifer avenues, and grafting and transplanting of trees by the head gardener William Barron during the 1840s, was matched in magnificence only by the yew topiary and series of strange inner gardens which lay enclosed behind high hedges (see pp. 248–49). The castle and estate at Elvaston lay in the flat plain of the River Derwent where there were few natural features or advantages of views. It did not appeal to Lancelot Brown, whose advice had been sought when he was at his peak of influence; finding the situation had no 'capabilities', Brown had declined its improvement but instead he gave the third earl six seedling cedars of Lebanon which were planted near the house. The seventeenth-century house was remodelled by Wyatt in 1817 and the fourth earl who succeeded in 1830 employed the young Scotsman, Barron, who had trained at the Botanic Garden in Edinburgh and worked at Syon House, to transform the garden. From then until the earl's death in 1851 a vast programme of 'improvements' took place, which included trenching and laying drains for four years prior to any planting. Eighty gardeners performed the work of planting, grafting and clipping, making a lake with a rugged picturesque rock garden, and laying out, besides the avenues and forests, an eccentric series of essentially symbolic gardens, which became private shrines to immortalize the romantic love between the earl and his actress mistress who later became his wife. Vast avenues 18 metres/60 feet wide, some stretching for a mile and a half into the plain to provide views to the Nottingham hills, were arranged in double or triple rows; in one there were upright yews, red cedars and deodars grafted in 'the side manner' described by Loudon in his *Arboretum et Fruticetum Britannicum*. Beyond the avenues there were extensive collections of pines and other conifers, some of which had been introduced only recently.

Even before 'bedding out' became the rage, many of the greater estates had reintroduced some form of Renaissance-style parterre layout on flat areas in the main lawns near the house. At Oxburgh Hall in Norfolk a parterre (restored by the National Trust in this century) was laid out according to the principles of Le Nôtre from a plan taken straight out of Dezallier d'Argenville. By far the most influential practitioner of the 'Italianate' style, based both on the surviving gardens of Renaissance Italy and on French seventeenth-century interpretations, was William Andrews Nesfield (1793–1881) who from the 1830s often worked with the architects Anthony Salvin (his brother-in-law) and Charles Barry in devising monumental schemes of terraces and parterres. His 'Italian' parterres were often lifted from the French pattern books. In England Nesfield's advice was 'now sought for by gentlemen of taste in every part of the country'.[1] Nesfield often used box scrolls, sometimes delineating the owners' monograms, set off by different coloured gravels and sands to create his effects. In 1862 he published some of his ideas of colour combinations in the *Gardeners' Chronicle*. In England it was an almost forgotten period style, while in many Continental gardens the French baroque embroidery system had been retained even while the rest of a garden had been extended to become fashionably naturalistic as a landscape park. Nesfield also proposed radiating avenues – the Broad Walk and the Syon vista at Kew are his work; he used plants as architecture, both in their natural shapes – such as upright Irish yew, common juniper and red cedar – as well as in more controlled topiary; large box, phillyreas, Portugal laurel were all welcome in cut and shaped forms. For the Horticultural Society's gardens at South Kensington in 1860 Nesfield devised a maze, a shrubbery, geometric flower-beds and box embroidery besides the rather dominant gravel walks, terraces and water basins which, in his style, tended to dwarf his plants.

PLANTS FOR BEDDING

The new trees and shrubs for permanent sites in a layout were further augmented by a vast number of colourful annuals which, reared in glasshouses as seedlings or cuttings, planted out and tended by bevies of gardeners, were best displayed massed in free-standing flower-beds for the summer months. Sheet glass was invented in 1833, and when the removal of the glass tax by 1845 reduced its price, greenhouses proliferated. It became within the means of quite modest gardeners to prepare massed annuals and tender plants – many of them, such as petunias, calceolarias, salvias and verbenas from South and Central America, with bright tropical colour – as well as prized South Africans, until now only grown in stove houses. Summer display in beds could be achieved in the gardens of suburban villas of the new middle classes as easily as on the large estates and in public garden layouts.

As it developed in the 1830s and 1840s, 'bedding out' of annuals and tender plants, grown from seed or overwintered as rooted cuttings, was a logical extension of the Reptonian flower-garden planting in which any suitable flower or sunk flower-pot would be used to make flower-beds bright with colour for as long as possible during a summer season (see pp. 250–51). As more and more annuals became available for bedding out for summer display, more and more space was given to the flower-filled beds, which to contemporary Victorians seemed in many ways to share an affinity with Tudor knots or later French-style flower parterres. Besides, this sort of 'temporary' planting implemented Loudon's concept of the 'changeable flower garden'; it gradually developed into a routine of concentric circles of purple heliotrope, yellow calceolarias, scarlet geraniums and salvias and blue lobelias filling flower-beds with colour from June until October. It was not until after 1850 that garden writers (such as Shirley Hibberd) and practitioners began to recommend extending the season with spring bulbs such as tulips and narcissus (the self-coloured Darwin tulips, now so popular, were not available until the 1880s and daffodil breeding did not really begin until the 1860s), hyacinths, anemones, pansies, biennial wallflowers and forget-me-nots, as well as pompon chrysanthemums for autumn flowering.

Whether the overall garden theme was based on 'old' Italian, French, Dutch or English styles, which had reigned supreme before the craze for sublime nature had swept away beds near the house, flower-filled parterres were now the rage. As early as 1826 the *Gardener's Magazine* could report that at Phoenix Park in Dublin alonsoas, pelargoniums and heliotropes were 'planted in distinctly separate beds throughout the flower garden where they blow through the summer and autumn in great luxuriance', a very different effect from sweet Williams, columbines and hollyhocks with a duration of three weeks' flowering. It seems that even as William Cobbett was describing beds massed with one sort of flower as largely out of fashion (except among florists), tastes were changing, mainly to accommodate the new seasonal flowers.

Moreover, by emphasizing the 'unnatural' or unspontaneous qualities of these long-flowering but temporary plants, the gardeners established the required triumph of art and horticultural skill over nature, as well as providing a much extended season of floral interest. In 1828 at Whitmore Lodge in Sunninghill in Surrey Robert Mangles had two parterres: one had a central bed massed with scarlet *Salvia splendens* (introduced only in 1823) surrounded by nine other beds carpeted with variegated- or ivy-leaved geraniums; the other was planted with alternating standard roses (new in 1818)[2] and *Calceolaria corymbosa* underplanted with scented mignonette.

As hybridization of pelargoniums, lobelias, petunias, verbenas and calceolarias brought increased variety, these, with the scarlet bedding salvias, between them covered all the main paintbox colours – yellow, purple, scarlet, blue, pink and white. As they became most widely used these often ousted other plants, which soon became unavailable as nurseries reduced their stock to accommodate massed supplies of the cultivars and hybrids most in demand.

At Trentham Park and at Shrubland Park there were new refinements. Scientific colour theories, describing how colours could alter and affect each other, produced more rather than less dogmatism. Colour controversy proved highly subjective. More subtle, and much more closely allied to sophisticated modern colour harmonies, were Lady Middleton's ideas for 'shading' at Shrubland Park, 'the highest style in the art of flower gardening' in

which groups of flowers of extremely similar colours were arranged to blend like rows in Berlin wool work. Within sight of the Italian Garden at Trentham Fleming laid out a serpentine bed of forget-me-nots, known as 'the rivulet', which wound down towards the lake in imitation of a meandering stream.[3] As colour schemes continued to be a subject of intellectual argument, shapes of flower-beds were in general simplified and the beds were arranged in symmetrical patterns.

At first, of course, the floral schemes existed only in select gardens but the displays at the Crystal Palace at Sydenham in 1854 were devised for public consumption and were the first to be generally influential; an elaborate unified scheme of flower-beds was dominated by yellow calceolarias and scarlet geraniums; in *Parks, Promenades and Gardens of Paris* William Robinson condemned it out of hand – 'a more horrid impression is received than in any part of Versailles'.

By the time the public had wholeheartedly adopted the 'bedding' system and extremes of colour contrast, the *cognoscenti* were ready to abandon it or modify its extremes. By the 1870s and 1880s many owners and gardeners in private estates toned down the garish schemes; others, resenting the short-term effects of annuals, in which plants were exhibited only at one stage of their life cycle, voiced a desire for more natural effects, with plants considered more as individuals than as a unit in massing. William Robinson, by the 1870s vehemently opposed to all features of the bedding system, was not a lone voice crying in the wilderness but rather expressed, if in somewhat insistent tones, a feeling already current in many gardening circles.

One of the reasons why Nesfield's Italianate style proved so popular during the 1840s was the belief that it resembled the English garden style which had existed before Kent and Brown had swept away all traces of ordered alleys, clipped trees and patterned parterres. Another Victorian giant was Joseph Paxton (1803–65), who not only designed greenhouses and filled them with tropical exotics – in 1849 he was the first to flower the South American water-lily *Victoria amazonica* – but was also a thoroughly knowledgeable gardener, extending Nesfield's Italian themes for private and public sites all over the country, and experimenting with foreign trees and other plants as soon as they could be procured. As head gardener and later agent to the Duke of Devonshire, Paxton planted cedars, monkey puzzles, Japanese aucubas and

FUCHSIA Magellanica.   FUCHSIA Magellanique. *Page 57.*

The first fuchsia (named for Leonhard Fuchs, whose *De Historia Stirpium* was published in 1542) was described by Charles Plumier in *Nova Plantarum Americanum Genera* (1703), but seems not to have been introduced until much later, in 1788. Plumier's fuchsia was almost certainly *Fuchsia coccinea*, found from southern Peru to Tierra del Fuego and grown by the Empress Josephine at Malmaison by 1800. Pierre Joseph Redouté (1759–1840) drew 306 of the illustrations for the *Nouveau Duhamel*; Plate 13 in Volume I (as shown above) is named as *Fuchsia magellanica*, one of the hardiest of the genus, but may, in fact, be *F. coccinea*. *F. fulgens*, the parent of most of our modern tender varieties, came from seed sent by Theodor Hartweg from Mexico to the Horticultural Society of London in the early 1840s.

laurels in quantity at Chatsworth, augmenting both the seventeenth-century garden and Brown's landscape park with exotic plant interest. In 1829 Paxton brought seedlings of Douglas's

newly arrived 'pines' (*Pseudotsuga menziesii*) to Chatsworth from London in his hat; by 1835 they had reached a height of 10.5 metres/35 feet.

RUSTIC ADORNMENTS

Mid-century horticultural writers such as Shirley Hibberd (1825–90) advised on rustic adornments for the modest garden with an emphasis on foliage plants to be grown in separate areas. Although not entirely against the practice of seasonal bedding out, Hibberd especially recommended using hardy trees, shrubs and perennials as well as hardy ferns and ivies planted in sensible places to produce enough interest and variety to keep the garden going through the winter months. Hibberd, although less well remembered than William Robinson, to whom he was an understanding patron, was a prolific writer and journalist. His writings seem the epitome of common sense. Where Robinson was dictatorial and aggressive, Hibberd cajoled, leading the reader through sweet reason to share his opinions. Most of his books, which include *The Fern Garden* (1869), *The Amateur's Flower Garden* (first published in 1871) and five volumes of *Familiar Garden Flowers*, are composed of extracts from his contributions to the *Floral World*, of which he was editor from 1858. Hibberd was essentially practical and wrote from his own experience for owners with small gardens and moderate means rather than those with great estates. His own garden in Lordship Terrace near Stoke Newington was still hardly in the London suburbs in the 1860s; he published plans of it, a typical long narrow town garden, in the *Floral World*, showing 'before', 'intermediate' and 'after' stages. Although not ostensibly against the fashionable practice of 'bedding' (he included a section on the parterre and suitable plants for it), Hibberd recommended it only for larger or municipal gardens, at the same time striking a few notes of warning: 'during the past twenty years there has been a constantly increasing tendency to superficial glare and glitter in garden embellishment, to the neglect of the more solid features that make a garden more interesting and attractive, not only today and tomorrow' but 'all the year round', and he deplored the 'tendency to regard gardens as exhibition grounds and tender plants of the geranium, verbena, and petunia type as their only proper occupants'. Equally, the detail of planting out in a bedding scheme could be a trap for the unwary or tasteless: 'in planting the

Shirley Hibberd (1825–90), the horticultural writer, recommended a delightful pelargonium pyramid, in which dwarf bedding hybrids, mostly derived from *Pelargonium zonale* and *P. inquinans*, give a fine display. The engraving is from the *Floral World* of 1866, of which he was editor. Hibberd, writing in the *Gardeners' Chronicle* in 1880, remarked that 'it must be evident to every cultivator of these flowers that the blood of a score or so of species is mingled in them'. Fashions swung between the circular flower with overlapping petals, a type preferred in Victorian England, to the Continental ideal of a two-lipped flower with separated petals. Today there are many fewer hybrids available than in the nineteenth century.

parterre it is as easy to make mistakes as in designing it'; he suggested not using primary colours in excessive quantity but experimenting with neutral tints to soften the effects: 'The stereotyped repetition of scarlet geraniums and yellow calceolarias is in the last degree vulgar and tasteless and the common dispositions of red, white and blue are better adapted to delight savages than represent the artistic status of a civilized people.' He felt the increasing use of varying leaf colours in more muted tones a 'great advance in taste'.

He was quite positive in what he could recommend, suggesting that flowers should have their beauties heightened by harmonious surroundings which should include outer boundaries of trees and shrubs, intersecting walks, belts of evergreens, mixed borders, 'air-inviting lawns', all combining to create a setting without the need for a parterre. He advocated a rose garden at some distance from the house, so that it need only be visited when actually in flower, as well as a rockery and fern garden, and an American Garden with soil suitable for all the Ericaceae including kalmias, rhododendrons and azaleas. If greenhouse and garden space allowed, there could be a sheltered area where soil could be warmed by the sun for large-leaved subtropicals as demonstrated by Mr Gibson at Battersea Park (see pp. 252–53).

In his advocacy of the hardy border Hibberd anticipated Robinson. 'The hardy herbaceous border is the best feature of the flower garden, although commonly regarded as the worst. When well made, well stocked and well managed, it presents us with flowers in abundance during ten months out of twelve. It is the best feature of the flower garden . . . while the bedding system is an embellishment the herbaceous border is a necessary fundamental feature.' The proper tenants of the border were hardy plants, among which should be included achilleas, aconitums, adonis, alstroemerias, aquilegias, asters, astilbes, camassias, dodecatheon, erythronium, hostas, cranesbills, gypsophila, hemerocallis, hollyhocks, lathyrus, phloxes, lilies (including *Lilium candidum, bulbiferum, auratum* and *longiflorum*), kniphofias, delphiniums, pinks, chrysanthemums, primulas, pyrethrums, potentillas, anemones, ranunculus, irises, oenotheras, foxgloves, campanulas, peonies, silene, smilacina, statice, symphytum (including ordinary comfrey and the grey-leaved *Symphytum caucasicum*), thalictrum, tradescantia and sisyrinchium. As usual Hibberd made very little fuss about how to grow these plants, stressing that as long as the soil was rich and dug deeply, most of the plants could be lifted, moved or divided 'as convenient and not by principles'.

THE WILD GARDEN: THE TASTE FOR NATURE REVIVED

Much of what Shirley Hibberd said was repeated by his protégé, the prophet of natural gardening, William Robinson (1838–1935), who revolutionized gardening attitudes with inflammatory writing in books and journals after the 1870s. Although at first much influenced by artificial schemes, particularly well achieved in the gardens of Paris, Robinson's theme song became the advocation of the 'natural' garden with hardy rather than tender plants used in all the garden schemes. Much of what he wrote expressed contemporary feelings of thinkers, art historians and painters such as the members of the Arts and Crafts movement who, in reaction to

Victorian industrialization and 'machine' production, preached a return to craftsmens' products and individual excellence, all with a strong bias towards natural rather than 'artful' stimulation. Robinson, aiming his writing at the new middle classes, made his most furious assault on 'the ugliest gardens ever made' in stylized Victorian formulas, and on topiary shapes which he described as 'the cramming of Chinese feet into impossible shoes'. Calling instead for gardens composed of predominantly hardy plants – foreign plants were allowed as long as they behaved like natives and did not need special techniques of growing in the English climate – he was really advocating ecological gardening. The gardener had to understand where and how plants grew in the wild and then place them accordingly, next to neighbours which required the same sort of environment and then allowing each group to spread into natural-looking drifts. *The Wild Garden* was published in 1870 and, illustrated by charming vignette paintings of happily naturalized plant groups by Alfred Parsons, introduced the reader to a new interpretation of the late-eighteenth-century 'picturesque' on a

flower-garden rather than a landscape scale. To make his point in the ordinary gardening world of the 1870s Robinson became a fervent crusader, battering readers with books and periodicals, encouraging them to grow old-fashioned hardy plants of the sort still then to be seen in gardens of cottage-like simplicity. He also became notorious for his quarrelsome advocacy of total informalism and condemnation of the architect's role in garden-making. Nevertheless it is the teachings of Robinson and his disciples such as Gertrude Jekyll, who used Robinsonian methods to turn

---

In *The Art and Practice of Landscape Gardening*, published in 1890, Henry Ernest Milner describes and illustrates his plans for Count Festetich's estate in Hungary on the shores of Lake Balaton. At Keszthely in 1885/6 Milner created undulations in flat areas north and east of the castle, planting trees and flowering shrubs on the mounds. Near the house Milner laid out flower gardens enclosed by yew hedges, displaying annuals and subtropical vegetation which did well in the summer heat of the Continental climate – with extremes very similar to that of the American Midwest – as well as dwarf rhododendrons, azaleas, heaths, pieris and pernettyas. To the south he planted a sunken garden with dwarf conifers.

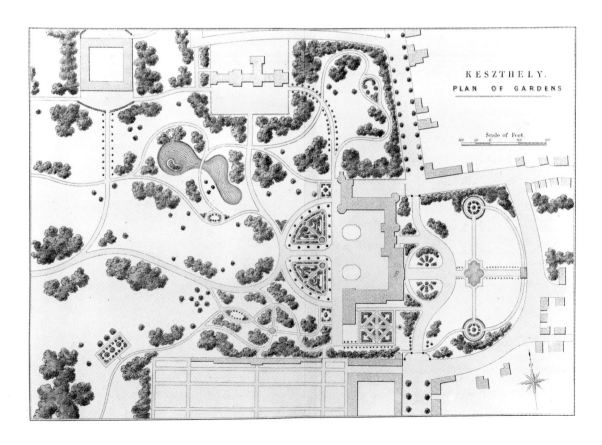

KESZTHELY.
PLAN OF GARDENS

Scale of Feet

borders and flower-beds into orchestrated dreams of beauty, that have most conclusively influenced the history of English gardening ever since. In more extreme climates, Robinson's and Jekyll's perennial growing is more difficult but, particularly in countries such as the United States with a vast range of garden flora of its own, the revival of the natural garden as a style has survived as a triumphant ingredient of modern gardening-making. The native plant garden in America remains a direct descendant of the Robinsonian ideal. The great plantsmen-collectors' gardens established in Europe at the turn of the century are in essence Robinsonian in style, with design schemes subordinated to the natural and beautiful development of plant growth.

Robinson's *The English Flower Garden*, published in 1883, went into fifteen editions during his lifetime, the last in 1933. The book, in two sections, with the first containing 'general' gardening advice pertaining to different garden themes and the second a catalogue of suitable hardy plants for growing in the open air in the British Isles, was in fact not written entirely by Robinson but had contributions by reigning experts on their own specialities – such as Gertrude Jekyll writing on colour schemes. Robinson's importance to posterity lies in his influence in general, often affecting gardeners who have neither heard of him nor comprehend the term 'Robinsonian'. He was the first to trumpet the desirability of planting in an ecological way so that plants would not only thrive in particular sites but would look well growing together. His *The Wild Garden* (its essence effectively captured in a section in *The English Flower Garden*) was revolutionary in its thinking at a time when great estates were planting mainly tender plants and annuals massed in beds for temporary seasonal effects.

In the next hundred years Robinson's revival of interest in hardy plants was as often misinterpreted as Loudon's definition of the 'gardenesque' early in the century; while 'gardenesque' came to represent a hotchpotch of stylistic muddle combined with an *ad hoc* collection of rare plants, Robinsonian labels have been given to

At Heale House on the Avon in Wiltshire, winter aconites (*Eranthis hyemalis*) and snowdrops (mostly *Galanthus nivalis*) spread in drifts in the light woodland. In other parts of the garden cyclamen, both *Cyclamen coum* and *C.hederifolium*, naturalize in equal profusion for winter and September flowering. William Robinson's encouragement of natural gardening, in which plants are encouraged to thrive and multiply on their own, has developed into a form of 'Robinsonian' gardening perfected in both Europe and in North America.

the ultimate in 'wild' and untidy gardening, often no more than tips of multiplying weeds.

For Robinson there were only two garden styles; that of the despised 'formal' garden (a new term only introduced by his arch enemy Reginald Blomfield in *The Formal Garden in England*, published in 1892) and that which with 'true humility and right desire . . . accepting nature as a guide' he himself advocated. Blomfield (and John D. Sedding in *Garden Craft Old and New*, published posthumously in 1891) both advocated a return to old-fashioned formality. In a new interpretation of the ideal architect-designed garden, they stressed the importance of linking house and garden styles together in the purest way of the Italian Renaissance. Blomfield relegated the gardener and his plants to a minor role and much of his historical argument was inaccurate; nevertheless his garden philosophies helped to establish both in England and in America a coherent Edwardian architectural style in which a profusion of plants was framed by walls, steps and hedges. These architectural layouts and those of garden designers such as Thomas Mawson remained anathema to advocates of the Robinsonian natural flower garden. In reality in the following century both styles were found to co-exist in admirable and amiable partnership.

It seems that the dialectic conducted during the last decade of the nineteenth century cleared the air for some of the finest gardening effects, in which the best plants accumulated and experimented with during a century of spectacular foreign introductions were combined with well-proportioned architecture. The compartmentalized garden, with Biddulph and other nineteenth-century gardens as earlier and grander models, developed to encompass a series of different architectural and plant themes in a cohesive whole.

At Gravetye, a Tudor manor set in a fold of the Sussex hills, William Robinson in 1885, owning a garden for the first time after twenty years of garden journalism and preaching to others, implemented many of the more naturalistic themes advocated in his writings (see pp. 254–55). Finally recognizing that a house needs a frame, he also laid out conventional straight-edged flower-beds, filled with his favourite violas, pinks and roses and, of course, other flowers, under pergolas tangled with more roses and clematis (some named for his gardener, Ernest Markham), on horizontal terraces round the house; in this area he tempered the layout to traditional geometry but inside each bed used informal free-style planting, a technique later exploited by Gertrude Jekyll, Lawrence Johnston and Vita Sackville-West to achieve new standards of cottage-style perfection. His 'wild' gardening took place appropriately in the open meadows which lay below the house, on sloping banks in woodland and beside the upper and lower lakes. Robinson also took advice from Robert Marnock (1800–89), for whom he had worked in the Royal Botanic Society's garden in Regent's Park when he first came to England from Ireland in 1861. Marnock, by now a respected designer and nurseryman, visited Gravetye several times from spring 1886 onwards, recommending the choice of site for the kitchen garden north of the house as well as general planting tactics such as incorporating fields into the park.

Robinson's gardening at Gravetye reflected the planting opportunities which were available to his contemporaries – albeit the more sophisticated ones – at the end of the nineteenth century. His dilemmas in choosing plants, and, in particular, in the need to rationalize collecting with some sort of coherence in design, remain as much dilemmas for gardeners in the late twentieth century as in other eras.

Robinson found native shrubs difficult to obtain from commercial nurseries but achieved plantings of water-elder or guelder rose (*Viburnum opulus*), dwarf gorse, sloe, cut-leaved bramble (*Rubus laciniatus*, grown since 1770 but origin unknown), honeysuckles, dyer's greenweed (*Genista tinctoria*), ivy, tamarisks, euonymus or spindle, sea buckthorn and bog myrtle or sweet gale (*Myrica gale*), interplanted with red-stemmed dogwoods (forms of *Cornus alba*, found from Siberia to Manchuria) to augment his natural-looking effects, in places where 'rhododendrons look prim and out of place'. Other successful plantations made in 1888 were of Austrian or Corsican pine (*Pinus nigra maritima*), which survived to make huge groves until the storm of 1987 – when 200, some of them 30 metres/110 feet tall, fell in one night. November frosts in 1890 killed off many evergreen shrubs including holm oaks, Oregon grape mahonias, South American escallonias and New Zealand shrubs, while American native rhododendrons such as *R. maximum* and *R. catawbiensis* as well as mountain laurel (*Kalmia latifolia*) proved hardy, especially if they had been planted in May or even June rather than in the autumn. Robinson was enthusiastic about the new water-lily hybrids from M. Marliac in France, who

experimented with crossing hardy and tropical nymphaeas, introduced after 1893.

In tree planting Robinson rivalled eighteenth-century landowners. During the decade before 1900 he planted 1,000 cedars of Lebanon, groves of Douglas fir, Crimean pine (*Pinus nigra caramanica*), larch, a few thousand sugar maples (*Acer saccharum*), a large collection of American hickories sent to him by Frederick Law Olmsted, American thorns (and other thorns) and crabs as well as lower-growing snowy mespilus (forms of the shadbush *Amelanchier*) and Siberian dogwood. In 1892 he planted a hedge of cockspur thorn (*Crataegus crus-galli*) grown from seed. A hundred *Clematis montana* and *C. viticella*, 100 evergreen honeysuckles (*Lonicera sempervirens* from North America) as well as climbing, tea and Dijon roses were all planted in 1892. In 1894 Veitch's nursery gave Robinson some of the acid-loving plants recently introduced from the Far East. *Rhododendron racemosum* came from the Yunnan in 1892, *Magnolia hypoleuca* and *M. parviflora* from Japan, and the Japanese garden hybrid *M. x watsonii* from these two parent plants. Other Veitch gifts from Asian sources included *Enkianthus campanulatus*, *Styrax japonica*, the lovely *Daphne genkwa* from China, *Daphniphyllum macropodum*, clerodendrons, *Cornus macrophylla*, the tender twining *Caesalpinia japonica*, *Lindera obtusiloba*, *Stachyurus praecox*, *Cleyera japonica* with marbled grey leaves, and the tender sun-loving species *Camellia sasanqua* (not generally available for another few years) as well as *Caryopteris incana* (the dominant parent of today's popular forms of *C. x clandonensis*).

At the same time Robinson was naturalizing 'noble hardy' perennials and biennials as recommended in his own books. Anchusas, rose campion, bellflowers, aconitums, goat's rue, Taurian cotton or scotch thistle (*Onopordon acanthium*), *Buphthalmum speciosum*, baptisias, 250 new starworts and giant heracleums were all planted where hopefully they could fend for themselves. In 1896 crocus and chionodoxa in thousands, red puccoon or bloodroot (*Sanguinaria canadensis*), *Scilla bifolia*, 1,000 fritillaries, tulips and narcissus (he planted more than 200,000 of these in cattle tracks and hollows, just covering them with mud) with 50 fair ladies of France (*Ranunculus aconitifolius*) and 50 blue alpine clematis are all mentioned. New trees included 100 honey locust (*Gleditsia triacanthos*) from North America, with new robinia clones (usually of French origin) and the shrubby *Exochorda racemosa* from China. In 1908 he planted 30 maidenhair trees (*Ginkgo biloba*) which

he underplanted with more *Narcissus poeticus* from the Bayonne.

The story of Gravetye is a microcosm of contemporary horti-cultural opportunity and practice, executed by one of Britain's foremost and most influential gardeners. In the developments at Gravetye Robinson's rather emphatic and didactic writings, aimed at influencing and changing the gardening habits of a nation, can be reinterpreted and modified by a real situation in which hazards of soil, climate and pests as well as plant behaviour require frequent rationalization of planting schemes. Robinson, gardening and living at Gravetye until his death in 1935, bridges the nineteenth and twentieth centuries and his precepts live on today in most modern gardens.

At Les Quatre Vents in Canada, 145 kilometres/90 miles north of Quebec on the St Lawrence river, Francis Cabot has expanded his short-season garden to include quite formal planting as well as more naturalistic woodland and open meadows above the house. In the photograph 'wild' flowers, including European lythrum and ox-eye daisies, are encouraged to compete with grasses to make naturalistic effects – Robinson would have approved. Mown paths are cut through the meadow and lead to the Music House glimpsed in the distance.

HUMPHRY REPTON

By the 1790s Humphry Repton (1751–1818) had taken on the mantle of Lancelot Brown (d. 1783) in the art of 'landscape gardening' – a descriptive phrase he himself invented; from then until his death he continued to reshape new and old landscapes (sometimes remodelling those of Brown himself), until by 1816 he had produced over 400 of the famous 'red books', each bound in red morocco, in which he wrote his reports for a client beside 'before' and 'after' watercolour sketches. These served as his working documents but they provide later generations with a chance of capturing his contemporary outlook and vision. Although many of Repton's parks have survived in part, we would have little idea of his flower-gardening repertoire without these records.

Even before he advocated the reinstatement of flowers near the house, Repton, while admiring Brown's 'clumping and dotting', developed his own views on planting in the park. Where Brown planted groves of trees for future generations to enjoy, Repton used his visual awareness of distance and his artist's eye to recommend filling with shrubbery below the canopy of the tree branches, thus creating quicker effects and making a more solid screen to add to the element of 'surprise'. In Repton's parks, instead of encircling perimeter tree planting, woods or smaller scale groves were planned so that different views were revealed at definite moments; the house glimpsed from a distant approach and then concealed by thick planting until again dramatically revealed almost on arrival.

Repton's proposals for flower-bed designs often included pots sunk in the ground to mix with more permanent planting. Herbaceous plants, roses, shrubs and geraniums – pelargoniums – were all proposed for the Prince Regent's garden at the Brighton Pavilion. The plans were not executed – the prince used Nash instead. John Adey Repton designed beds in the form of baskets, known as *corbeilles* or 'Hardenberg' baskets, for Glienicke at Potsdam, at the instigation of Prince Pückler-Muskau's father-in-law State Chancellor Hardenberg. These basket beds, with their handles and basketwork (later iron) edging, became fashionable in the 1820s and were adopted by the German designer Peter Lenné who used them in many of his gardens.

Repton differed most fundamentally from Brown in considering an employer's 'convenience'; he reinstated elegant terraces, gravelled paths and enclosed flower-garden areas near the house and designed 'hidden' rosaries or distinct flowery schemes for visiting in outer parts of the Pleasure Grounds. In 'Sunshine after Rain' (*left*), an aquatint taken from his *Fragments* published in 1816, an intimate garden with flower-filled box-edged beds, all enclosed by lattice-work fence and trellis, indicates his taste as it had developed by the early years of the nineteenth century. As more and more flowering plants became readily available, Repton joined with his clients in finding ways to use them while still retaining the more naturalistic outer landscape park.

The neo-classical greenhouse (*below*) at Sheringham Hall in Norfolk, designed by Humphry Repton and his son John Adey Repton in 1812, provides the architectural backdrop to some typical Reptonian flower-beds, in this case in free-flowing shapes dotted on the lawn. By 1803 Repton wrote, in his *observations on the Theory and Practice of Landscape Gardening*, 'a flower garden should be detached from the general scenery of the place . . . protected by an inner fence . . . within this enclosure rare plants of every description should be encouraged.'

At Endsleigh in Devon, Repton landscaped the view of the valley of the river Tamar for the sixth Duke of Bedford in 1814. As can be seen in the above 'before and after' illustrations, the terrace, with conservatory and rock walls for planting as a background, was levelled to give a more formal and 'narrowed' prospect. Repton ensured that the rugged characteristics of the hillside and river valley, with 'the foreground changed to a garden scene', would still contain all the elements of drama, with the ground falling steeply from the flat terraced walk. He believed that 'numerous class of rock-plants should have beds of rugged stone provided for their reception, without the affectation of such stones being the natural production of the soil'.

PRINCE PÜCKLER-MUSKAU

In Prince Pückler's park at Muskau the river Neisse flowed in a narrow valley through the undulating parkland which, he believed, could be opened up with views to distant mountains while still incorporating existing features – such as the arable land, the working of a local alum mine and the town – into the whole composition. In spite of inherently difficult sandy and marshy terrain, Pückler intended to use the natural topography to make a work of art. He was inspired by English landscape parks and planting schemes, particularly those of both Repton and Nash which he had admired during his two English visits. He was helped by his head gardener Heinrich Rehder (1790–1852) and at times 200 workers, widening the river valley to make lakes and using the spoil to alter the contours. Early on he took advice from Karl Friedrich Schinkel (1781–1840) whose ideas he also influenced, but, frustrated by financial failure, he often found himself unable to complete schemes. From 1845, forced to recoup by selling his beloved Muskau, he devoted his energies to improving the park of another of his properties at Branitz.

In his book, *Andeutungen über Landschaftsgärtnerei* (or 'Hints on Landscape Gardening'), he considered trees and shrubs and their grouping and more intimate flower-garden areas. In general Pückler produced rules to guide planting, such as: 'It is better in general . . . to group one kind in connected masses instead of planting too many single and isolated specimens . . . Only those plants which have in their beginning the same relative height that they attain in proportion to one another when full grown [are recommended].' Pückler's flower-beds, often as formal compositions placed before the main building, could be edged with basketwork (the best), alternatives were wooden or earthenware edgings, or those plaited simply with osiers. 'Flower-beds, star and rosette-shaped, surrounded by box borders, big vases, French parterres with gravel walks and elegant flower stands – all these are here in place with appropriate surroundings'.

The view from the castle (*left*), after the prince had redesigned the park. Having read Repton's *Fragments on the Theory and Practice of Landscape Gardening*, published in 1816, Prince Pückler invited Repton to come to Saxony. Repton was already dead, but his son, John Adey Repton (1775–1860), arrived at Muskau in the spring of 1822. On J. A. Repton's advice, which concurred with his own judgement, the prince removed twenty trees of the formal lime avenue to produce a more picturesque effect. Pückler also created a level area by filling in the moat. On this he laid out flower-beds in a style which seems a foretaste of the foliage schemes known as 'mosaïculture', adopted at the end of the century by all the grander gardens in Europe.

The oriental-style garden at Muskau has all the elements of the picturesque (*right*). Arranged on little hummocks, reached by steps and winding paths, kiosks and pavilions are framed with trees and shrubs. For his shrubberies, regretting the cold Prussian climate which limited the use of ornamental evergreens, Pückler advocated the styles recommended by Mr Nash, who massed shrubs closely together to allow grass to disappear in wide sweeps under the plants, thus preventing black earth from showing, and allowing the shrubs to develop as a thicket, augmenting the planting with herbaceous plants and annuals. He set various trees and larger shrubs as specimens in the lawn.

The rosary at Muskau had a strong resemblance to rosaries designed by Humphry Repton earlier in the century. Instead of garlands festooning chains, Prince Pückler grew his largest roses in tubs, arranging them around elaborate beds in a pattern based on the shape of a rose with flower petal segments; central stamens were represented by a basket filled with flowers.

LODDIGES NURSERY AND THE *BOTANICAL CABINET*

The Loddiges Nursery was outstanding among the many nurseries that proliferated towards the end of the eighteenth century. By 1817 they had such as assemblage of plants, that they began their own publication of a monthly illustrated periodical, the *Botanical Cabinet*, which was to continue for sixteen years. By 1823, the Loddiges Nursery, now under the founder Conrad's sons, George Loddiges and his brother William, covered 6 hectares/15 acres in Hackney. It probably had the greatest collection of plants in the world assembled together to be chosen and grown by English and European gardeners both outside and in hot-houses. In 1823, the year Douglas set out for the north-west coast of America, the Loddiges catalogue consisted of 48 pages, each of triple columns, of which the last twelve pages were limited to herbaceous and bulbous plants. This predated Robert Fortune's visit to China in the 1840s and also the introduction of the many annuals, including verbenas and petunias, from South America. Nevertheless the herbaceous section, starting with *Acaena*, includes 28 species of achillea, 53 aconitums, 47 alliums, 22 anemones including both single and double forms of the little woodland *Anemonella thalictroides* from North America, 8 aquilegias including the green-brown-flowered *Aquilegia*

Plate 1635 from the *Botanical Cabinet* shows *Eschscholzia californica*. Most of the 2,000 plates were drawn by George Loddiges and engraved by George Cooke and a few executed by Cooke's son Edward. The latter, who married George Loddiges's daughter, was later to become eminent not only as a marine painter but also as a garden designer, advising James Bateman at Biddulph Grange; ferns and orchids, ferneries and Wardian cases were among his special interests. Probably Cooke and Bateman first met at Loddiges's nursery in Hackney, where the Cookes lived in order to facilitate the portrayal of plants. George Loddiges was a major influence in Edward Cooke's development as painter and gardener.

viridiflora from Siberia and western China – still rare today – 11 artemisias, 8 asclepias, 44 different asters, and 60 campanulas. There were also 25 dianthus, 16 euphorbias and 19 different gentians, 37 thalictrums and 33 violas. The catalogue ends with the following note: 'In an establishment of this nature there of course must exist an ardent and continual desire of extending, as well as diffusing the collection. Persons in foreign countries, who are animated by a similar passion, are respectfully invited to a Correspondence, which can hardly fail to become mutually advantageous. A liberal price is at all times ready to be given for fresh seeds or living plants, if new or rare, from whatever quarter of the globe they may have been brought.'

A fine specimen palm (*Latania borbonica*) from Mauritius, once owned by the Empress Josephine at Malmaison, being transferred to the Crystal Palace. Moving the celebrated 9-metre/30-foot high palm tree was a feat in itself, requiring a 3.6-metre/12-foot square strong box bound with iron hoops, which itself weighed 760 kg/15 cwt; with the cart this made a total of 20 tons. Loddiges had a collection of 120 different palm species, most of which, after being refused by Kew when the nursery declined in the middle of the century, were bought by Sir Joseph Paxton for the Great Exhibition at Hyde Park; the rest were moved to Sydenham after 1851.

Much of the nursery's success in introducing plants was due to careful packing in the country of origin. A system which transformed conditions for plants that had to be kept growing during a voyage was Nathaniel Ward's invention of his completely sealed glass case, in which the moisture transpired by the plants was condensed to be used again in an endless cycle. This case was developed by experiments with ferns and other plants actually in the nursery and Edward Cooke, who contributed illustrations for Ward's *On the Growth of Plants in Closely Glazed Cases* (1852), also designed Wardian cases for the 1851 exhibition.

THE GARDENESQUE

The term 'gardenesque' has had a number of interpretations since Loudon adopted it in the 1830s. Looking back from the twentieth century, we see Loudon's recommendations for plants to be viewed as individual specimens as giving rise to a museum-like quality that detracts from any notion of the garden as a whole. The garden became a collection rather than a composed landscape and the style merely a way of incorporating the new exotic plants so that they could be most easily admired. Yet the fundamental inspiration for Loudon's views derived from the idea that 'Nature must acknowledge the supremacy of Art'.

For Loudon this was a simple conception, implying a method of ensuring that each individual plant should be allowed to develop its natural character as completely as possible – a situation more likely to be possible in gardens than in 'nature', where plants spring up in close proximity to each other, often 'spoiling' natural shapes and preventing a free development. Perhaps the idea was not so very different from Addison's early eighteenth-century pleas for trees to be allowed to grow freely into a natural conformation rather than being clipped and formed by man's hand. Loudon did not originate the style; instead he sought to give it rules and significance, and in this, during his lifetime,

he generally succeeded. By the 1860s and beyond, the 'gardenesque' became an excuse for almost any sort of free style that lacked coherence. In 1866, thirty-four years after the term was first adopted by Loudon, John Arthur Hughes defined the 'gardenesque' style as it had become accepted in the interval: 'The Gardenesque style is distinguished by the trees and shrubs, whether in masses or groups, being planted and thinned in such a manner as never to touch each other; so that, viewed near, each tree or shrub would be seen distinctly, while from a distance they show a high degree of beauty manifestly from the art which placed them where they are. The trees, shrubs and flowers are exotics, kept in a high state of cultivation, arranged in irregular groups with good outlines . . . Grace rather than grandeur is its characteristic.'[4]

Although Charles McIntosh's *Practical Gardener* was published in 1828 before the term 'gardenesque' was first coined, its frontispiece (*far left*) expresses many of the characteristics of the style. In the randomly scattered beds, herbaceous plants and shrubs are widely spaced for individual viewing.

Loudon suggested substituting exotic woody and herbaceous plants wherever possible for those which were indigenous. Sometimes he recommended simple exchanges of 'the cut-leaved alder for the common species'; the weeping poplar or the weeping willow and the paper birch (all characterized by an unusual habit) for the common forms, and especially, by natural water, using the introduced deciduous cypress (*Taxodium distichum*) as the prevailing species. An illustration (*left*) from the *Gardener's Magazine* in 1838 of an English garden and summer-house shows trees and shrubs planted so as to be admired as individual specimens exemplifying the 'gardenesque' style.

With so many new plants it was necessary to find new ways of showing them off. The 'gardenesque' linked the old-fashioned 'mixed' system and the 'massing' of both shrubs and flowers that developed later in the century. At first the term was applied mainly to the use of exotics, but it came to represent a style based on the isolation of individual trees, shrubs and flowers and often of garden features in a restless, non-cohesive way, as depicted in George Shepherd's painting of Battlesden gardens (1818). Its existence was already adversely commented on by the German architect Friedrich Ludwig von Sckell (1750–1823), the first German designer to be influenced by the English landscape style, and ultimately to reinterpret it for public parks in Germany and Poland. Prince Pückler-Muskau found fault when visiting English gardens in 1817, complaining that 'Each tree, and each shrub, has some particular charm to recommend it, and finally that none may be lost, he [the gardener] grasps them all. Thus I found the English gardens a real chaos of unconnected beauties'.

WILLIAM BARRON AND PLANTING AT ELVASTON CASTLE

One of the oddest gardens was that at Elvaston Castle, just outside Derby. There during the 1840s the fourth Earl of Harrington and his gardener William Barron collected together hundreds and thousands of conifers, literally in all sorts of shapes and sizes, for avenues and topiary work, as well as many other trees and shrubs, both common and recently introduced.

Moving trees of large size was one of Barron's specialities, for which he became well known, even though the public was seldom allowed inside the private kingdom of Elvaston to view his results. He had studied the methods of Sir Henry Steuart[5] and his

success in getting the trees established depended on replanting with carefully 'balled' roots on to little hillocks, some 2–3 metres/6–10 feet in diameter and 60 centimetres/2 feet above surrounding levels; moist loamy soil was then mounded up round the roots. Trees 'took' easily and successes were astounding; cedars already 13 metres/43 feet in height with a branch diameter of 14.6 metres/48 feet were moved to become speci-

mens in the east avenue, and vast yews from estates 20 miles away were brought in to give 'instant' effects.

Yews, golden and green, were cut into conical pyramids; at one moment there were more than a thousand of these specimens. A sport from a yew at Elvaston produced the stock of *Taxus baccata* 'Elvastonensis Aurea', the only 'golden' yew to have leaves which are wholly yellow. Barron also had a fine collection of hollies, with leaves in various forms of variegation, but found that box would not do in the rich moist soil. By 1850, when the Earl died and gardening activities had to be considerably reduced, with eight instead of 80 gardeners, there were 32 hectares/80 acres of pleasure grounds, 17.5 kilometres/11 miles of yew hedging (either dividing parts of the grounds from one another or enclosing spaces devoted to special subjects),[6] a 6.5-hectare/16-acre pinetum and 3.25 hectares/8 acres of kitchen gardens.

Many of the inner gardens at Elvaston, portrayed by E. Adveno Brooke for *The Gardens of England* (published 1856–7), were improved after 1840 and became the strangest creations: the painting (*left*) shows Brooke's *The Alhambra Garden*. In this garden a golden yew 12.8 metres/42 feet in diameter gave the appearance of a large group planted together. A visitor in 1859 described golden yews clipped to resemble an opening to a court, with colonnades all done in more yew, and columns clipped to resemble an eagle taking wing and a cock. A topiary crown had been 'formed by bending boughs into a proper shape with golden yew grafted on'.

Above right: Forests of yews clipped into strange shapes concealed the four 'ancient-style' gardens, each of more than 1.2 hectares/3 acres, in which monkey puzzles and variegated yews were planted as specimens. One garden had covered walks of arbor-vitae (*Thuja occidentalis*) , with a terrace of flanking yews forming a line of arches, all panelled with cydonias (*Chaenomeles japonica*) and with monkey puzzles growing as specimens in the lawn. A second garden was Italian in spirit, with urns and vases, a third had open lawns with specimen pines and firs, and a fourth had flower-beds in architectural forms surrounded by hedges of Oregon grape or evergreen mahonia (*Mahonia aquifolium*) from Oregon, only introduced by David Douglas in the late 1820s.

Below right: Grafting and shaping of trees and shrubs was also one of Barron's interests and he used his skills to convert upright trees to weeping ones and those with green foliage to exotic stripes and variegation, and, of course, to produce the huge number of trained and clipped topiary ornaments which became a feature of the garden. Deodar cedars were grafted on to cedars of Lebanon (at a height of about 3.6 metres/12 feet), purple and weeping beeches on to the common beech, and ash (grafted 12 metres/40 feet high) with the weeping variety. At a time when most horticulturists maintained that conifers could be grown only from seed, Barron grew them from cuttings and layers, as well as saving time by grafting variants on to mature specimens.

THE BEDDING SYSTEM

The availability of more and more plants that could be employed for sustained effects in seasonal growing led to a substitution of 'massed' rather than 'mixed' colour styles, in which plants could be grown in flower-beds laid out on flat terraces near the house. Dahlias, cosmos, *Zinnia elegans* and scarlet lobelias from Mexico, with arctotis, gazanias, blue lobelias (*Lobelia erinus* had been introduced in 1752), pelargoniums (although it was 1844 before the floriferous dwarf zonal pelargonium was produced commercially) from South Africa, and bulbs such as crinums, galtonias, and graceful angels' fishing rods (which could be treated as annuals and dried off after flowering) had all been introduced in the eighteenth century but were largely ignored until the bedding craze. Now Douglas's hardy annuals from California, including eschscholzias, clarkias and limnanthes, as well as collomias, collinsoas and platystemons, were largely superseded in popularity by 'half-hardies', many from South America. These could be grown from seed or cuttings in greenhouses and could be put out when already almost flowering. After 1820

Salvia splendens came from Mexico and *Calceolaria rugosa* from Chile; *Petunia nyctaginiflora* arrived in France and *P. violacea* in Scotland – both from Brazil – with the first bedding petunias hybridized by 1834. Verbenas arrived in Europe from Buenos Aires in 1826 and were so popular that, by the 1840s, Mrs Loudon could report seeing verbena growing on every balcony in London. Ernest Field, head gardener to Alfred de Rothschild at Halton in Buckinghamshire, 'once heard it said that rich people used to show their wealth by the size of their bedding plant list: ten thousand for a squire, twenty for a baronet, thirty for an earl and forty for a duke', but Rothschild himself had 41,000 to prove his supremacy over the aristocracy.

At Lednice in Czechoslovakia (*left*) impeccable bedding schemes are reminiscent of the concentric circles of colour used in the heyday of Victorian massed planting, when 'ribbon' borders, long narrow beds which lined pathways, were arranged with strips of successive colour. Blue nemophila, yellow calceolaria and scarlet Frogmore geraniums would line a path; at Enville Hall 'ribbons' seven strands wide lined a long walk. Neither then nor at Lednice today could the gardener be accused of imitating nature.

Head gardeners were especially influential in devising colour schemes, usually of vibrant primary hues. Among the leaders in this was John Caie, head gardener to the Duke of Bedford at Bedford Lodge

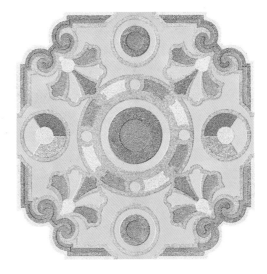

in Kensington, who extended his interest to 'clean, simple, and intelligible' concepts of solid colour massing with beds of different hues.
The new plants from hotter climates yielded much brighter and more distinctive flower colours than traditional plants from temperate regions.

At Cliveden today the parterre is of massed rosemary and santolina, taking the place of the colourful displays planned by John Fleming, head gardener to the Duke of Sutherland, in 1862. Then spring 'chain' patterns included tulips, blue and white forget-me-nots, yellow jonquils and pink silene. His summer effects would have been intended to last four months. They probably included perennials such as milkweed or silk weed (*Asclepias*), alstroemerias, Japanese anemones, polemonium, phlox, *Silene schafta*, cultivars of *Anagallis linifolia*, turtlehead (*Chelone*), as well as tender shrubs such as bouvardias, firecracker plants or Mexican cigar flowers (*Cuphea ignea* and *C. strigulosa*), fuchsias (the large-flowered hybrids were introduced by 1849), hydrangeas and both shrubby and perennial calceolarias, as in a scheme recommended for a nobleman's garden in 1850.

In reconstructing the English-style garden at the Parc Monceau in Paris after 1855, Jean-Charles-Adolphe Alphand (1817–91) and his horticulturist Jean-Pierre Barillet-Deschamps (1824–75) altered the annual bedding system of low-growing flowering plants which had been adopted throughout Europe during the middle of the century, in favour of creating new exciting effects using tender tropical or subtropical plants with large decorative green or coloured leaves. Tree ferns and bananas towered in exotic splendour above yuccas, agaves, caladiums, cannas and phormiums. All needed heated greenhouse protection in winter. This new style 'tropical bedding' was made even more effective with underplanting of silver-leaved cerastiums and centaureas, purple-leaved perillas, dark-folia-

SUBTROPICAL FOLIAGE: PARC MONCEAU AND BATTERSEA PARK

ged amaranthus, coleus and iresine and forms of tricolour geraniums. The French became adept at using large-leaved tropical plants as specimens or 'dot' features around which these low-growing plants, all clipped to one uniform level, could cluster as a collar, in circular or elliptical beds. In 1867 William Robinson described the system perfected at the Parc Monceau with enthusiasm. He admired a bed of variegated *Arundo donax*, made to 'spring from *Lobelia speciosa*', and *Ficus elastica* with 'the ground beneath perfectly

hidden by luxuriant mignonette'. The wigandia, from the tropical mountains of Central America, with large ornamental foliage, sprang 'from the little silvery sea produced by the mixture of the blue and white varieties of the Swan River daisy [*Brachycome iberidifolia* – a little Australian annual]'. Robinson continued, describing dracaenas rising above alternantheras and 'richly-toned' coleus, *Caladium esculentum* above 'a rich surface of flowering petunias', glowing hibiscus from gnaphaliums (*Anaphalis*), aralias from cuphea, erythrina from a 'sweet low carpet of soft purple Lantana'. A year later Robinson returned to admire variegated acers (*Acer negundo*) margined with rose-coloured geraniums, a banana framed by variegated tradescantia, with quantities of dahlias and salvias filling in spaces. There were groups of palms (including the hardy dwarf fan from Europe and the palmetto from the southern states of America), arching Japanese knot-weed, hibiscus, *Wigandia macrophylla*, silvery *Solanum marginatum*, and a mass of *Caladium bataviense* with 90-centimetre/3-foot leaves and dark stems. Robinson recommended the system to be 'grandly used in the most formal of gardens laid out on the ordinary massing system'.

Left: By 1864 Battersea Park, under John Gibson, showed that the English could rival the French in the use of subtropical and tropical plants. Sheltered on all sides except that fronting the lake by thickly planted trees and shrubs, the garden margins were broken up in a picturesque manner by deep indentations in which tender plants such as tree ferns (*Dicksonia*) and *Dracaena*, the much prized *Montanoa bipinnatifida* and *Wigandia caracascana* would find sufficient extra protection. Other mounds were clothed with trees and shrubs to make more protected valleys for tender stove plants and give those that required it shade. The different levels provided the drainage absolutely essential for these types of plant.

Successful tropical 'bedding' or 'dotting' with single specimens depended on the preparation of the soil so that heat was stored up in the materials on which each narrow bed was founded. The ground was dug out to 23 centimetres/9 inches below ground level and the excavated soil placed all round as an additional shield, with 45–60 centimetres/18–24 inches of brick-bats inserted to form at the side a slope of 25 degrees. Turf was laid face down on the brick-bats and then 25–30 centimetres/10–12 inches of compost added so that perfect drainage was assured. The brick-bats stored heat from the sun during hot days and gave it off to the soil at night or on cold days.

At the Parc Monceau exotic Abyssinian bananas (*Musa ensete*), growing naturally to a height of 9–12 metres/30–40 feet and with large leaves spined with red, towered above more modest-sized phormiums and agaves. These bananas, originally named plantains, were known to the ancient Egyptians and grown by the Emperor Babur in the early sixteenth century in his gardens near Kabul and in the Indian plains.

WILLIAM ROBINSON AND PLANTING AT GRAVETYE MANOR

William Robinson's own story of planting the garden at Gravetye Manor reveals frustrations and successes and the experimental nature of growing the exciting new plants coming in from different climatic regions of the world. In *Gravetye Manor; or Twenty Years' Work round an Old Manor House* (1911) and various *Country Life* articles, he described the development of the woods and garden, but this is even more explicitly documented in the source diary which he kept of Gravetye plantings from his acquisition of the property in 1885. As well as the small bulbs and plants for naturalizing, trees and shrubs were also planted on a vast scale during the early years. In 1887 silvery Bedford willows (*Salix fragilis* 'Russelliana'), rhododendrons and conifers were put in west of the house, where in later years varieties of starworts or Michaelmas daisies, found wild in the American woods, were introduced 'as graceful wreaths' to wave 'in the October winds ... making natural and picturesque effects' to complement the autumn green of the spring-flowering rhododendrons. He received plants from Glasnevin, Kew and Cambridge Botanic Gardens as well as from the Rev Charles Wolley Dod. These included *Aster acris* and *A. amellus* from Europe, and *AA. ericoides, lateriflorus* 'Horizontalis', *novae-angliae, novi-belgii* and the daisy starwort (*A. versicolor*) from North America. Beds in grass and gravel were large and simple in form with 'plants grouped in natural and picturesque ways' rather than 'set out' in the common style generally prevailing.

Golden, silver and 'fine green' hollies were planted to shut out the views to the new kitchen garden to the north; already 3.6 metres/12 feet tall, these were obtained from Knaphill Nurseries as 20-year-old specimens. Fifty young cardinal willows (*Salix alba* 'Cardinal') were planted on a moist slope 'and ever since it has been a pleasure to see the young trees'; medlars were in the orchard, and 6,000 hazels established as underbrush in the woods, with American azaleas planted on the sloping bank above. In 1890 the true laurel (*Laurus nobilis*) was planted in groves instead of the monotonous and rampant cherry laurel, but these were badly cut back in the succeeding cold winter.

Right: While practising his wild garden themes in the outer areas, Robinson had quite formal terracing and geometrically laid out flower-beds by the house, as shown in Beatrice Parsons' painting of *The Paved Garden, Gravetye Manor*. 'The real flower garden near the house is for the ceaseless care and culture of many and diverse things often tender and in need of protection in varied and artificial soils, staking, cleaning, trials of novelties, study of colour effects lasting many weeks, sowing and mowing at all seasons.' Robinson used old half-worn London York stone paving for his paths, edging them with pieces of broken stone about 25 centimetres/10 inches deep.

Opposite: Two of Alfred Parsons' illustrations for *The Wild Garden* (1870) show the 'White Japan Anemone' and *Myrrhis odorata* and white harebells combining to make 'A beautiful accident'.
Robinson advocated borders of hardy plants but, like any other gardener, would augment schemes of sturdy perennials with other types of plant. In his own flower-garden he sowed wood forget-me-not and Iceland poppy between the rhizomes of German irises 'to help furnish the border, and to extend the flowering season. The wild garden, Robinson considered, is for 'things that take care of themselves in the soil of the place . . . like narcissi on a rich orchard bottom, or blue anemone in a grove on the limestone soil'. During 1885 and 1886 Robinson sowed seed of Welsh poppies, and scattered seed of forget-me-not and blue lupin near watersides. Gifts of poet's daffodil from Bayonne, vernal snowflake (*Leucojum vernum*) and the species *Tulipa sylvestris* came from Edouard André in Touraine, as well as willow shoots, which were gnawed by rabbits during the first planting season. André also sent him 400 *Cyclamen hederifolium* and in April trilliums arrived from Pittsburgh (a note added in 1888 stated that these had been 'much worried by slugs and soil too dry'). Apennine anemones were planted round the boles of oak trees and bluebells (*Endymion hispanicus*) and aconites ('never did any good not liking soil') in wood and grass with 5,000 crocus near the house.

Beatrice Parsons

CHAPTER NINE

THE DEVELOPMENT OF NORTH AMERICAN HORTICULTURE

The first settlers, although examining American flora for its essential economic potential and for simple medicinal use, might well have been overwhelmed by the profusion of beauty growing wild. In 1670 Daniel Denton, in his *Brief Description of New York*, wrote, 'Yea in May you shall see woods and fields so curiously bedecked in innumerable multitudes of delightful flowers, not only pleasing to the eye but smell, that you may hold nature contending with the arts and striving to equal if not excel many a garden in England.' Others, of course, saw the new country only as a 'hideous, howling wilderness' full of swamps, rocks, predatory Indians and wolves, its natural vegetation only something to be hacked and cleared before life-providing crops could be planted.

Some information about plants had already percolated back across the Atlantic through Spanish sources. It also seems certain that before embarkation for the New World leaders of potential settlers familiarized themselves with John Frampton's 1577 translation, *Joyfull Newes out of the Newe Founde Worlde*, in which the Spaniard Nicolas Monardes (*c.* 1493–1588) placed on record in 1574 some of the earliest Spanish botanical discoveries. Clusius when he came to England in the 1570s was familiar with the work. If the settlers had not read it at least the idea of 'newe medicines and newe remedies' from the 'newe regions' and 'kyngdomes' of the Spanish will have been in their minds as they surveyed and

sought to overcome their new territories. Monardes described the sunflower or 'Hearbe of the Sunne' as 'a strange flower, for it casteth out the greatest flowers, and the moste perticulars that ever hath been seen, for it is greater than a great Platter or Dishe, the whiche hath divers coulers . . . it showeth marveilous faire in Gardines.' He also gave the earliest description of tobacco and mentioned sassafras, the wood of which was soon exported to the Old World. Both sunflower and tobacco are listed in Gerard's *Herball* (1597) and in all subsequent European florilegia and herbals.

However, although England had strong links with Spain during the sixteenth century, Gonzalo Fernandez de Oviedo's summary of the natural and general history of the Indies, published in 1526, had not appeared in English and the illustrated manuscript Badianus herbal, composed in 1552 by two Aztecs at Santa Cruz in Mexico, is unlikely to have been known to English settlers. The great works of Francisco Hernandez, physician to Philip II, researched between 1571 and 1577 in Mexico and containing valuable information on Mexican plants, animals and the extensive botanical gardens there, remained temporarily unpublished.[1]

THE NEW ENGLAND SETTLERS

At first, in their fenced rectilinear gardens, early settlers on the north-east coast tended to grow only the plants they brought with them or sent for in subsequent ships rather than those provided by the bounties of the New World; seeds of familiar medicinal and culinary herbs and pot vegetables, grafts of useful fruits and a few sweet-smelling flowers, rosemary, lavender, clary and hollyhock, as well as the eglantine rose. To these, as land was cleared, were soon

A modern photograph of the Carmel Mission in northern California shows a mixture of introduced and native plants. The calla or arum lily (*Zantedeschia aethiopica*) and native Californian poppies thrive against a background of red-flowered valerian (*Centranthus ruber*) in front of a wisteria-draped loggia. In the earliest Spanish missions, established towards the end of the eighteenth century, much of the planting was of fruit, flowers and vegetables introduced by the Fathers from the Old World or from more southern regions of the American continent.

added crops grown by the Indians: tobacco, corn, beans and squashes; many of the plants from Central and South America had already travelled northwards with Indian tribes and grew in the colder climate of New England. John Winthrop's garden on Conant's Island in Boston Harbor was known as 'The Governor's Garden'. Arriving in 1618 Winthrop, who with his neighbour George Fenwick did 'desire and delight much in that primitive imployment of dressing a garden', became the first governor of the Massachusetts Bay Colony. By 1630 he grew vines as well as mulberries, plums, raspberries, 'carrance' (possibly red or white currants, but these may have been grapes), chestnuts, 'filberds', walnuts, 'smalnuts, hurtleberries, and haws of white-thorne' and was able to help Fenwick get his orchard established.[2] When his son John Winthrop Junior joined him from England in 1631, he brought more seeds for his father's garden,[3] but it was not an inspiring collection. Besides useful herbs and vegetables the only decorative flowers are columbines, clary, hollyhocks, mallow, marigold, monkshood, poppy, sweet rocket, rosemary, stock-gilliflower (*Matthiola incana*), tansy and wallflowers, all grown in Europe for centuries past. The New England settlers were still pioneering colonists and had little spirit for over-indulgence in rarities. None of the new-fangled tulips, crown imperials or other delightful exotics recently introduced into Europe found a place.

In the 1670s John Josselyn reported both on native plants he had found growing in the wild and on the plants and flowers in the gardens seen in his earlier expeditions. ''Tis true the Countrie hath no Bonerets, or Tartarlands, no glittering coloured Tulpes; but here you have the American mary-gold, the earth nut [*Apios tuberosa*, a wild bean] bearing a princely flower, the beautiful-leaved pirola [*Goodyera pubescens*], the honied Colibry' as well as 'blew flower-de-luce, red lilies all over the country [*Lilium philadelphicum*], dragons [*Arisaema draconitum*]', skunk cabbage (*Lysichiton americanus*), pitcher-plants (*Sarracenia*), 'yellow bastard Daffodils' (*Erythronium*), white hellebore (*Veratrum viride*), one-berry (*Cornus canadensis*, now bunchberry), Bishop Compton's sweet fern (*Comptonia asplenifolia*) the new-found maize called 'Turkie-wheat', and tobacco.

Besides a wealth of trees, flowering shrubs and vines suitable for ornamental gardening, North America abounded in superlative wildflowers which later became essential perennials in beds and borders world-wide. To gardens in America the Old World con-

tributed flowering bulbs, trees and shrubs, later augmented by the exciting finds from the mountains of farthest Asia, which, linked geologically to the Appalachians, have plants which adapted especially well to conditions in north-east America. In Josselyn's time toadflax from Europe (*Linaria vulgaris*) was already naturalized and was soon to become a pest, which it is not in its native habitat, as John Bartram discussed with Peter Collinson a hundred years later. Other introduced plants also quickly became weeds; dandelions, ox-eye daisy, docks, mullein, Scotch thistle and even bouncing Bet (*Saponaria officinalis*) soon became a problem, still today carpeting areas of streamside and meadows near old settlements; to these we can add purple loosestrife (*Lythrum salicaria*), which in modern times threatens to block waterways, and the kudzu vine (*Pueraria lobata*), which spreads through southern regions.

Among flowers and herbs which Josselyn described in the settlers' gardens were cotton lavender, clary, clove carnations, hollyhocks and inula, tansy and perennial honesty or white 'satten' (*Lunaria rediviva*); lavender, rosemary, southernwood, rue and bay were not 'for the climate'. Josselyn's recommendation to plant eglantine and junipers close together is perhaps the earliest record of an American hedge, a century and a half before Washington tried out Christ's thorn or Jefferson the Washington thorn or the Osage orange. Samuel Sewall planted them in a ratio of one rose to two juniper bushes, making an impenetrable barrier within a few years.

Further research into seventeenth-century sources by Ann Leighton has added to Winthrop's and Josselyn's lists other flowers which must have been mainly for ornament, most of which have been naturalized: carpet or blue bugle (*Ajuga reptans*), the great celandine (*Chelidonium majus*), star of Bethlehem (*Ornithogalum umbellatum*) – like marvels of Peru, also called 'four-o'clocks', for their habit of opening up in the evening – moneywort or creeping Jenny (*Lysimachia nummularia*), the 'fair white lily' (*Lilium candidum*) growing in Plymouth gardens by the 1630s, marigolds (*Calendula officinalis*), masterwort (*Astrantia major*), mulleins, periwinkle, opium poppy, European Solomon's seal (probably *Polygonatum multiflorum*), yarrow (*Achillea millefolium*) and different forms of wormwood.

Josselyn was using Thomas Johnson's 1633 revised edition of Gerard for reference, and gardeners were probably dependent on it and Parkinson's *Paradisus* (1629) as their aids to identification, later in the century adding various editions of Culpeper's herbal. Parkinson's quite precise directions for laying out flower-bed pat-

terns for the 'garden of pleasant flowers' may have encouraged some attempts at more decorative schemes. *The Countrie Farme*, Richard Surflet's English version of Etienne and Liébault's *L'Agriculture et Maison Rustique* (1564), was first published in 1600 and was in the Winthrop library with William Lawson's two manuals; Leonard Meager's *The English Gardener* (London 1670) was owned by the third John Winthrop and included instructions 'concerning Arbors, and hedges in Gardens . . . whereby the meanest capacity need not doubt of success (observing the rules herein directed) in their undertaking', which must have remained a basis for seventeenth-century colonial garden design. All these practical books dealt with aspects of laying out orchards and kitchen garden areas as well as with more refined ornamental gardens.

Farther south, in what is now New York and along the Hudson, the Dutch and Huguenots early established fruit farms in New Amsterdam and New Netherlands. By 1655 Adrian van der Donck wrote that the Hollanders were growing white and red roses,

At Whipple House in Ipswich, Massachusetts, a seventeenth-century garden has been reconstructed with a rectilinear pattern, with shell walks and raised flower-beds to give an idea of the earliest colonial garden. Gardening was severely practical, with useful herbs, vegetables and fruit taking precedence over the few ornamentals such as hollyhocks and roses brought from the Old World, but, as John Josselyn pointed out, many traditional plants such as rosemary, sage and bay laurel could not survive a New England winter. American herbs and berries recommended by the Indians were used, but native plants, even when admired, were unlikely to be grown in gardens.

cornelian roses, and stock roses, besides several kinds of gilliflowers, 'jessoffelins' (?), fine tulips, crown imperials, white lilies, 'lily fritularia', anemones, violets, marigolds, etc. The clove tree had also been introduced, and he admitted that various indigenous trees had handsome flowers. Native flowers of merit were sunflowers, red and yellow lilies, mountain lilies, morning stars, red, white and yellow 'maritoffles' – 'a very sweet flower' – and several species of bellflower. As the century proceeded fine gardens multiplied. On Shelter Island north of eastern Long Island

Nathaniel Sylvester founded a garden in 1652; the plantation of box he set around it is the first record of this plant in the New World (it was presumably *Buxus sempervirens*, now called American box, rather than the smaller-leaved *B.s.* 'Suffruticosa', named English box in North America but commonly called Dutch or French box in Europe).

PHILADELPHIA

In a milder climate than New England's, William Penn founded Pennsylvania for the Quakers in 1682 and noticed the native flowers: 'I never saw larger; more variety, richer colours in curious gardens of England.' He felt strongly about houses having adjacent gardens: 'Let every house,' he wrote, 'be placed if the Person pleases in the middle of its plot so that there may be ground on each side for Gardens or Orchards, or fields, so that it may be a green Country Towne ... and will always be wholesome.' An ordinance of 1700 directed that 'every owner of a house should plant one or more trees before the door that the town may be well shaded from the violence of the sun in the heat of the summer and thereby be rendered more healthy.' Penn himself had gardeners from England working for him on his estate at Pennsbury, but although he was a pioneer in attempting to grow grape vines – a failure using the European grape – reports mention only cultivation of peach and other fruit trees, besides some salad herbs, although among 4,000 fruit trees sent by Penn from England to Pennsbury in 1684 there were some gallica roses. The gardener James remarked on the speed of growth during May: 'trees and Bulbes are shot in five weeks time, some one inch some two, three, four, five, six, seven, yea some are eleven Inches ... and seeds do come apace; for those seeds that in England take fourteen days to rise, are up here in six days or seven days.'

SOUTHERN ELEGANCE

By the end of the seventeenth century gardens were being laid out in Virginia, the most populous of the colonies, where the formal garden in America, considered as work of art, was probably first conceived. It is in Williamsburg, then the state capital, that the earliest record exists of a garden to be laid out in the Anglo-Dutch style then fashionable in England. In the spring of 1694 John

Evelyn wrote to John Walker in Virginia apprising him that through Bishop Henry Compton and the Revd James Blair, George London 'his majesty's gardener here at Hampton Court' was sending 'an ingenious servant of his, in Virginia ... on purpose to make and plant the Garden, designed for the new Colledge, newly built in yr country'. The gardener 'being sent thither' was James Road; he was also entrusted with making a collection of foreign plants to take back to the mother country and allocated over £200 for this purpose.[4]

It was a cousin of John Evelyn, Daniel Parke II, who was in charge of choosing bricks for the new College of William and Mary; building began in 1695. Later, one of Parke's daughters married John Custis of Williamsburg, and another William Byrd II of Westover, both of whom became important figures in the expanding contemporary horticultural world of the eighteenth century.

One of the Bodleian copper plates shows the College, probably modelled by Sir Christopher Wren, with ordered alleys of clipped

John White's views of the American Indian village of Secoton in North Carolina, painted in 1585, were engraved, with embellishments, by the German Theodor de Bry in 1590 for an illustrated edition of Thomas Harriot's *Briefe and true report* of the *new found land of Virginia* (translated by Clusius into both Latin and French). The illustration shows Cherokee Indians in the process of making a canoe out of 'Rakiock', the tall-stemmed tulip poplar or tulip tree (*Liriodendron tulipifera*). Farther north, Indians such as the Iroquois used the bark of paper birch (*Betula papyrifera*), strengthened with circles of wood, to make light canoes for easy portage.

evergreen trees before it, almost certainly yews brought from England, very much as described by William Dawson in July 1732 – 'planted with Ever-greens, kept in very good order' – and very typical of London and Wise's contemporary layouts in England. Another copper plate shows the Governor's Palace with oval flower-beds and stone paths.

As late as 1776 the college gardens remained 'ornamented with grand walks' with 'Trees, cut into different Forms'. After the Revolution it seems likely that Thomas Jefferson, as an admirer of the landscape styles he had glimpsed in England, was instrumental in altering the formal layout into a more pastoral scene.

Between 1700 and 1704 Francis Nicholson, the governor of Virginia, laid out a grid system of plots for sale for building and gardens over the uneven terrain of gullies and ravines at Williamsburg; this opened up possibilities for landscaping individual gardens on the edge of the town where they were, as the *Virginia Gazette* claimed, both 'retired' and 'healthful' – and rather larger for the wealthy citizens than the half-acre sites allocated in the town centre.[5] Nicholson was also curious about American plants (later in the 1720s, as governor in South Carolina, he facilitated the botanical research of Mark Catesby, author of *The Natural History of Carolina* (1720–47)). On several occasions he also sent to Bishop Compton a 'Collection of plants' for 'yr Lordsps paradise at Fulham'.

Books in Governor Nicholson's library attest to his lively interest in gardening. Among the recently published English gardening books he owned were John Evelyn's 1693 translation of La Quintinie's *The Compleat Gard'ner*, Evelyn's own *Sylva*, John Worlidge's *Systema Agriculturae* (1669), Leonard Meager's *English Gardener* (1670) and Moses Cook's *Manner of Raising, Ordering and Improving Forrest-Trees* (1676), as well as the botanist John Banister's manuscript *Treatise on the Flora and Fauna of Virginia*, dated 1680.

As early as 1705 Robert Beverley described Colonel William Byrd's plantation garden at Westover, half a day's riding up the James River from Williamsburg, as 'the finest in that country' with 'a Summer-House set round with the Indian honeysuckle, which all the summer is continually full of Sweet Flowers, in which these Birds [humming birds] delight exceedingly'. The Indian honeysuckle is *Lonicera sempervirens*, coral or trumpet honeysuckle, later to be grown, as it still is, to twine round pillars of Washington's Mount Vernon. Mark Catesby gave advice about the garden's improvement before his return to England in the 1720s. He, with

At Mount Vernon George Washington planted the evergreen native trumpet honeysuckle (*Lonicera sempervirens*) to twine over his loggia extension. Plants still thrive there today. William Byrd used this Indian honeysuckle at Westover near Williamsburg in the first years of the eighteenth century where it framed his summer house. It was introduced to England by John Tradescant the Younger in the 1630s. The orange-scarlet flowers of this honeysuckle attract humming birds for fertilization.

other naturalists such as John Clayton (after whom spring beauty – *Claytonia* – was named) and Alexander Garden, a doctor in Charleston (to his name we owe *Gardenia*), were influential in introducing gardeners to native trees and plants which they did not know and had not thought of using ornamentally. Catesby brought seed of the Indian bean tree (*Catalpa bignonioides*) to Williamsburg, as well as pink forms of the native dogwood (*Cornus florida*) and the lily-of-the-valley tree or sourwood (*Oxydendrum arboreum*). Trees for shade were essential and native *Liriodendron tulipifera* – the hardwood tulip trees or tulip poplars that could attain 60 metres/200 feet – were widely used around plantation houses in Virginia, with evergreen live oaks (*Quercus virginiana*) taking their place farther south.

William Byrd, son of Colonel William Byrd and married to one of Daniel Parke II's daughters, continued to improve the garden at Westover, remaining in Virginia from 1705 to 1716 and finally returning there from England in 1726. 'Mr Catesby directed how I should mend my garden and put it into a better fashion than it is at present,' he had written in his diary in June 1712, but from 1726, after visiting many English gardens, he embarked on more ambitious schemes. In 1740 John Bartram wrote to Collinson on the Westover improvements: 'Colonel Byrd is very prodigalle . . . with new gates, gravel Walks, hedges and cedars finely twined and a little green house with two or three orange trees . . . in short he has the finest seat in Virginia.' But not all the plants were brought from Europe; fine native trees such as tulip poplars were also planted, especially for shade. William Byrd himself observed that 'everyone has some of these trees in his gardens and around the house for ornament and pleasure'. At Nomini Hall avenues of tulip poplars, wider than the house, stretched for 300 yards to make an 'extremely pleasant avenue'. Today at Westover old specimens still grow between the house and the river as they do also at Carter's Grove farther down the James from Williamsburg.

During the 1730s and '40s another son-in-law of Daniel Parke II, John Custis of Williamsburg, exchanged plants with a fellow Quaker, Peter Collinson, and grew all the usual bulbs from the Levant and florists' flowers as well as horse-chestnuts, and box and yew shaped as topiary (see pp. 274–75). George Washington later married Martha, the widow of John Custis's son, Daniel Parke Custis. Custis's relatively large garden contained a formal area and different sections for flowers and vegetables as well as an orchard for fruit and nuts. Custis was 'curious' for his time in that he enjoyed collecting and growing different types of plants. But despite their contacts with English plantsmen, neither Custis nor his brother-in-law William Byrd II is likely to have adopted the 'natural' style in which Kent and Pope were just beginning to refashion English gardens by the end of the 1720s.

In the south, the development of slavery made it possible to grow labour-intensive crops like cotton, indigo, tobacco and rice, and plantations such as Middleton Place, Crowfield, Drayton Hall and Magnolia in South Carolina (all owned by the Drayton family) expanded to develop almost as self-governing kingdoms during the

The garden in Annapolis of William Paca, a signatory to the Declaration of Independence, was first laid out in 1772 and has been restored since 1965. Although still basically formal, Paca's garden tentatively reflected new inspiration gleaned from England, with the introduction of sinuous curves in the wilderness area to break the strict formality. No records existed of planting details, and the restoration has been achieved by using manuals describing contemporary garden practice. Philip Miller's *Dictionary* contained explicit cultural recommendations for hot beds and manuring and for the protection of plants with bell jars; these have been implemented successfully and add further historical interest for the visitor.

eighteenth century. Here ornamental garden developments were geared to estate farming practices. Descriptions of these plantation gardens indicate elements of a naturalistic style around formal features. Native trees – evergreen live oaks, festooned with Spanish moss (*Tillandsia usneoides*), southern magnolias and swamp or bald cypress (*Taxodium distichum*) provided a picturesque framework. At Middleton Place outside Charleston the steep slope to the Ashley River was terraced above ponds shaped like open butterfly wings designed as part of the system of rice growing, in which fields were alternately flooded and drained; the old rice mill still remains. Eliza Pinckney Lucas described what she saw in 1743 at Crowfield, today a ruin threatened by golf-course expansion: 'first the fruitful Vine mantleing up the wall loading with delicious Clusters; next a spacious basin of water in the midst of a large green'. The garden façade was flanked by walls running out away from the house for a thousand feet, on each side of which, 'nearest the house, was a grass plot ennamiled in a Serpentine manner with flowers . . . on the right . . . what immediately struck my rural taste, a thicket of young tall live oaks . . . opposite on the left . . . is a large square boleing green, sunk a little below the level of the rest of the garden with a walk quite round composed of a double row of fine flowering Laurel [*Kalmia latifolia*] and catulpas which form both shade and beauty.'[6] Beyond the mounts and wilderness, she explained, and 'to the bottom of this charming spott . . . [there was] a large fish pond with a mount rising out of the middle the top of which is level with the dwelling House, and upon it is a roman temple . . .' Beyond the 'fine prospect of water from the house . . . are the smiling fields dressed in Vivid green'. Modern garden archaeology has revealed the layout much as it was so picturesquely described.

In 1769 the Duc de la Rochefoucauld-Liancourt described Drayton Hall, built in about 1738: 'The garden is better laid out . . . than any I have hitherto seen. In order to have a fine garden, you have nothing to do but to let the trees remain standing here and there, or in clumps, to plant bushes in front of them, and arrange the trees according to their height. Dr Drayton's father began to lay out the garden on this principle; and his son, who is passionately fond of country life, has pursued the same plan.' Some of the new plants were those already cultivated in Europe; others, introduced by plant hunters such as André Michaux, were new exotics on trial for the first time in western gardens. The maiden-hair tree (*Ginkgo biloba*), camellias, the Chinaberry or Chinese bead tree (*Melia azedarach*), *Albizia julibrissin* and crape myrtle (*Lagerstroemia indica*) all flourished in the warm south. By the early nineteenth century evergreen Indian azaleas (*Rhododendron indicum*

and *R. mucronatum*) transformed spring in southern gardens to a riot of colour; in the twentieth century the bright-hued Kurume azaleas – introduced by E. H. Wilson – have 'modernized' the traditionally formal town gardens of Charleston and Savannah.

ADOPTING THE MORE NATURAL STYLE

Throughout the colonies, and even before the Revolution, other gardeners were beginning to translate geometric layouts into more naturalistic styles. Philip Miller, Batty Langley and the later Thomas Whately were all read. George Washington effected a judicious compromise between old-fashioned formality and the new pastoral styles, now at their height of popularity in England. Although laying out mirror-image walled gardens to flank his elegant mansion, Mount Vernon, he also followed some of Langley's recommendations, with serpentine rather than straight axial walks flanking the bowling green; he also allowed an open 'prospect' over the Potomac to the distant view of Maryland (see pp. 280–81). 'A large Virginian estate was a little Empire,' wrote Washington Irving in his biography of George Washington, and the principle of utility in organization will always have been borne in mind. In 1759, newly married to Martha Custis and intimate with details of her father-in-law's garden at Williamsburg with its trim box-edged beds, Washington's inclination and experience will have been towards retaining formality and keeping 'rude' nature at bay. Gradually his own style, combined with a passionate love of trees, developed along more naturalistic lines. In 1759 he looked forward to years of uninterrupted devotion to garden and estate but the demands and duties of public life kept him away for nearly twenty, and it was 1785 before he returned to Mount Vernon to finish his garden plans.

Thomas Jefferson (1743–1826), who had visited some of the new landscape and picturesque gardens in Europe during the 1780s, developed his own version of the natural style at his hilltop Palladian villa at Monticello, with curving walks and flower-beds between groves of native and exotic trees, but he retained geometry in the orchards and kitchen gardens (see pp. 282–83). These grand plantation owners were all avid for new plants for their woodland and flower gardens. Jefferson inherited the site of Monticello from his father when he was only fourteen. He finally moved there in November 1770, growing tobacco on the 2,025-

hectare/5,000-acre plantation until he substituted wheat as his main cash crop in 1794. Throughout his life he maintained an interest in introducing new crops to American farmers to improve the standards of living especially among the slaves and poorer settlers. He experimented with introducing olive trees and rice crops to South Carolina and Georgia and interested himself – unsuccessfully – in cultivating a grape which would produce wine comparable to that in Europe. The gardens and groves of Monticello became, in a sense, trial plots where new plants were nurtured; if found suitable they were passed on to neighbours in various parts of the country. Jefferson was not only enchanted by the beauty of flowers; he had a scientific interest in the natural world and made a study of plants, growing techniques and natural sciences in general, corresponding with many of the most eminent men of his day. He believed that 'The greatest service which can be rendered any country is to add a useful plant to its culture; especially a bread grain; next in value is oil.' His own farms rarely showed monetary profit during this difficult period of economic instability and agricultural depression.

By 1771 he had already begun tentative plans for landscaping and beautifying his grounds, thinning out trees, and covering the ground with grass interspersed with native Carolina yellow jessamine (*Gelsemium sempervirens*), as well as 'honeysuckle, sweet briar and even hardy flowers which may not require attention'. On the open ground to the west mainly native shrubs were not to exceed 3 metres/10 feet: alders (*Alnus rugosa*), blue false or bastard indigo (*Baptisia australis*), *Amorpha fruticosa*, barberry (*Berberis*), cassioberry, yaupon holly (*Ilex vomitoria*), chinquapin (*Castanea pumila*) and New Jersey tea (*Ceanothus americanus*), with higher trees such as catalpas, wild cherries, magnolias and mulberries, and clinging trumpet flowers and *Gelsemium*. While retaining more formal aspects of a large vegetable garden and orchard inside the structure of his working farm, he interpreted the European fashions and 'the genius of the place' in a distinctive and individualistic way. One of his most perused authors was Thomas Whately, whose *Observations on Modern Gardening* had accompanied him on his European visiting as a model guidebook. Following Whately's recommendations and implementing his own theories, he planted groves of both native and exotic trees at Monticello to shade and shelter the windswept house on the top of the 'mountain'. Jefferson recognized that the situation of the house and existing forest trees as well as the ever

important need for shade during the hot Virginian summers required a new approach. Further thick planting of trees and shrubs took place on the western and northern banks loosely flanking Jefferson's 'Roundabout' roads which encircled the hilltop on different contours. In 1793 Jefferson wrote from Philadelphia to his daughter Martha Jefferson Randolph: 'I never before knew the full value of trees. My house [here] is entirely embossomed in high plane-trees, with good grass below, and under them I breakfast, dine, write, read and receive my company. What would I not give that the trees planted nearest round the house at Monticello were full grown.' Even at the end of his life Jefferson continued to plant trees, writing to a friend in 1822: 'I thank you for the seeds . . . Too old to plant for my own gratification, I shall do it for posterity.'

Jefferson obtained his plants from many sources. His friend André Thouin in Paris sent him an annual parcel of seeds from the Jardin des Plantes, but the majority were obtained from Bernard M'Mahon's nursery in Philadelphia; some from William Hamilton at Woodlands in Philadelphia; and the American or Washington thorn (*Crataegus phaenopyrum*) for the hedges with which, in a fashion novel in North America, he enclosed his orchards and the vegetable garden, from Thomas Main, nurseryman in Washington. In 1803 Jefferson had as President organized the Lewis and Clark expedition; one of its purposes was the collecting of plants from western America for growing and possible 'use' in the east, and Jefferson through M'Mahon grew some of their plants. For reference and identification in his botanical studies he owned a copy of the 1768 edition of Philip Miller's *Gardeners Dictionary* and by 1806 he had received M'Mahon's *The American Gardener's Calender* which included many of the more recently introduced or discovered plants.

PLANT COLLECTING AND EXCHANGE

John Bartram (1699–1777), the Quaker plant hunter and the first American born botanist, was leader in the great exchange of plants with English collectors. He established his botanic garden *cum* nursery on the Schuylkill River outside Philadelphia, where he grew both native and exotic plants (see pp. 276–77). His 'exchange' of plants with Peter Collinson, Philip Miller (whose *Dictionary* Bartram was later to own) and many others in England

From 1844 Horatio Hollis Hunnewell, later a benefactor to the Arnold Arboretum, was one of the first in America to develop a pinetum for a collection of conifers, in Hunnewell's case those that could survive the New England winters. However, on the shores of Lake Wahan at Wellesley, Massachusetts, Hunnewell went far beyond collecting; he laid out seven Italian-style terraces on the steep slopes, and trimmed trees, including white pines, into topiary shapes. His main inspiration came from Elvaston Castle in Derbyshire; larch, hemlocks, arbor-vitae, Japanese yews and their hybrids – the English yew was not hardy – were all trained into cones, globes, pyramids and layered tiers.

and in Europe, helped to introduce to the Old World many of the plants – at least 200 during the period when he corresponded with Collinson between 1733 and 1768 – from the east coast of America; his descriptions of their native habitats improved Europeans' chances of succeeding in growing them. Linnaeus at Uppsala, Gronovius of Leiden and Dillenius of Oxford, the most substantial taxonomists of the day, all studied his plants to extend their range. Linnaeus pronounced Bartram 'the greatest natural botanist of his time'. In 1765 through Collinson's influence Bartram was appointed King's Botanist to George III with an annual salary of £50, little more than nominal as his freight charges were set against it. Among plants he sent to England in 1735 were gentians, asters, cardinal flowers, golden rod, Turk's cap or scarlet lily (*Lilium superbum*, which produced fifteen flowers with Collinson in 1738) and birches, as well as finding rhododendron (*Rhododendron maximum* – later to be transplanted direct from Bartram's garden to Collinson's at Peckham) along the Schuylkill River and by its source in the Blue Mountains. John Bartram collected during months in autumn when seeds would be ripe; on lengthy expeditions he kept his plants fresh inside an airtight ox-bladder. On one plant-hunting journey Bartram called at the farm of John Clayton (1694–1773) in Gloucester County to discover his garden containing only American plants, from among which he begged a specimen of devil's walking stick or Hercules' club (*Aralia spinosa*) for his own garden. He discussed shooting star (*Dodecatheon meadia*), a plant which he had found in the Shenandoah Valley years before (in the early 1740s) and had since grown in his garden and had sent to England to flower with Collinson. Clayton had never found it in the wild but grew other American native perennials from seed, including the blue-flowered *Amsonia* and a red-flowered turtlehead (*Chelone glabra*), and had also grown a fine cherry laurel (*Prunus laurocerasus*) from English seed. In Williamsburg Bartram admired the garden of John Custis, his four-acre 'square' plot planted up with silver and gilded hollies, fine yews, roses, Persian lilacs, 'Cornish cherries' (could this be a misprint for Cornelian cherry?), Arabian jasmine and many bulbs, all enclosed by an edging of Dutch boxwood. He also visited William Byrd at Westover where, inside high brick walls, flower-beds were edged with dwarf boxwood imported from England and orange trees grew in a greenhouse.

Although plant collecting seemed his main activity, Bartram considered that all nature was his study and saw that conservation and ecology as well as ornithology, zoology and palaeontology were all related. In his arboretum he sited plants carefully according to their ecological needs, allowing them to grow as they would in the wild with competition from more weedy plants. Alexander Garden described this 'garden' in 1754 as a 'perfect portraiture of himself, here you meet a row of rare plants almost covered over wt. weeds, here a beautiful Shrub, even Luxuriant Amongst briars, and in another corner an Elegant & Lofty tree lost in a common thicket . . . at every level spot a Parterre, where he nurses up some of his Idol Flowers & cultivates his darling productions . . .'[7] Bartram's fine appreciation of flowers and their colours found little expression in his hastily written journals. Some 25 years after his death it was estimated that 2,000 species of native American plants

were contained in a space of 6 acres. In 1751 Bartram published a list of native American medicinal plants as an appendix to Thomas Short's London edition of *Medica Britannica*.

Bartram's garden, kept going after his death in 1777 by his two sons, became a mecca for visiting botanists – among them Peter Kalm, after whom the mountain laurel *Kalmia* was named, and André Michaux (1746–1803), botanist to Louis XVI of France, a frequent visitor between 1786 and 1794. Other visitors, sometimes in search of rare plants, both foreign and native, included George Washington and James Madison, as well as botanists such as Benjamin Smith Barton, Gotthilf Muhlenberg from Pennsylvania, the Englishman Thomas Nuttall and the German Frederick Pursh. It also drew gardeners who found it a vital source of plants, although by now commerical nurseries such as that of Robert Prince, founded in Long Island in 1735, were extending their range to include native and exotic ornamentals rather than the fruit and vegetables hitherto so much sought after. Bartram's son Johnny wrote in the early years of the next century, 'these extensive gardens became the seminary of American Vegetables, from whence they were distributed to Europe, and other regions of the civilized world.' Today the site suffers from pollution and a complete restoration of Bartram's plants would be impossible. It was acquired by the city of Philadelphia in 1891, and the City Park Commission has in hand a replanting programme.

André Michaux visited John Bartram's garden in the spring of 1786, having arrived in New York late in the previous year. It was a good start to his eleven years of botanizing throughout the eastern States, during which time he often followed very similar routes to those taken by Bartram and his son William, and also often returned to the Bartram garden. But finding plants, particularly new timber trees which could be acclimatized to improve the forests of France, as well as new orchard varieties and ornamentals to ship to the king for his new garden at Rambouillet, was not Michaux's only purpose. He also introduced new plants from across the Atlantic to American gardens (see pp. 278–79).

Brought up near Versailles and trained by both Bernard de Jussieu and André Thouin at the Trianon and the Jardin du Roi in Paris, and already experienced as a plant hunter in Persia, Michaux was admirably suited to his new duties. His first task on arrival had been to purchase sufficient land at Bergen's Wood just outside New York to establish a nursery where seeds could be germinated

William Birch painted the house of William Hamilton, Woodlands, near Philadelphia, in 1787–89. Hamilton spent the years after the Revolution restoring his estate on the Schuylkill River and making a fine collection of plants, new to cultivation both native and foreign; he had a greenhouse, hothouse and 'exotic yard'. Thomas Jefferson coveted his *Albizia julibrissin* and had to ask for it more than once. Although entrusted by Jefferson with a share of the seeds from the Lewis and Clark expedition, Hamilton had a reputation for parsimony in sharing out his own acquisitions. Hamilton is one of the people credited with the introduction of the maidenhair tree (*Ginkgo biloba*) to America.

and young plants grown on to be sufficiently robust to withstand the long sea journey in pots. The Abbé Nolin, inspector of the Royal Nurseries under Louis XV and Louis XVI, gave him detailed instructions for preparing plants for the voyage. Within a year Michaux had persuaded authorities in France that another nursery was necessary in the south where he could cultivate a different range of plants, those unsuitable for the colder New Jersey climate. He bought 90 hectares/222 acres outside Charleston. This became his home and that of his son, François André. It was a measure of his success that, by 1796, Michaux had shipped 60,000 living plants and thousands of seeds – to the Royal Nurseries until 1789, and after the Revolution to the National Nurseries. To his disappointment many of the plants and even some of the dried herbarium specimens sent to Paris were neglected and lost during the troubled times succeeding the fall of the Bastille.[8] Nevertheless his discovery and classification of American plants, as well as his many introductions to American gardens, made his contribution to botany a major one. His son François André returned to the United States in 1801 to dispose of the two nursery properties in New Jersey and Charleston. In the latter garden many of the plants imported by his father still flourished, as did the American natives such as the rare *Pinckneya pubens*, *Oxydendrum arboreum*, the pawpaw (*Asimina triloba*) and *Gordonia lasianthus* (related to the *Franklinia*), all bearing copious seed which could be forwarded in the winter of 1801/2 to André Thouin in Paris before ownership of the garden was given up. In New York, where François André managed to visit Professor Hosack's Elgin Botanic Garden, plans instigated by Samuel du Pont were afoot to save the second nursery by renting it to the French gardener Paul Saulnier, on the condition of his continuing to supply France. The younger Michaux remained working in America, publishing *Histoire des Arbres Forestiers de l'Amérique septentrionale* or *The North American Sylva* between 1810 and 1813. It was partly illustrated by Redouté but not printed in America until 1841. The younger Michaux's life's work studying the utility of trees was instrumental in encouraging long-term forestry conservation and management in both America and Europe.

PLANT NOVELTIES

One of the more determined searchers-out of plant novelties was William Hamilton, of Woodlands, an estate up the Schuylkill River. Hamilton, a friend of Jefferson's, toured England between 1784 and 1786 and commented: 'the verdure of England is its greatest beauty and my endeavour shall not be wanting to give Woodlands some resemblance to it.' Hamilton carved out open spaces for his new exotics where they could be shaded by arbours of wild grapes and clumps of larger trees such as tulip poplars or tulip trees, assorted oaks and maples. He planned ahead, even before leaving England instructing his men at Woodlands to start a nursery for sowing seeds of a variety of American trees, from dogwood to magnolia, and to obtain 'handsome small plants' of other native trees and shrubs. He also sent out a great number of plants from England – 300 Portugal laurels in one order alone. Some died on the voyage and Hamilton's wrath exploded: 'pray am I to infer that all [those] plants are dead – pray are none of the eastern plane, the Portugal Laurels . . . the evergreen sweet Briar, Singleton's Rose, the evergreen Rose . . . now living? Did not any of the seeds vegetate of a Bushel of Horsechestnuts, a peck of Spanish chestnuts, 3 pounds of pistichia . . . or have they gone to the Dogs too?'

Hamilton is credited with the introduction of the Lombardy poplar (*Populus nigra italica*) and the ginkgo, although for the latter may have been by André Michaux. Hamilton favoured both hardy plants for outside and others for his greenhouse, and became famous and justly envied for his collections (he loved 'doubles' such as those of oleanders, convolvulus, crataegus, and daffodils). He was also admired by Jefferson for his 'new field of taste which has made Woodlands the only rival I have known in America to what may be seen in England'. Jefferson had to ask repeatedly for a plant of the tender *Albizia julibrissin* and Hamilton probably provided the *Acacia farnesiana* which grew in the glassed-in room at Monticello. Hamilton's pleasure grounds were described by Mannaseh Cutler in 1803 as 'formed into walks, in every direction, with borders of flowering shrubs and trees. Between are lawns of green grass, frequently mowed, and at different distances numerous copses of native trees, interspersed with artificial groves, which are of trees collected from all parts of the world.' He went on to judge the greenhouses: 'every part crowded with trees and plants, from the hot climates, and such as I had never seen . . . He assured us there was not a rare plant in Europe, Asia, Africa, from China and the islands in the South Sea, of which he had any account, which he had not procured.'[9] His collection can hardly have been typical of contemporary gardening.

Jefferson entrusted both Hamilton and Bernard M'Mahon, the Philadelphian seedsman and nurseryman, with seeds brought back from the Lewis and Clark exploration of 1804–6 up the Missouri to the Pacific; other seeds went to William Prince's nursery in Long Island. Hamilton is reputed to have given the germination of his share to David Landreth's Nursery, also in Philadelphia, which later specialized in rhododendrons, azaleas, magnolias, as well as camellias and roses; they soon added the Osage orange (*Maclura pomifera*), found in Arkansas and Kansas on the journey west, to their catalogue list. By the middle of the nineteenth century its use as a hedging plant in its native prairie country had been promoted so that by 1860 thousands of miles of 'fencing' of the handsome thorny 'orange' existed, only to be superseded by cheaper wire fences by the end of the century.

The Lewis and Clark expedition, the first in which a white man crossed the Rocky Mountains from within the United States, yielded many other treasures – some found again within twenty years by David Douglas for the Horticultural Society in London. The Oregon grape (*Mahonia aquifolium* named in honour of M'Mahon) was one of the most prized introductions, within a few years selling for $20 a plant. Other valuable ornamentals included the yellow-flowered currant (*Ribes odoratum*), the western snowberry (*Symphoricarpos rivularis*), and the western shad (*Amelanchier alnifolia*), of lower shrub-like growth than its eastern counterpart. The quamash, the beautiful blue-flowered *Camassia* with an onion-like bulb, a common food plant of the western Indians, was introduced to eastern gardeners. The botanist Frederick Traugott Pursh (1774–1820) worked at Woodlands before taking charge of 2,000 species of plants in David Hosack's Elgin Botanic Garden in New York. He also obtained specimens of the plants from the Lewis and Clark expedition, and, taking them to England without permission, in 1814 published their first description in his *Flora Americae septentrionalis* – 124 plants from the expedition were included with thirteen illustrations from Lewis's herbarium. He also named and popularized another American azalea discovered by John Bartram, *Rhododendron arborescens* from the mountains of Pennsylvania.

A *Flora of North America* by Dr William P. C. Barton was published in three volumes, the first appearing in 1821. There are detailed descriptions of each plant as well as of its geographical distribution, a factor of vital interest to a gardener. The roots of *Ixia acuta* in the illustration were brought from the Arkansas Territory in 1819/20 by the English plant hunter Thomas Nuttall, a pupil of Barton's; it was first flowered in Bartram's garden at Kingsessing, where the elderly William Bartram was able to compare it with his own *I. caelestina*, noted in Florida.

Thomas Nuttall, an Englishman who, as a student of the Philadelphian scientist Benjamin Smith Barton, named the native American wisteria (*Wisteria frutescens*, hitherto called *Glycine frutescens*), later also explored in the Far West, travelling up the Missouri River and finally in 1834 reaching the Pacific coast. He followed in the footsteps of Eschscholtz, who had found both the Californian poppy (*Eschscholzia californica*) and blueblossom or Cali-

fornian lilac (*Ceanothus thyrsiflorus*) in 1816, the latter proving a tender but much more garden-worthy plant than its hardy cousin, the New Jersey tea (*C. americanus*) from the east coast. Nuttall's most notable contributions to gardens include species of perennial *Coreopsis*, the aromatic-leaved California bay or bay rum (*Umbellularia californica*), the California chestnut (*Aesculus californica*) and the Oregon ash (*Fraxinus latifolia*), besides a description of the noble (but tender in most temperate climates) Californian sycamore (*Platanus racemosa*). Nuttall's *Genera of North American Plants* (1818) included trees from the Far West unknown to the younger Michaux, and Nuttall added a supplement to the first American edition of Michaux's *North American Sylva*, printed in 1841.

THE COMMERCIAL SIDE

For almost two hundred years after the first American colonies were established, any recorded nurserymen were fruit growers, selling or exchanging named varieties originally imported from Europe. Seed merchants would sell specially imported vegetable and flower seeds. In 1641 George Fenwick of Saybrook, Connecticut, was already writing to Governor Winthrop of the Massachusetts Bay Colony about his plentiful supply of cherries and peaches but how worms had destroyed his apple seedlings. By 1648 Henry Wolcott was selling apples, pears and quinces, some of them named varieties, but no one could call the trade brisk. Until the middle of the eighteenth century there were few operating nurseries in which American gardeners could purchase trees and flowers, but gradually the seedsmen began actually to propagate both the seeds they imported and the by now more familiar American natives and were able to provide young plants. In 1768 the Philadelphian gardener William Logan was still ordering vegetable and flower seeds, including sought-after broccoli, hyacinths and the South African geranium *Pelargonium inquinans*, from James Gordon's Mile End Nursery in London.

In 1735 Robert Prince's nursery at Flushing in Long Island both exported American plants to England and imported European varieties for the American market, following John Bartram's example but perhaps more commercially orientated. His son William Prince's first catalogue list was only of fruit trees but by 1790 he was offering most of the better-known American evergreens, mostly conifers but including 'Kingsbridge laurel' at 2*s.*, as well as timber trees and flowering shrubs both native and foreign. All are listed under colloquial names rather than Latin ones, so some are difficult to identify, with an English passion flower listed below an American one, and 'Fringe tree' (*Chionanthus virginicus*), or 'Venetian sumach' (*Cotinus coggygria*) listed together as if synonymous. By 1827 the nursery, now named the Linnaean Botanic Garden, offered more than 100 species of American plants as well as two species of eucalyptus and several of *Banksia*.

The contribution of Bernard M'Mahon (*c.* 1775–1816) to the development of American horticulture was twofold; he distributed seeds, both rare and ordinary, and wrote America's first practical gardening book, publishing the *American Gardener's Calender* in 1806 – Humphry Marshall (1722–1801) had written his *Arbustum Americanum*, in 1785, the first book on native trees and shrubs actually printed in America as *The American Grove*, and had established his own arboretum in Chester County. After arriving from Ireland in 1796 M'Mahon opened a seed store in Philadelphia; by 1804 he had fostered an international trade while also contributing the major part of the seed requirements of both exotic and native plants to enthusiasts such as Thomas Jefferson at Monticello. M'Mahon's greenhouse in Germantown sheltered seeds brought back from the Lewis and Clark expedition. M'Mahon, with a scientific approach, listed his seeds in a 'General Catalogue' in the closing pages of his book; using the Linnaean system of nomenclature all, including the vegetables, were given Latin as well as contemporary common names. Although some doubts may be expressed about genuine availability, the list remains one of the most important sources in determining which plants were being currently grown in American gardens. Of the deciduous trees and shrubs more than half of the 442 species were native ones found east of the Mississipi, with the 99 species of 'Hardy Evergreen Trees and Shrubs' divided in roughly the same proportion, while of his hardy bulbous and tuberous-rooted flowering plants, including 116 species, less than a dozen were of American origin. He listed 396 hardy perennials and biennials, of which 50 or 60 were American wildflowers. He also included many greenhouse and hothouse plants, among which some could be grown outside in the southern states. In his book M'Mahon gave directions for transplanting flowering plants from woods, fields and swamps; it remained the standard authority on American gardening for fifty years, going into eleven editions, the last in 1857, (See pp. 284–85).

The frontispiece to Andrew Jackson Downing's *Landscape Gardening* is of Blithewood on the Hudson River. There the natural scenery 'is nowhere surpassed in its enchanting union of softness and dignity . . . the lawn is studded with groups and masses of fine forest and ornamental trees, beneath which are walks leading in easy curves to rustic seats and summer houses . . . or to openings affording most lovely prospects.' Downing encouraged Americans to use their own native flora, but also urged them to discover the real lessons of landscape gardening in 'the steep hills sprinkled with picturesque pines and firs, and deep valleys dark with oak and hemlock'.

THE IMPROVEMENT OF COUNTRY RESIDENCES

American attitudes to ornamental gardening, and particularly those of the emerging middle classes, were addressed by the young Andrew Jackson Downing in his influential *Landscape Gardening: a treatise on the theory and practice of landscape gardening adjusted to America, with a view to the improvement of country residences*, to give it its full title, first published in 1841. Besides his book, Downing's reputation rests on descriptions of his created landscapes, of which few vestiges remain today, as well as on his less well known *Cottage Residences* of 1844.

With his father a nurseryman and his brother an expert on fruit trees, Downing had a strong background in horticulture. He was also brought up amid the romantic scenery of the Hudson River highlands. As an admirer of John Claudius Loudon's 'gardenesque' principles (with Loudon's original meaning rather than later Victorian understanding of the term) he exploited these for the American villa owner inside a general framework of 'naturalistic' gardening in which he re-interpreted both 'Capability' Brown and

Humphry Repton. He was also an early advocate for the development of the public urban park and of cemeteries, fields in which the United States was to lead the world. It was Downing's writing and influence which inspired the creation of Central Park in New York. In 1850 he brought to America the young English architect Calvert Vaux, who was to partner Frederick Law Olmsted in the project. Contemporary engravings or paintings of Downing's work show a general 'spottiness' in planting rather than much cohesion of design, probably derived from Loudon's desire to isolate individual plants, but in his writings he awakened Americans to an awareness that gardens and estates should have an artistic 'wholeness', a factor hitherto neglected in a nation still 'mainly occupied with the practical wants of life'. Downing really said very little about how to garden, but he was the first American to encapsulate theory in an almost Reptonian aesthetic concerning the difference between the 'beautiful' and the 'picturesque'. His encouragement to Americans to appreciate their own undoubtedly picturesque native landscape came at a time when the east was expanding westward more rapidly than ever before and a new nation of gardeners was avid for plants to grow and for information about them. The magazine of which he was editor, *The Horticulturist and Journal of Rural Art and Rural Trade*, inaugurated in 1845, was only one of many new gardening journals to fulfil this craving.

PLANTS AND PARKS FOR RECREATION

Three figures dominated the American horticultural scene in the second half of the nineteenth century. Two were pre-eminently plantsmen rather than gardeners, classifying and growing newly discovered introductions from the west and from abroad. Asa Gray, creator of the botanical department at Harvard and director before 1848 of its botanic garden (now obliterated by buildings), was also an author of standard botany books as well as of books specifically for the young. Charles Sprague Sargent, a pupil of Asa Gray, was given the task of establishing the Arnold Arboretum at Jamaica Plain in Massachusetts, one of North America's most important plant collections, which still today 'collects, grows, and displays as far as possible all the trees, shrubs and herbaceous plants, either indigenous or exotic, which can be raised in the open air' in the vicinity of Boston, as it was designed to do in 1872. Sargent was enormously influential in sending out plant hunters

and in introducing American gardeners to newly introduced exotics.

In developing the Arnold arboretum Sargent worked with the third dominating figure of the second part of the nineteenth century, Frederick Law Olmsted (1822–1903), successfully combining all the good features of a collection in a designed landscape. Olmsted, the father of landscape architecture in America, was involved in laying out more public park systems than any other designer, and although best remembered for his design for Central Park Olmsted is, like Gray and Sargent, remembered also for his great work in Boston.

In 1858 the plan entitled 'Greensward', one of 33 submitted anonymously (as was required) to the Commissioners for the design of Central Park, was successful. The winning plan was by Olmsted and Calvert Vaux.[10] The new urban space was to be laid out for public use between Fifth Avenue and Eighth Avenue (now Central Park West), and between 59th Street to the south and 106th Street to the north (a further 26 hectares/65 acres, to 110th Street, were acquired in 1963). The Olmsted and Vaux plan basically envisaged the creation of a pastoral landscape – with the exception of the more architectural Mall, with its double rows of flanking American elms terminating at the Terrace and Bethesda Fountain – a tract of rural scenery to be a haven 'where lawn, glade, water and wilderness weave in and out to push back the turbulent metropolis'. Olmsted himself wrote: 'It is one great purpose of the Park to supply to the hundreds of thousands of tired workers, who have no opportunity to spend their summers in the country, a specimen of God's handiwork that shall be to them, inexpensively, what a month or two in the White Mountains or the Adirondacks is, at great cost, to those in easier circumstances.'[11] This expressed the need; Olmsted also expressed his vision and conviction in an even more familiar if somewhat wordy quotation: '. . . that the Park throughout is a single work of art, and as such, subject to the primary law of every work of art, namely, that it shall be framed upon a single, noble motive, to which the design of all its parts, in some more or less subtle way, shall be confluent and helpful . . .' and 'every foot of the park's surface, every tree and bush, as well as every arch, roadway and walk has been fixed where it is with a purpose'.

A disciple of Andrew Jackson Downing, Olmsted became a ready convert to the idea of public access and was impressed by

Joseph Paxton's Birkenhead Park in Liverpool, which he visited in 1850. His plan for Central Park owed much to the English landscape tradition which had already spread throughout Europe, but was augmented by strong overtones of American romanticism and in particular the picturesque images of the Hudson River school of painting. Olmsted's own personal vision, influenced by his reading, was a compound of Virgil's *Georgics* and Gilpin's *Observations on the Picturesque*. But the plan was also eminently practical, containing an innovatory system of sunken transverse roads to keep the park itself clear of traffic, as well as arched underpasses for pedestrians, a network which still exists today to make the Park both functional and enjoyable. Olmsted and Vaux encountered many difficulties, but their scheme was virtually completed by 1877 (see pp. 286–87). Except for intrusions by features thought necessary for recreation or culture, Central Park still retains its basic integrity.

Working at a time in the mid-century when Joseph Paxton dominated much of English public design work and Adolphe Alphand, with the help of the horticulturist Barillet-Deschamps, was laying out Haussmann's boulevards in Paris, Olmsted created pastoral scenes in city parks for the relief of the workers. He was also in the forefront of schemes for forestry conservation and the development of National Parks, serving as an adviser at the Yosemite in California, the first state park established by Congress in 1864. Olmsted's interest in trees and shrubs is demonstrated by his advice to the Vanderbilts at Biltmore in North Carolina in 1888 where, besides laying out a geometric formal garden as an architectural extension of the French-style house, he recommended a scheme for the Vernal Garden, in a wooded dell. His firm continued laying out gardens all through the 'Country Place' era and well into the twentieth century.

ORDINARY GARDENERS

By the second half of the nineteenth century the ordinary American gardener, with access to all the plants currently available and popular in Europe, transferred his attention to tender plants that could be managed with glasshouses. Gardening styles and enthusiasms were not much different from those in the Old World. Reports of 'green' sofas embroidered in white gomphrenas with the message 'Sit Down', and Newfoundland dogs executed in pressed 'black' hollyhocks (could it be the same *Alcea rosea* 'Nigra' so popular today?) and greyish moss and carrying a basket of flowers (for which Miss Russell received a prize of $6) sound a trifle absurd, although not much more so than current extravaganzas at the Chelsea Flower Show. The bedding system and carpet and ribbon gardening followed similar routines as in Europe with an infinite variety of pelargoniums as well as foliage plants such as iresines, coleus and alternantheras, plants which enjoyed the hot summers, to create 'effects more brilliant than had previously been seen in gardens'. It was the same with subtropical gardening, as seen in parks in Paris and the famed Battersea Park in London, which soon became popular so that 'its groups of cannas, caladiums, dracaenas, tritomas, wigandias' and 'isolated specimens of palms, bananas, tree ferns, and similar exotic plants produced on our lawns an air of refinement and distinction previously unknown'. The American garden writer Peter Henderson suggested cutting holes in the lawn for single specimens of the castor oil plant, for a group of scarlet salvias 1.8 metres/6 feet high, or such a plant as *Amaranthus tricolor gigantea* which grew to the same height with leaves that 'exceed in brilliance of colour anything we know of in foliage: scarlet, crimson and gold predominating'.[12] In the 1880s Henderson regretted that the bedding system was not adopted in Central Park, due – he imagined – to 'incompetency or lack of taste'. Predictably such crazes had their opponents who preferred the old 'mixed' borders 1.2–1.8 metres/ 4–6 feet wide planted with hardy herbaceous plants as recommended by Shirley Hibberd and William Robinson in England.

THE WEST

As pioneers pushed across the American continent, new gardens were at first limited in scope by the climatic extremes of hot summers and cold winters in the central plains. With comfort and affluence once established, they settled down into patterns broadly similar to those in the east.

In 1859 Henry Shaw established a garden of exotic and native plants in St Louis, Missouri – a real botanic garden collection but one which was also intended for scientific research, the first to be established in America. The Shaw garden has developed into the Missouri Botanic Garden 'for the use of the public a Botanical garden which should be forever kept up and maintained', as Shaw

The lithograph of the annual blanket flower, the maroon-flowered *Gaillardia amblyoden* from Texas, by the Bavarian Joseph Prestele, is Plate 4 in Asa Gray's *Chloris Boreali-Americana* published in 1846. Wild flowers from the western regions of America, including abronias, Californian poppies, clarkias, Drummond's phlox, gaillardias and gilias, discovered in the first half of the nineteenth century, together with those from South America, augmented the older favourites, to make a brilliant assembly. In 1847 Thomas Bridgeman in his *Florist's Guide* was already suggesting gaillardias – 'galardia, orange and crimson' – to be used as annuals and in 1865 James Vick and Son's *Catalogue and Floral Guide* was recommending gaillardias massed in beds to flower 'early and continue until frost'.

himself confirmed in 1885. Arriving in St Louis from England in 1819, Shaw amassed a fortune by establishing a market in Sheffield cutlery. In his planning of the garden he was advised by Sir William Jackson Hooker of Kew and by Asa Gray of Harvard, but

it was a local physician and botanist, George Engelmann, who persuaded Shaw to make his garden a scientific institution.

In the Far West the first of a string of 21 Californian missions, designed to guard the Spanish dominions in Mexico 'from invasion and insult', was established at San Diego in 1769 by the Franciscans. Among the expedition's supplies were 'diverse seeds, vegetables, beans, and flowers to plant'. At first, agricultural crops, orchards and vegetables were all-important, but the Franciscans did introduce into California many useful Old World plants from Mexico, including oranges, lemons, figs and olives and many other fruits originally brought from Spain. By 1793 Captain George Vancouver found 'apples, pears, plums, figs, oranges, grapes, peaches and pomegranates together with banana, cocoa nut, sugar cane, indigo' and useful kitchen herbs growing in the mission gardens at San Buenaventura (a twentieth-century garden laid out by the Olmsted Brothers commemorates the Franciscans). Nor were climatic conditions easy; severe droughts could alternate with heavy rain and flooding and elaborate irrigation systems of dams and aqueducts were essential. Although there were functional hedges of the prickly pear (*Opuntia*) enclosing *huertas* (orchards) and vineyards, the first mention of ornamental plants comes with the pepper tree from Chile (*Schinus molle*) being grown from seed at San Luis Rey in 1825. Nevertheless the cultivated oases with their profusion of fruits, water supplies and welcome shade gave relief and shelter to many, including plant explorers such as David Douglas and his companions, in the barren treeless landscapes. By the time of the secularization, mission gardens, as opposed to the orchards, had a list of familiar ornamentals most of which had come via Europe: scented jasmine, nasturtiums, calla lilies, rose of Castile, four-o'clock, lavender, sweet peas, Madonna lilies, hollyhocks, stock, carnations and pinks, scabious, delphiniums, larkspur, valerian, iris, narcissus, poppies and French marigolds, although natives such as the Matilija poppy (*Romneya*), hollyleaf cherry (*Prunus ilicifolia*, after which Hollywood is named), Californian bay or bay rum (*Umbellularia californica*) and Monterey cypress were also grown. Edwin Bryant visited the Mission San Fernando in 1846, the year California became part of the United States. He found 'two extensive gardens surrounded by high walls'. Here were brought together fruits from many lands and plants from both temperate and tropical climates. Roses were in bloom in January, and lemons, figs and olives hung upon the trees, with blood red tuna – or prickly pear – looking very tempting.[13]

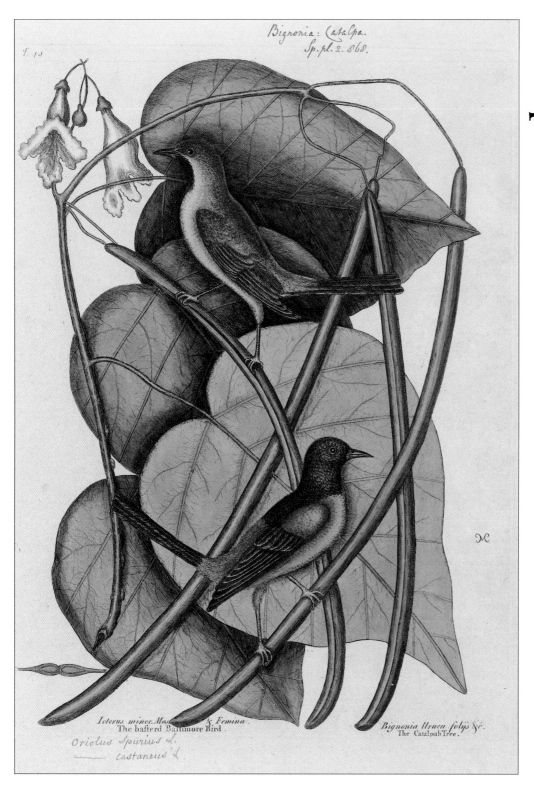

JOHN CUSTIS: A WILLIAMSBURG COLLECTOR AND GARDENER

There is nothing left of the most important private garden in Williamsburg, that of the wealthy John Custis, acquired in 1714 and gardened until his death in 1749. It was laid out to cover 1.6 hectares/4 acres (eight half-acre lots). His letter-book, including his correspondence with Peter Collinson in England between 1734 and 1746, is held in

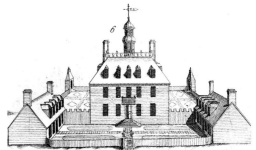

the Library of Congress; it documents Custis's gardening opinions and his 'exchanges' with English botanists. He was avid for more plants from Europe for his collection, while his correspondents pressed to have the chance to experiment with specimens of Virginian flora. Custis complained about the bad winters and an exceptional drought in 1737 when he 'made shades and arbours all over the garden allmost'. In his first year of correspondence with Collinson, Custis was able to boast of having 'a garden inferiour to few if any in Virga in which . . . my whole delight is placed.' Receiving plants in good condition could not be guaranteed: 'I had 100 roots of Dutch tulips sent me from . . . a gardiner at Battersy, but the ship came in so late that most of them split themselves; 2 or 3 came up which are now fine flowers.' In 1726 a long-awaited package was torn to bits by a dog, with carnations and auriculas spoiled, although some of the box and gooseberry trees lived; 'but the gardener . . . under whose care you put them I believe to be an ignorant and knavish fellow'. From England he had 'ews, phillyrea and gilded hollies; come safe to me and thrive very well; indeed any tree may be transported if carefully put in dirt and carefully minded.' In 1742 Custis lamented that a cruel frost had burned the south side of some of his topiary yews – 'balls or standards having heads as big as a pack and the pyramids in full shape ... established for more than 20 years'.

Left: The William and Mary College, built in the Virginia capital of Williamsburg (later the capital moved to Richmond) in the 1690s, had a garden in the Anglo-Dutch style. There were well-ordered alleys of evergreens – probably yews actually brought from England by the gardener James Road sent out by George London, William III's own gardener.

Far left: An illustration from Mark Catesby's *Natural History of Carolina* of the Indian bean tree (*Catalpa bignonioides*). Today at Williamsburg an avenue of *C. bignonioides* leads to the Governor's palace as it did probably in the time of John Custis. Seed of this native American tree was brought to Williamsburg by Catesby who was giving advice to settlers such as William Byrd at Westover and to Governor Nicholson before his return to England in 1720 and encouraging the use of native American trees and shrubs.

Mark Catesby referred to John Custis's garden in which Catesby had planted three pink-flowered native dogwoods (*Cornus florida*) (*right*) – by no means as common as the white-flowered form: 'In Virginia I found one of the Dogwood Trees with flowers of a rose-colour, which was luckily blown down, and many of the Branches had taken Root which I transplanted.' From prunings found in a well it has been established that Custis grew many other native trees in his garden, besides all the imported plants mentioned in his correspondence with Collinson; black walnut, coconut, honey locust, Virginia scrub pine, buckeye, red or sugar maple, loblolly pine, viburnum and sassafras all grew locally. The eighteen-century illustration is by Johannes Kerner.

687.

Cornus florida L

Franklinia alatamaha.

A beautiful flowering Tree.

discovered growing near the banks of the R. Alatamaha in Georgia.

JOHN BARTRAM AND HIS SON WILLIAM

Establishing one of the first plant collections in America in his 2.4-hectare/6-acre garden – extended later to become a much larger arboretum and nursery – at his home on the Schuylkill River, a few miles from Philadelphia, John Bartram was able to grow on plants and seeds he received from the Old World as well as those he collected in the wild. Double and breeding tulips, hyacinths, snowdrops and narcissus made welcome presents – to his brother William, living up the Cape Fear River, he sent European plants William lacked: buckthorn, angelica, lily-of-the-valley, iris, columbine, cowslips, saffron, althaea and violets. Plants he discovered on his journeys were used as 'stock' plants for his English and Continental correspondents; he found it simplest to gather seed each autumn out of his own garden to make up his famous 'five guinea boxes' containing American seeds for shipment abroad.

In 1734 Collinson sent Bartram hard-shelled almonds from his own garden, later followed by soft-shelled ones from Portugal, cuttings of vines, and of the 'great Neapolitan Medlar' (*Mespilus germanica*). Soon he sent some 'Spanish Nuts', a 'Lebanon cone' and seed of the 'China Aster' (*Callistephus chinensis*),

A watercolour from William Bartram's Fothergill Album *American Wild Flowers* of the white-flowered *Franklinia alatamaha*. John and William found the scarce and 'curious tree' in Georgia in 1765, *en route* for Florida. William returned to collect seeds of it in January 1777, too late for Bartram ever to see it flower – which it did four years later. William Bartram (1739–1823), besides being remembered for his illustrations of plants, birds, shells and other 'natural curiosities' commissioned by Dr John Fothergill and the Duchess of Portland, wrote an account of his *Travels, through North and South Carolina, Georgia, East and West Florida* (1791) made between 1773 and 1778. His vivid descriptions of plants and scenery inspired both Coleridge and Wordsworth in their romantic poetry.

describing the latter as 'the noblest and finest plant thee ever saw, of that tribe. It was sent by the Jesuits from China to France; from thence to us: it is an annual'. Within a week he sent 'sixty-nine sorts of curious seeds'. Bartram grew plants from other sources; in 1739 one of the few West Indian plants to survive transplanting from the tropics was Indian shot (*Canna indica*), which with Bartram grew to 1.2 metres/4 feet, producing a fine scarlet flower. In 1760 Bartram visited the nursery of Martha Logan at Charleston, who later sent a silk bag filled with seeds, including that of chokeberry (*Aronia arbutifolia*). Another female correspondent, Sarah Hopton, sent him a 'Golden Lilly'. He must have enjoyed his visit – 'Oh Carolina, Carolina a ravishing place for a Curious Botanist'; by September he could report that his garden 'now makes a glorious appearance with ye Virginia and Carolina flowers.'

Above left: In 1758, after more than twenty years of correspondence, Bartram made a sketch of his own garden, showing the part nearest the house, to send to Collinson. At the top is the two-storey stone house, built with his own hands in 1730. To the left a door opens from his study on to a path, sheltered by trees, and leads to the river some 400 yards away. Directly adjacent to the path and behind the house was the fenced 'common' flower garden, while to the left lay a 'new flower garden 25 yards long and 10 broad', intended for plants to come from England – a delicate hint to Collinson. A small shed at the back was Bartram's 'Seed House'.

Bartram's real tree and shrub collection was kept in a further 80–120-hectare/200–300-acre plantation.

Many of Bartram's plants flowering in Collinson's garden in England were used by Mark Catesby as models for illustrations to the second volume of his great *Natural History of Carolina, Georgia, Florida and the Bahama Isles* 1729–47. Among these was the mountain laurel (*Kalmia latifolia*) (*above*), which was known in England earlier, but failed to acclimatize there until sent by Bartram from the more similar climate of Pennsylvania.

ANDRÉ MICHAUX

André Michaux's mission to America in 1785 was a dual one of 'exchange'. As well as looking for suitable timber trees for afforestation in France, his brief was to introduce new plants, both ornamental and those useful in agriculture, to the victorious colonies. From Bartram's garden in Philadelphia he went on to visit George Washington on 19 June 1786 at Mount Vernon, his first experience of a working Virginia plantation. His gifts from Europe included 20 *Paliurus spina-christi*, the spiny Christ's thorn noted by Washington as 'very good to make hedges and inclosures for fields', as well as 46 of the aromatic-leaved pistachio nut (*Pistacia terebinthus*), 'seeds of the Pyramidical Cyprus 75 in number', and '4 of the Rhamnus Tree (an evergreen one)', which were planted 'one on each side of the Garden Gates' – this was the tender Mediterranean *Rhamnus alaternus*.

Some of the plants he introduced have become important street and garden trees. These include the crape myrtle (*Lagerstroemia indica*), sweet bay (*Laurus nobilis*), the mimosa or Chinese silk tree (*Albizia julibrissin*) brought by Michaux from Persia, which by 1806 Jefferson grew at Monticello, as well as pomegranates, *Lindera obtusiloba, Akebia quinata* and the tea tree (*Camellia sinensis*). He probably first brought the Japanese camellia (*Camellia japonica*) and *Azalea indica* 'Rhododendron luteum' to the southern states. Among other plants Michaux has the credit for introducing are: the maidenhair tree (*Ginkgo biloba*), often used as a street tree and which arrived in Europe only in 1727; the tallow tree from China (*Sapium sebiferum*), naturalized in the low country of the south-east and known as the popcorn tree for its white seeds which cling in clusters to the branches; *Melia azedarach*, the Chinaberry or Chinese bead tree (sometimes called Persian lilac) – although we know that Bartram had already received its seeds – and the spectacular varnish tree (*Firmiana platanifolia*, syn. *Sterculia platanifolia*), a relation of the cocoa tree, often called umbrella tree. The oldest camellias at Middleton Place are thought to be his gift to the Drayton family. Some of his plants have escaped to become 'naturalized' in suitable climatic regions.

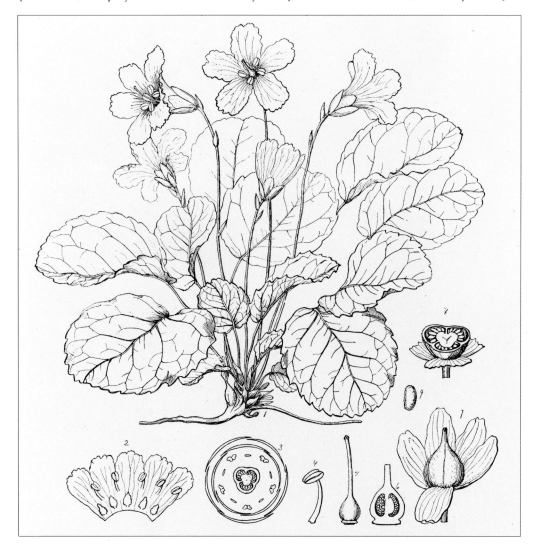

One of André Michaux's discoveries was nearly overlooked; the desirable Oconee bells (*Shortia galactifolia*) (*left*) was found near the headwaters of the Savannah River, and only preserved as a dry herbarium specimen in Paris, where it was discovered by Asa Gray in 1839. At first, despite directions given in Michaux's journal, the plant proved elusive. Finally it was located by chance in 1877, and by systematic search in 1886, almost a century after Michaux's original discovery. It is now propagated and used widely in gardens, although it is still scarce in the wild. The line drawing is by Charles E. Foxon.

The rare *Pinckneya pubens* (*above*), painted by Pierre Joseph Redouté for Michaux's *Flora Boreali-Americana* and named after Charles Pinckney, a distinguished statesman and general of the American Revolution, flourished in Michaux's nursery garden in Charleston; it was found still living there by Michaux's son during his mission to close the nursery in 1801. It provided seed which was sent to André Thouin in Paris. Known as the fever tree, Georgia bark or bitter bark, Michaux's pinckneya is difficult to grow, thriving only in shady low-lying swamps in southern states.

André Michaux discovered and documented large numbers of native American plants, many of which were quite rare and localized in range, and introduced them to American gardeners. His monograph on oaks, *Histoire des Chênes de l'Amérique* (1801), and the *Flora Boreali-Americana* (1803), the first flora of the North American continent, published posthumously and seen through the press by his son, were both illustrated by Pierre Joseph Redouté. In both books only species seen or gathered by the author himself were included. The illustration (*right*) is of the *Quercus prinus*, the chestnut oak.

View of Mount Vernon looking to the North. July 17ᵗʰ 1796. The portico faces to the East.

MOUNT VERNON

George Washington (1732–99) designed his garden at Mount Vernon himself, landscaping a full 200 hectares/500 acres of his 3,200-hectare/8,000-acre estate, with brick-walled flower gardens lying to the east of the mansion house and a lower terrace to the west reserved as a kitchen area, exactly mirroring each other in shape and extent. Today's restoration has involved research into Washington's own planting records.

In 1785 he rode out into his own woodland in search of trees to implement his schemes for his 'walks, groves and wildernesses', finding 'some young Crab apple trees and young pine trees ... and a number of very fine young Poplars-Locusts-Sassafras and Dogwood. Some Maple Trees on high ground & 2 or 3 Shrubs (in wet ground) which I take to be of the Fringe tree [*Chionanthus virginicus*]'. By February more pines, twelve catalpas, crab-trees and two magnolias were planted in the wildernesses. There followed twenty pines

(*Pinus virginiana*), four lindens (these from New York), aspens from Samuel Jankins, four horse-chestnuts from Colonel Lee of Stratford, three spruce and two hemlock from General Lincoln, and holly, maple, mulberry, sour or black gum (*Nyssa sylvatica*), poplar or yellow wood (another name for *Liriodendron tulipifera*), ash and elm from local sources.

He was enthusiastic to have the 'large magnolio [the evergreen *Magnolia grandiflora*] from So. Carolina' – in April 1786 he transplanted 46 from a box brought by his nephew of which '6 [went] at the head of each of the Serpentine Walks next to the Circle – 26 in the Shrubbery or grove at the South end of the House & 8 in that at the North end' – all of which proved a success. In the spring of 1792 he obtained plants, including the native swamp rose, *Rosa palustris*, from Bartram's nursery, but many failed and had to be re-

placed in November. He also had unspecified rarities from William Hamilton at Woodlands. Little remains of his planting except for two tall tulip poplars, some American holly (*Ilex opaca*), some elms, buckeye (*Aesculus octandra* var. *virginica*), white ash (*Fraxinus americana*) and some boxwood on the lower lawn.

Above: The View of Mount Vernon Looking to the North by Benjamin Henry Latrobe (1796). Latrobe described Washington's achievement in combining art and nature: 'Towards the East of the Mansion Nature has lavished magnificence, nor has Art interfered but to exhibit her to advantage. Before the portico a lawn extends on each hand from the front of the house and a Grove of Locust trees on each side, to the edge of the bank. Down the steep slope trees and shrubs are thickly planted. They are kept so low as not to interrupt the view but merely to furnish an agreeable border to the extension prospect beyond. The mighty Potomac runs close under this bank the elevation of which must be perhaps 250 feet.'

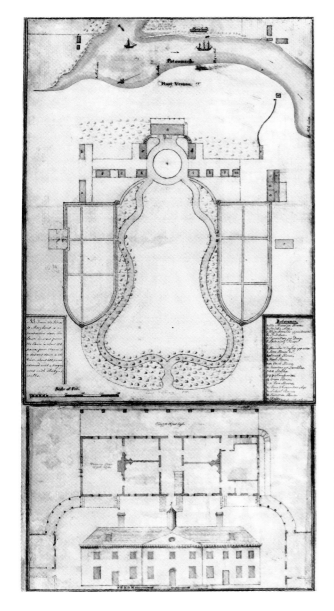

THE AUGUSTA ROSE.

Samuel Vaughan's plan of the gardens at Mount Vernon of 1787 (*above, top half*) shows the regularity of Washington's design, with only a hint of compromise with the new more naturalistic styles in the introduction of serpentine paths winding through the shrubbery. After establishing groves to the north and south of the mansion, Washington laid out the Bowling Green inside the regular frame made by the enclosing walls of the flower and the lower kitchen gardens. On his visit in 1796, Benjamin Latrobe commented scathingly on the old-fashioned air of the box-edged parterre in the flower garden: 'For the first time since I left Germany I saw here a parterre, clipped and trimmed with infinite care into the form of a richly flourished Fleur-de-Lis: The expiring groans, I hope, of our grandfathers' pedantry.'

Few plants have been introduced with as much excitement and suspense as the Augusta rose (*above*), discovered by visitors from Ohio on a January day in 1844 in the gardens of Mount Vernon. A seedling taken by a rose-fancier, Mathews, and named after his wife, produced a vigorous plant which in two seasons had shoots 4.8–5.5 metres/16–18 feet long, and blossoms large, double and fragrant, in colour a light pure yellow. Very similar to the rose 'Solfaterre' (also called 'Solfatare'), a seedling Chinese rose, it enjoyed popularity for a few seasons. The unsigned lithograph of about 1859 is by the Bavarian artist Joseph Prestele, who emigrated to America in 1843, and was probably prepared for a contemporary nursery catalogue.

JEFFERSON'S FLOWER GARDEN AT MONTICELLO

Thomas Jefferson's *Garden Book*, partly a diary of the garden, also contains notes of his many other interests. It was kept between 1766 (before he moved to Monticello) and 1824, two years before he died – with interruptions for his absences. So powerful is Jefferson's creative genius that the garden could almost have been reconstructed from correspondence alone, but in conjunction with the diary's entries, it has been possible for an extraordinarily authentic restoration to have been undertaken by the Garden Club of Virginia.

In 1807, at last anticipating his retirement from public life in 1809, Jefferson drew up a plan for making twenty oval flower-beds at the four corners of the house as well as informal beds laid out on either side of the main gravel 'roundabout' walk which curved to make an oval to the south-west of the house. It is possible that he had in mind some sort of arrangement similar to the flower-garden planting which he had seen at Philip Southcote's Wooburn Farm in England in 1786.

In 1811 Jefferson wrote to his grand-daughter, Anne Randolph Bankhead, on 26 May: 'The flowers come forth like the belles of the day, have their short reign of beauty and splendor, and retire like them to the more interesting office of reproducing their like. The hyacinths and tulips are off the stage, the Irises are giving place to the belladonnas, as they will to the Tuberoses.' Today the planting, for which there remained no precise detailed 'instructions', but which now includes all the plants mentioned by Jefferson, is as exciting as it must have been for him as he watched the seasons unfolding. Even his greenhouse, the glassed-in piazza at the south-eastern end of the house, contains the plants he preferred: the sweet acacia opopanax (*Acacia farnesiana*), the mimosa or Chinese silk tree (*Albizia julibrissin*), oranges and a lime.

A painting of the west front of Monticello by Jane Bradick, completed in 1826, the year of Jefferson's death, shows flower-beds in the lawn. For Jefferson – architect, philosopher and statesman – gardening was a continual delight, something he placed as a higher human pleasure than all his other interests. Near the end of his life, Jefferson wrote in 1811 that: 'No occupation is so delightful to me as the culture of the earth, no culture comparable to that of the garden . . . But though an old man, I am but a young gardener.'

A modern photograph of the 'roundabout' walk and informal beds south-west of the house. Without neglecting desirable natives from eastern America such as *Aquilegia canadensis*, lady's slipper (*Cypripedium acaule*), the twin-leaf (*Jeffersonia diphylla*, named for him), the Virginian bluebell (*Mertensia virginiana*), Atamasco lilies (*Zephyranthes atamasco*) sent to him by M'Mahon in 1812, and the cardinal flower, or long-grown favourites imported since earlier colonial times, Jefferson also collected a selection of rare, unusual and exotic flowers. By the end of his life he was probably growing almost all the perennials and annuals then available, which would thrive at Monticello. In spring bulbs such as crocuses, tulips, crown imperials, the new miniature 'yellow lily from Columbia' (*Fritillaria pudica*), narcissus and anemones flowered in his beds. Later performers included belamcandas, cornflowers, dictamnus, Chinese pinks, flag irises, everlasting peas, sweet peas (received as seed from Thouin in Paris in 1811), lavateras, lilies, *Lobelia cardinalis*, lychnis and bouncing Bet (*Saponaria officinalis*). In summer more tender annuals and bulbs augmented the planting: Texas bluebonnets (*Lupinus subcarnosus* from the Lewis and Clark expedition), celosias, amaranths and gomphrenas, double tuberoses (*Polianthes tuberosa*), four-o'clocks or marvels of Peru, heliotropes and mignonette were enlivened by the scarlet flowers of the Jacobean lily (*Sprekelia formosissima*) planted in an oval bed in the south-west angle of the house (M'Mahon had sent six bulbs in 1807).

EARLY NURSERIES AND BOTANIC GARDENS

American horticultural development was not only advanced by plant exchanges with Europe and the growing use of native plants. The establishment of so-called 'botanic gardens', plant collections rivalling those of collectors such as Bartram and Michaux, provided opportunities to learn about both exotics and American natives. The Elgin Botanic Garden, founded in New York in 1801 – situated roughly where the Rockefeller Centre is today – had its plants scientifically arranged and identified by both the Linnaean sexual system as well as by the natural orders advocated by the Jussieus. The garden, with a conservatory, was surrounded by a belt of forest trees and shrubs and a stone wall 2.1 metres/7 feet high and 75 centimetres/30 inches in thickness.

The Elgin Botanic Garden (*above right*) in New York was started by Dr David Hosack in 1801; Professor of Botany and Materia Medica at Columbia College, he purchased, at his own expense, 8 hectares/20 acres of land and established the botanic garden primarily for the cultivation of native plants, especially those possessed of medicinal properties. From 1807 to 1810 the botanist Frederick Pursh was in charge of Hosack's 2,000 species, which did finally include many exotics as well as natives.

David Landreth's seed house, also in Philadelphia, was founded in 1784. His son, another David (1802–80), further extended the seed business with a branch in Charleston, and by the 1820s entered the nursery trade as Landreth Nurseries, growing roses, camellias, rhododendrons, azaleas, magnolias and the prized Osage orange (*Maclura pomifera*) (*right*), originally from Lewis and Clark seed, and much in demand, especially in its native midwestern habitat, for hedges for agricultural purposes. The illustration is from Lambert's *Genus Pinus*, (1828); the appendix of the second edition included plants other than conifers.

André Parmentier, who came to New York from Belgium in 1824, and established his 'Botanic Garden' in Brooklyn, was a member of a horticultural family; his brother was the horticulturist at Enghien in Belgium (visited by the Caledonian Horticultural Society tour in 1817), where there were almost as many exotics as at Kew or at the Loddiges' Nursery in Hackney, while another brother grew roses in France. On Parmentier's arrival in America David Hosack had urged him to take over the flourishing Elgin Botanic Garden. Parmentier refused, but he did give Hosack advice for the layout of his garden at Hyde Park on the Hudson. Instead, Parmentier bought land and started propagating on a tract of some 9 hectares/23 acres where he grew fruit, grape vines and some 400 species of ornamental trees and shrubs, including the purple-leaved beech, *Fagus sylvatica atropurpurea*, as well as 200 kinds of roses and many flowers for outdoors and for greenhouses. His garden became famous for a 'rustic prospect arbor' or tower from which views of the surrounding countryside were revealed in a manner similar to a Tudor mount. Later Andrew Jackson Downing adopted this as a feature in his designs. Parmentier, who died in 1830, promoted the 'natural' style in gardening and much influenced Downing in his own development as the first important American landscape designer.

The American columbine, *Aquilegia canadensis*, with striking red petals and yellow spurs, is one of the most beautiful wild flowers of north-east America, thriving in open meadows or in light shade. It was originally introduced to England through John Tradescant the Elder and the Virginia Company, but also taken back personally by John Tradescant the Younger from one of his expeditions to Virginia, probably in 1637. Most of the plants with variants of the specific epithet *canadensis* were first identified by French missionaries or explorers in the sixteenth or seventeenth century.

The first tree in Central Park was planted in October 1858 as a gesture. Meantime two nurseries for 25,000 trees were established on park land, with seedlings obtained from local nurseries and some from Scotland. In 1862 alone, 74,730 trees and shrubs were planted; by 1873 four to five million trees, shrubs and vines had been planted, representing 402 different species of deciduous trees and shrubs, 149 broadleaf evergreens in open ground, 81 different sorts of conifers and 815 different hardy perennials and alpines. The man in charge of planting was Ignaz Anton Pilat (1820–70), an Austrian

OLMSTED AND PLANTING IN CENTRAL PARK

from the Imperial Botanical Gardens at Schönbrunn in Vienna.

In 1870 Olmsted and Vaux resigned, disliking the new city politics. By 1871 they were back in charge to find that for two seasons trees had been trimmed to resemble poles and 'no shrubbery or low growth seems to have been valued unless it could be seen within a clean-edged dug border'. In 1875 Olmsted

sent the superintendent, Mr Fischer, a copy of William Robinson's *The Wild Garden*, writing that Robinson expressed 'the views I have always had for the Ramble, the Winter Drive district and the more rocky and broken parts of the park. There can be no better place than the Ramble for the perfect realization of the wild garden and I want to stock it in that way as fully and rapidly as possible.' In those parts of the park where, owing to density of shade or the presence of rock, fine close turf would be out of character, liable to die from drought or very difficult to mow, Olmsted recommended thickets of low mountain shrubs such as broom, furze or heaths, or mats of vines or herbaceous plants such as asters, gentians, lobelias, hepaticas, southernwood, camomile, tansy, vervain, wild arum, wake-robin, epigaea, Solomon's seal, golden rod, lysimachia, lycopodium, convolvulus and vinca, 'to be diligently introduced in patches and encouraged to completely cover the surface'.[14]

Left: A bird's eye view of Central Park, New York, from the south, by John Bachmann (1863). By 1859 the quadruple row of elms had been planted along the straight Mall and planting under Pilat continued through the 1860s, with an emphasis on American native trees and shrubs; most evergreens, including pine, fir, hemlock, spruce, cedar of Lebanon and juniper, were planted along the West Drive or 'Winter', north of 77th Street.

Right: A view of Bow Bridge, the Island and Ramble from *Valentines Manual*. 1861. Olmsted was concerned about the view through the middle of the Ramble being kept clear between the Terrace and the Vista Rock, and recommended using evergreen shrubs, ferns, mosses, ivy, periwinkle, rock plants and common bulbs (snowdrops, dog's tooth violets, crocuses, etc), aiming at a much more natural wild character. Spruce, thuja and fastigiate conifers standing near walks and driveways had to be removed, and yews and chamaecyparis substituted, with thickets of barberry (*Berberis*), winterberry (*Ilex verticillata*), inkberry (*Ilex glabra*), holly, kalmia, andromeda (*Pieris*), mahonia, tree box and fiery thorn (*Pyracantha*).

The photograph shows Frederick Law Olmsted on the far left, with Calvert Vaux next to him, standing on Willowdell Bridge, east of the Mall, above one of the underpass roads. Olmsted's instructions to Mr Demcker, in charge of day-to-day supervision after 1871, give an idea of planting and pruning policy. In general scattered trees, growing singly and in small clusters or loose groups, were to border the North Meadows, The Green and the Playground, except where large rocks prevented it. They were to have low heads – but not so low as to prevent sheep from grazing. Oaks with horizontal limbs were to be trimmed with clean trunks to a height of 2.1 metres/7 feet, while those such as American elm might be left with branches lower. Where trees had been planted at regular intervals on the edge of a drive, they were to be shifted. On the transverse roads hedge plants, mainly spruce, were to be reduced and trimmed.

CHAPTER TEN

THE TWENTIETH CENTURY: CONSERVATION OF PLANTS IN GARDENING

In 1899 the nurseryman James Veitch summoned Ernest Wilson to discuss his departure for China and his search for the elusive but highly desirable *Davidia*, the dove or handkerchief tree. Veitch was quite specific, his directions precise. He was certain that all the 'best' plants in the mountain wilds of China had already been discovered and that Wilson should waste neither time nor expense in searching for new ones. Wilson himself was to disprove Veitch; there were many more finds of plants which have since become indispensable in western gardens (see pp. 302–3). Indeed, it is arguable that Wilson, the son of a humble signalman in Gloucestershire, was the most influential of all the plant explorers in his contribution to our range of magnificent garden plants. During his lifetime, tragically shortened when he and his wife were killed in an automobile crash in 1930, he encouraged amateur gardeners to experiment with both his and other explorers' recent introductions, and pressed nurseryman to cultivate and make all good plants available. Although wrong in detail Veitch was, of course, correct in his general approach. By 1900 the effect of the Asiatic plant influx on garden styles was already becoming well established. From then on new introductions, although avidly absorbed into ornamental gardening, did not have any major influence on gardening fashions. In fact, by the middle of the century the emphasis on plant discovery for garden embellishment had shifted to plant breeding, in which, with mysteries of chromosomes and genes unravelled, plants could be bred to satisfy or nearly satisfy market requirements. As in previous centuries, other circumstances, both economic and philosophical, helped to determine how the immense range of flowering species, hybrids and garden cultivars, the tools of the gardener's trade, would be chosen and arranged.

There is a further major consideration. Whereas the first decorative and useful gardens had been made as redoubts against threatening nature, gardeners in the twentieth century struggle to preserve some element of natural life in their gardens to insulate themselves from increasingly hostile man-made environments. After centuries of plant and seed hunting, nature itself is threatened by man's over-enthusiasm for collecting in the 'wild'; native flowers disappear from their habitats as escaped exotics can damage whole environments. The need for conservation has only recently been recognized. Even Sir Joseph Hooker, in his *Himalayan Journals* written in the middle of the nineteenth century, had no reservation in recommending the wholesale collection of the spectacular blue orchid (*Vanda coerulea*) for commercial gain. And in most western countries there is no longer such a thing as a 'natural' landscape; even natural features, especially in urban environments, have become increasingly scarce and whole countrysides have been altered by foreign tree and flower introductions. By the end of the last century, pioneers in the United States were in the forefront of developing garden styles using indigenous plants as the main ingredients. This movement, later extending to conservation of whole landscapes, is a fundamental part of late twentieth-century gardening.

Since 1957 at Le Vasterival, on the Normandy coast near Dieppe, Princess Sturdza has made a woodland garden containing plants, hardy in this favoured maritime climate, from all corners of the world. Naturalistic in style with island beds, each planted with three 'layers' (trees, shrubs and perennials) traversing hanging slopes and valleys, are all maintained at an inspirational level by thick organic mulches. This garden, providing a site for an eclectic twentieth-century collection of fine trees, rhododendrons, camellias, maples, hydrangeas and many other species and cultivars, demonstrates growing skills and potential. Here bluebells and *Tiarella cordifolia* underplant rhododendrons.

PLANTS FROM ASIA

By the end of the nineteenth century, following up the earlier discoveries of Philipp von Siebold, Robert Fortune and Sir Joseph Hooker in the Far East, the Asiatic regions had become increasingly accessible to plant collectors. Within twenty years of his interview with Veitch, besides the *Davidia*, Wilson himself had introduced the regal lilies, buddlejas, the tender *Jasminum primulinum* – now mass-produced for the American and British Christmas market, but by 1920 already a constant feature in Australian gardens – Kurume azaleas to enliven gardens of the American south in spring, and many more. His early finds first came to England, but after 1905 he collected for the Arnold Arboretum outside Boston under the direction of the great Charles Sprague Sargent. In 1926 Frank Kingdon Ward finally brought back the elusive blue poppy, *Meconopsis betonicifolia*. He was as excited as the French missionary Abbé Delavay had been in 1886 when he first saw the poppies. Although their culture is not easy, there is now no need to travel to the foothills of the Himalayas to share such experiences. The first Himalayan poppy had come earlier; *Meconopsis simplicifolia* flowered in England in 1848, forging a pre-Ice Age generic link with the little Welsh *M. cambrica*, a hardy British native. In 1910 Reginald Farrer discovered the scented winter-flowering *Viburnum farreri* (now superseded in popularity by the hybrid V. *x bodnantense* raised in Wales in 1935).

Many of the Asiatic plants proved to be particularly easily acclimatized to conditions in Britain and also, having survived from before the Ice Age, had a natural affinity to many plant genera on the east coast of America, where little radical plant adaptation had been necessary as the ice-cap retreated 10,000 years ago. In spite of seventeenth- and eighteenth-century enthusiasm, American trees and shrubs, particularly from the south-east, had never been easy in Britain; cooler summers prevented wood from ripening and cool, rather than cold winters, with frequent periods of warm weather encouraging premature growth, made growing them successfully difficult. Although in many English gardens it was possible to grow some of the best of the sun-loving Californian shrubs (including *Choisya ternata, Carpenteria californica, Ceanothus* and romneyas), many others, coming from individually specialized environments, proved difficult to establish. On the other hand English gardeners found that the Asiatic species of genera already

Among the most exciting finds of the late nineteenth century was the blue poppy first recorded in 1886 in Yunnan by the Abbé Delavay. In 1913 a dried specimen of this perennial poppy, *Meconopsis betonicifolia*, was sent to England by Colonel Bailey; it was finally introduced by Frank Kingdon Ward from south Tibet in 1926. He described his first sighting: 'Suddenly I looked and there, like a blue panel dropped from heaven – a stream of blue poppies dazzling as sapphires in the pale light.'[1] Within two years Kingdon Ward spoke of seeing the poppy massed in display beds in both Hyde Park and Ibrox Park in Glasgow.

known to them, such as *Cornus, Magnolia, Prunus, Betula, Spiraea* and *Viburnum*, were all more successful than their American counterparts, familiar since the middle of the eighteenth century. Cotoneasters took the place of *Crataegus, Weigela* of *Diervilla*; *Chionanthus retusus* did better than *C. virginicus* and Himalayan rhododendrons largely supplanted the American species which had so pleased eighteenth-century England and Holland. Although

Douglas's contribution of Monterey pines, Sitka spruce and Douglas firs had transformed forestry schemes, deciduous trees from eastern America had done less well as garden specimens; the American oak, maple, black walnut (which seldom ripens fruit in Britain), tulip poplar and black locust throve in the more extreme seasonal conditions of Central Europe but were often poor performers in Britain, even when provided with the essential acid loamy soil, and seldom produced the flaming autumn colours seen in their homeland. The woody plants from northern India, the foothills of the Himalayas, the mountain plains and valleys of western China and many of those from Japan (the latter generally demanding acid soil) proved themselves in British gardens as well as in suitable regions of east-coast America, even as far north as the Arnold Arboretum near Boston.

THE PLANTSMAN'S GARDEN

So much for the exciting new plants, but what of the gardens? In the opulent years up to World War I England, Europe and America continued to develop grand country gardens. On the one hand formal garden design at the end of the nineteenth century was mostly revivalist in style, but with historical layouts animated by the wealth of plants available. On the other, as Robinson preached to encourage a naturalistic approach to woodland, rock, water and meadows, the great plantsmen's gardens were being developed in an almost styleless way with an emphasis on the merits of plants themselves; plants were given priority over any sense of design.

As plants arrived from overseas in countless numbers, gardeners tended to forget any text-book rules or preconceived design formulations for their arrangement. Some of the greatest British collectors' gardens, established in favoured climatic regions – in Cornwall, on the west coasts of Scotland and of Ireland and on the High Weald in Sussex and Kent – were laid out round the turn of the century. A precursor was Holford's Westonbirt Arboretum in Gloucestershire, established in 1829. The eighteenth-century 'American Gardens in England', intended at the time they were made specifically for acid-loving trees, shrubs and perennials, could also incorporate the new exotics from the Far East. In general the planted woodland, in which exotic specimens were given an opportunity to show themselves off to their best ability,

Reginald Farrer was not only a plant collector and specialist in alpines, but stamped his own decided views on how a rockery should be designed. It had to both provide suitable conditions for fussy alpine plants – which needed excellent drainage, bright sunlight and circulating air, as in their natural habitat – and look as natural as possible. He abhorred the 'almond pudding' style of spikes and pinnacles as well as the 'dogs' graves' where stones were dropped anywhere without regard to usefulness. Farrer would have rejoiced in the late Lincoln Foster's garden in Connecticut, in which rock and woodland plants spread in unaffected drifts by waterside and between natural outcrops of rock. Native phlox, ferns, *Geranium maculatum*, trollius and *Caltha palustris* grow in harmony beside Lincoln Foster's stream.

seldom lent itself to any geometric system of arrangement although Westonbirt had been laid out on a grid system of forest rides. In Europe and America – or wherever they were – gardens on this scale became romantic paradises, idealized nature parks, in which the plants, especially trees and shrubs, became the dominant features. New Asiatic species of rhododendrons, maples, magnolias, dogwoods, roses and buddlejas could all be successfully established and surrounded by drifts of moisture-loving primulas, gentians, Japanese irises and meconopses to suit the soil and situation, plants which supplemented American woodland phlox, erythroniums and trilliums. It was all Robinsonian but on a vast scale; styles became personal expressions, with collections of types of plants more important than overall effects. As these gardens grew up, Robinson's views undoubtedly affected their refinement;

In Spain, even in the twentieth century, Moorish influence continues to dominate garden style and planting, and its themes and colours, adapted in similar climates for modern living, have become universal ones. Stylistically these gardens are equally appropriate around the Mediterranean and alongside the Pacific Ocean in California, where the first gardens were planted by Spanish missionaries using flowers and fruit from the Old World. Working in Seville just before World War I, the French designer J. D. N. Forestier used the traditional jasmine, myrtle and roses, bay, rosemary and citrus fruits already grown by Arab gardeners before AD 1000, but could also augment his schemes with Californian shrubs and wild flowers which would thrive in his Andalusian landscapes. The Maria Luisa garden in Seville was originally designed by Forestier and has recently been restored.

owners planting exotic trees and shrubs in groves or as single specimens began to see plant relationships as an ecological process, with taller trees sheltering successive layers of lower-growing plants, as in nature. Horticulturally speaking the large trees provided a protective overhead cover, small deciduous trees and shrubs sheltered lower-growing shrubs and perennials, and woodland bulbs, such as shade-loving anemones and lilies, grew under their spreading branches.

Besides choosing plants to be suitable 'cultural' neighbours, the skill lay also in matching plants to their new environment. These gardens, in spite of their lack of specific design elements, still provided emotional stimulus with transitions between dark and shady woodland groves and open sunlit glades; intellectual and aesthetic stimulus came from the superbly grown and often rare specimens and their association one with another. At Winterthur in Delaware, native American trees provided an overhead canopy for drifts of azaleas stretching back under the tall trees in symphonies of pink and white, the ground beneath covered with appropriate American native or foreign colonizers; may-apples (*Podophyllum peltatum*), mertensias, stylophorums, twin-leaf (*Jeffersonia diphylla*), woodland phloxes cheek by jowl with European bluebells and omphalodes and Asiatic primulas. In other areas groves of Asiatic trees and shrubs were planted with an eye to future effects. On the open slopes sun-loving American and Asian callicarpas provide spectacular turquoise fruit above drifts of yellow-flowered sternbergias, enjoying similar conditions.

Other gardens, particularly following Sir Joseph Hooker's triumphant journey to Sikkim in 1847–50, had developed as rhododendron parks, sometimes with hardy camellias thrown in for good measure. In these specialist gardens evergreen cover made low-growing associations more difficult to establish. Some of the first groves of *Rhododendron arboreum* were planted by John Veitch at Killerton in Devon even earlier, with old trees providing shelter and shade for them and for the exotic species and other genera later brought to the garden. From 1887 at Leonardslee in Sussex, pine, oak and birch country, Sir Edmund Loder began planting the steep slopes above a chain of hammer-ponds with cherries, magnolias, crab apples, sorbus and viburnums, as well as with exotic conifers. Above all he planted rhododendrons and camellias and the gardens became famous for the *loderi* rhododendron hybrids. Other Sussex gardens, such as Wakehurst and High

Beeches, belonged to members of the Loder family, a gardening dynasty comparable to the du Ponts of Delaware across the Atlantic, with their gardens such as Longwood, Winterthur, Mount Cuba, Hagley, Crowninshield and Nemours (see pp. 308–9). Wakehurst, with its acid soil and conditions especially favourable for plants from Chile and New Zealand, (now an invaluable extension to the Royal Botanic Gardens at Kew). High Beeches was stocked by plants acquired from the dispersal of Veitch's Nursery at Coombe Wood in 1916.

In Cornwall, conditions with high humidity and rainfall and little frost were even more favourable for the large-leaved Himalayan rhododendrons, sun-loving trees, shrubs and climbers from California and the Chilean and New Zealand plants. Crinodendrons and embothriums grew beside Himalayan magnolias and michelias, New Zealand leptospermums, hoherias and olearias, with drought-tolerant tap-rooted eucalypts and more moisture-seeking southern beech (forms of *Nothofagus*) also proving adaptable. Both Monterey pine (*Pinus radiata*) and cypress (*Cupressus macrocarpa*) were established as protective shelter belts against sea-borne salt winds. Today at Tresco Abbey in the Scilly Isles, where these perimeter shields established in the nineteenth century have succumbed to storm damage, another Californian, the bishop's pine (*Pinus muricata*), is proving a successful substitute.

Roberto Burle Marx studied music and painting, disciplines which influenced his development as a garden artist, creating work that is three-dimensional and deals with time and space. Using many native plants from Brazil in the sweeping swathes of his designs, Burle Marx believes that the plants in a created landscape should contribute to a work of art and express man's ability to manipulate nature: 'A garden is the result of an arrangement of natural materials according to aesthetic laws; interwoven throughout are the artist's outlook on life, his past experiences, his affections, his attempts, his mistakes and his successes.' The planting of Burle Marx's interlocking curvilinear beds in the Marina Stellin garden at Petropolis brings together yellow-flowered hemerocallis of Asian origin, *Iresine lindenii* 'Formosa' from Ecuador and green *Alternanthera ficoides*, native to Brazil.

INFORMAL PLANTING AND FORMAL SETTINGS

William Robinson's advocacy of permanent planting – using hardy plants in settings in which they could make natural drifts – has already been mentioned. His emphasis on plants and planting came into direct conflict with the architectural school of Reginald Blomfield and John Sedding, who believed that garden designing was simply an extension of house building. Gertrude Jekyll, who followed Robinson in many of his ideas of natural gardening, often using native trees and shrubs to link her garden landscape with the surrounding countryside, carried border planting to heights of sophisticated excellence (see pp. 304–5). By working with architects, she effected a compromise between the two extremes of thought, planting 'naturalistically' inside a tight framework.

During the Edwardian period 'old' English gardens, of the type praised by Sedding and Blomfield, were developed on quite grand scales in both England and in America. Designers were inspired to take a closer look at Italian style interpreted in its true spirit by Edith Wharton's *Italian Villas and their Gardens* (1904) and Inigo Triggs's *Art of Garden Design in Italy* (1906). Harold Peto working in England and in the south of France and Charles Platt in America designed architectural gardens as perfect settings for a wide range of plants both old and new. During the 1930s Beatrix Farrand, Edith Wharton's niece, also much influenced by what she had seen of European gardens in earlier travels, laid out Dumbarton Oaks in Washington DC as an American adaptation of an Italian garden (see pp. 312–13). In her foreword to *Beatrix Farrand's Plant Book for Dumbarton Oaks*, Diana Kostial McGuire stressed the significance of Dumbarton Oaks in America's cultural heritage: 'The gardens at Dumbarton Oaks represent a uniquely American adaptation of the classical Mediterranean garden form which travelling Americans came to admire in the late 19th century and which was eloquently described by Edith Wharton in *Italian Villas and their Gardens*.' The *Plant Book* is also a 'unique document that describes measures to be taken when plants need replacement, the various levels of maintenance required, the design concept of each part of the gardens, why particular choices were made, and why certain ideas were rejected. In addition, forty-two plant lists are included which give the scientific names of the plants growing in the gardens in 1941'. As a result of Beatrix Farrand's meticulous dedication in producing the book we have a unique historical record of the development of landscape gardening in twentieth-century America. Although written in 1941 and used by horticulturists connected with the garden in the interval, it was not finally published until 1980 under McGuire's editorship. Farrand used as reference books Liberty Hyde Bailey's *The Standard Cyclopedia of Horticulture* (1914–17) and the catalogue of the famous Bay State Nurseries in Massachusetts, the *Bay State Garden Book for 1938* (these have been updated by McGuire using the 1976 edition of *Hortus Third*). In the garden as it is today scale and planting do not always match the original intention.

As a designer Beatrix Farrand, influenced by Charles Sprague Sargent at the Arnold Arboretum, was unusual in her interest in the plants, their planting and their maintenance. For schemes for the campus at Princeton she especially recommended using American native trees in preference to exotics; among the deciduous ones she chose for the main planting, simply designed to show off the dignified buildings, were red oak, basswood (*Tilia americana*),

sugar maple, Eastern sycamore or buttonwood (*Platanus occidentalis*), sweet gum (*Liquidambar styraciflua*) and tulip poplars, leavened by drifts of flowering dogwood. Evergreens were planted in masses and included Douglas's exotics from the West Coast, which she used in all her designs.

In these Italian-inspired gardens wisterias from China and Japan and innumerable roses (with breeding possibilities increased by the introduction of the rampant Japanese *Rosa multiflora* and *R. wichuraiana*) climbed over enclosing walls and pergolas. Topiary patterns in yew and box became features both in Cotswold manor gardens and in the New World. The English designer Thomas Mawson advocated grafting golden yew on to green to produce dual-toned hemispheres as well as using distinctive golden hollies. In New England hardier Korean box took the place of European and Japanese yews and their hybrids were more reliable than English yew; in Maryland traditional boxwood needed more frequent trimming in the southern heat. Terraces and dry stone walling, linking the different levels, provided sites in which rock plants could find a 'natural' home, and the new hardy hybrid water-lilies, bred by M. Marliac in France at the end of the nineteenth century, could float on the surface of water basins.

In spite of Robinsonian strictures and Jekyllian flower-borders surrounding the smooth lawns, 'bedding out' for seasonal spring, summer and autumn effects remained fashionable until at least the outbreak of war in 1914. Since then and until the recent upsurge of interest in more formal layouts, bedding schemes have been the prerogative of municipal planners; their skilful use of annual and tender bedding plants, often in magnificent schemes designed primarily for bright colour effects, has ensured that breeding programmes continue and that a wide range of tender seasonal plants is maintained in stock. Even so the range available is very much reduced compared to the numbers of suitable seasonal plants listed in early Victorian nursery catalogues.

Some of the most influential gardens where plants were used in a new way were made by amateurs. Hidcote in Gloucestershire, laid out around the top of a windswept hill, was designed by its American owner Lawrence Johnston as a series of rooms, each geometric area protected by walls and hedges, with just two great sweeping vistas extending to the countryside. Johnston's first action was to purchase evergreen oaks from France to make a sheltering ring round the rim of the hill, enclosing house and

Warren Manning (1860–1938), a Boston landscape architect, worked for some years in the Olmsted office where, in adapting traditional designs, he developed his naturalistic style to suit the topography of a garden. At Stan Hywet in Akron, Ohio, Manning combined gentle lawns and groves of trees with strict alignments of alleys and vistas. Here we see the northern birch alley, which stretches for 150 metres/500 feet extending the axis of the house and framing the sky. An avenue of London plane trees underplanted with rhododendrons, and a vista cut from the main hall through flanking woodland stretches 12 kilometres/8 miles into the western landscape.

garden. One of Wilson's tall davidias guards the courtyard entrance. Unlike many of Gertrude Jekyll's gardens, Hidcote, now the property of the English National Trust, has survived to influence new generations; the Hidcote style of garden compartments and of planting has been copied or adapted not only throughout Britain but in the rest of Europe and in America, its combination of grandeur and simplicity especially appealing. Inside each intimate area cottage-type plants were tightly packed in glowing or pale colour schemes. The lavish planting was especially tuned to contrast with the architectural severity of the garden's firm Renaissance lines; while beyond the tighter hedged formality other areas by the stream were planted with Robinsonian abandon.

During and since the 1930s traditional herbaceous and mixed borders ceased to edge a path or wall in linear simplicity. Instead, following relaxed contours winding below tree canopies and curving out of sight at the end of a garden vista, they provided more planting opportunities in smaller-sized gardens. In rectangular town gardens their planted outline disguised straight garden perimeters. Often they became free-style island beds instead of borders. Plant shapes and colours, rather than hedges and walls, created the garden architecture. In a sense these softer shapes reflected a feeling for landscape and a desire to retain a slice of nature in the garden but, without careful planning, rapidly deteriorated into rather formless compositions. Percy Cane's meandering borders exhibited at the Chelsea Flower Show during the 1930s set a new fashion for informality in planting styles. His standardized choice of plants was conventional, with a concentration on roses, lilacs and plenty of flowering laburnums, cherries and brooms. In corners he used accent plants such as the horizontally branched *Viburnum plicatum* 'Mariesii' to give some architectural emphasis. Cane also planted island beds, designed to be viewed from all sides, using taller shrubs to make vertebrae down a ridged centre, and surrounding them with perennials. His planting schemes for Falkland Palace in Scotland, restored by the National Trust for Scotland, still survive.

Although new perennials were arriving from the Far East, they did not, as had the woody plants, supersede the popularity of the sturdy American varieties, many of which had already been 'improved' for gardening by British, Dutch and German horticulturists both for European gardens and for re-export for use in American perennial borders. The additional Asiatic perennials provided an extended range of hardy plants both for traditional flower borders and for the more informal Robinsonian areas in the outer garden. Many of them were moisture-loving and some, particularly from Japan, were intensely calcifuge. In America, in suitable climatic regions, these – among them astilbes, irises, kirengeshomas – throve in naturalistic woodland gardens, growing and associating with similar native flora. Some of the Asian perennials – plants such as hostas and both Chinese and Japanese anemones and day-lilies proved to be cultivars already, grown in Chinese and Japanese gardens for centuries. The American natives – Michaelmas daisies, chelones, eupatoriums, helianthus, monardas, phlox and rudbeckias as well as delphinium, lupin and penstemon cultivars, originally from farther west – many of them 'improved' in Europe, were grown in the popular English-style border layouts.

PLANTS TO SUIT THE SITE

The essence of natural gardening seems to be in allowing plants rather than architecture to shape the garden picture. For bog and stream gardens the plants from Asia were superb and added new dimensions to this gardening style; astilbes, irises, kirengeshomas, primulas, rheums, rodgersias, toad-lilies and hostas, most with distinguished foliage giving a semi-tropical atmosphere, as well as flowers in season, revolutionized the appearance of bog gardens. In favoured sites, the giant-leaved *Gunnera manicata* or prickly rhubarb, introduced from south Brazil in 1867, still dominated waterside planting as it does today. Bog gardening, growing moisture-loving plants around water so that their roots get adequate but not too much water, developed as a sort of stylistic offshoot of the western idea of a Japanese garden. The semi-wild water garden sometimes became almost stylistically synonymous with the rock garden, in which stones, casually distributed, provided shelves over which plants could creep in a natural sort of way. These 'constructed' water/rock gardens seldom feel appropriate in Britain, although the actual planting is often very successful. The rock pool at Sizergh Castle in Cumbria, constructed in 'local' limestone in 1926 and surrounded by groups of water-loving perennials, rock plants, dwarf maples and conifers and a fine collection of ferns, more nearly captures the spirit behind the idea than most. Modern rock and woodland gardens in New England with natural outcropping and a stream rushing through a steep gully effortlessly convey the required aesthetic effects while providing plants with conditions they enjoy. In the late Lincoln Foster's garden in Connecticut drifts of native woodland phlox and massed carpets of white-flowered meadow anemones (*Anemone canadensis*) follow the line of the stream. A mixture of native and exotic plants grows in the Garden in the Woods near Boston, where plants thrive in ecological settings (see pp. 316–17).

A new style of gardening, with planting of maximum informality inside a formal setting, was used by the American Lawrence Johnston at Hidcote in Gloucestershire from 1907. Divided up into a series of green rooms by tall tapestry hedges, each section of the garden is devoted to a separate plant or colour theme and is planted with the free abandon characterized by Gertrude Jekyll's teaching. Hidcote has been the prototype for other twentieth-century gardens, although these have often been on a more modest scale. The garden now belongs to the English National Trust.

True alpines needing rather specialized conditions hardly come into the scope of this book, but rock garden designs as settings for hardy mountain plants introduced from the European Alps, from mountains in Burma and from the Rockies are important features in many gardens. By the end of the nineteenth century, designs for growing these demanding alpines became more naturalistic in conception, with large firms such as James Pulham of Hertfordshire (in the 1870s Pulham had been using Pulhamite, a sort of concrete) and James Backhouse of York employing skilled 'rock' craftsmen to build layers of limestone brought from Westmorland to resemble natural rock strata. Reginald Farrer, condemning the more ridiculous rock garden fashions, recommended simple styles which, without looking obtrusive, provided alpines with deep pockets of soil for their questing roots to seek water without allowing their crowns to be waterlogged. Interestingly, modern alpine gardeners often abandon the attempt to grow these plants in any form of natural setting and, treating them instead as individual specimens with individual requirements, grow them either in microclimatic greenhouse conditions or in raised beds with specially prepared soil and aspect.

As the twentieth century developed, the Robinsonian garden ethic, which at first had expressed a revolt against Victorian

formalism – and in particular the use of plants in 'unnatural' ways in both bedding and topiary patterns – was extended to embrace a self-conscious attempt to cherish the last remnants of the rapidly disappearing natural world. While Percy Cane was revamping the traditional English border in more curvilinear style during the 1930s, in Germany Karl Foerster (1874–1970), nurseryman, plant breeder and writer, stressed the importance of the role of soft-stemmed plants in the garden; he liked to use taller perennials, ferns and grasses as important features, with less geometric and more organic designs spreading out from the house rather than distinctive beds and borders. In the Netherlands during the 1920s J. P. Tijsse, aware of how quickly the natural landscape was being

Meadow gardening, with summer-flowering perennials and annuals sown or planted among non-spreading grasses, is a popular way of achieving a more natural look in a garden. Rarely as labour-saving as anticipated, the most effective results are often achieved by rotavating the ground annually and reseeding. The photograph shows Sir John Thouron's garden at Glencoe in Delaware where annual cornflowers and field poppies (*Papaver rhoeas*) make a swathe of colour in tilled soil, a mixture also achievable in more temperate climates with cooler summers. In spring the Texan native blue-bonnets (*Lupinus texensis*), Indian paintbrush (*Castilleja*), gaillardias and coreopsis can be brilliant on roadside verges or in more self-consciously designed meadows; in warmer California the golden Californian poppy (*Eschscholzia californica*) can add further colour dimensions.

destroyed, developed public ecological gardens where people could be made aware of nature's beauty and meaning. Ultimately, as well as using natural environments and indigenous plants, spontaneous development of vegetation was encouraged.

American designers had even earlier taken up the theme of 'nature'; architects such as Frank Lloyd Wright had ideas of relationships between buildings and landscape which were further interpreted in terms of garden settings. Jens Jensen, with Lloyd Wright, established the Prairie Style in the Midwest, in which native plant material played a major role (see pp. 310–11). Jensen, a Danish immigrant working at first in quite a menial role as a gardener for the West Parks, part of the Chicago Public Park system, rose to be superintendent of Humboldt Park, only to be dismissed in 1900 for a stand against corruption and political graft. From then on he developed a private practice, although in 1906 he was appointed landscape architect to the entire West Park's system, a position he retained until 1920. He was a man of deeply held convictions, believing in landscaping with nature, using plants ecologically suited for a site – water supplies were already beginning to be a problem – rather than exotics, and asking the American people to save the natural landscape, and in particular the last prairie scenes, before it was too late. In this he was an early pioneer. It is said that visits early in his life to the Englischer Garten of Berlin, while a conscript in the German army, were of deep influence on his predilection for naturalism in landscape. He had a comprehensive knowledge of indigenous American trees, shrubs and wild flowers – a knowledge which already set him apart from many practising professional 'landscapers'. His most enduring public work, the Lincoln Memorial Garden at Springfield, Illinois, where planting was as in nature, with 'masses of young trees and shrubs planted close together for informal protection', is now so completely natural in atmosphere that it is hard to remember that it is an artificial creation. Jensen himself expressed some of his philosophies in *Siftings*, a collection of essays published towards the

end of his life. One of the few architectural motifs allowed in his gardens was a series of circular stone Counsel Rings, based on Indian culture, which he judiciously placed to act as meeting places or social centres. In spite of his beliefs, Jensen expressed the view that man can never successfully mimic nature: '. . . nature is not to be copied – man cannot copy God's out-of-doors. He can only interpret its message in compositions of living tones.' He used native plants distributed in such a way as to imitate natural distribution patterns, encouraging natural plant reproduction and succession to continue the process of the design work. His simple ideal of landscape seems rooted in his appreciation of the beauties

Wolfgang Oehme and Jim van Sweden have swept America with their 'New Style' perennial gardening, in which broad swathes of flowering grasses and foliage plants create abstract patterns for all seasons, with traditional 'foundation' shrubs and shade trees out of fashion. As appropriate in public as in private gardens, the massed foliage shapes and decorative flower-heads provide exciting textural contrast. This style, especially as a scheme matures, gives a 'natural' appearance, but in reality the planting is tightly planned and executed, with no space for extra specimens which could blur the design.

of his adoptive country; his ideas are a constant inspiration to modern ecological landscapers. 'There are two reasons why I turned away from the formal style that employed foreign plants. The first reason was an increasing dissatisfaction with both the plants and the unyielding design – I suppose dissatisfaction with things as they are is always a fundamental cause of revolt – and the second was that I was becoming more and more appreciative of the beauty and decorative quality of the native flora of this country.' Jensen spoke for an increasing number of Americans who are today even more aware of their natural inheritance and the need to preserve it.

Conservation movements, both public and private in origin, have influenced many ordinary gardeners towards a greater search for and appreciation of nature around them. Using native plants or adopting a natural style in gardening can also reduce maintenance and reduce the necessity for the use of environmentally sensitive herbicides and other chemicals as well as encouraging birds, butterflies and other forms of wild life (see pp. 318–19).

Particularly in the United States, where native plants stress the distinctiveness of the nation's geographic regions, meadow gardening, now a fashionable feature of private gardens, has been used to extend prairie restoration schemes on a public scale. Lady Bird Johnson's use of Texan flowers to flank highways has stimulated the conservationist's imagination. In England Robinson condemned constant lawn cutting as long ago as 1881: 'who would not rather see the waving grass with countless flowers than a close surface without a blossom.' Although growing bulbs, perennials and annuals in grass is not all that easy – too often strong grasses persist and eliminate the flowering plants – when successfully practised by experienced gardeners (Christopher Lloyd's mother at Great Dixter in East Sussex was an early pioneer) it can be immensely visually and emotionally satisfying. Gardeners intent on creating beauty rather than being ecological do not have to stick to native flora, and can extend the meadow theme with countless exotics. Annual meadows where yearly rotavating cleans the soil can be most effective even if less ecologically sound. In America new styles of planting, particularly by Wolfgang Oehme and James van Sweden, with broad sweeps of grasses and perennials, take up both Foerster's and Jensen's themes.

Not only are many native flora becoming rarer. Many cultivated garden flowers, grown for centuries, have also disappeared or are scarce. Over a long period garden cultivars, with suitable characteristics such as long flowering, larger flowers and leaves, and general sturdiness and adaptability, arose spontaneously and were selected for use. Many of these disappeared over the years, becom-

By the twentieth century gardens all over the world had eclectic collections of plants individually chosen to suit the climate and to fit in the scheme of the garden. At Barnsley House in Gloucestershire Rosemary Verey uses interesting flowering and foliage plants from many continents to complement a garden laid out with strong seventeenth-century axial lines and details. In the illustration of the water gates at Barnsley, New Zealand flax (*Phormium tenax*) is underplanted with Asiatic bergenias.

ing temporarily obsolete as gardening fashions changed and scientific breeding produced further popular novelties. Societies such as the National Council for the Conservation of Plants and Gardens in Britain and specialist societies in the United States, such as the Thomas Jefferson Memorial Foundation at Monticello are now devoted to searching for and saving old varieties. Historically authentic flowers are sought for period restorations of old gardens in both Europe and America.

E. H. WILSON: PLANT HUNTER

Veitch gave precise instructions: 'The object of the journey is to collect a quantity of seeds of a plant the name of which is known to us. That is the object – do not dissipate time, energy or money on anything else. In furtherance of this you will first endeavour to visit Dr A. Henry at Szemao, Yunnan and obtain from him precise data as to the habitat of this particular plant and information on the flora of central China in general.' So read Veitch's instructions to Ernest H. Wilson; the three-years' agreement was signed in March 1899.[2] The plant was the dove or handkerchief tree, *Davidia involucrata*. Wilson's successfully accomplished mission established his reputation; he sent seeds (it was an exceptional fruiting year) back to Veitch's Coombe Wood Nursery, from these most of the specimens presently grown in gardens are descended. Wilson had to admit to some bitterness when it was divulged that in 1897 M. Maurice de Vilmorin had also received seeds of a davidia; in 1898 *one plant only* was raised from this batch in his arboretum at Les Barres. From this plant, flowering first in 1906, and proving to be the smooth-leaved form *D. involucrata* var. *vilmoriniana*, a rooted cutting was sent to Kew Gardens and to the Jardin des Plantes in Paris, and a rooted layer to the Arnold Arboretum.

Wilson returned to China for Veitch's nursery in 1903 and from 1906 continued his plant explorations on behalf of the Arnold Arboretum, where he became assistant director in 1919. Wilson's most widely grown find was the regal lily (*Lilium regale*), which he brought back, after appalling hardship, from his fourth expedition to China in 1910. Hundreds of lily bulbs were dug and packed (later lily bulbs were embedded in clay for shipment) by Wilson's assistants and carried on men's backs to waiting boats.

Left: The regal lily (*Lilium regale*), which proved the most garden-worthy of Wilson's fine introductions from China, was brought back to the Arnold Arboretum from Hupeh in 1910. 'High up on the mountainside . . . this lily in full bloom greets the weary traveller [in June] . . . in hundreds, in thousands, aye, in tens of thousands. Its slender stems, each 2–4 feet tall . . . are crowned . . . with several large funnel-shaped flowers more or less wine-coloured without, pure white and lustrous on the face, clear canary yellow within the tube and each stamen tipped with a golden anther'. Breaking his leg in an avalanche, Wilson nearly lost his life on the expedition.

Sown in April 1901, the seeds of Wilson's *Davidia involucrata* (right) finally germinated in May 1902 after anxious months of waiting. Only those grown out-of-doors in prepared seed beds and subjected to winter frost were successful; those indoors hardly germinated at all. Wilson was able to pot up 13,000 plants from this original harvest, although in 1906 several thousand of these were burned by a maniac. He had also brought back three or four living plants, one of which first flowered at Coombe Wood in May 1911. The davidia has pendulous bracts of unequal size; the largest was as long and wide as 20 x 10 centimetres/8 x 4 inches, greenish-white turning to snow-white, which fluttered and stirred in a gentle breeze. Glowing accounts of it had been returned by both Père David in 1869 and Augustine Henry in 1888. The illustration is from Franchet's *Plantae Davidianae*.

d'Apreval ad nat. del. et lith.

Imp. Becquet fr. Paris.

Davidia involucrata, H. Baillon.

GERTRUDE JEKYLL AND THE BORDER

It fell to one of William Robinson's colleagues, Gertrude Jekyll, working with the talented young architect Edwin Lutyens, to bridge a gap between architects and gardeners. Miss Jekyll, trained as an artist but with increasing myopia in middle life, devoted herself to gardening and garden writing; throughout her life her love of rural craftsmanship and simple cottage-garden plants was an abiding force. Designing 400 or so gardens during her lifetime – including two in the United States – the strength of her ideas is still obvious to modern gardeners. She is best remembered for the border schemes in which she used any plants which would best sustain her colour vision. Small trees and shrubs, perennials, biennials and annuals, bulbs – and potted plants plunged into awkward seasonal gaps – were all arranged to reach her exacting standards. She was not particularly interested in newly introduced exotics – although, of course, she appreciated them – but primarily saw the plants as 'tools' which, when well managed, contributed to the composition, just as an artist uses his paint pigments on a canvas. What seemed like simple cottage-garden styling was in fact a sophisticated exercise in achieving a maximum amount of informality of planting inside the quite grand geometry of designs by Lutyens and other architects.

Although Miss Jekyll is better known, her contemporaries Louise Beebe Wilder and Mrs Frances King in eastern North America carried the 'colour' banner, advising on appropriate seasonal schemes for the more difficult American climate and recommending plants which would endure and continue to flower in the intense summer heat. Louise Beebe Wilder's *Color in my Garden*, first issued in 1918, has recently been reprinted with

In Miss Jekyll's own garden at Munstead Wood in Surrey, she had seasonal schemes for separate areas. A spring garden mainly of bulbs was given body with bold-foliaged veratrums and euphorbias; a May border was for peonies rising above the leaves of Lenten hellebores; roses were mixed and underplanted with other species. Unlike the main summer borders of most of her contemporaries, planned for a two-month peak in July and August, hers were backed up with dahlias and late-flowerers to carry the garden into September and early October.

plant names modernized. Outside Boston Mabel Cabot Sedgwick gardened at Beverly on the North Shore. Her book, *The Garden Month by Month* published in 1906, remains an invaluable inspiration to New England gardeners, although for ease of reading and usefulness the turn-of-the-century plant names need updating.

The garden at Upton Grey in Hampshire, designed by Gertrude Jekyll in the 1920s, has been lovingly restored with authentic planting, carefully researched. Jekyll developed her own colour harmonies in the garden, using the strong 'hot' flower tones – orange, reds, scarlet and crimson – in graduated sequences and the 'cooler' blues and yellows in complementary contrast. She was interested not only in bright flower hues but in leaf and flower textures as well as in the shapes of plants, so that each border scheme became a synthesis of balance and repetition.

The Lutyens/Jekyll partnership produced gardens which may be considered the very best in English garden style. By introducing a strong architectural framework, inside which plants in spreading drifts could look natural, both formalists and plantsmen were satisfied. Lutyens planned the garden layout at Hestercombe in Somerset in a series of different planes and levels, separating the garden into separate geometric areas; he liked to use traditional and where possible vernacular materials. Hestercombe, designed before World War I, with its framework and planting, is the supreme example of their complementary work, with Jekyll's flowing flowers and foliage decorating Lutyens's terraces and water rills.

THE GARDENS OF CHARLESTON IN SOUTH CAROLINA

Left: A view of Middleton Place showing the famed Cherokee rose (*Rosa laevigata*) and azaleas set amongst the trees. From the early eighteenth century, silk, indigo and rice were main cash crops on the fine plantations developed along the Cooper and Ashley rivers. For most, following the hard times after the Civil War, production of even rice ceased to be profitable, although grown still at Mulberry Plantation until 1902. André Michaux's 'French' Nursery at Goosecreek, established just outside Charleston in 1786, had introduced many settlers to American plants outside their normal experience. Foreign introductions of Japanese camellias (first planted at Middleton in 1786), the scented Lady Banks rose (*Rosa banksiae*), star or Confederate jasmine (*Trachelospermum jasminoides*) and Indian azaleas augmented plantation and Charleston gardens, with the specially colourful addition of E. H. Wilson's Kurume azalea, introduced to America in 1920.

Top right: Foreign plants such as *Rosa laevigata* from Asia, its date of introduction uncertain, have established themselves among native vegetation. The rose clambers up into tall trees and intertwines with native wisteria. Other introduced colonizers are the mimosa or silk tree (*Albizia julibrissin*), first grown from seed collected by André Michaux (in Persia and given by him to William Bartram), in 1785 and the Chinese bead tree (*Melia azedarach*), introduced in 1761. At first commonly cultivated in southern gardens, these plants have invaded forest margins.

Right: A small Charleston garden at 55 Church Street, the Benjamin Philips House of 1818, designed by Hugh and Mary Palmer Dargan. In these walled gardens, box-edged beds arranged geometrically and separated by sand-shell pathways edged with old Charleston brick, are planted with white-flowering pansies in spring and old camellia varieties. The flowering trees are Zumi crab apples (*Malus x zumi*). Today, although many foreign plants find it difficult to acclimatize to summer heat and humidity (especially the hot nights) many exotics flourish. Crape myrtles, gardenias, loquats (*Eriobotrya japonica*), Australian *Pittosporum undulatum*, red-leaf photinias, wax-leaf ligustrum (*Ligustrum japonicum*) and Chilean podocarpus (*Podocarpus andinus*) augment the native cherry laurels (*Laurocerasus caroliniana*), *Gelsemium sempervirens* and yaupon, and traditional European box (both 'English' and 'American').

Charleston in South Carolina has a mild winter climate, hot summers, fertile soil and sufficient rainfall to have an enviable range of natural vegetation, including live oaks (*Quercus virginiana*), usually festooned with grey Spanish moss (*Tillandsia usneoides*) – at Middleton Place, an old oak with a height of 26 metres/85 feet, circumference of 9 metres/30 feet and a 44-metre/145-foot spread, is thought to be pre-Columbian. There are also swamp or bald cypresses, dogwoods, evergreen magnolias, azaleas, cabbage palmettos (*Sabal palmetto*), purple or native anise (*Illicium floridanum*), red bay (*Persea borbonia*), redbud (*Cercis canadensis*), wisterias (*Wisteria frutescens*) and Carolina yellow jessamine (*Gelsemium sempervirens*). These plants, as well as plants from the Old World, original introductions and 'new' exotics, had been long grown both in the small walled gardens in Charleston and in the gardens surrounding the elegant houses built on the plantations on which the owners' fortunes depended. Loutrel Briggs, working in Charleston from the 1920s, restored and planted many historic walled gardens and plantation layouts.

At the end of the nineteenth century Olmsted's firm, now run by his sons and Charles Eliot, had made a design for Cannon Park in Charleston. Plants included were the Cherokee rose and its pink form (*Rosa laevigata* 'Anemonoides'), European ivy and periwinkle, bamboos, three different sorts of yucca (*Yucca filamentosa*, *Y. gloriosa* and *Y. angustifolia*), groups of hollies (*Ilex opaca*), *Ligustrum lucidum*, holly olive or devil wood (*Osmanthus ilicifolius*), Portugal laurel, American cherry laurel (*Laurocerasus caroliniana*), and hardy fruiting lemons (*Limonia trifoliata*), with Marliac's new hybrid water-lilies to grow in the ornamental pool. All these plants are still popular in Charleston today. Other native trees and

shrubs included in the plan of the park were willow-leaved oak (*Quercus phellos*), *Magnolia grandiflora*, loblolly bay (*Gordonia lasianthus*), yaupon (*Ilex vomitoria*), leather leaf (*Chamaedaphne calyculata*), *Illicium floridanum* and the little heath-like sand myrtle (*Leiophyllum buxifolium*), sent to Collinson by Bartram in 1736 but seldom found to thrive in British gardens. Introduced plants include cork oak (*Quercus suber*), pyracanthas, cotoneasters, Japanese pachysandra and rock roses. Today there are plans for a partial restoration of the Cannon Park scheme using the original plans that still exist.

In June 1990, in recognition of their servi-ces, the American Horticultural Society awarded its special National Achievement Award not to a single person but to the entire du Pont family. The list of gardens founded by the family which today remain of importance include Crowninshield, Doe Run, Hagley, Longwood, Nemours, Mount Cuba and Win-terthur, all in Delaware and Pennsylvania. Their first garden was established at the Eleutherian Powder Mills from 1803 by Eleuthère Irénée du Pont (1771–1834) and his wife Sophie.

Immigrants from France in 1800, the du Ponts first established themselves in New Jer-sey within a short distance of the Jardin de la République, founded at Bergen's Wood (Hagensack) by André Michaux in 1786,

THE DU PONT FAMILY

before moving to Hagley in Delaware. Du Pont, having attended lectures at the Jardin des Plantes in Paris, had also been trained as a powder-maker, working for the Government, and this, rather than professional horticulture or botany, was to be the foundation of the du Pont family's fortune at the Eleutherian Mills.[3]

At both Longwood and Winterthur there are strong architectural elements as well as fine plant collections. At the former, an exact reproduction of the water parterres at Villa Gamberaia, a theatre modelled on that of the Villa Gori at Siena – with hemlocks sub-stituted for soaring Italian cypresses and

'wings' of arbor-vitae (*Thuja occidentalis*) – show Italian influence. In the main Fountain Garden hedges of *Buxus sempervirens* 'Suffruti-cosa' and of the Japanese holly (*Ilex crenata*) and pleached Norway maple set off stonework and statues. A fine avenue of princess or empress trees (*Paulownia tomentosa*) provides a shady thoroughfare next to topiary yews, cut into neatly trimmed pyramids and domes.

In Chandler Woods at Winterthur, there is a fine stand of eastern climax forest with native trees, shrubs, wildflowers and ferns. A 300-year-old tulip poplar is the tallest tree in Delaware. Besides the woodland and meadows, there are formal gardens designed by Marian Coffin in the 1950s, in which box-wood and azaleas line steep steps descending to a reflecting pool.

Above: A *Cornus kousa* at Longwood in Pennsylvania, world famous for its horticultural excellence, spectacular conservatory and Italianate waterworks, and America's greatest pleasure garden, was the creation of Pierre S. du Pont, great-grandson of the original E. I. du Pont. Purchased in 1906 to preserve the notable 12-hectare/30-acre arboretum planted by the Quaker twins Joshua and Samuel Pierce after 1798, du Pont increased the acreage tenfold with a further 265 hectares/650 acres of woods and meadows. A row of swamp or bald cypresses (*Taxodium distichum*) still remains from the Pierce

planting, with the pagoda tree (*Sophora japonica*), ginkgos, and a massive cucumber tree (*Magnolia acuminata*).

Above right: Winterthur, first owned by members of the family in 1839, was first 'gardened' by Henry Algernon du Pont from the 1870s, but its greatest enrichment is due to the naturalistic planting genius of his son Henry Francis (1880–1969). The latter, among the first to use the evergreen Kurume azaleas introduced by E. H. Wilson in 1920 in an outdoor setting, expanded the garden into a dream

of beauty with drifts of pink and white azaleas spreading under native stands of tall tulip poplars. Steep banks are covered with 'woodlanders' such as may-apples, mertensias, Spanish bluebells and trilliums. His collections of Saunders peonies, Stout day-lilies and Dexter hybrid rhododendrons add botanical interest to an eclectic planting of cherries, dogwoods, lilacs, magnolias, redbuds, viburnums, a pinetum of fir, spruce, hemlock, pine and cedar, as well as lilies and irises, all interspersed with more open meadows bright with flowering bulbs in spring.

Louise du Pont Crowninshield was Henry Francis du Pont's elder sister. She and her husband restored the house at Eleutherian Mills (*above and left*), damaged by an explosion in 1890, and, after 1921, laid out a new romantic Italian garden on the foundations of the old Powder Mills and on the steep hillside which fell away to the Brandywine River below. The garden was a judicious blend of formal terraces and 'ruined' columns which gave architectural definition to naturalistic planting of dogwoods and azaleas. The Crowninshields lined flagstone and tiled mosaic pathways with box and tapering conifers for Mediterranean effects.

Jensen designed the Lincoln Memorial Garden on the shores of Lake Springfield in Illinois. Woodland rides lined with prairie thorn, crab, American plum, sumach, grey dogwood – all midwestern natives – fill in the horizontal plane of the Midwest landscape and link partially concealed open spaces filled by wildflowers, by the lakeside. Trees, shrubs and flowers, originally planted as seedlings or seeds by volunteers, unite to give a totally natural effect. Shown above is one of Jensen's circular stone Counsel Rings – a rare architectural motif in his design.

Completely out of tune with all formal geometric design, as exemplified by contemporary Italianate layouts for the great 'Country Places', Jensen's wild-nature technique – still known today as the Prairie Style – was particularly suitable to public parks.

JENS JENSEN AND
THE PRAIRIE STYLE

Jens Jensen (1860–1950), whose designs in the Midwest of America were characterized by broad open meadow scenes bordered by wooded 'peninsulas' and tree-edged trails curving out of sight to encourage exploration, was born in Denmark and emigrated to the United States in 1884. In his private gardens Jensen recognized the need for more formal elements near the house; cutting gardens, rose gardens and kitchen areas could all be incorporated in the right place, and to the end of his life he used old favourites such as day-lilies, hollyhocks, peonies and lilacs, all long associated with man's dwellings, to complement his obsessive interest in native garden flowers.

Few of his gardens remain intact. He worked for members of the Ford family in Detroit for many years, creating two land-scape masterpieces. From 1913 or 1914 he had a long association with Mr and Mrs Henry Ford at Fair Lane, during which he created his famous 'path of the setting sun' with trails leading through thicker planting to open 'rooms' of meadow and lakeside. His genius lay partly in his utilization of sunlight and shadow, placing sugar maples and sumach in places where the warm red rays of the setting sun would heighten their fall foliage, and paper birch and shadbush where their silver and grey bark would be illuminated by the early morning sun with mist rising from the lake behind. Flowering dogwood and haw-thorn trees underplanted with wildflowers edged the pathways. In his design he incorporated 'natural' ledgerock strata for 200 yards along the Rouge River. A beech and maple forest lay below the bluff towards the river's edge.

His relationship with the Fords was termin-ated when Mrs Ford wished to implant a formal rose garden into one of his meadow landscapes, an idea ferociously opposed by Jensen; but the landscape he designed at

Jensen's garden for Edsel and Eleanor Ford. Sugar maples and American elms, through which there are glimpses of the Cotswold-style house, curve round a central sunlit meadow oriented north-west and south-east for the setting and rising sun – Jensen's repeated theme song. Round a 'natural' rock pool (designed for swimming), paper birch, grey-stemmed amelanchiers, maple-leaved viburnums (*Viburnum acerifolium*) and dark hemlock are all underplanted with wildflowers. Virginian bluebells (*Mertensia*), trilliums, bunchberry (*Cornus canadensis*), claytonias, erythroniums and may-apples unite to create a magically beautiful small-scale woodland landscape.

Gaukler's Pointe on the shore of Lake St Clair for the Fords' son Edsel and his wife Eleanor during the late twenties and thirties remains a lasting memorial to his art.

In 1922, after a preliminary visit to Dumbarton Oaks, Farrand's report included all the main architectural features and themes which were later introduced. Letters were exchanged discussing the whole conception of the garden as a series of outdoor rooms. One small area, just below the Fountain Terrace in which seasonal flowering bulbs and annuals were framed by permanent shrubs and vines, is dominated by a wooden arbour, its framework based on the Montargis trelliswork shown by Du Cerceau in the sixteenth century. It was originally intended as a secret or private garden emphasising the contrast between sunlight and shade, the soothing sound of water and plantings of highly scented herbs. Today, plants in pots are its main decoration, placed beyond the wisteria-draped arbour. Farrand planted an aerial hedge of Leconte pear trees (*Pyrus x lecontei* 'Kieffer') to 'support' the eastern end of the Fountain Garden and the north side of this lower terrace, both of which protrude abruptly into the landscape.

BEATRIX FARRAND'S PLANTING AT DUMBARTON OAKS

Beatrix Farrand's strong architectural plant statements combine with a serenity of planting schemes at Dumbarton Oaks to make the whole garden an essay in contrasts of style, texture and colour so closely interwoven that there are no abrupt transitions to jar the mind, only a steady progression from one harmony to another. The relaxed planting with which Farrand framed the formal elements creates leafy passages from strong sunlight to dense shade, from soothing monotone green to an area of subtle flower colour.

There are few 'bright' hues – white azaleas and wisteria on the upper terraces, roses in the Rose Garden and spring-flowering trees, underplanted with blue scillas and golden daffodils, banked on the slopes beyond the more formal confines. Mildred Bliss herself once described 'the great billowing mass of forsythia tumbling down two hillsides turned to gold'. To Europeans the American dogwood (*Cornus florida*), making ghostly drifts in deciduous woodland, is a perfect theme song for eastern American gardens, just as the leafy shade-giving pines and evergreen oaks, soaring cypresses and boxwood speak to us all of the Italian garden.

Details in the *Plant Book for Dumbarton Oaks* are instructive. Beatrix Farrand used trees with weeping shapes to disguise abrupt changes in level; cherries, crab apples and willows were among those she found most useful. She liked to frame pathways with architectural plants, both trees and shrubs. A pair of Himalayan cedars (*Cedrus deodara*), and not Farrand's preferred more stately cedars of Lebanon, flanked the main north terrace steps. For lower-level accents she used different broad-leaved evergreens: both sorts of box, small-leaved Japanese hollies, American holly (*Ilex opaca*) and Japanese yew (*Taxus cuspidata*). Of the ramped Box Walk she wrote

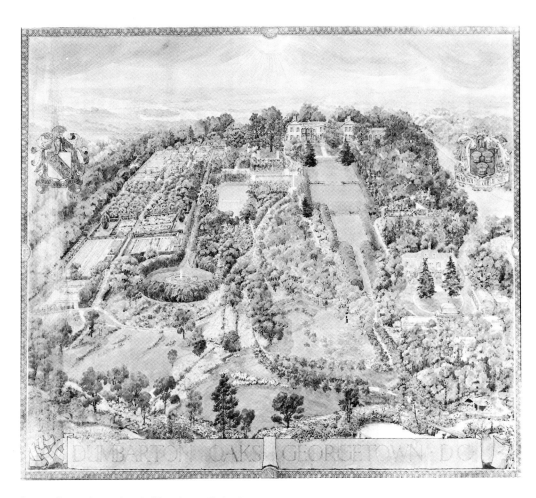

Beatrix Farrand was already fifty when called in by Robert and Mildred Bliss to redesign the 11 hectares/27 acres round the original Federal-period house in Georgetown. She did not find a totally blank canvas: oaks, silver maples, Japanese maples and katsuras (*Cercidiphyllum japonicum*) already existed. Nor was the site flat; even the north-facing slope had deep valleys and rising hills, constantly changing the contours and aspects for planting effects. In fact the very unevenness of the terrain allowed for Farrand's development of both formal and informal spaces, with geometric alleys and enclosures flanked by loosely planted 'natural'-looking groves of trees. The watercolour (*above*) is by Ernest Clegg, 1935.

in 1941: 'Nothing will ever be quite as beautiful as the rumpled masses of Box as they follow the slope of the hill.'

Above: Ninfa, on the banks of the river below the Lepini mountains south of Rome, remained an abandoned village from the fourteenth century until the early years of this century when members of the Caetani family – descendants of the seventeenth-century plant collector Francesco Caetani – reclaimed the land, canalized the water, tidied up the ruins and made a garden. Even in the intervening centuries its favoured situation with land fed by abundant water had made Ninfa famous for its wild flowers.

Right: Calla or arum lilies (*Zantedeschia aethiopica*) line the water channels to make May spectacular and Ninfa unforgettable. Since the 1900s three generations of Caetanis have made the garden at Ninfa one of the most romantic in the world. At first tidying up the ruins and canalizing water courses – Ninfa gets its water supply from a reservoir fed by natural springs situated just above the village – they planted plane trees, cypresses, cedars, evergreen oaks and pines, all of which helped establish the main 'bones' of the garden.

NINFA

In the eighteenth century, Gregorovius, the German historian, described how 'over Ninfa waves a balmy sea of flowers'; later Augustus Hare saw flowers which 'grow so abundantly in the deserted streets, where honeysuckle and jessamine fling their garlands through the windows of every house, and where the altars of the churches are thrones for flame-coloured valerian'. By the 1920s Ada Wilbraham Caetani, the Duchess of Sermoneta, with her son Prince Gelasio Caetani, had begun to add rarer plants and above all roses. The next generation, Roffredo Caetani and his American-born wife, continued to expand the planting. Lelia, their daughter, with her English husband Hubert Howard, devoted her life to gardening and it is her 'eye' as garden planner – she was also a painter – which has framed the romantic profusion of the garden's appearance today. She and her husband also created a nature reserve in the surrounding area.

Many of the plants Lelia Howard added to the garden were obtained through English nurseries but were cosmopolitan in origin; there are lists kept of annual planting between 1950 and her death in 1972. Wisterias, *Caesalpinia japonica*, trachelospermums, climbing hydrangeas, schizophragmas and scented jasmine from the east, and ceanothus from West Coast America clothe the walls; tender pines from Mexico (*Pinus montezumae*, *P. patula*, and *P. jeffreyi*), fine dogwoods and magnolias from America and Asia, buddlejas, maples, viburnums and rare trees such as *Cladastris sinensis*, which takes twenty years to flower, grow as neighbouring specimens.

At Ninfa, besides the romantic garden in the old village, high seventeenth-century walls make an enclosure below the medieval Castello; here Francesco Caetani may have grown some of his vast collection of tulips, anemones, hyacinths and tuberoses. Modern planting of citrus fruit (oranges, lemons and grapefruit) also reflect that period.

At Ninfa acclimatization was possible for a wide range of plants from very varied habitats. In essence the garden has an English flavour, its only formal definition given by the original layout of the ancient medieval streets and the high walls, over which wisteria and roses cascade today, and by an avenue of cypresses (each entwined with a rose) which leads from one of the ruined churches down to the river on the banks of which grow tropical gunnera. Occasionally a pair of pines or cypresses flanks a pathway, more to indicate direction than to introduce a formal note, and hedges of rosemary line mown paths.

THE GARDEN IN THE WOODS

The founders of the Garden in the Woods at Framingham in Massachusetts in 1934 were Will Curtis and Howard 'Dick' Stiles. They believed that by collecting together wildflowers from all over America in a flower sanctuary 'where plants will be grown, their likes and dislikes discovered, and the knowledge gained passed on in an effort to curb the wholesale destruction of our most beautiful natives.' It would be their lasting contribution to conservation.

Curtis was a trained landscape designer, a follower of the garden designer Warren Manning (he worked in Manning's office), but ultimately was intent only on making gardens with a strongly naturalistic appeal. Dick Stiles was the avid horticulturist. Together for over forty years they collected thousands of wild flowers, ferns, shrubs and trees and established them in natural and modified settings, developing woodland groves, rockeries, swamps and lily ponds, pine barrens, meadows and screes to provide very varied 'habitats' and microclimates.

In 1965 they entrusted the Garden's future to the New England Wild Flower Society, which already had a chartered purpose to promote the horticulture and conservation of native American plants. Today the Garden is

These flowers are not arranged as 'specimens' but as natural-looking drifts, growing as they do in a natural environment. Nor does the Garden in the Woods appear like a botanic collection, although that is what it is, but rather as a collection arranged in an ecological twentieth-century style. It is also what its name implies: a real 'garden', just as carefully landscaped to create environmental beauty, provide education and stimulate future conservation as Le Nôtre's vast seventeenth-century layouts, with their plants regimented and clipped to play required roles, were designed to represent fashionable attitudes to controlling nature. Here the plants are given, as nearly as possible, conditions which they crave, with easily accessible winding paths separating different 'culture' areas.

the Society's headquarters and is renowned for its collection of rare natives, now scarce in the wild. These include Oconee bells, the elusive *Shortia galacifolia* so long searched for by nineteenth-century botanists, familiar with it only from Michaux's Paris herbarium and the spreading globeflower (*Trollius laxus*) from swampy regions from Delaware north to Michigan.

In the end the originators of the garden did not stick only to American flora. The planting of exotics cheek by jowl with broadly similar natives adds extra interest, a harking back to before the Ice Age when continents were linked not separated. The greater purpose behind the Garden is that of conservation and propagation of species in order to make them available to the public. The Garden in the Woods covers an area of more than 18 hectares/45 acres in which grow over 1,500 varieties of plants.

Top right: The site, with mainly acid soil, already had many old trees, groves of hemlocks, sugar maples and birches, as well as a typical New England vegetation of viburnums, fothergillas, huckleberries, blueberries and dogwood, many of which produce vivid autumnal colours. The pockets of diverse soils make it possible to establish a wide range of plants with different requirements. On a site of glacier-carved terrain with winding steep-valleyed eskers, streams and kettlehole ponds and wooded bogs, Curtis and Stiles pioneered the largest landscaped collection of wildflowers in north-east America.

Right: For Curtis and Stiles albino flowers and other mutants such as 'doubles' became a special interest quite early on. These now include white cardinal flowers (*Lobelia cardinalis* 'Alba'), white forms of the wild American roses (*Rosa virginiana* and *R. setigera*), 'white' red trilliums (*Trillium erectum*) and double-flowered *T. grandiflorum petalosum*, white wild geraniums (*Geranium maculatum*), white-fruited partridgeberry (*Mitchella repens*), double-flowered bloodroot (*Sanguinaria canadensis* 'Flore-Pleno'), variegated wild oats (*Uvularia sessifolia*) and a double-flowered trailing arbutus (*Epigaea repens*), the main type now quite rare in its native East-Coast woodlands.

THE DRY GARDEN IN THE WEST

A xeriscape, or dry garden, is a new ecological approach to gardening in arid regions or in drought-prone areas. It is designed with certain specific aims in view. The most important is the effectiveness of saving water, or using water in a sensible way. Plants from the region in which the garden is placed are an obvious solution to water shortages. If suitably planted the garden will be of correspondingly low maintenance, with soil improved with some sort of organic material to hold any available moisture and ensure efficient watering, and both 'hard' landscaping and mulches used to prevent moisture evaporation. In other words the garden should be ecologically perfectly adapted to its site. In an area of great summer heats and low rainfall plants survive in natural circumstances. Depending on local rainfall the plant range used can be extended or restricted.

The xeriscape movement was first formulated in 1981 in Denver, Colorado, a region with only 355 millimetres/14 inches of rain a year, in response to an awareness of water deficits in the coming years. Before this, gardeners in arid California, Arizona and parts of Colorado, semi-desert country, had been persistent in copying the cultural ideals of European gardens, making green lawns a necessary part of their gardening efforts, with watering of grass accounting for almost half their water consumption. Numerous native and introduced plant species can be used for this sort of landscaping; the only criterion is choosing plants which thrive in an existing situation. Every region can assemble lists of Californian, desert, Australian and Mediterranean plants with suitable minimum water requirements. For lawns, if they are necessary, buffalo and blue grama grasses can be substituted for ordinary fescues. Under pressure to save water, the public now demands the availability of more native and drought-resistant plants from nurseries, and new irrigation techniques with drip systems and leaky hose pipes substituted for extravagant spray systems. Forecasts of 'greenhouse effects' to be felt world-wide make this sort of water-conservation gardening worth considering even in countries which in the past have had high average rainfalls.

Left: In Santa Fé, New Mexico, native planting of gaillardias (*Gaillardia aristata*), mahogany-red and yellow Mexican hat (*Ratibida columnaris*), combine with blue flax (*Linum lewisii*) and native grasses to give naturalistic garden effects in front of pinyon pine (*Pinus edulis*). These plants and grasses need little water and maintenance during the hottest summers.

Below: Lotus Land in Santa Barbara was partly designed for Madame Ganna Walska by Lockwood de Forest, the well-known Santa Barbara designer, and partly by Ralph Stevens, the son of the previous owner of the estate, whose speciality was desert plants – he even constructed a motorized flowering clock of cacti and succulents. The beautiful Cycad Garden, with over 50 different species of *Encephalartos*, was designed by Charles Glass and Robert Foster in 1975. There is an Aloe Garden, with soaring flowers in orange and yellow, and a Cactus and Euphorbia Garden (euphorbias are succulents and no relation to cactus), containing a flowering *Cereus peruvianus* 'Monstrosus'. The illustration shows the blue-foliage garden with *Festuca glauca* growing under Atlas cedar and blue palm (*Erythea armata*).

In the Grier garden at Lafayette north of San Francisco native plants from the area form the bulk of the planting. Various blue-flowered ceanothus and the white *Ceanothus thyrsiflorus* 'Snow Flurry', underplanted with low-growing *Baccharis pilularis*, are seen through the red stems of the east-coast American shrub, *Cornus stolonifera*, which leafs out later in the season. Native-plant gardens in the west seldom maintain all-the-year-round effects and in many gardens, where saving water is considered essential, Mediterranean plants, thriving in similar conditions, are used to supplement the main themes of *Ceanothus*, grey-leaved buckwheat (*Eriogoron arborescens*), *Arctostaphyllos* and *Baccharis*.

AUTHOR'S ACKNOWLEDGEMENTS

I am very grateful to Colin Webb of Pavilion for suggesting that I should write about the history of garden design. In adapting this theme to a book about plants in garden history Helen Sudell at Pavilion has been a continual support. She and her team, with the designer Bernard Higton, have made the book beautiful. I owe special debts to Sandra Raphael and to Penny David. As an adviser, Sandra has answered questions, stimulated alleys of research and corrected errors, feeding me from her vast store of knowledge, particularly in the field of botanical illustration. Penny, always an expert editor, has also travelled with me in spirit through areas of research, going far beyond her editorial brief. Caroline Taylor's reading of the proofs was invaluable. Jenny de Gex has been indefatigable in her successful search for illustrations. Without her the book would lack that extra visual dimension.

So many others have helped me. Dr Brent Elliot and the assistant librarians at the Lindley Library have been untiring; their expertise and depth of knowledge illuminating research. To garden historians in general I owe a vast debt; much of my material is drawn from their scholarship and previous assessments. In almost every chapter Dr John Harvey, either in person or in his books and articles, has provided the meat and pointed the way to further reading. A chance meeting with Professor William Stearn in the gardens at Kew directed me to new reading. Others who have given me advice include Georgio Galleti from Italy, Louise van Everdingen, Dr Wernt Grimm, Liliane de Rothschild, Pierre-André Lablaude, Count Jan van Aspeck, Carla S. Oldenburgger-Ebbers, Mrs van de Greer from Het Loo, Lord Bridges, Esme Howard, Paul Miles, Elizabeth Mclean in Philadelphia, John Kirkpatrick and Peter Hatch at Monticello, and many others both in Virginia and Charleston, Ken Brinkley, Wesley Green and Robin Wooley at Williamsburg, Dean Norton at Mount Vernon, Sarah Hammond and Kristin Jacob in California, Mary Ellen Ray in Savannah, William Frederick in Delaware, Bernadette Callery in the library of the New York Botanical Garden, and Linda Lotte, librarian at Dumbarton Oaks. The late Elizabeth Woodburn from New Jersey introduced me to American garden literature and suggested suitable reading. In England Mavis Batey, Anthony Huxley, Mark Laird, Hazel Le Rougetel, Jean O'Neill and Patrick Taylor and many others have answered my questions and suggested routes for research.

Penelope Hobhouse

PICTURE ACKNOWLEDGEMENTS

The Publishers wish to extend particular thanks for all kind help and advice to Dr Brent Elliot, Librarian of the Lindley Library at the Royal Horticultural Society, and to Eileen Tweedy for her copy photography.

The following sources have been abbreviated thus:

BNP/DES Bibliothèque Nationale, Paris (Cabinet des Dessins et Estampes)
BNP Bibliothèque Nationale, Paris (Manuscrits)
BOD Bodleian Library, Oxford
BL/IOL British Library/India Office Library, London
BL/MS British Library, London (Manuscripts)
BL British Library, London (Printed Books)
BM British Museum, London
RMN Réunion des Musées Nationaux, Paris
RBG Royal Botanic Gardens, Kew
RHS Royal Horticultural Society, Lindley Library, London

Illustrations are identified by page number.

Endpapers *The Planter's Guide*, J. Meader. 1779 RHS. **Half-Title page** *Tacuinum Sanitatis*, f. 38. Österreichisches Nationalbibliothek, Vienna. **2** *Florilegium*, Kickius, Courtesy of the Duchess of Beaufort. **6** Spinette cover, Van Valchenborch. Germanische National Museum, Nürnberg/Scala. **9** *Wild daffodil*, Jacques Le Moyne de Morgues. E. T. Archive. **10** Wall painting from Tomb of Minnakhte, c. 1475 BC. Metropolitan Museum, New York, Rogers Fund, 1930. **13** Dr Lisa Manniche. **15** RBG. **16, 17, 18** BM. **19** *Les Jardins*, Arthur Mangin, 1867. RHS. **21** National Museum of Athens/Scala. **22** Ancient Art and Architecture Collection. **23** Dimitrios Harissiadis/George Rainbird Ltd/Robert Harding Picture Library. **24** *Florilegium*, Emmanuel Sweert, 1612. RHS. **27** Museo delle Terme, Rome/Scala. **28** Jay Venezia. **29** Casa del Bracciale d'Oro, Pompeii/Scala. **31** Gianni Dagli Orti, Paris. **32L** *The Manners and Customs of the Ancient Egyptians*, J. Wilkinson, 1847. BL. **32R** RBG. **33** BM. **34** George Rainbird Ltd/Robert Harding Picture Library. **35T** William Macquitty Collection. **35B** Museo Nazionale, Naples/Scala. **36** *Codex Vindobonensis*, Med Gr f.26 verso. Österreichisches Nationalbibliothek, Vienna. **37** *Codex Neapolitanus*, MS Gr. 1 f.148. Biblioteca Nazionale Vittorio Emanuele, Naples/Pedicini. **38** Weidenfeld & Nicolson Archives. **39** Ancient Art & Architecture Collection. **40** OA 1969.3 – 17, 0. 1. BM. **42** MS Or Smith Lesouef 198 f.1r–2v. BNP. **43** Staatsbibliothek Orientabteilung, Berlin/Bildarchiv Preussischer Kulturbesitz. **45** IS 48–1956. Courtesy of the Board of Trustees of the Victoria & Albert Museum, London. **47** MS Arabe 2964 f.54 v. BNP. **48** MS Or Arabe 2850, f.89 v. BNP. **50** Musée Historique des Tissus, Lyon/Studio Basset. **51** Rare Book Department, The Free Library of Philadelphia. **52** Burrell Collection, Glasgow Museums and Art Galleries. **54** *Amoenitatum*

exoticarum politico-physico-medicorum, engraving by E. Kaempfer, 1712. BL. **56** A. G. E. FotoStock, Barcelona. **57** Arxiu MAS, Barcelona. **58** *Icones Plantarum Medico-oeconomico-Technologicarum*, Vietz, Vol. IV Tab 772, 1819. RHS. **59** MS Bodl. 130 f.44r. BOD. **59** MS Or 338 f.110a. BL/IOL. **60** Bayerische Staatsgemäldesammlungen, Schack-Galerie, Munich/Artothek. **61L** *Los Jardines de Granada*, Prieto Moreno. Private Collection. **61R** Mick Hales. **62** MS Add. 27257 f.44b. BL/IOL. **63L** MS Add. 27261 f.47b. BL/IOL. **63R** MS Add. 19766 f.81a. BL/IOL. **64** OA 1921. 10–11, 0.3. BM. **65L** IM 276A and 276–1913, Courtesy of the Board of Trustees of the Victoria & Albert Museum. **65R** MS Or. 3714 f.407r. BL/IOL. **66L** MS Or. 3129 f.61v. BL/IOL. **66R** MS Or. 2157 f.612. BL/IOL. **67** MS Or. 3129 f.49v. BL/IOL. **68** Topkapi Palace Museum MS H 1524. Sonia Halliday Photographs. **69T** Godfrey Goodwin, Royal Asiatic Society, Leiden. **69B** Sonia Halliday Photographs. **71** Städelsches Kunstinstitut, Frankfurt-am-Main/Artothek. **72** Department of Special Collections, Kenneth Spencer Research Library, University of Kansas. **73** *Apuleius Platonicus Herbarium*, MS 204 f. 45r by permission of the Provost and Fellows of Eton College. **75** MS Add 38126 f.110. BL/MS. **76** Capilla Real, Granada/Scala. **77** MS Lat 1, 99, f.831r. Biblioteca Nazionale Marciana, Venice. **78** Andrew Lawson. **79** University of Arizona Museum of Art, Tucson (Gift of Samuel H. Kress Foundation). **81** *La Teseida*, Boccaccio Cod 2617 f.53. Österreichisches Nationalbibliothek, Vienna. **82** *Historia Naturalis*, Pliny, MS Book XXII. Courtesy of the Board of Trustees of the Victoria & Albert Museum, London. **83** Metropolitan Museum of Art, New York, Gift of John D. Rockefeller Jr, the Cloisters Collection, 1937. **84** Palazzo Medici Riccardi, Florence/Scala. **85** Alte Pinakothek, Munich/Scala. **86TL** NAL 1673 f.32. BNP. **86TR** *Tacuinum Sanitatis* f.40. Österreichisches Nationalbibliothek, Vienna. **86BL** *Tacuinum Sanitatis* MS Leber f.34 v. Bibliothèque Municipale, Rouen. **86BC** ibid f.4v. **87BR** ibid f.19r. **86TC** *Tacuinum Sanitatis* f. XVII. Biblioteca Casanatense, Rome. **87TL** ibid f. LXVIII. **87R** ibid f. LXIX. **88L** MS Canon Misc 482 f.62v. BOD. **88R** *Warburg Hours* MS 139. Library of Congress, Washington DC, Rare Book Collection. **89** Galleria degli Uffizi, Florence/Scala. **90** MS Egerton 3781 f.lr. BL/MS. **91** Metropolitan Museum of Art, New York, Bequest of George Blumenthal, 1941. **92** Gunter Mader. **93L** MS Egerton 1069 f.1. BL/MS. **93R** MS Royal 6E IX f.15v. BL/MS. **94L** *Opus Ruralium Commodorum*, MS Add 19720 f.214. BL/MS. **94R** MS Fr. 12330, f.105r. BNP. **95** *Le Livre des Prouffs Champestre et Ruraux*, MS 232 f.157. Pierpont Morgan Library, New York. **97** *Verzameling van Bloemen naar de Natuur geteekend*, c. 1630. RHS. **98** *Viceroy Tulip* from *Verzameling van een meenigte tulipaanen*, P. Cos, 1637. Wageningen Agricultural University Library, Netherlands. **99L** Galleria degli Uffizi, Florence/Scala. **99R** Graphische Sammlung Albertina, Vienna. **101** MS 12322 f.143v. BNP. **102** Richard von Hünersdorff, Rare Books and Manuscripts, London.

104L MS Ashmole 1504, f.9v. BOD. **104R** *Ibid*, f.21. **105** *A New Orchard and Garden*, William Lawson, 1618. RHS. **107** National Trust. **109** Jerry Harpur. **110** *The Gardener's Labyrinth*, Thomas Hill, 1577. RHS. **111** *Le Jardin du Roy très Chrestien Henri IV, Roy de France*,' Pierre Vallet, 1608. RHS. **112** By kind permission of the President and Council of the Royal Society, London. **113** *Wild violets*, Jacques Le Moyne de Morgues. E. T. Archive/Victoria & Albert Museum. **114** Courtesy of the Duchess of Beaufort. **115** Windsor Castle, Royal Library (c) 1992, Her Majesty the Queen. **116** *Commentarii in Libros Sex pedacii Dioscoridis*, p. 85, P. A. Matthiolus. RBG. **117L** *Herbarium Vivae Eicones*, p. 61, Otto Brunfels. RBG. **117R** *De Historia Stirpium*, Fuchs, 1542. RHS. **118L** *Hortus publicus academiae Lugdunum-Batavae*, P. Paaw, 1601. Hortus Botanicus, University of Leiden. **118R** *Rariorum Aliquot Stirpium*, Clusius, 1576. RHS. **119** Hortus Botanicus, University of Leiden. **120L** *Gerarde's Herball*, (L. l. 5. Med) 1597. BOD. **120C, 120R** *Gerarde's Herball*. RHS. **121** *Paradisi in Sole, Paradisus Terrestris*, John Parkinson, 1629. RHS. **122R** *Hortus Eystettensis*, Besler. Bibliothèque Centrale du Museum National d'Histoire Naturelle, Paris. **122L, 123** ibid/Dominique Genet/Editions Citadelles and Mazenod, Paris. **124** *Description du Jardin Royal des plantes medicinales . . . à Paris*, G. de la Brosse, 1636, Sherard 392 (2). Department of Plant Sciences, Oxford. **125L** *Horti Medici Amstelodamensis*, Jan Commelin, 1699–1701. Courtesy of the Board of Trustees of the Victoria & Albert Museum. **125R** *Gymnasium Patavinum*, P. Tomasini, 1654. BL. **126L, R** Department of Western Art, Ashmolean Museum, Oxford. **127L** Department of Rare Books and Special Collections, University of Rochester Library, New York. **127R** *Plantae Selectae*, C. J. Trew, 1750–65. RHS. **128L** *Hesperides*, G. B. Ferrari, 1646. RHS. **128R, 129** *Florilegium*, Emmanuel Sweert, 1612. RHS. **130** *Hortus Floridus*, Crispin de Passe, 1614. RHS. **131L** *Flora*, John Rea, 1665. RHS. **131R** *Nawkeurige Beschryving der Aard-Gewassen*, Abraham Munting, 1696. RHS. **132T** *Des Semis et Plantations des Arbres*, Duhamel, 1760, Plate VI. RHS. **132B** *Silva*, John Evelyn 2nd edition, 1776. RHS. **133** *Greenwich from One Tree Hill*, Johannes Vorsterman. National Maritime Museum, Greenwich. **134T** Private Collection. **134B** *Nouveau Duhamel*, 1801–25, Vol II Plate 11. RHS. **135** Devonshire Collection. Reproduced by permission of the Trustees of the Chatsworth Settlement. **136** Prado, Madrid/Scala. **138** Balthazar Korab. **139** Museo di Firenze com'era, Florence/Scala. **141** Galleria degli Uffizi, Florence/Scala. **142** Villa d'Este, Tivoli/Scala. **143** Royal Collection, St. James's Palace (c) Her Majesty the Queen. **145** *Li Giardini di Roma*, Falda 1683. RHS. **146** *Hesperides*, G. B. Ferrari, 1646. RHS. **148–9** Musée des Arts Decoratifs, Paris/E. Sully–Jaulmes. **150** Gunter Mader. **151TL, BL, TR** *Hypnerotomoachia Poliphili*, Francesco Colonna. Private Collection. **152–153** Museo di Firenze com'era, Florence/Scala. **153T** K TOP LXXXII.12CI. BL Maps. **153B** Gabinetto dei Disegni e delle Stampe, Uffizi, Florence.

SELECT BIBLIOGRAPHY

General

BAZIN, Germain. *Paradeisos.* London, 1990.
BISGROVE, Richard. *The National Trust Book of the English Garden.* London, 1990.
BLUNT, Wilfrid. *The Art of Botanical Illustration.* London, 1950.
BLUNT, Wilfrid, and RAPHAEL, Sandra. *The Illustrated Herbal.* London, 1979.
COATS, Alice. *The Book of Flowers.* London, 1973.
— *The Quest for Plants.* London, 1969.
COWELL, F. R. *The Garden as a Fine Art.* London, 1978.
DUHAMEL DU MONCEAU, H. L. *Traité des Arbes.* Paris, 1755.
— (Revised and enlarged edition, edited by E. Michel and others, and usually known as the *Nouveau Duhamel.*) Paris, 1880–19.
FISHER, John *The Origin of Garden Plants.* London, 1982.
GALINOU, Mireille, editor. *London's Pride.* London, 1990.
GOTHEIN, Maria Luise. *A History of Garden Art,* translated by Laura Archer-Hind. New York, 1928 (reprinted 1979).
GRISWOLD, Mac. *Gardens of Pleasure.* New York, 1987.
HADFIELD, Miles, HARLING, Robert, and HIGHTON, Leonie. *British Gardeners.* London, 1980.
HALL, James. *Dictionary of Subjects and Symbols in Art.* Revised edition. London, 1979.
HARVEY, John. *Early Gardening Catalogues.* London and Chichester, 1972.
— *Early Nurserymen.* London and Chichester, 1974.
HOBHOUSE, Penelope, and TAYLOR, Patrick. *The Gardens of Europe.* London, 1990.
HUXLEY, Anthony. *An Illustrated History of Gardening.* London, 1988.
— *The Painted Garden.* London, 1988.
JELLICOE, Geoffrey, and JELLICOE, Susan. *The Landscape of Man.* London, 1975.
JELLICOE, Geoffrey, JELLICOE, Susan, GOODE, Patrick, and LANCASTER, Michael, editors. *The Oxford Companion to Gardens.* Oxford, 1986.
MOSSER, Monique, and TEYSSOT, Georges, editors. *The History of Garden Design.* London, 1991 (also Boston, 1991, as *The Architecture of Western Gardens*).
PREST, John. *The Garden of Eden.* New Haven and London, 1981.
RAPHAEL, Sandra. *An Oak Spring Pomona.* Upperville, Virginia, 1990.
— *An Oak Spring Sylva.* Upperville, Virginia, 1989.
RIX, Martyn. *The Art of the Botanist.* Guildford and London, 1981 (also New York, 1981, as *The Art of the Plant World.*)
STEARN, William T. *Flower Artists of Kew.* London, 1990.
— 'The origin and development of garden plants', *Journal of the Royal Horticultural Society,* XC, 1965, pp. 279–91, 322–40, 350.
TAYLOR, Patrick. *Period Gardens.* London, 1991.
THACKER, Christopher. *The History of Gardens.* London, 1979.
WHITTLE, Tyler. *The Plant Hunters.* London, 1970.

Periodicals

Garden History (the journal of the Garden History Society), 1972–
Journal of Garden History, 1981–
Journal of the Royal Horticultural Society, 1866–1975; continued as *the Garden,* 1975–

Botanical references

BAILEY, L. H. *Standard Cyclopedia of Horticulture.* New York, 1922 (and later reprints).
CHITTENDEN, Fred J., editor. *The Royal Horticultural Society Dictionary of Gardening.* Oxford, 1951.
— *Supplement,* edited by P. M. Synge. Second edition. Oxford, 1969.
The Plant Finder. 1991 edition.

Chapter 1 The Origins of Gardening in the West

AMERICAN SCHOOL OF CLASSICAL STUDIES. *Garden Lore of Ancient Athens,* edited by Dorothy Burr Thompson. Princeton, 1968.
BONAVIA, Emmanuel. *The Flora of the Assyrian Monuments and its Outcomes.* London, 1894.
COLUMELLA. *On Agriculture and Trees,* translated by H. B. Ash, E. S. Forster, and E. H. Heffner. London and Cambridge, Massachusetts, 1951–5.
DIOSCORIDES. *De Materia Medica (Codex Vindobonensis* facsimile). Graz, 1965–70.
DUDLEY, Donald. *Roman Society.* Harmondsworth, 1970.
HEPPER, Nigel. *Pharaoh's Flowers.* London, 1990.
HIGHET, Gilbert. *Poets in a Landscape.* Harmondsworth, 1957.
HOMER. *The Odyssey,* translated by E. V. Rieu. Harmondsworth, 1946.
HUXLEY, Anthony. *Green Inheritance.* London, 1984.
MacDOUGALL, E. B. and JASHEMSKI, W. F., editors. *Ancient Roman Gardens.* Washington, DC, 1981.
MANNICHE, Lise. *An Ancient Egyptian Herbal.* London, 1989.
MARINATOS, Nanno. *Art and Religion in Thera.* Athens, 1984.
The Monuments of Egypt and Nubia. London, 1834.
PLINY the Elder. *Natural History,* translated by H. Rackham and W. H. S. Jones. London and Cambridge, Massachusetts, 1949–80, especially volume VII, second edition, 1980.
PLINY the Younger. *The Letters of the Younger Pliny,* translated by Betty Radice. Harmondsworth, 1967.
SCOTT-JAMES, Anne, DESMOND, Ray, and WOOD, Frances. *The British Museum Book of Flowers.* London, 1989.
VIRGIL. *The Georgics,* translated by Robert Wells. Manchester, 1982.
XENOPHON. *Oeconomicus IV,* translated by E. C. Marchant. London and New York, 1923.

Chapter 2 The Gardens of Islam

Arabesque et Jardins de paradis: collections français d'art islamique, edited by Marthe Bernus-Taylor and others. (Catalogue of an exhibition at the Louvre, 1989/90). Paris, 1989.
BABUR. *The Babur-Nama in English,* translated by A. S. Beveridge. London, 1922.
BELL, Gertrude. *Letters,* edited by Lady Bell. London, 1927 (reprint, Harmondsworth, 1953).
— *Persian Pictures.* London, 1928.
BELON, Pierre. *Les Observations de plusieurs singularitez . . .* Paris, 1554.
BERNIER, François. *Travels in the Mogul Empire,* edited by Archibald Constable. London, 1891.
BROOKES, John. *Gardens of Paradise.* London, 1987.
CASTEJOHN, Rafeal. *Medina Azahara.* Leon, 1977.
CHARDIN, Sir John. *Travels in Persia,* translated by E. Lloyd. London, 1927.
ELDEM, Sedad H. *Türk Bahçeleri.* Istanbul, 1976.
GONZALEZ DE CLAVIJO, Ruy. *Embassy to Tamerlane 1403–1406,* trs. by Guy Le Strange. London, 1928.
HARVEY, John. 'Gardening books and plant lists of Moorish Spain', *Garden History,* 3 no. 2, 1975, pp. 10–21.
— 'Turkey as a source of garden plants', *Garden History,* 4 no. 3, 1976, pp. 21–42.
HERBERT, Sir Thomas. *A Relation of Some Years Travaile.* London, 1652 (reprint, New York, 1971).
LEHRMAN, Jonas. *Earthly Paradise.* Berkeley, 1981.
MacDOUGALL, E. B. and ETTINGHAUSEN, R., editors. *The Islamic Garden.* Washington, DC, 1976.
MOYNIHAN, Elizabeth. *Paradise as a Garden in Persia and Mughal India.* New York, 1979.

PORTER, Sir Robert Ker. *Travels in Georgia, Persia, Armenia, . . .* London, 1821–2.

STEVENS, R. B. *The Land of the Great Sophy.* London, 1962.

TITLEY, Norah M. *Plants and Gardens in Persian, Mughal and Turkish Art.* London, 1979.

TITLEY, Norah M. and WOOD, Frances. *Oriental Gardens.* London, 1991.

VILLARS-STUART, C. *Gardens of the Great Moghuls.* London, 1913.
— *Spanish Gardens.* London, 1929.

WILBER, Donald. *Persian Gardens and Garden Pavilions.* Rutland, Vermont, and Tokyo, 1962.

Chapter 3 The Medieval Gardens of Christendom

BOCCACCIO, Giovanni. *The Decameron,* translated by Richard Aldington. London, 1957.

COGLIATI ARANO, Luisa. *The Medieval Health Handbook: Tacuinum Sanitatis,* translated and adapted by Oscar Ratti and Adele Westbrook. London and New York, 1976.

CALKINS, Robert G. 'Piero de' Crescenzi and the medieval garden', in E. B. MacDougall, editor, *Medieval Gardens,* Washington, DC, 1986, pp. 155–73.

HARVEY, John. *Medieval Gardens.* London, 1981.

MacDOUGALL, Elisabeth B., editor. *Medieval Gardens.* Washington, DC, 1986.

POWER, Eileen. *The Goodman of Paris.* London, 1928.

STOKSTAD, Marilyn, and STANNARD, Jerry. *Gardens of the Middle Ages.* (Exhibition catalogue, Spencer Museum of Art, Lawrence, Kansas.) Lawrence, Kansas, 1983.

WALAHFRID STRABO. *Hortulus,* translated by Reaf Payne, with a commentary by Wilfrid Blunt. Pittsburgh, 1966.

Chapter 4 Botanists, Plantsmen and Gardeners of Renaissance Europe

ARBER, Agnes. *Herbals: their origin and evolution.* Second edition. Cambridge, 1938.
— Reprint, with an introduction and annotations by William T. Stearn. Cambridge, 1986.

BESLER, Basilius. *Hortus Eystettensis.* Nuremburg, 1613.
— *The Besler Florilegium,* edited by Gerard G. Aymonin. New York, 1987.

BLOMFIELD, Reginald, and THOMAS, Inigo. *The Formal Garden in England.* London, 1892.

DUTHIE, Ruth. 'The planting plans of some seventeenth-century gardens', *Garden History,* 18, 1990, pp. 77–102.

EVELYN, John. *Diary,* edited by Esmond de Beer. Oxford, 1955.
— *Sylva, or a Discourse of Forest-trees.* London, 1664.
— *Silva . . .* with notes by Alexander Hunter. York, 1776.

GERARD, John. *The Herball or General Historie of Plants.* London, 1597.
— Second edition, enlarged and amended by Thomas Johnson. London, 1636.
— *Leaves from Gerard's Herball,* arranged by Marcus Woodward. Second edition. London, 1931 (reprint, London, 1985).

GILBERT, Samuel. *The Florists Vade-mecum.* London, 1682.

GREEN, David. *Gardener to Queen Anne.* Oxford, 1956.

HANMER, Sir Thomas. *The Garden Book [1659],* with an introduction by Eleanour Sinclair Rohde. London, 1933.

HENREY, Blanche. *British Botanical and Horticultural Literature before 1800.* London, 1975.

HILL, Thomas. *The Gardeners Labyrinth.* London, 1577.
— Edited with an introduction by Richard Mabey. Oxford, 1987.

LAWSON, William. *The Countrie Housewifes Garden.* London, 1617.
— *A New Orchard and Garden.* London, 1618.

LEITH-ROSS, Prudence. *The John Tradescants.* London, 1984.

MARKHAM, Gervase. *The Countrie Farm* (Based on various editions of C. Estienne and R. Liébault, *La Maison rustique.*) London, 1616.

MATTIOLI, P. A. *Commentarii in sex libros Pedacii Dioscoridis Anazarbei de medica materia . . .* Venice, 1565.

MEAGER, Leonard. *The New Art of Gardening.* London, 1697.

PARKINSON, John. *Paradisi in Sole Paradisus Terrestris.* London, 1629.

PASS, Crispin van de. *Hortus Floridus.* Utrecht, 1614.
— The text translated from the Latin by Spencer Savage, with an introduction by Eleanour Sinclair Rohde. London, 1928–9 (reprint, London, 1974).

RAPHAEL, Sandra. *The Mattioli Woodblocks.* London, 1989.

RAUWOLF, Leonhard in John Ray, *A Collection of Curious Travels and Voyages.* Volume I. London, 1693.

RAVEN, Charles. *John Ray: Naturalist.* Cambridge, 1942.

REA, John. *Flora Ceres & Pomona.* Second edition. London, 1676.

RIDDELL, John. 'The Long Acre Garden 1600–1650', *Journal of Garden History,* 6, 1986, pp. 112–24.

STRONG, Roy. *The Renaissance Garden in England.* London, 1979.

TURNER, William. *A New Herball.* [Part one.] London, 1551.

VEENDORP, H. and BAAS BECKING, L. G. M. *Hortus Academicus Lugduno-Batavus, 1587–1937.* Leiden, 1938 (reprint 1990).

WORLIDGE, John. *Systema Horti-culturae: or, The Art of Gardening.* London, 1677.

Chapter 5 Gardens of the Italian Reniassance

ALBERTI, Leon Battista. *The Ten Books of Architecture,* translated by J. Leoni. London, 1755 (reprint, New York, 1986).

CASTELLI, Pietro. *Exactissima Descriptio Rariorum Quarundam Plantarum quae continentur Romae in Horto Farnesiano.* Rome, 1625.

CLARICI, P. B. *Istoria e coltura delle painte.* Venice, 1726.

COFFIN, David R. editor. *The Italian Garden.* Washington, DC, 1972.

COLONNA, Francesco. *Hypnerotomachia Poliphili.* Venice, 1449.

DEL RICCIO, Agostino. *Il Giardino del Re.* (Manuscript of the late 16th century in the Biblioteca Nazionale, Florence.)

FERRARI, G. B. *Flora.* Rome, 1638.
— *Hesperides.* Rome, 1646.

GURRIERI, Francesco, and CHATFIELD, Judith. *The Boboli Gardens.* Florence, 1972.

LANZARA, Paolo, and others. *Roma e il suo Orto Botanico.* Rome, 1984.

LAZZARO, Claudia. *The Italian Renaissance Garden.* New Haven and London, 1990.

MADER, Gunter, and NEUBERT-MADER, Laila. *Les Jardins italiens.* Fribourg, 1987.

MASSON, Georgina. *Italian Gardens.* London, 1961.
'Italian Flower Collectors' Gardens in Seventeenth Century Italy' in David R. Coffin, editor, *The Italian Garden,* Washington, DC, 1972, pp. 63-80.

MONTAIGNE, Michel de. *Journal of Montaigne's Travels,* translated by W. G. Waters. London, 1903.

SERLIO, Sebastiano. *The Book of Architecture.* (Translator anonymous.) London, 1611 (reprint, London, 1970).

SITWELL, Sir George. *An Essay on the Making of Gardens.* London, 1909.

TASSI, Alessandro. *Ulisse Aldrovandi e la Toscana.* Florence, 1989.

VASARI, Giorgio. *Lives of the Painters, Sculptors and Architects,* translated by A. B. Hinds. London, 1900.
— Edited and introduced by W. Gaunt. London, 1963.

VREDEMAN DE VRIES, Hans. *Hortorum viridariorumque elegantes et multiplicis formae.* Amsterdam, 1583.

Chapter 6 The Origin and Development of French Formality

ADAMS, William Howard. *The French Garden, 1500–1800.* New York and London, 1979.

ANDROUET DU CERCEAU, Jacques. *Les plus excellens bastiments de France.* Paris, 1576–1607.
— *French Châteaux and Gardens in the XVIth Century,* edited by W. H. Ward. London, 1909 (reprint, Farnborough, 1972).

CAUS, Salomon de. *Hortus Palatinus.* Frankfurt, 1620.

DEZALLIER D'ARGENVILLE, Antoine-Joseph. *La Théorie et la pratique du jardinage.* Paris, 1709.
— *The Theory and Practice of Gardening,* translated by John James. London, 1712.

DUVAL, Marguerite. *The King's Garden,* translated by Annette Tomarken and Claudine Cowen. Charlottesville, Virginia. 1982.

ESTIENNE, Charles. *L'Agriculture et maison rustique,* translated by J. Liébault. Paris, 1570. (Later editions augmented and revised by Liébault, 1586, 1598.)
— *Maison Rustique or the Countrie Farme,* translated by Richard Surflet. London, 1600.

FIENNES, Celia. *The Illustrated Journeys 1685–1712,* edited by Christopher Morris. London, 1988.

GROEN, Jan van der. *Der Nederlandtsen Hovenier.* Amsterdam, 1669.

GUIFFREY, Jules. *André Le Nostre,* translated by George Booth. Lewes, 1986.

HARRIS, Walter. *A Description of the King's Royal Palace and Gardens at Loo.* London, 1699.

HUNT, John Dixon, and DE JONG, Erik. *The Anglo-Dutch Garden in the Age of William and Mary.* (An exhibition catalogue, also issued as numbers 2 and 3 of volume 8 of the *Journal of Garden History.*) London, 1988.

JACQUES, David, and HORST, Arend van der, editors. *The Gardens of William and Mary.* London, 1988.

LAISSUS, Yves. *Nicolas Robert et les vélins du Muséum National d'Histoire Naturelle.* Paris, 1980.

MacDOUGALL, Elisabeth B., editor. *The French Formal Garden.* Washington, DC, 1974.

MOLLET, André. *Le Jardin de Plaisir.* Stockholm, 1651.
— *The Garden of Pleasure.* London, 1670.

MOLLET, Claude. *Théâtre des Plans et Jardinages.* Paris, 1652.

SERRES, Olivier de. *Théâtre d'Agriculture et mesnage des champs.* Paris, 1600.

VALLET, Pierre. *Le Jardin du Roy très chrétien Henri IV.* Paris, 1608.

WARNER, Marjorie. 'The Morins', *National Horticultural Magazine,* July 1954, pp. 168–76.

WOODBRIDGE, Kenneth. *Princely Gardens.* London, 1986.

Chapter 7 The Eighteenth-century English Landscape

BATEY, Mavis. 'William Mason, English gardener', *Garden History,* 1 no. 2, 1973, pp. 11–25.

BLAIKIE, Thomas. *Diary of a Scottish Gardener,* edited by Francis Birrell. London, 1931.

CALMANN, Gerta. *Ehret: Flower Painter Extraordinary.* London, 1977.

CHAMBERS, Sir William. *A Dissertation on Oriental Gardening.* London, 1772.

DILLWYN, Lewis Weston. *Hortus Collinsonianus.* Swansea, 1843.

HENREY, Blanche. *British Botanical and Horticultural Literature before 1800.* London, 1975.

HINDE, Thomas. *Capability Brown.* London, 1986.

HYAMS, Edward. *Capability Brown and Humphrey Repton.* London, 1971.

JACQUES, David. *Georgian Gardens.* London, 1983.

KING, R. W. 'John Spence of Byfleet', *Garden History,* 6 no. 3, 1978, pp. 38–64; 7 no. 3, 1979, pp. 29–48; 8 nos. 2 and 3, 1980, pp. 44–65, 77–114.
— 'The Ferme Ornée: Philip Southcote and Woburn Farm', *Garden History,* 2 no. 3, 1974, pp. 27–60.

KNIGHT, Carlo. *Il Giardino Inglese di Caserta.* Naples, 1986.

LABORDE, A. L. J. de. *Description des nouveaux jardins de la France.* Paris, 1808.

LAIRD, Mark. 'An approach to the conservation of ornamental planting in English gardens, 1730–1830.' MA thesis for the University of York, 1984.
— '"Our equally favourite hobby horse": the flower gardens of Lady Elizabeth Lee at Hartwell and the 2nd Earl Harcourt at Nuneham Courtenay', *Garden History,* 18 (1990), pp. 103–54.

LANGLEY, Batty. *New Principles of Gardening.* London, 1728.

LE ROUGETEL, Hazel. *The Chelsea Gardener: Philip Miller 1691–1771.* London, 1990.

LYTE, Charles. *Sir Joseph Banks.* Newton Abbot, 1980.

MARSHALL, William. *Planting and Rural Ornament.* Second edition. London, 1796.

MASON, William. *The English Garden: a poem.* London and York, 1772–81.

MEADER, James. *The Planter's Guide.* London, 1779.

MILLER, Philip. *The Gardeners Dictionary.* London, 1731 (and later editions).

PEVSNER, Nikolaus, editor. *The Picturesque Garden and its Influence outside the British Isles.* Washington, DC, 1974.

PRICE, Uvedale. *An Essay on the Picturesque as compared with the Sublime and the Beautiful.* London and Hereford, 1794–8.

REPTON, Humphry. *The Art of Landscape Gardening,* edited by John Nolen. Boston, 1907.
— *Observations on the Theory and Practice of Landscape Gardening.* London, 1803.

SPENCE, Joseph. *Observations and Characters of Books and Men,* edited by J. M. Osborn. Oxford, 1966.
— Papers in the Osborn Collection, Yale University Library.

STROUD, Dorothy. *Capability Brown.* London, 1975.
Humphry Repton. London, 1962.

SWINDEN, Nathaniel. *The Beauties of Flora Display'd.* London, 1778.

SWITZER, Stephen. *Ichnographia Rustica.* London, 1718.

SYMES, Michael. 'Charles Hamilton's plantings at Painshill', *Garden History,* 11, 1983, pp. 112–24.
— 'Charles Hamilton's sowings of grass at Painshill', *Garden History,* 13, 1985, pp. 4–8.

WALPOLE, Horace. *On Modern Gardening.* London, 1771 (in Walpole's *Anecdotes of Painting;* the first separate edition – in English and French – was published in 1785).
— Edited by Rebecca Moore. London, 1987.

WHATELY, Thomas. *Observations on Modern Gardening.* London, 1770.

WOODBRIDGE, Kenneth. 'The planting of Ornamental Shrubs at Stourhead: a history, 1746 to 1946', *Garden History,* 4, 1976, pp. 88–109.

Chapter 8 The Nineteenth Century: Experimentation and Expansion

ALLAN, Mea. *William Robinson: Father of the English Flower Garden.* London, 1982.

BROOKE, E. Adveno. *Gardens of England.* London, 1858.

CARTER, George, GOODE, Patrick, and LAURIE, Kedrun. *Humphry Repton: Landscape Gardener 1752–1818.* (Catalogue of an exhibition at the University of East Anglia and the Victoria and Albert Museum.) Norwich, 1988.

CARTER, Tom. *The Victorian Garden.* London, 1984.

COBBETT, William. *The English Gardener.* London, 1829, reissued 1833 (reprint, Oxford, 1980).

DESMOND, Ray. 'Victorian garden magazines', *Garden History,* 5 no. 3, 1977, pp. 47–66.

DOUGLAS, David. *Journal kept during his Travels in North America 1823–1827,* edited by W. Wilks. London, 1914 (reprint, New York, 1959).

ELLIOTT, Brent. 'Master of the Geometric art', *Garden,* CVI, 1981, pp. 488–91.
— 'Mosaïculture: origins and significance', *Garden History,* 9, 1981, pp. 76–98.
— *Victorian Gardens.* London, 1986.

FARRER, Reginald. *The English Rock Garden.* London, 1922.

GIROUARD, Mark. *Sweetness and Light: the Queen Anne Movement 1860–1900.* Oxford, 1977.

GORER, Richard. *Living Tradition in the Garden.* Newton Abbot, 1974.

HARRIS, John, editor. *The Garden: a Celebration of one thousand years of British Gardening.* (A guide to an exhibition at the Victoria and Albert Museum.) London, 1979.

HAYDEN, Peter. *Biddulph Grange, Staffordshire.* London, 1989.

HIBBERD, Shirley. *The Amateur's Flower Garden.* London, 1875.
— *Rustic Adornments for Homes of Taste.* London, 1870.

HUGHES, John Arthur. *Garden Architecture and Landscape Gardening.* London, 1866.

JEKYLL, Gertrude. *Colour in the Flower Garden.* London, 1908.
— *Home and Garden.* London, 1900.
— *Wall and Water Gardens.* London, 1901.
— *Wood and Garden.* London, 1899.

LOUDON, Jane Wells. *The Ladies' Companion to the Flower-Garden.* London, 1849.

LOUDON, John Claudius. *Arboretum et Fruticetum Britannicum.* London, 1835–38.
— *Encyclopaedia of Gardening.* Third edition. London, 1825.
— *The Suburban Gardener and Villa Companion.* London, 1838.

MacDOUGALL, Elisabeth B., editor. *John Claudius Loudon and the Early Nineteenth Century in Great Britain.* Washington, DC, 1980.

M'INTOSH, Charles. *The Flower Garden.* London, 1838.

MILNER, H. E. *The Art and Practice of Landscape Gardening.* London, 1890.

PÜCKLER-MUSKAU, Hermann, Prince. *Andeutungen über Landschaftsgärtnerei.* Stuttgart, 1834 (reprint, Stuttgart, 1977).
— *Hints on Landscape Gardening,* translated by Bernard Sickert and edited by Samuel Parsons. Boston, 1917.

ROBINSON, William. *The English Flower Garden.* London, 1883 (and later editions).
— *Gleanings from French Gardens.* London, 1868.
— Gravetye Manor (manuscript in the Lindley Library, Royal Horticultural Society).
— *The Parks, Promenades, and Gardens of Paris.* London, 1869.
The Wild Garden. London, 1870.

SEDDING, John D. *Garden-Craft Old and New.* London, 1891.

SIMO, M. L. *Loudon and the Landscape.* New Haven and London, 1988.

VEITCH, James. *Hortus Veitchii.* London, 1900.

Periodicals

Gardeners' Chronicle, 1841–
Gardener's Magazine (edited by John Claudius Loudon), 1826–43.
The Cottage Gardener, 1848–61; continued as the *Journal of Horticulture,* 1861–1915.

Chapter 9 The Development of North American Horticulture

BARTRAM, William. *Travels through North and South Carolina . . .* Philadelphia, 1791, and London, 1792.
— Facsimile edited by Robert McCracken Peck. Salt Lake City, 1980.

BERKELEY, Edmund, and BERKELEY, Dorothy Smith. *The Life and Travels of John Bartram.* Tallahassee, Florida, 1982.

BEVERLEY, Robert. *The History and Present State of Virginia.* London, 1705 (reprint, Charlottesville, Virginia, 1968).

BRIDGEMAN, Thomas. *The Florist's Guide.* New York, 1847.

BROWN, Tom. 'Gardens of the Gulf Missions', *Pacific Horticulture,* 49, 1988, pp. 3–11.

BUIST, Robert. *The American Flower Garden Directory.* Philadelphia, 1841 and 1854.

CATESBY, Mark. *The Natural History of Carolina, Florida and the Bahama Islands.* London, 1729–47.

DOWNING, Andrew Jackson. *A Treatise on the Theory and Practice of Landscape Gardening.* New York, 1841 (reprint, Sakonnet, 1977).

DUTTON, Joan. *Plants of Colonial Williamsburg.* Williamsburg, Virginia, 1979.

HEDRICK, U. P. *A History of Horticulture in America to 1860.* New York, 1950 (reprint, Portland, 1988).

HOCKADAY, Joan. *The Gardens of San Francisco.* Portland, Oregon, 1988.

HUME, Audrey Noël. *Archaeology and the Colonial Gardener.* Williamsburg, Virginia, 1974.

JEFFERSON, Thomas. *Garden Book 1766–1824,* edited by Edwin Morris Betts. Philadelphia, 1944.
— *Notes on the State of Virginia 1787,* edited by William Peden. New York, 1954.

JOSSELYN, John. *An Account of Two Voyages to New England.* London, 1673.
— *New-Englands Rarities Discovered.* London, 1672.

KORNWOLF, James D. '"So good a design": a William and Mary garden at William and Mary', *Journal of Garden History,* 10, 1990, pp. 173–88.

LEIGHTON, Ann. *American Gardens in the Eighteenth Century.* Boston, 1976.
— *American Gardens in the Nineteenth Century.* Boston, 1987.
— *Early American Gardens.* Boston, 1979 (also London, 1979, as *Early English Gardens in New England*).

MACCUBBIN, Robert P., and MARTIN, P., editors. *British and American Gardens in the Eighteenth Century.* Williamsburg, Virginia, 1984. (Originally published as a special issue, new series volume VIII number 2, of *Eighteenth Century Life*).

McGUIRE, D. K. and FERN, L., editors. *Beatrix Jones Farrand.* Washington, DC, 1982.

MARSHALL, Humphry. *Arbustrum American: the American Grove.* Philadelphia, 1785.

MICHAUX, André. *Histoire des Chênes de l'Amérique.* Paris, 1801.

MICHAUX, François-André. *Histoire des Arbres forestiers de l'Amérique.* Paris, 1810–13.
The North American Sylva. Paris, 1819.

MORGAN, Keith. *Charles A. Platt: the Artist as Architect.* Boston, 1985.

NEWCOMB, Peggy Cornett. *Popular Annuals of Eastern North America, 1865–1914.* Washington, DC, 1985.

NEWTON, Norman T. *Design on the Land.* Cambridge, Massachusetts, 1971.

PRENTICE, Helaine Kaplan. *The Gardens of Southern California.* San Francisco, 1990.

REED, H. H. and DUCKWORTH, S. *Central Park.* New York, 1967.

SAVAGE, H. and SAVAGE, E. *André Michaux and François-André Michaux.* Charlottesville, Virginia, 1988.

SCOTT, Frank. *Victorian Gardens. Part I. Suburban Home Grounds.* New York, 1870 (reprint, New York, 1982).

SPONGBERG, Stephen P. *A Reunion of Trees.* Cambridge, Massachusetts, 1990.

SWEM, E. B., editor. *Brothers of the Spade: the Correspondence of Peter Collinson . . . and John Custis . . . 1734–46.* Worcester, Massachusetts, 1949.

Chapter 10 The Twentieth Century: Gardening as Conservation

ADAMS, William Howard. *Roberto Burle Marx: the Unnatural Art of the Garden.* New York, 1991.

BALMORI, Diana, McGUIRE, Diane Kostial, and McPECK, Eleanor M. *Beatrix Farrand's American Landscapes.* Sagaponack, New York, 1985.

BRIGGS, Loutrel. *Charleston Gardens.* Columbia, South Carolina, 1951.

CHURCH, Thomas. *Gardens are for People.* New York, 1983.

FARRAND, Beatrix. *Beatrix Farrand's Plant Book for Dumbarton Oaks,* edited by D. McGuire. Washington, DC, 1980.

FORESTIER, J. C. N. *Gardens,* translated by Helen Morgenthau Fox. New York, 1924.

JENSEN, Jens. *Siftings.* Chicago, 1930.

MAWSON, Thomas. *The Art and Craft of Garden Making.* London, 1901.

WILKINSON, Norman. *E. I. du Pont, Botaniste.* Charlottesville, Virginia, 1972.

WILSON, E. H. *Aristocrats of the Garden.* Boston, 1926.

Periodicals

Garden Design (American Society of Landscape Architects), 1982–
Horticulture, 1904–
Magnolia (the journal of the Southern History Society)
Pacific Horticulture, 1976.

REFERENCE NOTES

Chapter 1 The Origins of Gardening in the West

1   The vast hypostyle hall at Karnak was constructed round a colonnade of carved and painted pillars of huge diameter, made to resemble bunched papyrus stems with capitals of papyrus flowers.

2   Quoted in F. R. Cowell, *The Garden as a Fine Art* (1978), p. 26.

3   Xenophon, *Oeconomicus,* tr. E. C. Marchant (1923), pp. 20–5.

4   In Greece a grove meant not only trees but meadows and streams within it as well.

5   Homer, *Odyssey,* tr. E. V. Rieu (1946), p. 115.

6   Cato, *De Re Rustica,* tr. W. D. Hooper (1934), pp. 52, 113.

7   Xenophon, *Oeconomicus,* p. 395.

8   A translation by Sir Arthur Hort was published in 1916.

9   Columella, *On Agriculture and Trees,* tr. H. D. Ash and others (1951–5), Book X, lines 95–108.

10 Cicero, *Letters to his Friends,* including *Epistolae ad Quintum Fratrem,* tr. W. G. Williams (1690) Vol. III, Book III. I. 5, p. 553.

11 Pliny, *Letters,* tr. Betty Radice (1963), Book II letter 17 to Gallus, pp. 75–7, and Book V letter 6 to Domitius Apollinaris, pp. 139–43.

12 Columella, *On Agriculture . . .* Books X and XI.

13 Pliny, *Natural History,* tr. H. Rackham and W. H. S. Jones (1949–80). Book XVIII deals with forestry and agriculture, Book XIX with kitchen gardens, and Books XX–XXVII with all sorts of herbs and flowers and their medicinal uses, as well as hints on growing and propagation.

Chapter 2 The Gardens of Islam

1   John Harvey in *Garden History,* 4 no. 3 (1976), pp. 30–41.

2   John Harvey in *Garden History,* 3 no. 2 (1975), pp. 10–21.

3   Translated by James Dickie in 'The Islamic Garden in Spain' in *The Islamic Garden,* ed. E. B. MacDougall and R. Ettinghausen (1976), p. 94.

4   Harvey in *Garden History,* 4 no. 3 (1976), p. 23, and R. Pinder-Wilson, 'The Persian Garden' in *The Islamic Garden,* ed. MacDougall and Ettinghausen (1976), p. 83.

5   Sir Robert Ker Porter was a court artist in Russia, and his book of *Travels* (1821–2) is illustrated with beautiful drawings.

6   Kritovoulos, *History of Mehmed the Conqueror,* tr. C. T. Riggs (Princeton, 1964; reprint Westport, Connecticut, 1970).

Chapter 3 The Medieval Gardens of Christendom

1   Columella, *On Agriculture and Trees,* tr. H. B. Ash and others (1951–5), Book XI lines 11–14.

2   Translated by John Harvey in *Medieval Gardens* (1981), p. 4.

3   Translated in M. L. Gothein, *A History of Garden Art,* tr. L. Archer-Hind (1928), vol. I, p. 178.

4   Translated by John Harvey in the *Oxford Companion to Gardens* (1986), p. 438.

5   Ibid., p. 439.

6   Translated by John Harvey in *Medieval Gardens,* p. 10.

7   John Trevisa's translation of Bartholomew's *De Proprietatibus Rerum* was printed in 1495.

8   Crescenzi, Book VIII chapters 3 and 4.

9   Eileen Power, *The Goodman of Paris* (1928).

10 Translated by R. G. Calkins in *Medieval Gardens,* ed. E. B. MacDougall (1986), p. 273.

Chapter 4 Botanists, Plantsmen and Gardeners of Renaissance Europe

1   A translation by Nicholas Staphorst of Rauwolf's account of his journey was published in the first volume of John Ray's *Collection of Curious Travels and Voyages* in 1693.

2   *Journal of Montaigne's Travels,* tr. W. G. Waters (1903).

3   H. Veendorp and L. G. M. Bass Becking, *Hortus Academicus Lugduno-Batavus, 1587–1937* (1938), p. 58.

4   John Parkinson, *Paradisus* (1629), p. 430. This book appeared a few years earlier than Thomas Johnson's revised edition of Gerard's *Herball* (1633, reprinted 1636).

5   Parkinson, *Paradisus,* p. 65.

6   Edited and published by John, Lord Hanmer, in 1876 in *A Memorial of the Parish and Family of Hanmer.*

7   See John Riddell on Parkinson's Long Acre garden 1600–1650 in *Journal of Garden History,* 6 (1986), pp. 112–24.

8   Prudence Leith-Ross, in Appendix III (pp. 252–92) of *The John Tradescants* (1984) lists all the Tradescant plants with their modern Latin names. This incomparably useful compendium is a great

help in identifying and bringing up to date the names in other sixteenth- and seventeenth-century books too.

9   Evelyn's *Kalendarium* originally formed part of his unpublished gardening encyclopaedia, *Elysium Britannicum,* but it was detached and added to successive editions of *Sylva* from the first one in 1644, as well as being published separately in 1666 and many times thereafter.

Chapter 5 Gardens of the Italian Renaissance

1   Luigi Zangheri in *The History of Garden Design,* ed. M. Mosser and G. Teyssot (1991), pp. 59, 64.

2   Georgina Masson, *Italian Gardens* (1961), p. 59–60.

3   L. B. Alberti, *The Ten Books of Architecture,* tr. J. Leoni (1755), Book IX.

4   F. Gurrieri and J. Chatfield, *The Boboli Gardens* (1972), p. 17.

5   L. Puppi, 'The Villa Garden of the Veneto from the Fifteenth to the Eighteenth Century' in *The Italian Garden,* ed. David R. Coffin (1972), pp. 83–114.

6   Soderini, *Trattata della Cultura,* vol. II p. 41, written in the 1580s or 1590s.

7   Alberti, 'Libri della Famiglia', translated by R. N. Watkins (1969) and quoted in C. Lazzaro, *The Italian Renaissance Garden* (1990), p. 293 note 77.

8   There is an inventory of the plants in Appendix 3 of Lazzaro's book, pp. 328–32.

Chapter 6 The Origin and Development of French Formality

1   Translated by Kenneth Woodbridge in *Princely Gardens* (1986), p. 295 note 23. Quotations from Claude Mollet are all Woodbridge translations; those from André Mollet are from *The Garden of Pleasure,* the 1670 translation of his book.

2   Belon quoted in M. Duval, *The King's Garden,* tr. A. Tomarken and C. Cowen (1982), p. 16.

3   Dezallier d'Argenville, *The Theory and Practice of Gardening,* tr. John James (1712), p. 17.

4   Ibid.

Chapter 7 The Eighteenth-century English Landscape

1   M. Iljin, 'Russian Parks of the 18th Century', *Architectural Review* (February 1964), pp. 110–11.

2   Pope, *Epistle to Lord Burlington* (1731).

3   Addison in the *Spectator,* no. 414 (25 June 1712).

4   Spence in a 19 September 1751 letter to Robert Wheeler, printed in his *Observations . . .* ed. J. M. Osborn (1966), vol. II pp. 646–52 esp. 649.

5   J. C. Loudon, *Arboretum et Fruticetum Britannicum* (1838), vol. I, p. 70.

6   Switzer's letter is quoted in John Harvey, *Early Nurserymen* (1974), p. 171.

7   Switzer, *The Nobleman, Gentleman, and Gardener's Recreation* (1715), vol. III. pp. 88–9.

8   Quoted in Mavis Batey, 'The Way to View Rousham, by Kent's Gardener', *Garden History,* 11 (1983), p. 129.

9   Quoted in R. W. King, 'Joseph Spence of Byfleet. Part IV', *Garden History.* 8 no. 3 (1980) pp. 81, 84, 96. See also E. C. Nelson's supplementary note in *Garden History* vol. 15 No. 1 pp. 12–18.

10   Walpole was writing to Lady Hervey on 11 June 1765.

11   Charles Marshall, *An Introduction to the Knowledge and Practice of Gardening* (1796).

12   Laird on the flower gardens at Hartwell and Nuneham Courtenay in *Garden History,* 18 (1990), pp. 103–54.

13   Quoted in Dorothy Stroud, *Capability Brown* (1975), p. 157.

14   Repton, *The Art of Landscape Gardening,* ed. J. Nolen (1907), chapter IV.

15   The Collinson quotations are taken from his manuscript 'Day Book' in the library of the Linnean Society in London, or from L. W. Dillwyn's *Hortus Collinsonianus* (1843).

16   Loudon, *Arboretum . . .* (1838), vol. I, pp. 57–8.

17   Ibid., vol. IV, p. 2402.

18   Ibid., vol. I, p. 71.

19   Spence was writing in 1752. The description is in his *Observations . . .* ed. J. M. Osborn (1966), vol. I pp. 424–6.

20   Carlo Knight's books on Caserta (1986) gives a detailed history of the garden.

Chapter 8 The Nineteenth Century: Experimentation and Expansion

1   See the *Gardener's Magazine,* XVI (1840), pp. 49–58.

2   Richard Gorer, *Living Tradition in the Garden* (1974), p. 47.

3   Brent Elliott, *Victorian Gardens* (1986), p. 91.

4   J. A. Hughes, *Garden Architecture and Landscape Gardening* (1886), p. 148.

5   Sir Henry Steuart, *The Planter's Guide* (second edition, 1828).

6   Barron in *Journal of Horticulture and Cottage Gardener* (3 January 1901), p. 13.

Chapter 9 The Development of North American Horticulture

1   Part of Hernandez' work was published in Mexico in 1615. A fire then destroyed much of the manuscript, but its rescued remains were published in three volumes in 1784 and again in 1959–60.

2   See Ann Leighton, *Early American Gardens* (1979), p. 66.

3   The list of seeds is in a bill from Robert Hill dated 26 July 1631, printed in Leighton, *Early American Gardens,* p. 190.

4   See James D. Kornwolf, '"So good a design": a William and Mary garden at William and Mary', *Journal of Garden History,* 10 (1990), pp. 173, 175, 186 note 2. The plates were given to the Bodleian Library in Oxford by Richard Rawlinson in 1755. The one showing Williamsburg was recently given to the Colonial Williamsburg Foundation.

5   The most accurate copy of the system extant is one drawn (but not until 1782) by an anonymous Frenchman.

6   The 1743 letter from Eliza Pinckney Lucas is quoted by George C. Rogers in *British and American Gardens,* ed. R. P. Maccubbin and P. Martin (1983), pp. 151–2.

7   The letter of 17 November 1754 from Alexander Garden is quoted in *The Life and Travels of John Bartram,* by E. and D. S. Berkeley (1982).

8   Michaux's arrival home was disastrous, for his ship sank within sight of the Belgian coast and his unconscious body was dragged ashore. Some of his plant specimens were saved, but the notebook containing the journal of his American experiences was lost. In 1803 he died of fever in Madagascar, where he was trying to re-establish a botanical collection and nursery garden.

9   Cutler's description is quoted by Elizabeth McLean in *British and American Gardens,* ed. R. P. Maccubbin, and P. Martin (1983), p. 142.

10   The judges were Edward Kemp, the English landscape architect (and author of *How to Lay Out a Small Garden* (1850)) who had helped Joseph Paxton in the design of Birkenhead Park in Liverpool between 1843 and 1847, and an anonymous Frenchman.

11   The Olmsted quotations are printed in H. H. Reed and S. Duckworth, *Central Park* (1967), pp. 2 and 46.

12   Peter Henderson, journalist and author, wrote, among other books, *Gardening for Pleasure: A Guide to the Amateur in the Fruit, Vegetable and Flower Garden* (1875).

13   Bryant's description is quoted in *The Gardens of Southern California,* by H. K. Prentice (1990), p. 9.

14   The Olmstead quotations are in Reed and Duckworth, Central Park, pp. 354–55.

Chapter 10 The Twentieth Century: Gardening as Conservation

1   Frank Kingdon Ward.

2   Veitch's directions are printed in *Ernest Wilson, Plant Hunter,* Edward Farrington 1931.

3   See N. Wilkinson, *E. I. du Pont, Botaniste* (1972).

INDEX